O. M. Barnes
March 1, 1875

The History of Switzerland.

THE

HISTORY OF SWITZERLAND,

BY

HEINRICH ZSCHOKKE.

TRANSLATED BY

FRANCIS GEORGE SHAW.

NEW YORK:
ALBERT MASON, PUBLISHER.
1875.

TRANSLATOR'S PREFACE.

WHILE studying the history of Switzerland on Swiss soil, I was charmed by the simple beauty, the conciseness and impartiality of Zschokke's popular work, which is used as a textbook in many, if not in all, of the Confederate Cantons; and, with the assent of pastor Emil Zschokke of Aarau, the worthy continuer of his late celebrated father's labors, I made the following translation from the ninth enlarged edition.

Having myself felt a want of information on the subject, I now present this translation to my fellow-citizens of these United States, in the hope that a more extended acquaintance with the history of our sister republic may teach us to shun the perils through which the Swiss people have passed at the cost of so much suffering, and may aid us to appreciate our own more favorable position as a nation.

STATEN ISLAND, New York,

NOTE.—As the Swiss, in different parts of their country, speak different languages (German, French, Italian, and several distinct idioms), there is necessarily a great diversity also in their nomenclature. I have followed that of the author, which is German, or employed that locally prevalent, except in cases where a person or place is better known to us by some other name.

CONTENTS.

CHAPTER		PAGE
I.	How it was in the beginning..........................	1
II.	The first exploits of the ancient Helvetians, and how the Cymbri came to them. [B. C. 100.]....................	3
III.	All the country becomes Roman. [B. C. 50.]............	5
IV.	Of the Roman dominion in the land. [A. D. 1 to 300.]....	10
V.	How the whole country became a prey to foreign nations. [A. D. 300 to 550.]................................	13
VI.	Dominion and rule of the Franks. [A. D. 550 to 900.]....	16
VII.	The Christian religion penetrates the land...............	18
VIII.	How the country becomes part of the German empire, and cities are built. [A. D. 900 to 1200.]..................	21
IX.	More about the cities and the great signiors in the country. [A. D. 1200 to 1290.]...............................	26
X.	Of the communities in the mountains of Schwyz, Appenzell, Rhetia and Valais. [A. D. 1200 to 1290.]..............	30
XI.	About the good emperor, Rudolf of Habsburg, and the evil designs of his son Albert. [A. D. 1291 to 1307.].......	34
XII.	Of William Tell and the three men in Rutli. [A. D. 1307.]	38
XIII.	The New-Year's morning of 1308. Battle for freedom at Morgarten. Lucerne joins the Confederates. [A. D. 1308 to 1334.]..	41
XIV.	Berne vanquishes the power of the nobility near Laupen; and knight Brun changes the constitution of Zurich. [A. D. 1335 to 1340.]...............................	46
XV.	Origin of the perpetual bond of the eight ancient cantons of the Confederacy. [A. D. 1341 to 1360.].............	50
XVI.	How the Swiss increase, and the Guglers and the counts of Kyburg are ruined. [A. D. 1360 to 1385.].............	55

CHAPTER PAGE

XVII. The battle for freedom near Sempach. [A. D. 1385 to 1387.] 59

XVIII. The battle for freedom near Nafels, and its consequences. [A. D. 1388 to 1402.] 62

XIX. The heroic days of the Appenzellers. [A.D. 1403 to 1411.] 67

XX. The Confederates conquer Aargau and establish common bailiwicks. [A. D. 1412 to 1418.] 73

XXI. The Mazza of Valais against Raron. The battle of Arbedo, and the cunning of lord Zoppo. [A. D. 1419 to 1426.]. 78

XXII. In the Highlands of Rhetia, the Upper-league, the God's-house-league and the League of the Ten-jurisdictions are formed in behalf of liberty. [A. D. 1426 to 1436.] 83

XXIII. Quarrel respecting the Toggenburg-inheritance. [A. D. 1436 to 1443.] 88

XXIV. War of all the Confederates against Zurich. The Heroes-death near St. Jacques. Peace. [A. D. 1443 to 1450.]. 93

XXV. Rheinfelden is devastated. Freiburg falls into the power of Savoy. Thurgau becomes a common bailiwick of the Confederacy. [A. D. 1450 to 1468.] 99

XXVI. Union of the three Leagues in Rhetia. Discord in Berne. Commencement of the Burgundian war. [A. D. 1469 to 1476.] 104

XXVII. Result of the Burgundian war. Freiburg becomes free. [A. D. 1476 to 1477.] 108

XXVIII. The glorious day of Giornico. Nicholas von der Flue. Freiburg and Solothurn in the Swiss Confederacy. Death of John Waldmann at Zurich. [A. D. 1478 to 1489.] 114

XXIX. The Suabian War. Formation of the Confederacy of the thirteen cantons. [A. D. 1490 to 1500.] 120

XXX. The savage manners and mercenary wars of the Swiss; they conquer Valtelina and the Italian bailiwicks. [A. D. 1500 to 1525.] 126

XXXI. Beginning of the religious schism in Switzerland. [A. D. 1519 to 1527.] 131

XXXII. Progress of the discord in church-matters. [A. D. 1527 to 1530.] 136

XXXIII. The war of Kappel. Death of Zwingli. Avoyer Wengi of Solothurn. [A. D. 1531 to 1533.] 140

XXXIV. Geneva separates from Savoy. Berne subdues Vaud. [A. D. 1533 to 1558.] 143

CHAPTER PAGE

XXXV. Religious hatred in the Italian bailiwicks, in Grisons and everywhere. Dispute about the calendar. The Borromean-league. [A. D. 1558 to 1586.] ... 148

XXXVI. Insurrection at Muhlhausen. The Rhodes of Appenzell separate. The duke of Savoy tries to surprise Geneva. [A. D. 1587 to 1603.] ... 153

XXXVII. Troubles in Bienne. Conspiracy against Geneva. The black death. Commencement of civil war in Grisons. [A. D. 1603 to 1618.] ... 158

XXXVIII. Terrible destruction of Plurs. Massacre in Valtelina. Civil war among the Grisons. [A. D. 1618 to 1621.] ... 162

XXXIX. The Grisons are brought under the Austrian yoke. [A. D. 1621 to 1630.] ... 167

XL. The Grisons recover their liberty. [A. D. 1630 to 1640.] 171

XLI. Of the troubles among the Confederates during the Thirty years' religious war in Germany, and how Switzerland's independence of the German empire was established. [A. D. 1618 to 1648.] ... 175

XLII. How the peasants in the cantons of Lucerne, Berne, Solothurn and Bâle undertake to revolt, and lose thereby. [A. D. 1648 to 1655.] ... 180

XLIII. Another religious war. The battle near Villmergen. Commotion in Bâle. The pestilence. [A. D. 1656 to 1699.] ... 189

XLIV. How the Toggenburgers were deprived of their ancient liberties by the abbot of St. Gallen, and what happened in consequence. [A. D. 1700 to 1712.] ... 194

XLV. The Toggenburger war. Second battle near Villmergen. Peace concluded at Aarau. [A. D. 1712 to 1718.] ... 199

XLVI. Condition of the Swiss at the commencement of the Eighteenth century. Thomas Massner's quarrel. [A. D. 1701 to 1714.] ... 204

XLVII. Disturbances in Zurich, Schaffhausen and the bishopric of Bâle. [A. D. 1714 to 1740.] ... 208

XLVIII. Insurrection of the Werdenbergers against Glarus. [A. D. 1714 to 1740.] ... 213

XLIX. Party-rage and disturbances in Zug. Power and misfortunes of landammann Schumacher. [A. D. 1714 to 1740.] ... 216

L. Quarrel of the Harten and Linden in the Outer-rhodes of Appenzell. [A. D. 1714 to 1740.] ... 221

CHAPTER PAGE
LI. Henzi's conspiracy at Berne. [A. D. 1740 to 1749.]..... 225
LII. Of the rebellion in the valley of Leventina. [A. D. 1750 to 1755.].. 229
LIII. How the ancient Confederacy fell into still greater decay. The Helvetian society. [A. D. 1755 to 1761.]......... 233
LIV. King Frederick the Great, as prince of Neuchâtel, behaves nobly towards his subjects. [A. D. 1762 to 1770.]..... 238
LV. Party-quarrels in the city of Lucerne. History of land-ammann Suter of the Outer-rhodes of Appenzell. [A. D. 1770 to 1784.]................................... 241
LVI. Disturbances and insurrections in the canton of Freiburg. [A. D. 1781 to 1790.]............................. 247
LVII. Disturbances in the bishopric of Bâle, in Vaud and Grisons. [A. D. 1790 to 1794.]............................. 251
LVIII. History of parties and excesses in Geneva. [A. D. 1707 to 1797.].. 256
LIX. Of the ancient district of St. Gallen and the wise abbot Beda; how disturbances also broke forth on the lake of Zurich. [A. D. 1794 to 1797.]...................... 262
LX. Destruction of the old Confederacy. Entrance of the French into the land. [A. D. 1797 and 1798.]........ 268
LXI. How the Swiss suffered great calamities, until a new Confederacy was formed. [A. D. 1798 to 1803.].......... 274
LXII. Napoleon Buonaparte gives to the Swiss an "Act of mediation." [A. D. 1803 to 1813.]...................... 279
LXIII. The Swiss annul Napoleon's "Act of mediation," and divide, until foreign powers once more put an end to their division by founding a new Confederacy of twenty-two cantons. [A. D. 1814 and 1815.]................ 284
LXIV. Renewed loss of liberty, and weakness of the Swiss. [A. D. 1815 to 1829.]............................. 289
LXV. Thirteen cantons recover their liberty. Troubles in Schwyz, Neuchâtel and Bâle. [A. D. 1830 to 1832.]... 293
LXVI. The league of Sarnen. Five hundred Poles enter Switzerland from France. [A. D. 1832 to 1833.]............. 300
LXVII. Breach of the peace. Peace restored by the Diet. [A. D. 1833.].. 304
LXVIII. Conclusion... 307

CONTINUATION.

CHAPTER PAGE

LXIX. Expedition against Savoy. Occurrences at Steinholzlein. [A. D. 1834.] ... 311

LXX. Dispute with France. [A. D. 1835 and 1836.] ... 315

LXXI. Protocol of the Baden-conference; its occasion and consequences. [A. D. 1834 to 1836.] ... 320

LXXII. Constitutional quarrel in Glarus. Contest between the Horners and Klauens in Schwyz. Louis Napoleon. [A. D. 1837 and 1838.] ... 326

LXXIII. Explosion at Zurich. [A. D. 1839.] ... 331

LXXIV. Bitter consequences. Convent-rebellion at Aargau. [A. D. 1840 and 1841.] ... 336

LXXV. Revolution in Lucerne, in Ticino and Geneva. [A. D. 1840 to 1841.] ... 343

LXXVI. Termination of the convent-question. Formation of the Sonderbund. [A. D. 1842 to 1843.] ... 348

LXXVII. Party-hatred in Valais and fratricide on the Trient. [A. D. 1844.] ... 352

LXXVIII. The Jesuits invited to Lucerne. First free-corps expedition. [A. D. 1844.] ... 357

LXXIX. Revolution in Vaud. Second free-corps expedition. [A. D. 1845.] ... 362

LXXX. Painful consequences. [A. D. 1845 and 1846.] ... 368

LXXXI. The crisis approaches. [A. D. 1846 to 1847.] ... 372

LXXXII. The Sonderbund-war. [A. D. 1847.] ... 376

LXXXIII. The new Swiss Confederate-bond. [A. D. 1848.] ... 387

HISTORY OF SWITZERLAND.

CHAPTER I.

HOW IT WAS IN THE BEGINNING.

THE wonderful deeds of the heroes, our fathers, their good and evil fortunes, have been frequently told and as frequently recorded; but I wish to freshen those ancient traditions in the minds of the whole nation; and I relate them to the free men of the mountains and of the valleys, that their hearts may be inflamed with new love for their noble fatherland.

Attend, therefore, to my tale, old men and young. The history of past ages is a tree of the knowledge of good and of evil.

Where the Rhone, which rises from under the glaciers of Valais, at last rushes into the Mediterranean, begins a chain of lowly mountains. As they stretch further to the east, they raise their summits higher in the air, and, approaching Italy, lift them still higher, veiling their rocky tops in clouds and everlasting snows. They are three hundred leagues in length from their beginning until they reach Hungary. There the mountains sink by degrees and become hills. These mountains are the Alps,* and

* *Alp* means an elevated pasture: hence the name of the mountains on which such pastures exist.

Helvetia was the ancient name of the country where their snowy summits, their bared cliffs and inaccessible peaks rise highest, far above the fields of men and above the clouds of heaven.

Beyond the high Alps, furrowed by narrow gorges and covered with glaciers, the sources of innumerable rivers, the country extends to the north, in progressively enlarging valleys, as far as the calcareous mountains of the Jura. These curve in the form of an immense half-moon, from lake Leman (lake of Geneva) to the lake of Constance (Boden-see). And from Schaffhausen to Bâle, the Rhine rolls its waves along the base of the Jura, as in a moat at the base of a rampart. Thus has God begirt our fatherland, like an immense citadel, with steep mountains and deep waters. But a citadel is strong only when men are in it.

In ages of which no man knows, all this country was an ocean. The water stood fifteen hundred fathoms above the fields and meadows which we now cultivate. At that period, the summits of the mountains were separate islands. The high rocks still bear the marks of the mighty flood. Plants and shell-fish, which once lived at the bottom of the sea, now lie petrified in the mud which has become rock. The finger of God has written in the veins of the mountains, and the voice of Nature cries to us from the depths of their caverns, that this earth, before being the abode of man, underwent more than one overwhelming convulsion.

After the waters had subsided, and the dried bottom of the sea had become covered by moss, grass, shrubs and forests, ages passed ere a human voice resounded through the silence of this wilderness. No one knows who first wandered with his herd along the woody shores of our lakes and rivers. The earliest families must have established themselves in the broad and temperate valleys; long afterwards, they ascended into the wilder regions, and, at last, discovered the solitudes enclosed among the high Alps.

Six hundred years before the birth of Christ, the valleys above which the Rhine has its source were still uninhabited. Then, according to tradition, some fugitives from Italy first peopled them. The Gauls, a warlike and powerful nation, had penetrated into Italy, and, conquering the inhabitants, had slain them, or driven them from the abodes of their fathers. Trembling before the sword of their enemy, many fled from the maritime country of the Rasennes, where now flourish the cities of Genoa and Florence. With their wives, their children and their household gods, they found an asylum in the recesses and wildernesses of the high Alps. There they fixed their abodes in secluded valleys, among dense forests and lofty mountains, safe from the fury of the Gauls. They were called Rhetians, from the name of their god or hero, Rhetus. Hence the country about the sources of the Rhine and of the Inn, the strong home of the free Grisons, is, even in our day, called Rhetia.

CHAPTER II.

THE FIRST EXPLOITS OF THE ANCIENT HELVETIANS, AND HOW THE CYMBRI CAME TO THEM.

[One hundred years before the birth of Christ.]

For several centuries, the people increased slowly in the valleys between the Alps and the Jura, between lake Leman and the lake of Constance. Surrounded by rocks, woods and rivers, they lived on the products of the chase, of the soil, of their herds, unknown to the world, in savage freedom. They formed as many independent communities as there were separate valleys. Their valiant young men pursued the game through gloomy forests, fought with serpents in caverns and morasses, with wild beasts in the mountains, or, from time to time, made predatory excursions into the neighborhood. Skins formed their clothing; lances, clubs, bows and arrows were their arms. For offence and defence, several communes united into a Gau (district or province). That of the Tigurins, upon the banks of the Rhine and Thur, was the first of which the name is known (Thurgau).

Then it happened that a terrible people, coming from distant countries, crossed the forests of Germany. They were three hundred thousand warlike men, called Cymbri, that is: Confederates from various nations. Many of them are said to have come from Friesland and Sweden, and from Norway, where the inhabited world lies chilled in snow and ice. The tradition is that they had been driven out by hunger, when the sluices of heaven were opened upon their homes, and valleys and heights became lakes and swamps. Now they came, fighting and conquering, to the Rhine, and over the Rhine, to the cities of the Gauls, in the country which is now France. There they obtained an enormous booty.

When the young men in the district of the Tigurins heard of this, they were desirous to share in the glory and booty of the Cymbri. All who could bear arms went and joined those powerful conquerors. Much plunder was taken, much blood was shed. The people of Gaul uttered cries of terror, and implored help from Rome.

Rome immediately sent a strong army. It marched over the snowy Alps towards lake Leman. This frightened the Tigurins who were with the Cymbri; they thought that their homes in the mountains were threatened. They at once hastened against the Romans near lake Leman. A young hero, named Divikon, was their leader. As soon as he saw the enemy's camp, he drew the sword. A frightful carnage ensued; the bodies of the Romans covered the field; at last, they asked for quarter. Then Divikon raised two posts, over which he placed a beam. Beneath this gallows-yoke he compelled the disarmed enemies to crawl, to the eternal glory of his own people, and to the shame of Rome. Then he sent them home over the mountains.

Elated by this victory, Divikon rejoined the Cymbri, his companions in arms, and with them ravaged Gaul. Afterwards, they crossed the high Alps, entered Italy, and threatened Rome. Then the Romans rose in their strength, and many bloody battles were fought. But fortune deserted the Cymbri. Most of them fell by the edge of the sword. Those who escaped sought safety with Divikon in the security of the Helvetian mountains.

Thus, men driven from the cold North by flood and famine, came to establish themselves in Helvetia. They fixed their abode on the shores of the lake of the Waldstatten,* at the foot of the Haken and the Mythen, near to Bruch-land, which means marshy land, and cleared the forests. Hence they were called Bruchen-buren (peasants of the marsh). Schwyz is thought to have been founded by the brothers Switer and Swen. Family names, common in Sweden, are even now heard in those valleys.

Thence the people, as they became numerous, spread into the uninhabited woody valleys on the lake, into the country about Kernwald, over the black mountain Brunig, and thence through Hasli in Weissland, at the foot of the white ice mountains, from valley to valley, as far as Frutigen, Obersibnen, Sanen, Afflentsch, and Jaun.

So say the most ancient, uncertain traditions.

CHAPTER III.

ALL THE COUNTRY BECOMES ROMAN.

[Fifty years before the birth of Christ.]

For a long while after the exploits of Divikon and the Cymbri, tales were told of the fat pastures and rich country which had been seen in Gaul. There, was a more temperate sky, under which flourished the olive and the vine, and the snows of winter were seldom known. These tales excited the longings of the people in rugged Helvetia, especially when they heard them confirmed by travellers, or by their neighbors beyond the Rhine, with whom a friendly intercourse was maintained.

* *Lake of the forest-cantons;* usually called Vier Waldstätter See, *Lake of the four forest-cantons,* because enclosed by the cantons of Uri, Schwyz, Unterwalden and Lucerne.

At this time, there lived in the country a man of note, named Hordrich. (The Romans called him Orgetorix, and he is now known only by this altered name.) Ten thousand men and women servants cultivated his fields and herded his cattle; he enjoyed much consideration among the neighboring Gauls, and associated with their small princes. This man aspired to great things. He spoke first to the chief persons of his own district, then to those of the others, and, lastly, to the people in the communes. "Why should we exhaust our strength on a rough and rocky soil, to obtain a bare subsistence for ourselves and our animals? We must migrate into Gaul, here are plenty of fruitful fields open to a valiant people." These speeches inflamed all minds, and, soon, every one thought of going. The communes assembled and unanimously decided to prepare for a general emigration. During three years they were to cultivate their fields and make provision for the long journey; while, in the interval, they engaged allies and assistants, and did whatever was necessary to give security to their hazardous enterprise.

Orgetorix, delighted with the success of his appeal, exerted himself to ensure a prosperous result. He displayed great activity, constantly traversed the different districts, passed the Rhine to communicate with the bordering people and their chiefs; he asked a free passage for his nation, made great promises, talked more and louder than was prudent. He even gave his daughter in marriage to one of the neighboring princes, and acted as if he were himself already lord and king of the Helvetians.

This made his fellow-countrymen suspicious, and they began to think that he intended to betray the people and to destroy their ancient liberties, in order to become absolute master. But there was a law in the Helvetian districts that whoever attempted to infringe the rights and liberties of the people should be burnt to death; and Orgetorix was summoned to appear and reply to his accusers. He refused, and tried to arm his servants in his defence. Then the communes rose against him. Seeing that all was lost, he killed himself.

When the three years of preparation had elapsed, the

people in the four districts began their emigration. The men bearing arms opened the march. Old Divikon, who had defeated the Romans at lake Leman fifty years before, was their leader. Then followed the women and children, the wagons and carts laden with provisions and articles of value. They burned all their dwellings behind them, twelve cities and four hundred villages, that no one might long to return to his old home. Many thousands of allies came from lake Constance, and the Rauraques from the Rhine country, which now constitutes the Frickthal and the territory of Bâle. All joined the Helvetians.

Thus the long, interminable train of warlike emigrants crossed mountains and valleys. The Helvetians were 260,000 in all. They directed their march towards Geneva, then a city of the Allobroges, a small but courageous people, and allied to Rome.

At this time, about sixty years before the advent of Jesus Christ, Rome was the most powerful city in the whole world. She had become such through the liberty, the heroism and the wisdom of her citizens. Her arms and laws ruled over Italy and from Gaul to Judea. The greatest of her generals, Julius Cesar, was at Geneva to protect the Allobroges.

When Cesar heard of the approach of the Helvetians, and of their intention to cross the Rhone at Geneva, he immediately built, along the stream, in front of the city, a wall 9000 paces long and 16 feet high, with numerous towers, and opposed the passage of the emigrants. But they turned towards the gorge of the Jura, through which the Rhone precipitates its waters into Gaul. They clambered along steep rocks, by narrow footpaths. Beneath them were abysses and the roaring flood.

They were hardly across the mountains, on the plains of Gaul, when Cesar was there also. He attacked the rear-guard of Tigurins. Grey-haired Divikon approached Cesar and said: "What have I to do with thee and thy Romans? Let me go on my way in peace, or remember the conflict of lake Leman, and beware lest I make this place, also, celebrated by a Roman defeat!" Cesar answered: "The Gods formerly granted good fortune to thee by lake Leman, in order that thy present bad fortune might be doubly bitter. Nevertheless, I will let thee go thy way, provided thou respect my allies, restore to them what thy soldiers have plundered on their passage, and give me hostages for thy truth." "Not so, Roman," replied Divikon, "we have learnt from our ancestors to take, instead of giving hostages."

Thereat, the Helvetians journeyed on, slowly and with difficulty, followed closely, during fourteen days, by the Roman host. Suddenly the Helvetians turned, full of anger and in arms. A general battle took place in the fields of the Gallic city of Bibracte (Autun); it lasted from morning until sunset. Valiantly, but without skill, fought the Helvetians; not less valiantly, but with more experience in war, the Romans. This gave the victory to the latter. The Helvetians fled in disorder to the hill where their wives, children and property were enclosed by a rampart of wagons. The enemy followed and broke through the wagons; old men and warriors, women and children, fell by the swords of the victors; many by their own, that they might not survive freedom and honor; others fled shrieking, wandered in every direction, and were given up by the Gauls to Cesar. He said to the vanquished, prostrate at his feet and imploring his mercy: "Lay down your arms; return home whence you came; rebuild your huts; live as before, contented in your mountains, under your own laws. Every country is good for man, when man is good for the country. You shall not be the slaves of Rome, but shall share her alliance and protection."

Full of shame and sorrow, numbering hardly 110,000, they returned to the valleys whence they had come, and rebuilt their huts upon the ashes. But Cesar erected, near Geneva, on the lake, a new fortress, called Noviodunum, now Nyon. This he did to watch the Helvetians. Other garrisons were also placed here and there in the land.

Roman troops were also stationed at Octodurum (perhaps Martigny), at the foot of the Alps, in what is now Lower Valais, to guard the road over the mountains into Italy. The inhabitants of this broad valley, through which the

Rhone finds its way to the lake, then lived a free and savage life; they had no connection with either the Helvetians or the Romans; they enforced a toll on all merchandise that crossed their Alps, and committed depradations upon it. When they saw foreign soldiers thus established and entrenched on their territory, they became furious. Rushing from their mountains and their valleys, they attacked the Roman garrisons in their entrenchments, and harassed them until they drove them from the country. But the Romans soon returned into the valley with such increased forces as made all resistance vain. Nearly ten thousand of the inhabitants, fighting for the freedom of their homes, were slain, and, on every side, villages sank in flames. From this time, Valais, also, was Roman.

The Rhetians alone, behind their ice-mountains and their lakes, deemed themselves invincible. Along the Inn, in the valleys of what is now Tyrol, and in the Vindelecian plains (now Suabia), were their allies and confederates, as advanced guards. They lived a wild life, pillaged travellers, or, suddenly issuing in numerous hordes from the gorges of their mountains, surprised and plundered the neighboring Italian cities. From among their prisoners they sacrificed victims on the altars of their Gods.

Irritated by this, the emperor Augustus, in whose reign the Savior of the world was born, sent two armies at once to penetrate that fearful and elevated region. One passed the Alps and descended towards the Inn; the other crossed the Vindelecian lake (lake of Constance); and the whole country was subjugated after bloody conflicts. It is related that the wives of the Rhetians rushed into the ranks of the combatants, and dashed their nursing infants upon the faces of the enemy, as if in their mountains all life must become extinct with liberty.

CHAPTER IV.

OF THE ROMAN DOMINION IN THE LAND.

[A. D. 1 to 300.]

LIBERTY did indeed become extinct in the mountains, but life remained, subject thenceforth to the Roman emperor Augustus, who ruled, all-powerful, from the rising to the setting of the sun. He sent his prefects, governors and soldiers into the inhabited valleys of Helvetia, and caused strong fortresses to be erected, to keep the people in subjection and obedience. He saw that the snowy Alps and the Jura were an insurmountable bulwark for Italy, where he sat on the throne in the rich city of Rome.

Still the emperor treated the conquered Helvetians with humanity, and respected their manners and customs, that they might thus become more easily habituated to his rule, and forget their disgrace. He even permitted them to live according to their ancient laws, and under magistrates of their own choice. All matters relating to the interests of a district were discussed in an assembly of deputies from each commune. But the emperor reserved to himself the right to enact general laws, to decree taxes and contributions, and to make war and peace.

All this took place at the time when Jesus Christ was born in Judea. After the death of the emperor Augustus, his successors long showed themselves favorable to the Helvetians. They founded many new colonial cities, and connected them with each other by broad highways. The Roman prefects, governors and military men, accustomed to a more comfortable life than were the poor, rude Helvetians, built everywhere magnificent dwellings and pleasure-houses, introduced fruit-trees from Italy, and instructed the people in all kinds of trades and manufactures, in commerce, and in the arts and sciences; thus, by degrees, the country acquired riches and comforts, previously unknown.

Many places became populous, and grew into magnificent cities, with immense palaces, baths, temples and theatres. The great city Aventicum was ten times more extensive than now is Wiflisburg (Avenche) on the same spot. The boats of the lake of Morat then landed under the walls. At the place where we now see two little villages (Augst in Bâle, and Augst in Aargau) at the confluence of the Ergolz and the Rhine, was a flourishing city, Augusta Rauracorum, the ruins of which still attest its former magnificence. But greatest and most magnificent of all was the city of Vindonissa (Windisch, in Aargau). In the vast space covered by its fortresses, its palaces and its suburbs, we now see three villages and a city (Brugg).

These things pleased the Helvetians. They were delighted at the clemency of their masters, willingly paid taxes and contributions, and sent their sons to serve in the Roman armies. In their new comforts, they forgot the ancient liberty for which their fathers had fought and bled.

But comfort without liberty is an uncertain good. Let not the bird rejoice in his golden cage, for his master can kill him at his will!

About seventy years after the birth of Jesus Christ, an emperor, named Galba, was assassinated at Rome, and another elected in his stead: Vitellius, who was not satisfactory to all. The Helvetians were ignorant of the death of the old emperor, but the chiefs of the Roman garrisons in the country, being early informed, leagued together in behalf of Vitellius, and sent messengers in every direction. This astonished the Helvetians, who thought that the leaders meditated a revolt against the emperor Galba. The soldiers of the garrisons, especially those of Vindonissa, were moreover insolent and undisciplined, and had even seized the pay belonging to the garrison of Baden, composed entirely of young Helvetians. These, therefore, intercepted the messengers and letters of Aulus Cecina, governor-general of Vindonissa.

When Cecina received news of this in Vindonissa, he was greatly exasperated, and marched out with his troops, who were called, and were, "terrible." He stormed and destroyed the fortress and city of Baden, which had become flourishing in consequence of its warm healing springs on the Limmat, plundered the country and vanquished the resisting Helvetians in a bloody combat. He pursued the conquered beyond the Bœtzberg, one of the Jura mountains. In their flight down the mountain, the fugitives were met by a numerous body of Thracian cavalry. Thousands of the Helvetians were slain in this encounter, or dispersed among the woods and cliffs; others were taken and sold as slaves.

This massacre did not appease the wrath of Cecina, but he swept over and ravaged the whole country, as far as Aventicum. Here lived a rich and respected Helvetian, Julius Alpinus. The cruel Roman ordered him to be seized, as the originator of the revolt, to be loaded with bonds and chains, and led forth to an ignominious death. In vain did many persons testify to the old man's innocence; in vain did his daughter, Julia Alpinula, a priestess, throw herself at Cecina's feet. Her beauty, her youth and her tears could not touch the heart of the ferocious warrior. The grey-haired old man was put to death.

The whole land was filled with sorrow and complaints. The people now learned, too late, that the emperor to whom they wished to remain faithful, had been killed, and that Vitellius was lord of the world. Embassadors were sent in haste to the new emperor, to implore his mercy. Prostrate in the dust at the foot of his throne, the Helvetians begged for pardon with tears and sobs. That which they solicited with contemptible submission as trembling subjects, was contemptuously granted to them as vile slaves. Such is the lot of vassalage, which prefers the comforts of life to freedom from foreign bondage.

But neither the carnage of Bœtzberg, nor the desolation of Aventicum, nor the disgrace before the imperial throne, could restore to the Helvetians their pristine vigor. It had been extinguished and destroyed by long effeminacy. They forgot past sufferings, and lived as before, in enervating pleasures; sought for riches, sensual delights, and the refinements of luxury, and cared not for that heroism which lives only in free hearts.

Their Roman rulers were pleased to see that the people, thoughtless of better things, remained effeminate and tribu tary; that, unaccustomed to fighting, they unlearned the art of war, and that, instead of strengthening the union between their districts, they awaited their weal or woe, in slavish silence, from the hand of their masters.

Woe to the country in whose tribunals foreigners sit, and whose gates are guarded by foreigners! Woe to the people who are proud of the support of a foreign power, and divided among themselves by hatred! Woe to the nations who amass gold and know not the use of steel, by which life is protected!

The Helvetians, thoughtless of defence, were exposed to constant peril. As they had forgotten the past, they foresaw not the future. Thus they were ripe for destruction. Thus the day of their terrible and total ruin found them entirely unprepared.

CHAPTER V.

HOW THE WHOLE COUNTRY BECOMES A PREY TO FOREIGN NATIONS.

[A. D. 300 to 550.]

At this period, great and wonderful things took place upon the earth. Rome, for so many ages queen of the world, in losing her virtues had lost the pillars of her power. Paganism, despised, had no longer any hold upon men, and they forsook the altars of idols for the unknown God. From the bosom of the East, the light of Christianity blazed forth as a newly risen sun, and enkindled with its rays the hearts of multitudes in three quarters of the world.

It seemed as if a voice from heaven had said: "I will mingle together the nations of the earth, like chaff in a whirlwind, that the sparks of holy faith may be scattered over the world, and all the countries of men be set on fire thereby. The false gods shall become dust and ashes. Old things shall be destroyed, and all shall become new."

And now, from the depths of unknown regions, issued nations upon nations, driving all before them at the point of the sword. They came from the rising of the sun, and from the unconquered countries of the North.

First came the Allemanni, savage warriors of Germanic race. During two centuries and a half of continued warfare, they penetrated deeper and deeper into the Roman territory, and drew nearer and nearer to the Helvetian mountains. At last they broke, like an overwhelming torrent, through the passes of the Jura, and spread themselves over the land. From the Black Forest to the foot of the Alps, all was desolation. The magnificence of Aventicum and of Vindonissa lay heaped in ruins. Romans, as well as Helvetians, if spared by the sword of the enemy, became slaves. The Allemanni divided among themselves the whole country, with its riches and its inhabitants, from the Rhine and the lake of Constance to the lake of the Waldstatten and the Aar. They loved war, liberty and herds. They despised cities, as the prisons of free men. The memories of Rome and of ancient Helvetia were sunk in shameful oblivion.

Shortly after these, the Huns swarmed forth from the wildernesses of Asia in numberless hordes. They pillaged the world. Their faces were so hideous that they could hardly be called human ; their deeds were still less human. These destroyers traversed Germany, Gaul and Italy. Some of their bands passed through the Helvetian territory, penetrated into Rhetia, into the districts on the Aar, and spread over the neighborhood of Augusta Rauracorum and of Basilia (Bâle), formerly a Roman city. They stopped nowhere; but everywhere flames, blood and tears marked their passage.

Then came the Burgundians, a vigorous race. They established themselves in Gaul, on both sides of the Jura, in Savoy, on lake Leman, in Lower Valais, and as far as the Aar, where the French language is now spoken. They built strong fortresses, raised Geneva from its ruins, and, probably, Avenche on the ashes of Aventicum. On the heights near lake Leman, where Roman Lausonium formerly stood, they founded Lausanne anew, and several other places.

Then, from the South, over the highest Alps, came the

powerful Goths. Italy was already their prey; all Rhetia, with her valleys and mountain pastures, shared the same fate. The power of the Goths extended far beyond the lake of Wallenstatt even to the Sitters (the small rivers of Appenzell), over the St. Gotthard into the valleys of Uri and not less into Glarus. Fear was in all places.

These successive invasions effaced the arts and industry of olden time; the laws, customs and languages formerly in use. Even the name of Helvetia was lost. Men heard only of the Allemanni, the Goths and the Burgundians.

Wherever the Allemanni came, they destroyed the cities. They dwelt in isolated farm-houses or in hamlets. Their bondsmen, with their wives and children, served them as shepherds, husbandmen and mechanics. Whenever they wished to favor one of these, they gave him inalienable lands, at ground-rent and man-service. Their herds supplied them with meat, milk and cheese. The whole country was pasturage and undivided common. The soil formerly cultivated became a wilderness. Bushes grew where once the Roman plough had been. Around the lake of Constance were immense forests, full of bears and wolves.

In Upper Rhetia, the Goths preserved their warlike spirit, but their manners were more gentle. They made the people serfs, it is true, but left to them their ancient customs. They did not destroy the Roman fortresses they found, but built new ones. Living in their high towers, the signiors and counts governed their tributary valleys in the name of their king, who dwelt in Italy.

The Burgundians showed themselves the most humane of all. They appropriated only a third part of the land and serfs. They did not exterminate the ancient inhabitants, but made them subjects, and inferior in rights. They established themselves among them, mingled their own language and customs with theirs, so that at last the two became one people. Even in our day this people is distinguished from the rest of the Confederates by the hereditary but disfigured idiom called Romain, of the districts of Vaud, Freiburg, and Neuchâtel.

The dominion of all these foreign nations was of short

duration. Another people made their appearance, more powerful, more daring, more shrewd than those who had preceded them. These were the Franks. They came from afar, across the Low Countries, and with fire and sword quickly made themselves masters of all Gaul. They established themselves in the conquered cities, and the country, from them, was called France. When they encountered the power of the Allemanni on the Rhine, a long struggle took place between the two people. At last the Allemanni were completely and irretrievably vanquished in a terrible conflict, and those who dwelt along the Rhine, in Suabia and in Helvetia, fell under the dominion of the victors.

A short time afterwards, the Burgundians also perished by discord and the vices of their princes. The Goths took possession of the Burgundian Alps and of Geneva; the Franks, of the rest of the Burgundian territory.

But the latter, only, kept what they won; not so the Goths. When their dominion came to an end in Italy, their power over the Alpine region perished also. The Frank king, Dietbert [Dagobert?], did not hesitate. He marched with his troops, and conquered Rhetia and the rest of the country.

Thus, at last, after more than five centuries of vicissitudes and changes, all Helvetia was again united under the sceptre of a single sovereign, as it had been under the Romans.

CHAPTER VI.

DOMINION AND RULE OF THE FRANKS.

[A. D. 550 to 900.]

THE new masters divided the country into two parts, because they had acquired possession of them at different times, and because the inhabitants themselves spoke different languages. The country occupied by the Allemanni, and where German was spoken, that is, Rhetia and Thurigau,* was united to Suabia. The other districts, in which Romain was spoken, or which had been taken from the Burgundians, as Geneva, Valais, Neuchâtel, and what now belongs to Berne, Solothurn, Freiburg, and Vaud, were united with Savoy, and called Little Burgundy.

The mighty kings of France, chiefs of a warlike people, organized the governments of countries as they did their armies. They placed a general-in-chief, or duke, over a broad territory; commandants, or counts, governed separate portions of this territory, or districts; and other valiant captains received large domains in these districts, in fee or fief. In those times money was rare. Kings therefore recompensed the services of their warriors with lands and their revenue. Among the property which they gave away in conquered countries, all the inhabitants, with their houses, farms and cattle were included; then the inhabitants became serfs. The serf could own no property, as he was himself the property of his signior, and must account to the latter for all he held. Thurigau and Rhetia were under the duke of Suabia or Allemannia, and the rest under the duke of Little Burgundy.

Thus the whole country was divided, with its inhabitants and cattle; what the king had not given or enfeoffed to his counts, nobles, or officers, remained his own property, and was managed for his profit. The free Franks only, however few in number, constituted the nation; the multitude of subjugated inhabitants were counted for nothing, had no civil rights, were serfs, infamous and defenceless. The lot of these serfs was lamentable, indeed, in the early times; their master could, at his will, punish them, give them away, sell them, even put them to death, without being called to account. They were hardly looked upon as human, but rather as a kind of cattle; thus they were united without any marriage ceremony, and the new-born children became the property of the mother's master, when the father belonged to another lord.

So barbarous and savage were those times.

* All the region enclosed between the lake of Constance and the Rhine on one side, the Aar and the St. Gotthard on the other, was then called Thurigau.

CHAPTER VII.

THE CHRISTIAN RELIGION PENETRATES THE LAND.

THROUGH the midst of the darkness of the times came messengers of God, pious men, to preach to the heathen the kingdom of heaven, and to announce the crucified one. They were military men who had heard the word of eternal salvation in other countries; men of elevated rank, often kings' sons, who, like the holy apostles, renounced the pleasures of the world to confess Jesus among the heathen. It is said that, even in the time of the Romans, hardly two centuries after the birth of the Savior, such a king's son, named Lucius, had sown the seed of the faith among the Rhetian mountains, under danger of death. Somewhat later, others came among the Burgundians, and others also among the Allemanni in Thurgau. They gathered around them pious families, baptized young and old in the name of God, established small Christian communities, built churches and chapels. They also founded convents for the promotion of education, prayer and faith, and instituted bishops, who were called superintendants, over the other Christian teachers and communities. Even before the country became Frank, there was a bishop at Coire (Chur) in Rhetia, a city which first became important towards the close of the Roman dominion; also at Augusta Rauracorum, at Vindonissa and at Aventicum, as well as at Geneva and at Octodurum in Valais.*

But when the Franks, already Christians, became masters of our country, then the work of conversion was for the first time carried forward with zeal; priests were protected, bishops revered, churches and convents endowed. A tithe was imposed on the products of the soil for the

* The seats of the Christian bishoprics have not remained in all these cities, but in a long course of disasters have been removed to undestroyed places. Thus the bishop's see was transferred from the ruins of ancient Augusta Rauracorum to Bâle, that of Aventicum to Lausanne, that of Vindonissa to Constance on the lake of this name, that of Octodurum to Sion (Sitten) in Upper Valais.

support of ecclesiastics; voluntary contributions increased the magnificence of God's service. As money was rare, contributions were more easily made in products of the soil and in real estate. That which was conferred on religious institutions was looked upon as given, not to mortal men, but to God, and to the saints of God, who were revered, and as a loan to be repaid by endless enjoyments after death. Thus, by degrees, churches and convents became wealthy, rich in lands and rents.

From foreign countries came an always increasing number of preachers of the Cross, to extirpate the last remains of paganism. For, in the thick forests which bordered the lake of Zurich, and in the remote valleys among the mountains, long dwelt half-savage men without any knowledge of the living God. Upon the heights of the hills and in the depths of the woods they sacrificed cattle and horses as victims to their idols; at the beginning of each new year they made a horrible uproar with cries and shouts, and by beating on noisy instruments, to drive away wicked spirits, sorcerers and witches; but welcomed the opening of spring with huge bonfires on all the mountains, as thank-offerings to the good gods. Many superstitious fears about ghosts and spirits tormented these poor blinded heathen; they believed in all kinds of presages and predictions, in the influence of good and evil days, and in similar self-deceptions.

Therefore the pious men who brought the tidings of salvation to these heathen are to be held in high esteem. Sigebert came from the country of the Franks, and preached in the wildernesses of Rhetia. He built his cell in the rough angle of the mountains, where the convent of Disentis now stands. Columban and Mangold long taught upon the Aar, the Reuss and the lake of Zurich, as did the zealous Gallus. The latter finally established his hermitage in the solitude of the high mountain-valley, near the lake of Constance, where, in memory of him, stands the convent of St. Gallen. Among the mountains which border the lake of the Waldstatten, the word of God was announced by pious Meinrad, who built his cell in the dark forest (Finsterwald) near the Sihl, where in our days flourishes the convent of Einsiedeln (Our Lady of the Hermits). A duke founded the chapter of canons upon the hill near Zurich, and endowed it with much property on the Albis; his brother built another monastery on the lake of the Waldstatten, where once, probably in the Roman time, there had been a simple light tower for vessels, and where the city of Lucerne now shines. Shortly afterwards, the rich count Bero erected near the same place another convent or monastery, even now called Beromunster.

But I should be long in coming to an end, if I tried to name all the pious works of that period. The poor pagans in the districts saw the consecrated walls of churches and convents rising on every side; all day long they heard the words of salvation and of the Cross, and all the night long the hymns and prayers of the monks in their cells. Their hearts were moved, and they went to baptism.

It must be acknowledged that the Christianity of those early days was very poor and feeble; conversions were too numerous and too sudden; the teachers were often as rude and ignorant as the hearers of the word. Whoever was baptized, had learnt a prayer, attended church, and could make the sign of the cross, was called a Christian, even though he had not given up his savage customs and heathen superstitions. Saints were frequently placed upon the seats of idols, and pagan feasts changed by name to Christian festivals. The fear of the devil was more powerful than the love of God. Sinners thought they could easily purchase their everlasting salvation, and redeem themselves from hell by ceremonies, and gifts to convents and churches.

Nevertheless, the new religion did not remain entirely inefficacious. Dawn always precedes the brightness of broad daylight. The belief in the one living God, in the compensations of eternity, and that we men here below are all children of the Father in Heaven, became general. Many pious priests and bishops, with their wives, shone as bright examples among the rest of the households; for, in those days, marriage was not forbidden to priests and bishops. Many Christian lords bettered the condition of their subjects, and many serfs received privileges which rendered their lot more endurable. In many convents schools were established, and the writings of ancient sages collected and copied; for the art of printing was not discovered until several centuries later. The light of science especially shone forth from the cells of the abbey of St. Gallen upon the darkness of the land. The people were instructed in agriculture and rural economy by the hermits and monks, who, in their wildernesses, extirpated the forests and cleared the soil; fallow lands were broken up. The people were taught to burn lime and to build with stone; until then they had only miserable wooden huts; they learned to weave wool and to use woollen clothes, instead of the linen and skins they had previously worn. They even began to plant vines upon the heights of lake Leman and of the lake of Zurich.

All this was not, indeed, the work of the monks alone, but more especially of the Franks, when they established themselves in the country; they brought with them domestic economy, the ox and the plough, wherever their king had granted to them, in fee or in fief, lands with men and women slaves thereon.

CHAPTER VIII.

HOW THE COUNTRY BECOMES PART OF THE GERMAN EMPIRE, AND CITIES ARE BUILT.

[A. D. 900 to 1200.]

THE kings of powerful France were for a long time more mighty than all the others, and the most mighty was king Charlemagne. He caused himself to be crowned at Rome, as emperor of the ancient Roman empire, which he proposed to reëstablish, and by the name of emperor he wished to show that he was a king of kings. But his sons and grandsons were always quarrelling among themselves, and, often, men of weak minds. Each wished to have a portion of the sovereignty, and they divided that vast empire. One took France, another Italy, a third Germany, and they carried on great wars against each other without cessation. In consequence of this division, that portion of the Helvetian territory which had, until then, been attached to the duchy of Suabia, became part of the German empire.

As there were so many kings, and they were continually at war with each other, great confusion prevailed every where. This pleased the principal officers and governors of the kings, that is, the dukes and counts. They ruled thenceforward without fear of responsibility, and, at their deaths, gave their offices to their sons, considering the duchies and counties as hereditary fiefs, or even as their own properties. The duke of Suabia would obey no one; the duke of Burgundy assumed the title of king. As the dukes revolted against the kings, so the counts revolted against the dukes, hired troops and acted as sovereigns. Even the bishops did not remain idle. Eminent and powerful in their dioceses and domains, they imitated the counts and dukes, made themselves independent of the secular arm, donned casque and cuirass, and rode at the head of their troops. As did the bishops towards dukes and counts, so did the pope of Rome towards emperors and kings; assumed authority over them, over all the bishops and churches in their dominions, and, finally, over their people.

At last, as a consequence of this general confusion, the signiors and counts established in Helvetia, no longer paid respect to the dukes of Suabia, but, ruling by their own authority, they feared only the kings or German emperors, or flattered them for ambitious purposes. Usually at variance with each other, only a common danger could unite them.

Such a danger threatened them all at the time when Henry, surnamed the Fowler, ruled the German empire. From the regions of the East, from the Black Sea and along the Danube, once more appeared a warlike and savage people, all on horseback, numerous as the sands of the sea. They were called Hungarians. With sword and fire they quickly swept over Germany, quickly over Italy. Nothing stopped them, neither rivers nor mountains. But they did not attack strong fortresses and castles, because they did not understand the art of besieging. This was nine hundred years after the birth of Christ.

Then the emperor ordered that all large villages in the country should be surrounded with walls, ramparts and ditches, against these terrible enemies. Thus St. Gallen and Bâle were encircled by walls, because they were on the frontiers, as well as Zurich on the lake. These were like fortresses for the people, to which they could flee with their property in case of need. One-ninth of the free and noble men, those who had but little landed estate being selected, were obliged to dwell in these national fortresses, to defend them in war, and govern them in peace. Thus were founded the cities and their councils. The free nobles, charged with the city government, assumed the name of patricians.

The example once given, many people's fortresses or cities were soon built, as Lucerne and Solothurn; and, later, Schaffhausen, at the landing-place of the Rhine, where this stream makes its mighty rush over the rocks, took the place of the cluster of boat-houses (Schiffhausern). As in German Helvetia, so also in Burgundian Helvetia, when the emperors at last added this also to the German empire, and made the dukes of Zahringen imperial bailiffs over it. Here were already the very ancient cities of Geneva and Lausanne. To these the imperial bailiff, Berthold, duke of Zahringen, added the city of Freiburg, which he built in Uechtland* (in 1179), as a means of offence and defence against the power of the refractory lords and counts of the neighborhood. His son did the same, and built the city of Berne on a peninsula formed by the river Aar, in 1191.

All these, and other cities, which rose up here and there, as open villages were walled and fortified, received the political organization, the franchises and privileges enjoyed

* *Uechtland:* waste or pasture land; applied to what was probably the ancient Pagus Aventicensis of the Romans, embracing much of the present territory of Berne, Neuchâtel, Freiburg, &c., which had been devastated by the Allemanni.

by the most ancient cities of Germany. The laborers and artisans who established themselves in a city acquired the rights of burghership, were obliged to keep a spear and a sword for defence, to pay taxes and contributions, to have a fire-bucket ready in each house; for the houses in cities, as well as in villages, were then built of wood. Important matters were discussed in a general assembly of the citizens, but the government of the commonwealth was entrusted to a council chosen by the burghers, and presided over by an avoyer or burgomaster. Small disputes were decided by the council, but the higher jurisdiction (blutgericht, jus-gladii) belonged to the imperial bailiff, the vicar of the abbot, or the count's lieutenant, in short, to the governor of the city, whoever he might be.

The security found behind their walls against inimical attacks, attracted many people to the cities; the increase of population fostered trade, commerce and the mechanic arts. Markets were established, to which the countryman brought the surplus products of his fields and flocks, and where the citizen gave in exchange the fruits of his industry. The comforts of the citizens increased with their ingenuity, and softened their manners; their union and strength caused them to be respected more and more by the signiors and nobles who dwelt in the neighborhood, in isolated castles and fortresses. Dukes, kings and emperors liked to stop on their journeys, and enjoy the comforts of the cities, to which they, in return, granted various privileges and franchises. But the prosperity of the cities excited the jealousy of the counts, knights and signiors of the country. They also strove to increase their power and revenues; and to obtain new fiefs and grants, served with redoubled ardor the kings, dukes and convents; or made small war upon their neighbors, for the sake of plunder. Several, who knew their best interests, lightened the yoke of servitude which pressed upon their subjects, and were pleased to see the people increase upon their lands. As by right of conquest all the soil, with man and beast and tree (mit Wohn' und Weid' und Wald), had become their property or fief, they divided the land, when arable or pasture, into large farms or single house-lots (usually of twelve acres), among the householders, who paid therefor in body-service, in rent and tithes. Thus villages, farms and plantations were multiplied. Every new house on signioral land paid a tribute in fowls and eggs. At the death of a vassal, father of a family, his children gave to their signior, or to the convent from which they held, the best dress from the chest, the best piece of furniture from the house, and the best beast from the stable. After thus satisfying the "right to the best chattels" (todfalls), the heirs kept the rest as if it were their own inheritance and property.

Thus the revenues of the signiors were increased by the body-service and rents due from their vassals. The undivided lands, mostly thick forest, remained the lord's property. He allowed to his subjects and vassals all the wood they required, and, at his good pleasure, granted to them, on a rent-charge or as a gratuity, permission to gather acorns for the fattening of their swine, as well as free range for cattle, as far as the limits of the next hamlet or farm.

But, without permission of the signior, no one could cut, burn or clear, in whole or in part, those forests of lofty growth, to convert them into meadows or fields. Still, the signiors were pleased to see households multiplied and new farms established. Thus they allowed portions of their woods to be cut and cleared, and received ground and clearance-rent therefor from the new comers. In this manner were formed numerous villages, even now called Schwanden or Schwændi, Ruti or Reuti.* But the farmers, if not before free, remained serfs, as their fathers had been, and all their possessions were considered the property of their signior. For the latter furnished to them, not only the soil, but also the wood for a house and stable, a plough, a cart, seeds for the field, a hatchet and ladder for housework, a cow for the stable, a sow and pigs, a cock and hens for the yard. This is why they owed rent for everything, with man-service in their lords' fields, cart-work to his

* Both these words signify to clear; the first by burning, the second by felling or uprooting, the trees and bushes.

castle, tithes and taxes on their crops, with cheese, cloth, hens and eggs.

Such was the origin of the cities and of numerous villages in Switzerland.

CHAPTER IX.

MORE ABOUT THE CITIES AND THE GREAT SIGNIORS IN THE COUNTRY.

[A. D. 1200 to 1290.]

THUS, in proportion as the peasants gained in comforts, the greater revenue did the numerous imposts paid by them yield to the counts, nobles, abbots and other signiors. But especially did these latter become free and independent when the dukes of Zahringen died out; as, at their extinction, the dignity and office of imperial lieutenant, or bailiff, ceased to be hereditary, and was conferred temporarily, sometimes on one count, sometimes on another. From this moment, the nobles had no reason to fear the overpowering force or authority of any one among their peers. Each endeavored to be first, or hoped to become so.

At that time flourished many noble families which are now extinct. The counts of Savoy had extensive domains, fiefs and rights, in Valais and in Vaud, where the bishop of Lausanne also reigned as sovereign on a small scale. The counts of Neuchâtel, who granted great franchises to the city of that name, reigned over French and German districts on the lake of Bienne (Biel), as well as on the Aar and Zihl. The counts of Kyburg, who were masters of all the country between Zurich and the lake of Constance, and who built upon their own territory the cities of Diessenhofen on the Rhine, and of Winterthur near Zurich, acknowledged no one in the country more powerful than themselves. Still, near them, in Aargau, were the counts of Habsburg, already long possessors, in their own right, of a large domain in the region where ancient Vindonissa had flourished. They were, moreover, patrons of the rich abbey of Seckingen, which held much property in Glarus;

then they received in fief the very ancient Burgundian county of Rore, in Aargau. This county extended as far as Muri, where, two centuries before, the wife of a count of Habsburg, then called counts of Altenburg, had founded a Benedictine abbey (1025). On extinction of the counts of Rore, their domains had fallen to the counts of Lenzburg, from whom descended also the counts of Baden, and whose great riches now increased the eminence of the counts of Habsburg.

The counts of Rapperswyl, also, who built the city of that name on the lake of Zurich, were powerful and respected in the Marches of Rhetia; but the rich counts of Toggenburg were even more so. The original residence of this family was on a rock not far from the convent of Fischingen. It was there that a count Henry of Toggenburg, in a fit of jealousy, threw his beautiful wife Ida from a window of the lofty castle, because he had seen her wedding-ring on the finger of one of his servants. A raven had stolen the ring from an open window, and afterwards dropped it. But Ida, as she fell, seizing fast hold of some bushes growing out of the precipice, was saved by divine providence, and her innocence manifested. She closed her life in a cell at Fischingen, as she could no longer love her husband; who, besides wreaking his anger upon her, had caused the innocent servant to be dragged to death at the tail of a wild horse.

I could also name many other families of counts and barons, then very powerful signiors, such as the counts of Werdenberg and Sargans, of Montfort and Sax, of Vatz and Rhezuns, in Upper Rhetia, and others in Burgundian and German districts. But who would care to know them all, when nothing is now left of them but the obscure remembrance of their wars, or the traditions of their atrocities, which still float around the ruins of their fallen rock-castles.

Many of these ancient and noble families became extinct and forgotten at a very early period. This happened quite frequently when the opinion prevailed that religion and honor required men to make a pilgrimage to Jerusalem, sword in hand, for the purpose of rescuing the holy sepulchre from the possession of heathens and infidels. Armed pilgrims from all Christian nations united in countless numbers, and departed, year after year, for the promised land, all conspicuous by the sign of the Cross sewed upon their garments. Young and old went, even children, princes, kings, emperors, nuns and princesses. But of thousands and thousands, only a few ever returned from these crusades; for most of them died on the way, or perished in Asia and Africa, by hunger, disease, the sword, the plague, leprosy, or in the prisons of the infidels. This widowed many a noble lady, made many a mother childless.

That which proved the ruin of counts and knights, benefited the serfs in the villages and farms, and even the burghers in the cities. The serfs were treated with more humanity, to induce them to remain at home and not seek freedom under the banners of the Cross. Privileges were granted to them that they might be employed as soldiers in internal wars. And the burghers of the cities enriched themselves by all kinds of trade and traffic for the arming, equipment and provisioning of the troops which incessantly departed for the Holy Land. An extensive interchange of merchandise took place through Hungary with Greece, and through the ports of Italy with Egypt and the East. Bâle, especially, flourished by this commerce, in which even Cyprus wine was brought there; and Zurich, where the manufacture of costly silks was established.

As comforts and riches increased in the new cities, the burghers became more enterprising, acquired greater privileges, and extended their city-territory by purchase. Some ransomed their cities from the oppressive sovereignty of the bishops, abbots and convents, under which they had long lived, and gladly placed them under the protection of the German empire, that they might be subject to no one but the emperor himself, or to an imperial bailiff acting in his name. The Solothurners made themselves independent of the convent of St. Ursus, which had possessed great influence in their municipal affairs, because it had largely contributed to the foundation of the commune.

The abbot of the rich convent of Allerheiligen (All Saints) had signioral rights over the borough of Schaffhausen, and exercised them by a bailiff. But now the citizens allowed him to nominate only one half of their council, themselves choosing the other half. Soon they excluded the convent from all share in the government, and placed themselves, like other cities, under the protection of the empire. The people of Bâle did the same with their bishop, so that, by degrees, they became their own masters, under the safeguard of the empire, as Berne and Freiburg had long been, by imperial favor.

Many small cities followed the example of the larger, as they found opportunity. They took advantage of the troubles of the empire. When the kings or other signiors, from whom they held, needed money, they opened the city purse; in times of common danger, they were ready with hand and sword. Every citizen was plain and economical at home, but liberal for the public good. The private houses were small, but the public edifices, council-halls and churches large and stately. The artisans rivalled each other in producing good work, and in improving their trades by care, industry and ingenuity. The trades corporations were watchful to prevent negligence. Thus industrial pursuits became lucrative and honorable, and no one endeavored to appear more than he really was. In the houses prevailed piety, good faith and industry; in the councils, justice, prudence and disinterestedness. No one thought of living at the public expense, but the citizens were always found ready to provide for the wants of the commonwealth, and to contribute to useful establishments and institutions.

Through these means the cities increased, became powerful and acquired valuable franchises, real estate, the right of levying taxes, and other advantages. All therefore endeavored to hold directly of the emperor and empire, and to be free of other lords, that they might choose their own magistrates and judges, and have the sole management of their municipal property. For this purpose they willingly paid the imperial tribute. The emperor's rights were administered by an imperial bailiff, who had the higher jurisdiction also, because, as a stranger, he could be more impartial than one citizen towards another. In case of war, the cities chose, as protectors and general, some powerful and valiant signiors and counts, whom they paid. For greater security, they often formed leagues with each other, as well as with the imperial cities in Suabia and on the Rhine.

Thus after long subjection and servitude, liberty began to raise her head among the convents and castles, and especially in the cities. No signioral tyranny, whether from within or from without, can flourish on Swiss soil. Here noble freedom finds a home, as does the eagle on the rocky summits of the land.

CHAPTER X.

OF THE COMMUNITIES IN THE MOUNTAINS OF SCHWYZ, APPENZELL, RHETIA AND VALAIS.

[A. D. 1200 to 1290.]

Behind the lakes, at the foot of the high Alps, whither, in very ancient times, probably after the Roman victories, the last Cymbri had fled, lived their descendants, separated from the world. No Allemann, no Burgundian, no Frank, had wished to venture into their poor and frightful wildernesses. Undisturbed, they fed their herds upon unknown mountains. No knight's castle was to be seen upon their rocks, no city in their valleys. The Bruchen-buren long had but a single church ; it stood in the Muottathal ; thither came the people from Schwyz, Unterwalden and Uri. The inhabitants of these three valley-districts were all of the same race ; as they long had but one church, so they lived under a common government, formed of experienced and upright men, chosen from among themselves.

But when the people multiplied, each valley built its own church, and chose its own landammann, council and tribunal. Thus Schwyz, Uri and Unterwalden separated their commonwealths, but acted, in important matters, as one undivided community. Later (about 1150) the people of Unterwalden above the (forest of) Kernwald separated their interests from those who dwelt in the villages below the Kernwald, and each part of Unterwalden, thenceforth, had its own council and tribunal. Those above the Wald (Obwaldeners) had, according to ancient usage, been obliged to pay two-thirds of the common expenses, probably because they were originally more numerous than those below the Wald (Nidwaldeners), and this was felt to be burdensome when the latter had become as strong and wealthy as themselves. Although thus separated, they remained united for important purposes, and always formed, as now, but one district or canton.

No one pretended to any sovereignty over all these mountains, except the emperor, and the people were pleased to be under the protection of that powerful prince. In internal disputes, they usually had recourse to some imperial judge, and most willingly to the counts of Lenzburg.

In their neighborhood still existed vast wildernesses and unexplored mountain-valleys. The emperors considered such lands as unappropriated, and, consequently, imperial domains, and often conveyed them to signiors or convents as gifts or fiefs. When the wildernesses were cleared, the peasants paid rent therefor to the kings, to the counts of Lenzburg and Rapperswyl, to the convents of Einsiedeln, Zurich and Beromunster, or to such other ecclesiastical and secular signiors as had been invested by the emperor. A pious baron, Konrad of Seldenburen, even built a convent, called Engelberg (1083), in a rough mountain-valley of Unterwalden, at the foot of snow-covered mount Titlis. This so pleased the pope of Rome that he took it under the immediate protection of the holy see.

The monastery of Einsiedeln, in the same region, was much older and richer. The flocks of the abbot fed on all the mountains, because all the surrounding wilderness had formerly been conveyed to his community. The shepherds of Schwyz, ignorant of worldly affairs, knew nothing of such a donation until they suddenly found themselves in conflict with the abbot, who sent his flocks into

Alps which from time immemorial had descended to them from their fathers. The abbot appealed for assistance (1113) to the emperor, who decided in his favor. The Schwyzers were astonished at this, and said: "If the protection of the emperor and the empire be of no avail in securing our rights, we have no need of it." Those of Uri and Unterwalden held with them, said as they said, and ceased to obey the emperor. This irritated the emperor; he put them under ban, and the bishop of Constance anathematized the land, so that no bell should be rung in it, and no holy sacrament be administered to the living or the dead, until the emperor was obeyed. This did not intimidate the Schwyzers, but they compelled their priests to celebrate divine service as before, and drove the recusants out of the country. Their flocks multiplied, and their Alps remained fertile, in spite of the bishop's anathema; and the peasants freely sent the products of their flocks to the public markets of Zurich and Lucerne. Afterwards, when the emperor was in need, and wanted valiant men for his army, he sent the count of Lenzburg with a friendly message to them. He said: "The emperor loves valiant men; go to the war for him as your fathers did, and care not for the talk of the priests." At this, six hundred young men followed him to war for the emperor, to obtain glory and booty, and not one of all the people cared for the talk of the priests.

In the high mountains near the lake of Constance, also, lived many free people, long under the protection of the emperor and the empire. There the abbot of St. Gallen had always possessed extensive domains, and bonded serfs who cultivated his land, and were called abbey-people. On the Sitter, at the foot of the high rocky Alps, was the abbot's house and cell, whither the signior often came, to maintain his rights. Many people built houses at this place, and about the abbot's cell (Abteszelle) sprang up the borough of Appenzell, from which the whole mountain country finally took its name. Over his abbey-people the abbot placed his bailiff, but the freemen at Appenzell, Hundwyl, Urnaschen and Teuffen, under the immediate protection of the emperor, like the free communities on the lake of the Waldstatten, chose their landammann, council and tribunal from among themselves, and had their imperial bailiff.

Still the abbots of St. Gallen by degrees acquired constantly increasing rights over the whole land by purchase or donation; at last they even obtained from the emperor the imperial tribute, the penal jurisdiction and the sovereignty of these four small imperial states. As this did not prejudice the ancient liberties of the people, they considered it the same thing whether they paid their tribute for protection to an imperial bailiff or to a powerful abbot. On the other hand, the convent of St. Gallen was well content with the fine tribute and dues, and did not seek in any way to diminish the long-inherited rights of the shepherd-people; and, that the peculiar abbey-people might not be too different from the rest who were free, the abbot granted to them authority to choose a landammann, with other important privileges. This was in recompense for the fidelity and valor with which they had often served their warlike abbots in battle.

The poor people in the Rhetian highlands did not enjoy such good fortune. Hundreds and hundreds of strong castles of counts and barons hung on the steep rocks in all their valleys, like a slave-chain on the neck of their country. There were the bishop of Coire, the abbots of Disentis and Pfeffers, the counts of Bregenz, Werdenberg, Montfort, Metsch and Misox, the rich barons of Rhezuns, Montalt, Aspermont, Batz, and many other powerful nobles. The city of Coire alone enjoyed important rights under the sovereignty of her bishops, and here and there an isolated valley, such as the Pregallerthal, on the Italian border, possessed hereditary privileges. All the rest of the people, who generally spoke Romantsch,* were and remained tributary, subject to labor-dues, and serfs. Only the Walsors, who spoke German, were free in their farms and hamlets, as the Franks had found them when they conquered the land. It is said that these Walsors were

* Said to be the ancient popular Latin idiom, the language of fugitives from Italy, driven out by the Gauls.

fugitives of Allemannic race, who sought refuge here in the time of the Gothic dominion, and inhabited secluded mountain-valleys, the rough Avers, and Brettigau in the Rhinewald, at the foot of the Rhine glacier. The same people, also, first inhabited and rendered productive the frightful solitudes of Davos, which they received in fief from the baron of Batz (1250).

Many counts and signiors also ruled in Valais, where the city of Sion preserved its municipal privileges, with great difficulty, under a burgomaster and council. In Lower Valais, the count of Savoy was long among the most powerful, but in Upper Valais, the bishop of Sion. The mountaineers in the valleys and communes of Upper Valais, all speaking German, had also valiant German hearts, and maintained the ancient freedom of their forefathers. They had divided their country into seven Zehnten (tithings). The council of the country was formed of representatives from the Zehnten, and presided over by their captain-general. Thus, under the protection of their own laws, they fed their flocks on the banks of the Rhone. even to its sources among the everlasting ice of the mountains.

CHAPTER XI.

ABOUT THE GOOD EMPEROR, RUDOLF OF HABSBURG, AND THE EVIL DESIGNS OF HIS SON ALBERT.

[A. D. 1291 to 1307.]

At this period, no signior in Switzerland was so respected for his humanity and probity, as well as valor, as count Rudolf of Habsburg. His castle was on the Wulpelsberg in Aargau. The cities of Aarau, Baden, Melli gen, Diessenhofen, Sursee and others had him for their bailiff. The Schwyzers also requested him to be theirs, in consequence of the trouble then existing on account of the quarrel between the emperor and pope. Already (in 1251), Uri, Schwyz and Zurich had formed a league with each other to withstand the nobles in their castles. Zurich chose count Rudolf for her general.

Rudolf was not so much beloved by the burghers of Bâle, though more than were his noble brothers-in-arms and friends. In consequence of these latter having, on a day of the Carnival, insulted the beautiful wives and daughters of Bâle, many bloody conflicts took place, and several of the audacious nobles fell under the blows of the vigorous citizens. The defeat of his friends offended the count of Habsburg, and, to avenge them, he marched against the city with numerous troops.

This war, however, came to a speedy and happy conclusion. For the dukes and princes of Germany, on the death of their emperor, having long disputed who should be their king, at last elected count Rudolf of Habsburg.* "They chose him," as said the elector of Cologne, "because he was wise and just, and beloved of God and men."

When the Bâlese learnt that their enemy had become their king, they issued from their gates with every mark of respect, and invited him and his people to enter the city. Friendship was sworn on both sides. Joy and astonishment filled all the land. The principal men of the cities and of the country hastened to Brugg to congratulate the count and his wife.

Although upon the first throne in Christendom, and in a distant country, emperor Rudolf, during his whole life, remained attached to the people of his native land. He granted new dignities to their nobility, new franchises to their cities, or confirmed by his kingly word those they already possessed. The people of Zurich, Schaffhausen and Solothurn were to be held to answer only before their own judges and according to their own laws; Laupen and Lucerne received the same franchises as Berne, and Lucerne held directly from the empire; Bienne received the same municipal franchises as Bâle; Aarau was not obliged to recognize any other judge than her own avoyer; Winterthur, Diessenhofen and other cities acquired other and similar rights. He confirmed to the three Waldstatten

* King of the Germans and emperor of the Holy Roman empire.

(Uri, Schwyz and Unterwalden) the perpetual right of immediate dependence on the empire; he elevated the bishop of Lausanne and the abbot of Einseideln to the dignity of princes of the empire. In the Romain districts, where the counts of Savoy domineered, he reëstablished the imperial power by force of arms, relieved Lausanne and Freiburg from the yoke of Savoy, and made again free of the empire whatever places had formerly been so. For these things, the cities and country testified their gratitude to him by abundant supplies in money and men.

But other times came, when he was dead and his son Albert ascended the throne.* It was soon known that the latter looked only to the extension of his family domain by the incorporation of foreign territory, and that he disregarded the franchises of the cities and the country. Therefore all feared for themselves. Then the people of Uri, Schwyz and Unterwalden, anticipating evil and dangerous times, assembled (1291) and swore to a Perpetual Bond,† by which they agreed to defend themselves and their families, with goods and chattels, against all and every, whoever they might be, and to assist each other with advice and arms. Thenceforward they were called Confederates (Eidsgenossen: bound together by oath). The bishop of Constance also united in league with the counts of Savoy and with other counts and signiors against the king's designs, as well as with the abbot of St. Gallen and the city of Zurich. The German princes hated him no less, and chose count Adolph of Nassau for their sovereign.

Now partisan wars spread everywhere, for and against Albert of Austria, from country to country, from city to city. Berne held with the count of Savoy, and made a league with Freiburg and Solothurn. Albert, with an army of Austrians, immediately invaded and ravaged the territory of the bishop of Constance. In a bloody battle he took from king Adolf victory, life and the imperial crown. Then the confederates of the Waldstatten sent to him at Strassburg, to request him to guarantee their ancient fran-

* The counts of Habsburg had also become dukes of Austria.

† *Bund:* league, compact, treaty. I use the word *Bond* to distinguish that between the Swiss cantons from all others.—Tr.

chises, as his father of glorious memory had done. But he answered that he thought of shortly proposing a change in their situation. This reply greatly terrified the Confederates.

Cries of war and the clash of arms resounded through all Uechtland, from Solothurn to lake Leman. The signiors and counts, who were partisans of Albert, and hated the cities and their increasing power, marched against Berne. But the valiant burghers of the city, with auxiliaries from Solothurn and other places, and commanded by the experienced Ulrich of Erlach, totally defeated (1298) the superior forces of the enemy at Donnerbuhl, took and destroyed many castles and towers of the nobles, so that the renown of the city became great throughout all the land. Thereupon king Albert himself entered the country and encamped before Zurich, on a hill whence he could look into the streets of the city. The Zurichers did not close their gates, though they were prepared for a vigorous resistance, but sent word that they were ready to acknowledge him as king, provided he acknowledged their franchises. As he had brought but few besieging engines with him, and saw so many armed people in the city (for even the wives and daughters had taken arms), he showed peaceful inclinations and confirmed the free constitution of the city.

But he informed the Confederates in the Waldstatten that he wished to have them as dear children of his royal house, and that they would do well to place themselves under the protection of Austria, as faithful subjects; that he would make them rich by fiefs, knighthoods and booty. But when the mountaineers replied that they much preferred to remain in the ancient rights of their fathers, and in immediate dependence on the empire, he sent to them, as imperial bailiffs, severe and wicked men from his own territory, to oppress and harass them, that they might be desirous to detach themselves from the empire, and put themselves under the sovereignty of the house of Austria. He sent Hermann Gessler of Brunegg and the knight Beringer of Landenberg. They did as imperial bailiffs had never before done, and took up their abode in the land. Landenberg went to the king's castle, near Sarnen in Obwalden, and Gessler built for himself a tower in the country of Uri. The taxes were increased, the smallest offences punished by imprisonment and heavy fines, the country-people treated with haughtiness and contempt. Gessler, passing on horseback before Stauffacher's new house, in the village of Steinen, cried out insultingly, "Shall peasants be allowed to build so finely?" And when Arnold Anderhalden, of Melchthal in Unterwalden, was condemned for some slight offence to lose a yoke of fine oxen, Landenberg's servant took the oxen from the plough and said, "Peasants may draw the plough themselves." But young Arnold, irritated by this insult, struck the servant and broke two of his fingers. Then he fled into the mountains. In revenge, Landenberg put out both the eyes of Arnold's old father.

Whoever, on the contrary, adhered to the bailiff and did his will, was treated with indulgence and was always in the right. But all did not escape, who, trusting in the protection of the bailiff, thought themselves entitled to do evil; and, as there was no longer any justice to be had in the land, each man helped himself, and this occasioned many disorders. But the bailiffs laughed and persisted in their tyranny; they not only trod under foot the chartered franchises of the people, sanctioned by emperors and kings, but disregarded the everlasting right to life which God has given to every man.

CHAPTER XII.

OF WILLIAM TELL AND THE THREE MEN IN RUTLI.

[A. D. 1307.]

WHILE the oppressors laughed and the oppressed groaned in the valleys of the Waldstatten, the wife of Werner Stauffacher, in the village of Steinen, said to her husband: "How long shall the oppressors laugh and the oppressed groan? Shall foreigners be masters of this soil, and heirs of our property? What are the men of the mountains good for? Must we mothers nurse beggars at our bosoms, and bring up maid-servants for foreigners? Let there be an end to this!"

Thereupon Werner Stauffacher, without a word, went down to Brunnen on the lake, and over the water to Uri, to Walter Furst, in Attinghausen. With him he found concealed Arnold of Melchthal, who had fled across the mountain from the wrath of Landenberg.

They talked of the misery of their country, and of the cruelty of the foreign bailiffs whom the king had sent to them, in contempt of their hereditary franchises and liberties. They also called to mind that they had in vain appealed against the tyranny of the bailiffs before the king, and that the latter had threatened to compel them, in spite of the seals and charters of former emperors and kings, to separate from the empire and submit to Austria; that God had given to no king the right to commit injustice; that they had no hope but in God and their own courage, and that death was much more desirable than so shameful a yoke. They therefore resolved that each should talk with trustworthy and courageous men in his own district, to ascertain the disposition of the people, and what they would undertake for security and liberty.

Subsequently, as they had agreed, they met frequently by night, at a secret place on the lake. It lay about midway between Uri, Schwyz and Unterwalden, in a small bushy meadow at the foot of the rocks of Seelisberg, opposite the little village of Brunnen. It is called Rutli, from the clearing of bushes; there they were far from all human habitations. Soon each brought the joyful news that death was more desirable to all the people than so shameful a yoke.

When, on the night of 17th of November, 1307, they came together, and each of the Three had brought with him to the meadow of the Rutli, ten true and honorable men, determined to hold the ancient liberty of their fatherland before all, and life as nothing, the pious Three raised their hands to the starry heavens, and swore to God the Lord, before whom kings and peasants are equal, faithfully to live and to die for the rights of the innocent people; to undertake and carry through every thing in unison and not separately; to permit no injustice, but also to commit no injustice; to respect the rights and property of the counts of Habsburg, and do no harm to the imperial bailiffs, but also to prevent the bailiffs from ruining the country. And the thirty others raised their hands and took the oath, like the Three, to God and all the saints, manfully to assert liberty; and they appointed New Year's night for the work. Then they separated; each returned to his valley and to his cabin, and tended his cattle.

The bailiff, Hermann Gessler, was not easy, because he had an evil conscience. It seemed to him that the people began to raise their heads, and to show more boldness. Therefore he set the ducal hat of Austria upon a pole in Uri, and ordered that every one who passed before it should do it reverence. By this means he wished to discover who was opposed to Austria.

And William Tell, the archer of Burglen, one of the men of Rutli, passed before it, but he did not bow. He was immediately carried to the bailiff, who angrily said, "Insolent archer, I will punish thee by means of thine own craft; I will place an apple on the head of thy little son; shoot it off and fail not!" And they bound the child, and placed an apple on his head, and led the archer far away. He took aim. The bowstring twanged. The arrow pierced the apple. All the people shouted for joy. But Gessler said to the archer, "Why didst thou take a second arrow?" Tell answered, "If the first had not pierced the apple, the second would assuredly have pierced thy heart."

This terrified the bailiff, and he ordered the archer to be seized and carried to a boat in which he was himself about to embark for Kussnacht. He did not think it prudent to imprison Tell in Uri, on account of the people; but to drag him into foreign captivity was contrary to the privileges of the country. Therefore the bailiff feared an assembling of the people, and hastily departed, in spite of a strong head wind. The sea rose, and the waves dashed foaming over the boat, so that all were alarmed, and the boatmen disheartened. The further they went on the lake, the greater was the danger of death; for the steep mountains rose from the abyss of waters like walls to heaven. In great anxiety, Gessler ordered the fetters to be removed from Tell, that he, an experienced steersman, might take the helm. But Tell steered towards the bare flank of the Axenberg, where a naked rock projects, like a small shelf, into the lake. There was a shock, a spring. Tell was on the rock, the boat out upon the lake.

The freed man climbed the mountain, and fled across the land of Schwyz; and he thought in his troubled heart, "Whither can I fly from the wrath of the tyrant? Even if I escape from his pursuit, he has my wife and child in my house as hostages. What may not Gessler do to my family, when Landenberg put out the eyes of the old man of Melchthal on account of a servant's broken fingers? Where is the judgment-seat before which I can cite Gessler, when the king himself no longer listens to the complaints of the people? As law has no authority, and there is no one to judge between thee and me, thou and I, Gessler, are both without law, and self-preservation is our only judge. Either my innocent wife and child and fatherland must fall, or, bailiff Gessler, thou! Fall thou, therefore, and let liberty prevail!"

So thought Tell, and, with bow and arrow, fled towards Kussnacht, and hid in the hollow way near the village. Thither came the bailiff; there the bowstring twanged; there the free arrow pierced the tyrant's heart.

The whole people shouted for joy when they learnt the death of their oppressor. Tell's deed increased their courage; but the night of the New Year had not yet come.

CHAPTER XIII.

THE NEW YEAR'S MORNING OF 1308. BATTLE FOR FREEDOM AT MORGARTEN. LUCERNE JOINS THE CONFEDERATES.

[A. D. 1308 to 1334.]

The night came. One of the young men who had taken the oath at Rutli, went to the castle of Rossberg in Obwalden, where lived a young girl beloved by him. With a rope the young girl drew him up from the castle-ditch intc her chamber. But twenty others were waiting below whom the first drew up also. When all had entered, they mastered the steward and his servants and the whole castle.

When it was day, Landenberg left the royal castle near Sarnen to attend mass. Twenty men of Unterwalden met him, bearing, as customary presents, fowls, goats, lambs, and other New Year's gifts. The bailiff, in a friendly manner, told them to enter the castle. When under the gate, one of them sounded his horn. At once, all drew forth sharp spear-heads, fastened them upon their staves, and took the castle, while thirty others, who had been hidden in a neighboring thicket, came to their assistance. Landenberg, terrified, fled over the meadows towards Alpnach. But they took him, and made him and all his people swear to leave the Waldstatten forever. Then they permitted him to retire to Lucerne. No injury was done to any one.

High blazed the bonfires on the Alps.

With the people of Schwyz, Stauffacher went to the lake of Lowerz, and seized the castle of Schwanau. The people of Uri marched out, and Gessler's tower was taken by assault.

High blazed the bonfires on the Alps.

That was Freedom's New Year's day. On the following Sunday, deputies from the three districts assembled, and, with an oath, renewed their original bond for ten years; and the bond was to endure forever and to be often renewed. They had reässumed their ancient rights, had shed no drop of blood, and had done no harm to any, belonging to the king or to Habsburg, in the land.

When king Albert learnt what had taken place, he was exceedingly incensed, assembled troops, and, in company with many noble lords, rode into Aargau. With him was also his nephew and ward, duke John of Suabia, from whom he had withheld his patrimony. As, on the 1st of May, 1308, having left Baden, he was crossing the Reuss near Windisch, duke John cried out, "This is the reward of injustice!" and pierced the monarch's throat with his lance. Other lords, who had conspired with the duke, followed his example. Knight Rudolf of Balm plunged his sword into the king's bosom, Walter of Eschenbach clove his head. The rest remained motionless, in horror at the crime. Finally, they all dispersed. The emperor of Germany expired in the arms of a poor woman, who passed, by chance, along the road.

This crime occasioned horror everywhere. The murderers wandered and died, cursed of men. Zurich closed her gates against them; the Waldstatten would grant no asylum to the assassins of their enemy. But the children of the murdered man, duke Leopold of Austria, and Agnes, queen of Hungary, and his widow, queen Elizabeth, wreaked their vengeance on innocent and guilty. The most cruel of all was Agnes. Many castles of the suspected were reduced to ashes: Wart, Fahrwangen, Maschwangen, Altburen. When, at Fahrwangen, the blood of sixty-three guiltless knights flowed at the feet of Agnes, she is said to have exclaimed: "See, now I am bathing in May-dew!" In vain did the wife of knight Rudolf of Wart beg before her in the dust for the life of her husband. His limbs were broken, and, still living, he was exposed on the wheel* to the voracity of birds of prey. From the wheel, while dying, he consoled his faithful wife, who alone knelt near him, and prayed and wept till his dear soul had fled. But Agnes and her mother built the rich convent of Kœnigsfelden on the spot of the emperor's assassination. She herself retired thither, to close her days in devotion. But brother Berthold Strebel, of Oftringen, filled with indignation, said to her, one day, as she was inviting passers-by to enter her church: "Woman! that is poor God's-service, which sheds innocent blood, and builds a convent with the spoil!"

Neither did duke Leopold forgive the Waldstatten for

* A person suffering this punishment was first fastened, face upwards, upon a large wheel raised horizontally on a shaft; then his limbs were broken by repeated blows with an iron bar, and he was left to die, unless, in mercy, a final blow upon the chest terminated his torments and his life together.

their resistance to his father, especially when he saw that they preferred the emperor, Louis of Bavaria, to his brother, Frederick of Austria. He marched against them with many knights and signiors, and a large force. Count Otto of Strassburg crossed the Brunig against Obwalden, with four thousand men. More than a thousand soldiers were sent by the governors of Willisau, Wollhausen and Lucerne, to attack the country of Unterwalden from the lake. The duke himself advanced with the best of his troops from Aegeri, by Morgarten, against the mountains of the Schwyzers. He carried with him numerous ropes to hang the leaders of the people.

The Confederates, to oppose his power, stationed themselves, thirteen hundred strong, on the height near the march of Einsiedeln. Four hundred of Uri, three hundred of Unterwalden, had joined the Schwyzers. Also, fifty men to Schwyz, who had been banished, came and begged permission to show themselves worthy of restoration to their country by deeds of valor. As, on the 16th of November, 1315, the many thousand harnessed knights, in the rosy dawn of morning, were ascending the mountain, the Confederates, with loud cries, rushed upon them at a small plain near the Hasellmat, and on the broad grassy slope of the mountain. The fifty banished men rolled down huge masses of rock from the heights of the Siegler-Flue, then broke forth from the morning-mist upon the disarrayed enemy. There was great disorder among the troops of the duke, then flight and rout. Leading the Schwyzers with word and deed were Henry of Ospenthal and the sons of old Reding of Biberegg, who had given the plan of the battle. The enemy were driven into the defile below at Aegeri. The flower of the nobility fell at Morgarten under the halberds and maces* of the shepherds. Leopold saved himself with difficulty from the victorious pursuers. Then, on the following day, the victors hastened across the lake of the Waldstatten towards Unterwalden; there they defeated the Lucerners, many of whom were drowned in the lake. Strassburg saw this, and fled terri-

* Called Morgensternen: morning stars; clubs armed with iron points.

fied. After this great heroic day, the Confederates renewed their ancient bond, to die, all for each, each for all; to enter into no engagement with foreign powers except with consent of all; to respect foreign property and rights in the country, as their own. Thus the name of Schwyzers (Swiss) became world-renowned, and afterwards was the name of all the Confederates. The aid of their formidable arms was soon demanded in the wars of the empire. Their intercession saved the liberties of Zurich and St. Gallen, when the emperor, in want of money, wished to pledge these imperial cities to the dukes of Austria. But Schaffhausen, Rheinfelden and Neuchâtel fell into the power of Austria, as mortgaged property. This greatly grieved those cities. Lucerne learnt by sad experience the heavy pressure of a prince's yoke. Dependent upon Austria, the burghers of Lucerne, to their great detriment, had been compelled to fight against the Waldstatten and in all foreign wars, for many long years. Besides this, the dukes, making use of their princely power, had increased the taxes. At last, the citizens could bear no more. Thereupon, they concluded a truce of twenty years with the Waldstatten; but, seeing that the nobles and principal families, devoted to the service of the dukes, meditated projects injurious to the city, on this account, they united in a perpetual bond with the Confederates, that they would stand by them, each for all, all for each, but without detriment to ancient rights.

Thereat the nobility dwelling in Aargau declared war against the city in the name of Austria. The burghers valiantly defended their good right. The Waldstatten fought with them against the nobles. But the principal families in Lucerne itself sided with the foreign nobles. For caste does not forsake its caste. The nobles of Lucerne conspired to make a nocturnal massacre, and to give up the city to the duke, after the friends of the Waldstatten had been murdered in their beds. They were already assembled in arms, in the darkness of the night, in a cellar near the lake, under the tailors' hall, when a boy chanced to overhear their projects. They seized and would have killed him. However, his life was spared, and he was forced to take an oath to tell to no man what he had heard. But he went into the hall of the butchers, where some burghers were still drinking and playing, and there, in a loud voice, related to the dumb stove that which he had sworn to tell to no man. All the burghers listened wondering, hastened away and roused the city. They made the conspirators prisoners, called in auxiliaries from Unterwalden, and took the government of the city forever from those principal families which had until then been invested with it. The chief persons were exiled. Three hundred burghers thenceforth formed the council; but the city-property, the taxes, war and alliances were controlled by the commune. Thus the prudence and patriotism of a child saved the liberties of Lucerne.

Afterwards, the dukes, burdened or exhausted with other wars, willingly made peace with Lucerne, as soon as nine arbitrators of Bâle, Berne and Zurich had declared: that the perpetual bond of the four Waldstatten was blameless, and in no wise injurious to the rights of Habsburg-Austria.

CHAPTER XIV.

BERNE VANQUISHES THE POWER OF THE NOBILITY NEAR LAUPEN; AND KNIGHT BRUN CHANGES THE CONSTITUTION OF ZURICH.

[A. D. 1335 to 1340.]

At this period the city of Berne also was compelled to engage in a war for life or death against the nobles of Uechtland and their allies. The counts and signiors of the neighborhood were displeased to see Berne flourishing by her arms, her industry and her agriculture, powerful by the public spirit of her citizens, strengthened by the purchase of Hasli and Laupen, and respected more and more throughout the country. And when the city refused to receive the money struck by count Eberhard of Kyburg with imperial sanction, and to recognize the emperor Louis of Bavaria, because the pope had excommunicated him, the nobles joyfully seized this pretext to punish the recusants. Thereupon count Rudolf of the French house of Neuchâtel, who had given city rights and walls to his villages Erlach and Nidau, convoked all the enemies of Berne at his tower in Nidau. And they determined that the city must be destroyed from the earth. They collected many troops in Aargau, Savoy, Upper Burgundy, Uechtland and Alsace. There came 700 lords with coronetted helms, 1200 harnessed knights, with more than 15,000 men on foot and 3000 on horseback.

The Bernese were not terrified at the tidings of these great preparations, neither did they insult their enemies by too confident a security; they resolved to satisfy all just claims, but to repel force by force. When all peaceful negotiations proved fruitless, they prepared their arms.

With uplifted hand, the ancient avoyer, John of Bubenberg, swore to sacrifice property and life in defence of the city of Laupen, under the walls of which the enemy's forces were assembled. And he went to reinforce the garrison with 600 trusty men. While the Bernese were deliberating in their council-hall upon the choice of a general to whom the command of their soldiers should be confided in this war, there rode into the city knight Rudolf of Erlach, son of that Ulrich of Erlach who had defeated the nobility on the Donnerbuhl, forty-one years before. They at once chose him for their general, for he was an experienced soldier, and had helped to gain six great battles in foreign lands. At the call of Berne, 900 valiant men, from Uri, Schwyz and Unterwalden, crossed the Brunig to her assistance; 600 came also from Hasli and Siebenthal (Simmenthal). Solothurn, also, sent 80 cuirassed horsemen, gratefully remembering the day on which Berne had succored her, when besieged by duke Leopold of Austria with a numerous army. (But, on that occasion, Leopold was vanquished less by arms than by the furious inundation of the Aar and the magnanimity of the Solothurners. The swollen waters of the Aar had carried away the duke's bridge of boats, and the generous burghers of the city saved from death their enemies perishing in the flood.)

With these auxiliaries, and with 4000 citizens and inhabitants of Berne, Rudolf of Erlach took post in front of the enemy not far from Laupen, upon a height whence he could overlook the army of the nobles. The battle began immediately. The enemy's squadrons ascended the height. Erlach gave the signal. The slingers commenced. The iron war-wagons thundered down the hill, and broke the ranks of the enemy's array. Then followed the banners, the halberds and the maces. The hindmost of the Bernese alone quailed in terror at the sight. Then cried the quick-witted hero Erlach: "Good! The chaff is separated from the wheat! Cowards will not share the victory of the brave!"

And the victory was theirs. Count Rudolf of Nidau lay under the foremost of the slain; about him 1500 of his party. This was in the year 1339. Nevertheless, the war lasted four years, with skirmishes here and there. Many places were plundered and burnt. Freiburg in Uechtland suffered greatly, for she was compelled to side with the nobles against Berne. At last, peace came; especially glorious for Berne, though she acquired no foot of land as compensation or by conquest; but the city which was threatened with destruction from the face of the earth, had become so victorious that she threatened the destruction of all her enemies. Forces ten times superior in numbers had been vanquished by her citizens, all animated by one mind, by one heart, by love for their country, by no thought of self. Thus men work miracles.

After peace was concluded, the Bernese hung up their arms, and resumed their occupations. The knightly hero, Rudolf of Erlach, quietly cultivated his paternal field, asked for no pay, honors or title, and lived happily to an advanced old age. But one day, Jobst of Rudenz, from Unterwalden, his son-in-law, entered his chamber, and they disputed with each other on the subject of dowry. Jobst saw the sword of the victor at Laupen hanging against the wall. In sudden anger he seized it and plunged it into the heart of the old hero. Then he fled, pursued by his father-in-law's hounds, and was never seen more.

The avoyer, John of Bubenberg, who had rendered

great services to his city in the most difficult times, experienced a still sadder fate. His haughty manners made him odious to the citizens. He was therefore accused of governing with immoderate pride, not like a citizen, but like a prince, and of undertaking no business without a present. He was banished from the city with all his friends, for one hundred years and a day. Then, after fourteen years, when he was old and weak, the people took pity on him and received him back. In a free commonwealth, the virtue of a citizen may often obliterate the remembrance of past faults, but former services can never excuse subsequent misdeeds.

About the same time, still more deplorable was the lot of the council-lords of Zurich, where four nobles of the city and eight of the most eminent burghers always held the government for four months, and then chose their successors. Thus the power was in the hands of a few knightly and military families, who were called Konstafflers. The other citizens, and the mechanics distinguished by their riches, acquirements and courage, were displeased at being subject to these families, against whose government, moreover, many complaints were made. The lords, it was said, cared only for their own and families' interests, gave no account of the city moneys, treated the simple citizens quite haughtily, and knew no law but their own caprice. These complaints continued until one of the council itself joined the dissatisfied people, and made common cause with them. This was knight Rudolf Brun, a man of talent, but ambitious. Instigated by him, the burghers at last summoned the council to give an account of the city moneys. Rudolf Brun, his friend Rudiger Manesse and some others of the council supported the demand as just. The rest of the councillors thought that this was only a momentary effervescence of the burghers, which would soon die away, and they made use of small manœuvres to procrastinate the matter. They understood the council-chamber, but not the temper of the people.

After six weeks, Brun caused a report to be spread, that the lords of the council were only trifling with the commons. Then the people flocked to the lower bridge, near the council-hall, where the council was in session. As the crowd and clamor increased, those in the house became terrified. Some declared in favor of the citizens; the others, anxious for their personal safety, made their escape and hastily left the city. Full powers were given to knight Brun, and it was decided that the lords should suffer in honor, person and property. They were banished with their partisans.

Then knight Brun, with the advice of his friends, drew up a new constitution, divided all the artisans into thirteen corporations, the chiefs of which had seats in the council; the Konstafflers he classed as a single body, that they might have no great influence in the other corporations. The council, composed half of citizens, half of nobles and patricians, was to be renewed every six months. Brun caused himself to be appointed burgomaster for life, and retained great power. The people gladly swore to this constitution in 1336. As the artisans had a voice in the council, they were enabled to prohibit the competition of foreign mechanics, the exportation of raw materials, the importation of manufactured articles, as if the whole city existed for the benefit of their trades, not their trades for the benefit of the city.

But the banished lords of the council, and their friends without, meditated a bloody vengeance against Zurich.

CHAPTER XV.

ORIGIN OF THE PERPETUAL BOND OF THE EIGHT ANCIENT CANTONS OF THE CONFEDERACY.

[A. D. 1341 to 1360.]

THE exiles had retired to Rapperswyl and into the castles and towers of their friends; thence they made small war against the Zurichers, and harassed them by every means in their power. But the Zurichers were courageous men, and Brun brave as well as talented. When the ex iles found that they did not accomplish any thing, they conspired to make a nocturnal massacre in Zurich. Several counts and nobles entered the city, either openly under various pretexts, or secretly. It was agreed that when they had got possession of the city in the horrors of a dark night, the gates were to be opened, and numerous troops from Rapperswyl admitted. The night came. The conspirators assembled in a friend's house. There a baker's apprentice, half asleep behind the stove, overheard their plot. He immediately revealed it to his master; his master to knight Brun. The latter, in armor, hastened, barefooted, to the council-hall. The alarm bell was rung. All the citizens rushed at once to arms. The conspirators tried to escape, but the women threw stones, earthen pots and tiles upon them from the windows, and Brun, at the head of the citizens, met them in the market place. A long and bloody conflict ensued. The conspirators were vanquished. Those who could escape fled. Many were slain, others taken prisoners.

Brun thought only of vengeance. The bodies of the dead lay three whole days unburied on the market-place, until they were so disfigured by the horses and carts that passed over them, that they could no longer be recognized. Thirty-seven citizens, engaged in the conspiracy, among them ancient magistrates of the city, were beheaded or broken on the wheel in the streets in front of their houses. Then Brun led his troops against Rapperswyl. The fortress was taken and demolished, the inhabitants driven into the open fields, the walls thrown down, every thing, even to the last hut, burnt. Thus Brun's vengeance struck down the innocent with the guilty. This was in 1350.

In the following year, when duke Albert of Austria threatened a severe reprisal, the burgomaster applied to the Confederates in the Waldstatten for assistance, and to be allowed to join in their perpetual bond. Uri, Schwyz, Unterwalden and Lucerne, who had long esteemed Zurich as their rampart and their market, willingly assented, on the 1st of May, 1351, and swore with her to a perpetual bond, to assist each other with life and property against all enemies, and in case of difference among themselves, to settle the dispute in a friendly manner by arbitrators. All the rights of the king and of the holy Roman empire, and all ancient treaties were maintained, but in new treaties with foreigners the Confederacy was to be preferred.*

Now, duke Albert, giving vent to his anger against Zurich, came and demanded satisfaction for the destruction of Rapperswyl, which had belonged to his relatives, and for the injuries suffered by the servants and subjects of Austria. He advanced at the head of 16,000 men, and required Glarus also to send auxiliaries. But the people of Glarus refused and said, "It is indeed our duty, under the protection of the empire, to take arms for the defence of the abbey of Seckingen, to which our country belongs, but we have nothing to do with any other wars of Austria." This answer irritated the duke. He resolved to send troops into Glarus, because he was patron and protector of the abbey of Seckingen, and because, from Glarus, he thought to intimidate the people of Uri and Schwyz, so that they might not assist those of Zurich. But the Confederates suddenly issued from the Waldstatten in the depth of winter, and occupied Glarus for their own security. The people of Glarus swore to hold with the Swiss, sent two hundred men of their valley to reinforce the city of Zurich, beat Walter of Stadion when he entered their country with an Austrian force from Rapperswyl, and destroyed the castle of Nafels.

This valor pleased the Confederates, and they received Glarus into their perpetual bond, reserving the just sovereignty and revenues of the duke and of the princess-abbess of Seckingen, on condition that these acknowledged the ancient franchises of Glarus. This took place in 1352, while in the year before (26th December, 1351) Rudiger Manesse, of Zurich, with less than 1500 men, had vanquished more than 4000 Austrians near Tatwyl, and (16th December, 1351) forty-two Schwyzers kept at bay more than a thousand Austrians near Kussnacht, on the lake of

* Zurich received the title of Vorort, or chief canton of the Confederacy, and was the seat of the federal authority, if any existed that could be so called. She enjoyed this distinction on account of her superior wealth and importance, but had no political supremacy.

the Waldstatten, and avenged the burning of Kussnacht by the destruction of Habsburg on the Rothenflue, near the same lake.

The duke of Austria had as yet achieved no single exploit, while the renown of the Confederates and of their rapid victories flew afresh from valley to valley, from land to land. And they were greatly praised, because they did not war like princes, but as freemen, and did not plunder the conquered countries, or make the vanquished inhabitants tributary serfs and subjects, but received them as faithful and free confederates.

Therefore, the country-people on the lake of Zug, and in the rich fields and mountains of the neighborhood, preferred them to all others, and gave them advice, assistance, and important information on many occasions. The city of Zug, on the contrary, remained faithful to her lords of Austria, closed her gates, and garrisoned her strong walls against the Confederates. Many a noble family here enjoyed the right of citizenship. The ancient counts of Lenzburg are said to have first fortified the village on the lake.

But when the Confederates, to the number of about 3000 men, appeared before the walls and gates of Zug, and were joined by all the people of the neighboring country, the burghers of the city were frightened, as they had only a weak garrison of Austrians. They therefore sent in haste to duke Albert, to ask help from him in their need.

The messenger found the duke near Kœnigsfelden; but this prince hardly paid attention to his complaints, talking with his falconer about the pleasures of the chase, while the messenger wept. To bring down a bird from the high clouds seemed of more consequence to this lord than to save a city. Full of indignation at such indifference, the burghers of Zug opened the gates of their city to the Confederates, and joined in their perpetual bond, reserving all the rights and revenues of the house of Austria.

The duke had said to the messenger from Zug: "I will soon recover every thing." He trusted in his powerful allies. With him came all the nobility of Aargau, Thurgau and Uechtland, troops from the allied cities of Schaffhausen, Bâle, Strassburg and even Berne. The elector of Brandenburg also brought soldiers from Germany. He immediately besieged the city of Zurich with more than 34,000 men. It was valiantly defended by the Confederates.

The elector of Brandenburg soon perceived that no glory was to be won against people so steadfast, so united, so intrepid as the Swiss, and, moreover, supplies and provisions began to fail, and famine to threaten, in the duke's crowded encampment. He therefore offered his friendly mediation to the duke, and sent two confidential messengers to the Swiss. The latter had hardly given an answer, when, on the next morning, they saw the enemy depart from before their walls; the Bernese alone remained, more attached to the Confederates than to the duke.

At Lucerne, the elector negotiated the peace, in which, as always, all ancient rights and treaties were maintained. But the Confederates here received Berne also into their perpetual bond. This was in 1353.

After this peace the duke of Austria tried to persuade the people of Zug to withdraw from the Swiss bond. They answered: "The Swiss bond is recognized in the treaty of peace; we owe obedience to the duke, only in those things which concern his rights." The duke complained to the emperor, and the emperor condemned the perpetual bond of the Confederates, saying: "Members of the empire can form no compact among themselves without consent of the chief of the empire." And he himself came into the country and before Zurich, with a large force. But when he saw the strength, the union and the loyalty of the Confederates, and that the duke had in view only the aggrandisement of Austria, he changed his purpose, and left the Swiss as they were; and peace was made and the perpetual bond remained unbroken.

Two years after this peace (in 1360) burgomaster Rudolf Brun died, hated for his ambition and despotism. He was a man who cared only for himself. A year before his death, he had secretly sworn to the dukes of Austria, to serve them and their officers, but not against the Confederates. And for this they were to pay him one thousand guilders, and an annuity of one hundred guilders.

CHAPTER XVI.

HOW THE SWISS INCREASE, AND THE GUGLERS AND THE COUNTS OF KYBURG ARE RUINED.

[A. D. 1360 to 1385.]

WHAT made the Confederates strong and steadfast? That they valued liberty more than ease and gold, and more than fleeting life; that they readily took arms to defend their rights, never to destroy the rights of others; that they held together as brothers in danger and in death, and no selfishness divided them. This made the Confederates strong and steadfast. Their perpetual bond was engraved on all their hearts more plainly than it was written on the parchment.

Having now made peace with Austria, they put their internal affairs in order, labored diligently at their trades, economised in their households, and amassed gold, not that they might live luxuriously and splendidly, but that they might purchase for their commonwealths the rights and revenues which the impoverished nobility were always ready to sell. Thus they increased their strength and freedom by just means. And justice is the foundation of all noble freedom.

The shepherd-commune of Gersau on the lake of Lucerne, reserving their prerogatives, united with the four Waldstatten in the perpetual bond. Hergiswyl and Alpnach purchased themselves free from the sovereignty of their signiors, and joined Unterwalden. Lucerne bought from the barons of Ramstein their rights over Weggis on the lake; Zurich, many imperial fiefs, by contributions from her citizens. Berne, like Zurich, obtained franchises and privileges from the favor of the emperor, and, with ready money, the signiory of Aarburg and several villages. Other cities also, not of the Confederacy, increased their ancient territory under their ecclesiastical or secular signiors; such were Schaffhausen, Bâle, Lausanne, St. Gallen, Bienne and Solothurn. But the power of the bishops and counts was weakened by continual discord, their treasuries exhausted by endless wars. This, more than force or violence, helped all the people to gain privileges and strength. The Appenzellers, also, obeyed their own laws rather than the commands of the abbot of St. Gallen. So the valleys of the country above the lake of Thun lived in hereditary freedom under the mild sovereignty of their counts, whose power was no longer unlimited. Saanenland bought herself entirely free from the counts of Gruyeres. Oberhasli and Brienz wished to free themselves by force from the dominion of the bailiff at Rinkenberg. But the Confederates would not help them. They said: "No freedom without justice."

On the other hand, when a member or ally of the Confederacy was threatened with danger or war, the Confederates flew promptly to her assistance, as when Arnold of Cervola, with undisciplined hordes from England, ravaged France and threatened Bâle. But when Ingelram of Coucy, count of Soissons, made war against Austria, and the dukes, fearing for their possessions in Aargau, which had been assigned to Ingelram as his wife's dowry, called upon the Waldstatten and Lucerne for assistance, the people cherished in their breasts too strong an anger against Austria. But Zurich, on the contrary, and Berne, who feared for their own frontiers in consequence of the proximity of Aargau, promptly seized their arms. Ingelram did in fact enter Aargau with several thousand men. This frightened the country not a little, even Lucerne and Unterwalden. The most courageous of the Austrian subjects prepared for resistance without delay; the most ardent were the men of Entlibuch (a populous valley in the present canton of Lucerne). They assembled in arms; the young men of Lucerne and Unterwalden, desirous of conflict, joined them. Three thousand English were posted at Buttisholz; with them were many noble lords and knights. The Entlibuchers saw them. They and their companions, only 600 strong, at once attacked the enemy and routed them after a very bloody fight. The Entlibuchers rode home in triumph on the horses they had taken, in the armor of the knights they had vanquished. This sight saddened the old noble lords in the country, and one of them, Peter of Dorrenberg, said with a sigh: "O noble lord of noble blood, must a peasant wear thine armor?" But the Entlibucher replied: "Why, my gentleman, we have taken arms, and mingled blood of noble and blood of horse together." The people of Berne, Laupen and Aarberg also achieved heroic deeds near Ins and the convent of Fraubrunnen, against the hordes of Guglers, as Ingelram of Coucy's men were called, in consequence of their pointed helmets. Here his strength was broken. Therefore this lord sadly returned home into Alsace, over the Hauenstein.

Six years after this (1382), the free imperial-city of Solothurn was in great danger. Not far from the city lived count Rudolf of Kyburg, in the mountain-castle of Bipp, which he had received on pledge from the counts of Thierstein. He was grieved that so much property had been alienated from his very ancient and formerly wealthy family, in consequence of the poor economy of his father. Thun, the city of his ancestors, had fallen to Berne on mortgage; so had Aarberg. He had some claim on Solothurn, in virtue of certain rights. He thought he could recover the whole by a bold stroke. He secretly enlisted auxiliaries on the right and left. He intended to surprise and take Solothurn in the darkness of the night. The prior of the church of St. Ursus, in that city, was his uncle. A canon of the cathedral, John Amstein, who lived on the city-wall, was to admit the soldiers through his house, and to muffle the alarm-bell with cloths. Every thing was ready. The night came, and the enemy were already advancing towards the city in the darkness.

But John Rott, a peasant of Rumisberg, ran ahead of them in the midnight hour, and informed the watchmen at the east gate of the count's murderous projects. They tried to ring the alarm-bell, but in vain. Cries of terror resounded through the streets. All seized their arms; all hastened to the walls. When Rudolf of Kyburg saw this unexpected vigilance, he retired with shame. John Amstein, the traitorous canon, was punished by quartering; to recompense John Rott, on the contrary, it was decreed, that

Solothurn should, every year thenceforward, give to the eldest of his descendants, a new coat in the colors of the city, red and white.

From this day, the affairs of lord Rudolf of Kyburg went from bad to worse; Solothurn and Berne, to avenge themselves, ravaged his property and that of his friends. The want of money deprived him of all assistance. He took this much to heart and died. His brothers, however, fought valiantly for their heritage. Many noble lords embraced their cause. Then Berne called on the Confederates. Great misfortunes befell Kyburg, and the counts made a disadvantageous peace; abandoned in perpetuity Thun and their office of bailiff over woody Grussisberg, and sold to the Bernese Burgdorf, already besieged by their troops. Berne paid the Confederates for their assistance, and Solothurn for the expenses of the war, in money.

Thus the bloody enterprise of the Kyburgs against Solothurn terminated in their own ruin, and Berne derived the greatest advantages from her valor and prudence; and Berne did this at a time when within her own walls dwelt an enemy much more dangerous to liberty than all the power of Kyburg.

Either by the abuse or mal-interpretation of the laws, or by the indifference of the citizens, a small number of families in Berne had by degrees acquired supremacy in the council, and assumed the whole government and the management of public affairs. These families treated the common citizens haughtily, disregarded the laws, and divided the best offices among their own members. Nevertheless, the spirit of freedom was still rife among the citizens in their corporations and trades. When they met on Shrove Tuesday, 1384, to elect the magistrates of the city and the common council, according to ancient usage, they deposed all the obnoxious councillors, with one exception, and took a personal oath; for themselves and their posterity, that, in future, magistrates and citizens should live together like brothers; that the important officers should be changed annually, as well as the majority of the council; that the bannerets and their assessors should yearly select two hundred honorable men from among the artisans of the city for a great common council, in which no two brothers should sit at the same time, and that the council elect should first appear before the general assembly to be confirmed by it, and should then swear, in its presence, to observe all the laws and ordinances contained in the records.

Thus did they and swore they, at Berne; but, with time, much was forgotten; the commons by degrees neglected the annual renewal, and did not even remember the names of those who belonged to the Two hundred.

CHAPTER XVII.

THE BATTLE FOR FREEDOM NEAR SEMPACH.

[A. D. 1385 to 1387.]

I WILL now tell of the very bloody battles for freedom which were fought against Austria and the knights in the fields of Sempach and Nafels.

The nobility, as always, implacably hated the freedom of the people. They oppressed the subject-peasants, and treated the Confederates with haughtiness. They thought themselves all-powerful, because they were upheld by the duke of Austria, who showed his hostility to the Confederates by establishing new tolls in his hereditary estates to impede their commerce. As, one day, a troop of bold Lucerners, full of wrath, went to the castle of Rothenburg, where a new toll had been established, and razed its walls to the ground; and as, on the same day, the much-harassed Entlibuchers, whose taxes their lord, Peter of Thorberg, had increased, requested the Lucerners to enter into a brotherly league with them for the defence of their rights, and Lucerne acceded to their request, the war against the signiors began.

Peter of Thorberg ignominiously executed those men of Entlibuch who first proposed the alliance with Lucerne, and ravaged the country to the city-gates. And duke

Leopold of Austria came and swore to take vengeance on the insolent Confederates, for all the damage they had already done to him and his house. Then arose cries of war and the noise of a general arming. The Confederates hastily assembled a Diet. Berne alone held back, because her truce with duke Leopold had not yet expired. In the mean while, one hundred and sixty-seven ecclesiastical and secular signiors declared war against the Confederates in the space of a few days, swearing their destruction and total ruin.

The latter, unterrified, at once seized their arms. Many castles were destroyed by them in a short time. Rumlang on the Glatt, Morsburg, Schenken on the mountain near Sursee, Windegg in Gasterland. The enemy, on their side, not inactive, and assisted by the treachery of the burghers of Mayenberg, killed many of the men from Zug and Lucerne who garrisoned that city; the place itself was reduced to ashes. Reichensee, faithful to the Confederates, paid for its fidelity by the burning of its houses and the massacre of most of its inhabitants; the unconscious infant at its mother's breast was not spared.

Thereafter, duke Leopold, with a formidable army and many noble knights and auxiliaries from his domains, marched from Baden, through Aargau, by Sursee, against Sempach, to chastise the citizens with a rod of iron for their attachment to the Confederates. Then he intended to attack Lucerne. But when he came to Sempach he found the banners of the Confederates already assembled on the heights. At once, without waiting for his infantry, he caused his thousands of cuirassed knights to dismount, because he feared lest the horses might create confusion in a hill-fight, ordered them to close up, man to man, like a wall of iron, and advance, with levelled lances, on the Confederates. Thereat the nobility shouted. Brave Hans of Hasenburg, however, spake warningly, "Arrogance does no good!" But duke Leopold said, "Here, on my own land, for my people, I will conquer or die!"

It was in harvest-time. The sun was high and hot. The Swiss fell on their knees and prayed. Then they rose: four hundred of Lucerne, nine hundred from the Wald statten, one hundred from Glarus, Zug, Gersau, Entlibuch and Rothenburg. All rushed furiously against the iron multitude. In vain; it was unshakeable. Man fell on man. Sixty Confederates bled upon the ground. All wavered.

"I will open a path for freedom!" suddenly cries a voice of thunder; "faithful and dear Confederates, take care of my wife and child." Thus spake Arnold Struthahn of Winkelried, the knightly Unterwaldener, and immediately clasping with both arms as many of the enemy's lances as he could, he buried them in his bosom, and fell. And over his dead body, the Confederates rushed furiously through the breach thus made in the iron wall, crashing as they went. Casque and cuirass cracked under the blows of the maces. Many hundreds of splendid banners became blood-red. Thrice the chief banner of Austria sank from dying hands, thrice it was raised again over the press, bathed in blood. Many a lord and count lay slain. The duke himself died despairing. He fell; a Schwyzer slew the prince's son. Thereat dismay spread through the ranks of knights. They fled, shouting for their horses. But the servants, in affright, had already ridden away with them. With difficulty, in their heavy iron armor, heated by the rays of the sun, fled the unfortunate knights; close behind them nimbly followed the vigorous Confederates. Many hundred counts, barons and knights from Suabia, Etschland and Aargau, fell with thousands of their foot-followers. Schaffhausen lost her banner, vainly defended, to the last drop of blood, by thirty-four nobles and burghers of the city. The banneret of Lenzburg, Werner of Lo, fell under seven, the avoyer of Aarau under fourteen, of his fellow-citizens, and Nicholas Thuet, avoyer of Zofingen, under twelve of his. The latter, seeing his death near, destroyed his city's banner, that no enemy might boast of having captured it. Even in death, he held the staff of the banner fast between his teeth. The citizens of Mellingen and Bremgarten fought with as much bravery as the Confederates, but with less good-fortune. Such was the issue of the battle of Sempach, on the 9th of July, 1386; such the ever glorious result of the heroism and martyrdom of Arnold of Winkelried.

Now Berne, also, joined her ancient Confederâtes and brothers-in-arms against Austria and her partisans in the mountains. She destroyed many a noble's strong tower; took the Obersibenthal (a valley rich in pasturage in the south part of the present canton of Berne) under her protection, and vanquished Freiburg in the field of Bumplitz. The banners of Zurich and Lucerne floated victorious over the domains of Habsburg, in valley and plain. The Austrian city of Wesen in Gaster was obliged to yield to Glarus, Zurich and the Waldstatten, who pressed around its walls with fire and sword, by land and water.

Austria, reduced to extremity, negotiated. A truce was concluded for eighteen months; a truce to arms, but not to hatred. Such was the animosity against Austria and the nobility, both mortal enemies of the liberty of the Confederates, that no man dared to wear, upon hat or casque, the peacock's feather which was the usual symbol of the Austrian dukes; no peacock was allowed in all Switzerland; and, one day, at an inn, a man broke his glass, in fury, because the rays of the sun, refracted through it, reproduced the brilliant colors of that bird

CHAPTER XVIII.

THE BATTLE FOR FREEDOM NEAR NAFELS, AND ITS CONSEQUENCES.

[A. D. 1388 to 1402.]

But the nobility and Austria still had faithful partisans in many places.

Although Glarus governed with great mildness the little city of Wesen which she had conquered, its inhabitants did not forget their ancient grudge against their neighbors, and their pride suffered more under the sovereignty of their equals than under that of a mighty prince. They conspired to avenge the house of Austria on the Swiss. For this purpose they secretly came to an understanding with the neighboring counts and lords; introduced into the city Austrian soldiers in disguise or concealed in casks, and kept them hid in their cellars and outhouses. The better to deceive the people of Glarus, they asked for a stronger garrison of Confederates. Glarus, mistrusting nothing, sent fifty men.

Suddenly, on the appointed night (St. Matthew's Eve, 1388) Austrian troops, numbering about six thousand, arrived before the city from all the neighborhood, overland and over the lake of Wallenstat. Every thing was silent in the streets, and in the houses where the citizens and concealed soldiers awaited the signal for their work of death. It came. Immediately every window was illuminated, every gate opened to admit the troops; then the massacre began. Konrad of Au, in Uri, bailiff and governor of the city, was killed, and with him fell more than thirty Confederates. Twenty-two leaped from the city-walls and escaped by swimming.

Glarus was filled with terror, and sent a weak handful of faithful men to the Landmarch against the invaders. The enemy advanced. The paths over the high alps were covered with snow. There was no hope of speedy assistance from the Confederates. They fought for several days in the Landmarch. In great distress, Glarus sent to the enemy and asked for an equitable peace. The Austrian nobles replied haughtily and imperiously to the landammann and communes of Glarus: "You must obey the duke of Austria, your proper sovereign, as serfs; have only such laws as your lord shall give to you; pay to him quit-rent and taxes; be subject to labor-dues and the right to the best chattel, as he shall prescribe; there shall no longer be among you any family free from imposts; you shall give up to him the parchment of the perpetual bond you have entered into with the Swiss, and serve him against them; you shall compensate the city of Wesen for all the damage she has suffered, and expiate your misdeeds until you deserve the grace of the duke."

Glarus answered and said: "We willingly acknowledge the princess-abbess of Seckingen as the lady of our land, and the duke of Austria as having the protectorate. We will pay the customary dues, and even compensate the city of Wesen; but we ask to retain our ancient rights and our harmless bond with the Confederates."

The Austrian councillors and lords haughtily disregarded this request, and marched at once with six thousand men against the barrier near Nafels, where captain Matthias Am Buel was posted with two hundred men of Glarus. Women and children fled for safety to the mountains; messengers hastened over the Alps to Uri and Schwyz; the landsturm (comprising old men and boys, all who can handle a weapon) rushed forth. But the overpowering army of the Austrians forced the defences of the barrier. Fighting with barely 500 heroes, Am Buel retired towards mount Ruti, that it might cover his rear; in front, was a rough plain, strewed with rocks. This stony ground impeded the movements of the Austrian cavalry; the people of Glarus threw down masses of rock on horse and man, so that confusion soon spread among the multitude of the enemy. They were still fighting valiantly, when warlike and encouraging shouts were heard on the mountain. They came from thirty men of Schwyz, hastening to the rescue. The enemy, ignorant of their number, were terrified. The alarmed cavalry, already in confusion, retreated. Seeing this, the Austrian infantry thought that all was lost, and fled in dismay. Hurrying upon their footsteps, the spears and swords and maces of Glarus made horrible carnage. More than 2500 men were slain in the orchards and meadows; many threw themselves into the waters of the Linth. The bridge of Wesen broke under the mass of fugitives, and the lake swallowed up the cuirassed corpses. Such was the battle of Nafels on the 9th day of April, 1388. Even at this day the people celebrate its anniversary on the first Thursday of April, and hear recited the names of the heroes who fell, and of the heroes who conquered, on the holy battle-field of freedom.

Before the fame of this exploit reached the Confederates, they were already assembled under their banners. Zurich, with auxiliaries from all the Confederates, attacked the newly-fortified city of Rapperswyl, but in vain. The Bernese, aided by the Solothurners, conquered Buren,

Nidau, Unterseen, gained a battle before Freiburg, ravaged Aargau, destroyed the family-castle of Peter of Gauenstein, and returned home through the Frickthal laden with booty.

When the dukes of Austria heard of so many reverses, and saw that all their possessions in Thurgau and Aargau were in great danger, their armies beaten and dispersed, their treasures exhausted, they desired to make peace, and concluded one for seven years. The Swiss held all the districts which had sworn to come under their jurisdiction; they only gave up Wesen, but on condition that no one of those who had broken the oath and taken part in the massacre, should dwell there during the peace.

What Leopold, fourth of this name among the dukes of Austria, had not been able to accomplish by force, he attempted by craft. He tried at first to sow dissension among the Swiss, and did, in fact, gain over burgomaster Rudolf Schon and some lords of the council, at Zurich. But their treachery was discovered and frustrated. The burghers of Zurich banished this dangerous man and his adherents, and in order to prevent future abuses, swore to an act which limited the power of the burgomaster and council. And the eight cantons of the Confederacy, assembled in diet at Zurich, with Solothurn, agreed among themselves to a general law respecting future wars (10 June, 1393,) and swore: "To avoid useless feuds, but to unite all their efforts in case of necessary war; never to stop fighting even when wounded, until the decision of the affair; not to flee, but to remain masters of the field; not to pillage, except by permission of the general; to spare churches, convents, and defenceless wives and daughters." This law of the Confederates, made on occasion of the war commenced by the battle of Sempach, and for the better ordering of their forces, was called the Convention of Sempach.

When Austria demanded a prolongation of the peace, it was fixed at twenty years, and observed.

The Confederates were glad to have this fine respite, that they might increase their franchises and commonwealths by ransom and purchase. Then no one was poor, but every one rich, when contributions and imposts were required for the glory of the fatherland; as, in the day of battles every one was rich in courage and blood. That was indeed a golden age.

Then the Zurichers bought from the impoverished Austrian nobility the bailiwicks of Kussnacht on the lake of Zurich, of Hongg and Thalwyl; obtained the signiories of Grunenberg, Regensberg and many others; the Lucerners acquired all Rothenburg, Ebikon, rights over Merischwanden and neighboring villages on the lake of the Waldstatten; received on mortgage the castles of Wollhusen, Russwyl and Entlibuch; the Bernese secured many places and rights in the mountains of the Oberland, the valley of Frutigen, fertile Emmenthal, the county of the lords of Kyburg in Burgundy, from Thun as far as the bridge of Aarwangen. The cities of Solothurn and Bâle also extended their rights and territories more rapidly with gold than they had done with the sword. The always free people of the valley of Urseren, on the St. Gotthard, united with Uri in a perpetual community of rights; and when the people of the duke of Milan, in consequence of a dispute respecting tolls, took from some men of Obwalden and Uri the cattle which the latter were driving to the yearly fair at Varese, Uri and Obwalden advanced their banners over the St. Gotthard mountain, and caused the people of the valley of Leventina to come under their protection and to swear allegiance to them. No one opposed this, for even the lords of Bellinzona, from fear of the Confederates, made an offensive and defensive alliance with them.

Thus, during the days of peace, the Swiss enlarged their territory by purchase and negotiation, embellished their cities and villages, and ameliorated their constitutions. Freiburg in Uechtland abjured her ancient enmity against Berne, made a treaty of everlasting friendship and co-burghership with the latter, and a perpetual league with the city of Bienne. Schaffhausen remodelled her constitution on that of Zurich, with greater freedom. But the city of Zug had a quarrel with the three communes of Menzingen, Baar and Aegeri, respecting the custody of the banner and seal of the canton, so that there was danger of a civil war, until the Confederates reëstablished peace and justice by an armed intervention. Glarus ransomed herself from the tithes and rights of the abbey of Seckingen, so that every one was free from tribute.

Such were the works of peace among the Confederates after the battles for freedom of Sempach and Nafels.

CHAPTER XIX.

THE HEROIC DAYS OF THE APPENZELLERS.

[A. D. 1403 to 1411.]

THE people in the mountains of Appenzell, on the streams of the Sitter, heard of the great battles and doings of the Confederates. And they thought with sad hearts of the abbot of St. Gallen, what a hard man he was, how immoderately he had increased the imperial tribute, and of the arbitrary conduct of the officers whom he set over them. Impositions, which they could hardly bear, were laid with inhumanity. The bailiffs in Schwændi levied a heavy toll on cheese, milk and butter, and whoever attempted to pass the toll-house without paying was seized by two trained hounds. The bailiff at Appenzell, to assert his right to the best chattel, under which the best coat of the dead belonged to him, caused a grave to be opened, that he might take from the corpse the garment in which poor children had buried their father.

At last the people were filled with indignation, and would no longer bear such an abuse of power. They said, "This must not continue;" and one day they attacked the castles and drove away the officers. Abbot Kuno, at the moment, had neither troops on foot, nor money with which to hire them. He therefore applied to the ten Suabian imperial cities, with whom he was in league, and asked for assistance. The imperial cities sent threatening messages to the Appenzellers. These said to the messengers: "We will willingly pay all our dues to the abbot, but we cannot endure injustice. We only ask that the abbot shall choose his officers from among the upright men whom we will nominate to him." The imperial cities held council at Ravensburg, refused the proposition of the people, and reinstated the ejected officers, who now added revenge to cruelty.

Abbot Kuno also had a dispute with the flourishing city of St. Gallen, which had already received great franchises from the emperors, and was in league with other cities. This city, enriched by the activity of her commerce and manufactures, would gladly have made herself independent of the abbey. As Appenzell and St. Gallen had the same fears and the same needs respecting their rights, they made a compact with each other, mutually to defend their ancient franchises. This displeased the abbot greatly. He increased his harshness towards the Appenzellers, disregarded their complaints, and tried to break their league with St. Gallen. Thereat the people became indignant, demanded an explanation from the abbot, and seized their arms. Kuno, affrighted, fled to his estate at Wyl. The ten imperial cities assembled anew and decided: "The abbot shall fill his offices with people of the country, but without previous nomination; the amount of the imperial tribute shall be fixed by the emperor, but the compact which those of Appenzell swore to with St. Gallen is and shall be null and void." St. Gallen submitted to this sentence. But the people in the mountains of Appenzell cried out that it was treachery. They saw clearly that the lords of the Suabian cities were arrogant and proud, and preferred the interests of a prince-bishop before those of common peasants. Then the people of the mountains assembled together, and the Rotten or Rhodes (cohorts, bands) of the country swore to their chiefs, and all the communes to the landammann, in the village of Appenzell, to hold together in danger and in death for defence of their rights.

As they were deserted by the city of St. Gallen, they asked the cantons of the Confederates, excepting Berne, to be allowed to enter into the bond with them. Five of these timidly refused, but Schwyz received Appenzell into her alliance, and Glarus proclaimed: "Whatever courageous lover of liberty wishes to help the Appenzellers, is free to do so."

At news of this, the imperial cities reiterated their threatening warning to the people of Appenzell, and afterwards, in concert with the abbot, resolved to reduce the peasants to subjection by force. They armed cavalry and infantry, and sent them to the city of St. Gallen, where the abbot entertained them magnificently. Then they advanced; the cavalry, with brilliant coats of mail, in front; behind them five thousand infantry. The army passed over the Linsenbuhl, through the sunken way, towards the height of Voglinseck, where is the village of Speicher. It was the 15th of May, 1403, in the early morning.

The Appenzellers, well-informed, had with them two hundred men of Glarus and three hundred of Schwyz, and when the watchers on the mountain-heights gave notice of the enemy's approach, the landsturm came forth. Each manfully took leave of wife and child, resolved to risk all for all; and the old men, who could not go with them, blessed their sons. Two thousand hastened to the top of the Voglinseck. Eighty Appenzellers took post in the upper part of the sunken way; on the left and right, near them in the woods, lay the men of Glarus and Schwyz.

The enemy's cavalry rode courageously up the mountain; there the eighty attacked them with spears and slings; there the men of Glarus and Schwyz came out upon their flanks from the ambush on each side of the sunken way. The cavalry in the narrow pass could neither fight nor wheel; they spurred wildly up the mountain to reach the plain above, but there all Appenzell advanced in armed cohorts, led by Captain Jacob Hartsch. When the enemy's generals saw this, they determined to return through the sunken way, and await the Appenzellers below. They gave the order, "Back!" and at once, through the whole troop on the mountain, resounded "Back! back!" Thereat the rear ranks thought that all was lost above, and that flight was ordered. Terror seized upon them. But Appenzell, Glarus and Schwyz rushed at once, from all sides, into the sunken way, slaying therein above and below. Then ensued a rout and a despairing flight towards St. Gallen. Six hundred knights, clothed in armor, lay dead in the sunken way; others dashed through their own infantry. Close upon their footsteps followed the murderous sword and spear and mace of the Appenzeller.

Now there was great mourning in the ten imperial cities for lost fathers and sons, and the cities would risk no more for the abbot, but concluded peace. The abbot, on the contrary, heaped insults on the cities and on the Appenzellers, who destroyed all his castles in their country, and ravaged his domains. He applied to duke Frederic of Austria, and said: "Appenzell will become a second Switzerland, if not prevented; and, in case she joins the Confederates, the nobility and Austria will lose everything in the upper country."

After many parleyings, duke Frederic promised assistance, and assembled many noble knights and a large army. Then he divided his forces, and advanced upon Arbon and St. Gallen, to invade the country on both sides at once. But, previously, Rudolf of Werdenberg had appeared before the general assembly of the Appenzellers and said: "I have been informed that the duke is raising troops in Tyrol to fight against you. The oppressed must hold together; therefore I come to you. You all know me. Behind these rocks is Werdenberg, the inheritance of my fathers; my ancestors were sovereigns in the Rheinthal.* Austrian rapacity has robbed me of everything; nothing is left to me but my heart and my sword. These I bring to you. Let me remain among you, a free countryman of Appenzell, and live and fight with you."

Thus said he, laid aside his armor and rich count's dress, put on the common shepherd's clothes, and lived among them. Such conduct in this heroic warrior pleased them all, and they made him their general-in-chief. They built ramparts in the defiles, and renewed their old alliance with the city of St. Gallen.

* A valley on the left bank of the Rhine, in the present canton of St. Gallen.

On a rainy day (17 June, 1405) the largest body of duke Frederic's forces marched from Altstatten in the Rheinthal, ascending towards the frontiers of Appenzell and up the Stoss mountain. The way was difficult, the ascent slippery upon the short grass of the slope, wet with rain. Four hundred Appenzellers, with a few men from Glarus and Schwyz, rolled rocks and trunks of trees from the heights down upon the troops. These latter had hardly reached the middle of the ascent when Rudolf of Werdenberg gave a signal. Then the cohorts of Appenzell rushed with loud shouts upon the already broken array; Rudolf at their head, barefooted like all the Appenzellers; thus they had a surer foothold on the slippery soil. The enemy could not use their cross-bows, because the strings were slackened by the rain. It was only sword and spear, against sword and spear. Austria fought with desperation. Suddenly, upon the heights behind, appeared a large fresh troop of Appenzellers, who seemed determined to cut off the Austrians' retreat. At once the terrified enemy hurried down the mountain, Appenzell slaying as they went. But those on the heights were the wives and daughters of Appenzell, all in shepherd's frocks. They wished to die for freedom with their husbands, lovers and brothers, or to help them conquer. Now, blood and rain flowed mingled, in the mountain-streams. Six hours long lasted the combat and the flight to the Rheinthal. Then Appenzell returned to the Stoss, and, kneeling on the battle-field, thanked God for this great victory.

In the mean while, duke Frederic, ravaging everything on his passage, arrived with his splendid cavalry before the walls of the city of St. Gallen. But when he found the city too strong, and was returning towards Arbon, the burghers of St. Gallen, divided into several small troops, fell upon his disorderly march, and killed many Austrians on the Hauptlisberge. This disgrace troubled the duke sorely; but he was still more troubled when he heard of the defeat of his people on the Stoss. Then he swore not to retire without vengeance. He caused a report to be spread that he was retreating homewards from Arbon into Tyrol, and he did, in fact, march to the Rhine with his troops. But, having reached the village of Thal, he suddenly wheeled about, to cross the Wolfshalde against Appenzell. He hoped to surprise and terrify the shepherd-people. But the Appenzellers were already forewarned. Four hundred of them, uttering loud shouts, attacked the Austrian soldiers, who marched without mistrust and without order. The latter hastily took up an advantageous post near the church. The combat was terrible. Forty Appenzellers were killed before the duke's ranks could be broken. But then the Austrians fled in a body down the Wolfshalde. Every slain Appenzeller was avenged by the death of ten flying enemies.

Then the duke cursed this war, and rode back into Tyrol. The Appenzellers, the glory and fear of whom spread far over the land, now made a league for nine years with St. Gallen; gratefully avenged Rudolf of Werdenberg on Austria, and restored to him the inheritance of his fathers; gratefully assisted the Schwyzers to take the valley of Waegi and the Lower March (which now forms the northern part of the canton of Schwyz and lies north-west of Waegi, in the same canton) from the dukes of Austria, and penetrated by the Vorarlberg into Tyrol, near Landeck, where they vanquished the duke's mercenaries. Then said the Tyrolese peasants on the Inn and the Etsch: "What do we care? Let us become free Swiss!" Then the Appenzellers were informed that the duke was collecting the forces of the empire against them, on the lake of Constance. Therefore they hastened home from Tyrol. But they found no enemy.

This war raged for five years. Appenzell, victorious, feared by all her enemies on the lake of Constance, the Thur and the Inn, took more than sixty castles, destroyed more than thirty of them, and at last besieged the city of Bregenz, but without success.

Peace was not thought of until after great desolation in all these regions. The king of the Germans himself wished to settle the difficulty, but Appenzell considered his decision partial. By the mediation of Schwyz, abbot Kuno had his legitimate revenues restored to him; but he lost forever all sovereign power and rights over Appenzell.

Austria made a peace for several years, and resumed possession of the Rheinthal.

The Appenzellers, satisfied with freedom and independence in their mountain-home, on St. Catherine's day, 1411, entered into a league with the Confederates, but not then with Berne; agreed not to undertake another war without the consent of the Swiss, and, in case of war, to assist the latter with all their force and at their own expense. The Swiss, on the other hand, reserved to themselves united, and to each canton separately, the right to extend or to limit this league, and, if they were obliged to aid the Appenzellers in a war, it was to be at the expense of the latter.

The formation of this league, which did not give equal rights to both parties, shows how much the Appenzellers feared for the maintenance of their newly-acquired independence, since they were willing to purchase the league with the Confederates at any price; and how much, on the other hand, the Confederates feared being drawn into bloody conflict with foreigners by the warlike people of Appenzell.

CHAPTER XX.

THE CONFEDERATES CONQUER AARGAU AND ESTABLISH COMMON BAILIWICKS.

[A. D. 1412 to 1418.]

After the brave people in the mountains of Appenzell had obtained their liberty and formed a league with the Confederates, they were well contented, and no longer desired war. Duke Frederic of Austria, also, saw that it was useless to contend with a people strong in union for their right, preferring independence to life. He saw, moreover, that the Confederates were so powerful that their friendship was more desirable to him than their enmity. Therefore duke Frederic opened a negotiation with them, and concluded a treaty for fifty years with the eight republics or cantons who composed the Confederacy (on the 28th of May, 1412) and recognized their right to all they held. They, on their side, recognized the mortgages, fiefs and other rights which the duke held in their country. This fifty years' peace was assented to by sixteen cities in the duke's hereditary domains, viz.: Schaffhausen and Waldshut, Laufenburg, Seckingen, Rheinfelden, Diessenhofen, Baden, Rapperswyl, Brugg, Bremgarten, Zofingen, Sursee, Lenzburg, Mellingen, Aarau and Frauenfeld.

But this peace lasted barely three years. Then it happened that Sigismund, king of the Germans, went to Constance, where, at the same period, a great council was assembled to put an end to the many differences in the Christian church. Thither came the principal prelates from countries far and near, and embassadors from the kings and princes of Italy, Germany, France, England, Poland, Denmark, Sweden, Hungary and many other kingdoms. An arrangement and settlement had become necessary, because a priest, named Huss, had preached, at Prague in Bohemia, a new doctrine, opposed to that of the catholic church, and had found many followers. Besides this, the catholic church was divided in herself, as, instead of one pope, she had three popes, in Italy and France, who anathematized and excommunicated each other. This occasioned much scandal in Christendom.

While the spiritual and temporal princes were assembled at Constance, duke Frederic had a quarrel with emperor Sigismund. The duke refused to go to Constance to receive his fiefs from the hand of the emperor, according to ancient custom. The fathers of the council were also incensed against the duke, because he had taken under his powerful protection one of the popes, named John, whom they wished to depose. As the duke obstinately refused obedience to the church-council, they pronounced against him the anathema of Judas and the greater excommunication. The emperor declared him guilty of high treason against the imperial majesty and against the empire, stripped him of all princely honors and deprived him of his fiefs. All faithful subjects of the empire were summoned against the duke, as were the Confederates also.

The emperor summoned the city of Schaffhausen against the duke, her lord, and, as an inducement, offered her independence, that she, like other free cities, might hold directly from the empire. The people of Schaffhausen eagerly seized this offer. Frauenfeld, Diessenhofen and almost all Aargau listened to the same or similar proposals from the emperor.

But the Confederates felt a just scruple at violating the fifty years' treaty they had recently concluded with the duke. The holy assembly of the church, it was true, declared such a course exempt from all sin, and the emperor said: "The territory which you may conquer from Austria, your hereditary enemy, shall remain your property in all time." But those in the Waldstatten, as well as Zurich, Zug, Lucerne and Glarus, answered: "We cannot persuade ourselves that such a breach of faith can be honorable."

Berne, however, thought differently. The opportunity appeared favorable to increase her own domains and to diminish the power of Austria in her neighborhood. Until this time, the city had enlarged her territory, not by the sword, but by negotiation and principally by purchase. But now Berne said to Zurich: "Justice and honor permit the war, since empire and church command it; the hour for the destruction of all the enemies of our forefathers has now struck!" As the Confederates still hesitated, the emperor sent frequently renewed messages to them, and the church-council, several times, threatened to excommunicate all the Confederates, if they did not march against the duke.

Berne speedily armed her troops. When Zurich saw this, she wished not to be behind, but to have her share of the booty. Then the other Confederates* obeyed the summons of the emperor and of the church; but Appenzell did not.

When the cities and nobles in Aargau were informed of these things, and of the disgrace of their sovereign, duke

* Zug appears to have remained firm in her refusal, and to have taken no part in the expedition.

Frederic, they assembled in diet at Sursee, in the spring of 1415. And the cities said, "Let us remain neutral between Austria and Switzerland, and maintain our prince's rights with our own liberties. The time has come when all Aargau should make a perpetual league for the protection of all. Then she can enter the Swiss Confederacy as a single free state, without fear of a greater, without subjection to her equals, and on a par with all the cantons of the Swiss in honor and dignity."

The pride of the barons and nobles would not allow them to make common cause with the cities. They preferred to serve a prince rather than to have burghers for equals. So the Diet separated without result. But the cities resolved to place themselves under the protection of the whole Confederacy. This, also, was already too late.

For, when the deputies of the cities started, in the early morning, on their mission to the Confederates, they saw, on all the heights, the Swiss signals of attack, and their banners and troops on the march. Sadly they returned home.

The Bernese troops marched upon Zofingen, harassed the city several days, and compelled it to abjure the duke and to take an oath to the empire and to Berne. To the right of Zofingen are the Wyken, four towers upon rocky summits; the Bernese took three, the Lucerners carried the fourth. On the left of Zofingen is Aarburg, the fortress, next to the little city on the Aar; Berne took both, as well as the two Wart-burgen (watch-towers) on the neighboring mountain-summits. Then the troops marched upon Aarau, having been reinforced from Solothurn, Bienne, Neuchâtel, and Neustadt. Aarau, notwithstanding the opposition of some of her citizens, yielded herself, with reservation of her franchises, into the protection of the Roman empire and of the cities of Berne and Solothurn. Brugg and Lenzburg also capitulated on similar conditions; many castles in Aargau did the same: Trostburg, which was destroyed by fire, Ruod, Brunegg, and others. Thus the Bernese, in a few weeks, by the rapidity of their attack, subjected seventeen strong castles and walled cities, without loss to themselves. Only before the castle of Wildegg, where the valiant barons of Hallwyl made a vigorous resistance, were four men slain.

At the same time, the Lucerners unfurled their banners over Sursee, subjected the upper countries on the Sur, Wiggern, Aa, and Winna, until they reached the limits of the Bernese conquests. Towards the east, they conquered the fertile country near Reichensee, Meyenberg, and Villmergen.

The Zurichers had already passed Mount Albis into the free bailiwick of Knonau, which they compelled to take the oath to them. Another troop went by the Limmat against Baden in Aargau, taking Dietikon.

In the region where the Limmat and the Reuss approach the Aar, the troops of the seven cantons of the Confederacy united, and together conquered what remained of the hereditary domains of Austria: Mellingen, Bremgarten, Baden. Mellingen maintained her faith to the duke for four days; Baden made a still stronger resistance. In the castle, the Stein, above Baden, was the lord of Mannsberg with a numerous force. But when the engines of the Bernese had battered down a part of the walls, and water failed the besieged, the Stein of Baden, also, was surrendered and destroyed. Far over the land shone the flames of that ancient castle.

After their conquests were concluded, the Confederates organized their new domains. What Berne, Zurich and Lucerne had conquered by their individual arms, each of the three cities kept for herself, with the rights which Austria had possessed. What had been conquered in common, was to be the individual domain of all, only Berne was excluded from participation, because she already had so much.

But Uri said: "We learn that the emperor has been reconciled to duke Frederic. Let us rather give back to the emperor what we have taken, that he may restore to the duke what is his. For this war was not ours, but the emperor's. We, O Confederates! we men of Uri will have no share in what is not our own. Our fathers have transmitted to us the custom of esteeming an inviolable fidelity above all other things."

The other Confederates laughed at this, and said: "How scrupulous and godly these men of Uri are! They must always be peculiar!" And they decided: "Inasmuch as Uri refuses, Zurich, Lucerne, Schwyz, Unterwalden and Glarus shall alternately send a bailiff, for two years, into these common bailiwicks, and, every year, deputies from all the participating cantons shall examine into the government and the management of the revenues."

Thus the Confederates kept their conquests, and were confirmed in them by the emperor. They reigned over these countries in the place of Austria, and, though free burghers in cities and cantons, had, like princes, greatly increased the number of their subjects.

CHAPTER XXI.

THE MAZZA OF VALAIS AGAINST RARON. THE BATTLE OF ARBEDO, AND THE CUNNING OF LORD ZOPPO.

[A. D. 1419 to 1426.]

A CENTURY had now hardly elapsed since the deed of William Tell, and the cities and cantons of Switzerland, formerly subject, had made others subject, and were feared by those before whom they had themselves trembled. And the sons of the old warriors and knights, who, from their castles on the rocks, had formerly threatened the cities, now humbly asked for the right of citizenship in them, or sold to them their lands, and went into other countries, that they might not be compelled to obey plebeian burghers.

Therefore the cities and cantons of the Confederacy felt their strength and a military pride, which could not be wounded with impunity, either by friends or foes. This was seen in the quarrels occasioned by Wichard of Raron, captain-general of Valais.

At the time when the Confederates, with the people of Uri, conquered the Leventina, they also took possession of the neighboring valley of Ossola, and left there a weak garrison. The duke of Milan, unwilling to leave Ossola to the Swiss, sold it to the duke of Savoy. The latter sent troops to Ossola through Valais; the baron of Raron showed them the way over the mountains, and the few Swiss were compelled to retire.

The baron of Raron said: "If I had been there, no Swiss should have been left alive." These arrogant words embittered the people of Unterwalden and Uri; they accused the baron in vain before Berne, where he was a citizen; therefore they excited against him the peasants of Valais. The latter had already many subjects of complaint against him: that he had made a compact with Savoy contrary to their will; that he and the grandees of the country violated the ancient customs, and wished to introduce serfdom. The men of Brieg said: "If Valais is to retain her ancient rights, the great lords must be bitted and curbed; all honest men must lend a hand for this."

And, according to a very ancient custom of the country, some men took an enormous club, on which they carved a human face with an expression of sadness, and surrounded it with thorns; this represented oppressed justice, and was called "La Mazza" by the Valaisians. They raised it on high in an open square, the people came around it, and a bold man stood by the club, as chief of the Mazza, and held it. Then many of the people addressed the image and said: "Mazza, why art thou here?" But it answered not. Others said: "Mazza, we wish to help thee; tell us, against whom? Art thou afraid of the Sillenen? Does Asperling or Henngarten (signiors of the country) trouble thee?" The Mazza remained motionless and silent. But when they named the captain-general Raron, it made a low affirmative bow. Thereon they removed the Mazza, and carried it from village to village, through all the Zehnten of Valais, and it was proclaimed that the Mazza was aggrieved by the captain-general and all his partisans, and by the bishop of Sion, his nephew.

When the baron of Raron saw the excitement of the angry people, he fled into Savoy, and implored the duke's assistance. But the peasantry destroyed his great castle on the height above Sierre (Siders), and the bishop's fort above

Leuk in Asche, and besieged his strong castle Beauregard, on the high rock over Chippis. They ravaged all his estates, and the duke of Savoy dared not assist him.

So he hastened to Berne, where he was a citizen, and asked for help and succor. But those of Valais applied to Uri and Unterwalden, and, as free peasants, concluded a mutually defensive alliance, and promised to aid them to retake Ossola, which valley borders on Valais. Those of Uri and Unterwalden at once crossed the highest Alps; Schwyz, Lucerne and Zurich went with them; the Valaisians did the same, and the whole valley of Eschen or Ossola was reconquered.

But Berne carried the case of the baron of Raron before all the Confederates, and demanded justice. Long parleyings ensued. Berne wished to march against Valais, and summoned the Confederates. But Unterwalden and Uri refused, as did Lucerne. A war between the Confederates themselves was imminent. To prevent this, the neutral cantons formed a diet at Zurich, and, after having heard those who were for and against Raron, decided: "First of all, Valais must restore to the baron the property which has been taken from him; then he shall do justice to the country on all complaints."

But the party-leaders in Valais did not like this decision, and persuaded the people to an obstinate resistance. They assembled some peasants, entered Oberhasli, seized and drove away the flocks of sheep, on pretext that the baron of Raron had before, with men of the Oberland, invaded Valais and committed ravages. Immediately, for the security of her passes, Berne sent a force against Valais. Schwyz and Zurich tried once more to mediate. But the Valaisians would not give back, and preferred war to moderation.

Then the Bernese, joined by the banners of Freiburg, Solothurn, Neuchâtel and others, thirteen thousand strong, marched over the highest Alps against the Zehnten of Gombs, and over mount Sanetsch against Sierre in Valais. They also received reinforcements from Schwyz, but neither Uri nor Unterwalden sent any to the Valaisians, on account of the obstinacy of the latter. Many villages fell in flames. Terror spread throughout the whole of Valais.

But a common peasant, Thomas Brantschen, restored courage to his fellow-citizens by his intrepidity, and, as he saw the plundering enemy advancing towards the village of Ulrichen: "What," said he, "has become of Valais, the ancient hero-land? Did not our fathers formerly defeat the duke of Zahringen in a bloody battle near Ulrichen? Let us once again conquer here for the fatherland and our ancient liberty, or die a glorious death."

Thus cried he, and, with four hundred valiant Valaisians, rushed from an ambush upon the thousands of Confederates, as they marched without mistrust. Brantschen fought like a hero. Forty Bernese lay dead before him; then he also fell, the lion of Valais. Terror was in the ranks of the Bernese. They wavered. Then appeared the array of Schwyz, and compelled the Valaisians to retreat to their first position. No one pursued them. On the next day the Confederates marched out of Valais. The Bernese troops from Saanen had also met with a terrible resistance from the Valaisians, near Sion.

Fresh propositions of peace were made. Finally, the Valaisians unwillingly consented to restore his signiories to the baron of Raron, to pay him ten thousand guilders (20,800 French francs) for all damages; the same sum to Berne for the expenses of the war, and four thousand to the chapter of Sion. This was in 1420, a few months after the heroic action of Thomas Brantschen. But the baron of Raron died, far from his native land. The splendor of his family was forever tarnished, because he had not known how to win the love of the people.

In the mean while, the duke of Milan had not forgotten the valley of Ossola, and he was the more angry when he also learned that the Confederates had bought from the barons of Sax, then signiors of Bellinzona, that city and all the district which extends from the Leventina to Lago Maggiore, for twenty-four hundred guilders. He armed secretly, and, with a large force, invaded Ossola and Bellinzona. These, as well as Leventina, were compelled to swear fealty to him.

Too late for vengeance rose the Confederates. Since the

conquest of Aargau their ancient concord had no longer prevailed among them. This delayed them. Discord also tarnished the glory of a bloodily-purchased victory, when they passed the St. Gotthard, and met the Milanese forces in the plain of Arbedo, not far from Bellinzona. There, from morning to evening, the Confederates had to contend against Italian skill and despair. There fell many valiant heroes of Switzerland: John Rot, landammann of Uri; Henry Puntiner, banneret of Uri; and old Peter Kolin, ammann and banneret of Zug. Kolin fell dying with his banner in front of his troop. One of his sons drew the banner from under his father's body, and raised it, bloody, over the combatants. Death took him also, but the enemy did not take the banner. John Landwing saved it. This was on the 30th of June, 1422.

Saddened by so many deaths, and by their poor victory, each reproaching the others, the Confederates marched back over the St. Gotthard. They left only a garrison in Leventina. For several years they disputed among themselves as to what should be done, adopted half measures with half minds, and accomplished nothing against Milan.

This disgusted Petermann Rysig, a stout-hearted countryman of Schwyz. He assembled five hundred courageous men, and with them passed the St. Gotthard, then to the right into the valley of Ossola over the mountains, drove out the Milanese garrison, and kept possession. All the forces of Milan marched against the valley. But Petermann Rysig kept possession. Now first waked the Confederates, aroused by the deed of the few Schwyzer heroes, and marched towards Ossola. From Solothurn, Valais, Toggenburg and Rhetia came auxiliaries. Thereat the duke of Milan was discouraged; but what he could not hope to gain by force of arms, he expected to accomplish by cunning.

And he said to his chamberlain Zoppo: "Go with my gold to the Confederates, and negotiate with them." Then came lord Zoppo, cunning as a fox and discreet, talked in a friendly manner with the council-lords, and was very liberal; divided their interests from each other; first persuaded Uri, Nidwalden and Lucerne to make a separate peace for themselves, and afterwards gained over the others by secret negotiations. And, in the year 1426, the Confederates gave up to the duke of Milan the valleys of Ossola, Bellinzona, and even Leventina, for thirty-one thousand and some hundreds of guilders, and for certain franchises and toll-gratifications in favor of their merchants and petty dealers. The Confederates returned home. The heroic action of Petermann Rysig was made of no avail; in vain had the blood of the noble Kolins dyed their banner before Arbedo. Truly, in all ancient and modern times, no powerful enemy has been so formidable to the Swiss as a lord Zoppo.

CHAPTER XXII.

IN THE HIGHLANDS OF RHETIA, THE UPPER LEAGUE, THE GOD'S-HOUSE LEAGUE, AND THE LEAGUE OF THE TEN JURISDICTIONS ARE FORMED IN BEHALF OF LIBERTY.

[A. D. 1426 to 1436.]

WHILE the Confederates were selling for money what had cost them the blood of so many heroes, a far different spirit prevailed in the elevated valleys of the Rhetian mountains: the spirit of liberty, of everlasting justice and concord.

In mountainous Rhetia, the people, from the old Frank times, had been tributary, subjects and serfs of the bishop of Coire, the abbots of Disentis and Pfeffers, and other ecclesiastical lords, and of numberless counts, barons and nobles. The city of Coire had, it is true, many franchises, but she also endured many vexations from her bishop. And the poor people in the villages suffered severely in the wars constantly carried on by the many great or small lords, and suffered just as severely in peace from the harshness and cruelty of their masters. Never had Uri, Schwyz and Unterwalden worse tyrants than had Rhetia; but Rhetia had also her Tells.

When the despotism, selfishness, injustice and pride of the ruling signiors had reached their height, then the poor people in Rhetia remembered that they also were men, and, moreover, that God had given to them, as his children, rights which no tyrant should violate. And the courage of a few honest men, in separate valleys, awakened the courage of the whole people in defence of their everlasting rights.

In the high verdant valley of Engadine, from the glaciers of which the Inn rushes forth towards Tyrol, stood the castle of Gardoval, the terror of the country, on the rocks above the village of Madulein. There dwelt the bailiff of the convent of Coire, a cruel and arbitrary man, who governed and judged in the name of the bishop of Upper Engadine. He saw the beauty of a young girl in the village of Camogast, which lay across the Inn, on the mountain, sheltered by the forest. And he sent his servants to bring the young girl to him that same day. The maiden's father, whose name was Adam, was filled with terror, his daughter with despair. But Adam mustered courage, and said to the servants: "Tell your lord that I will bring my child to him at the castle to-morrow morning."

As soon as they were gone, the father hastened to his neighbors and friends, with rage in his soul, fire in his eyes. He told them what had happened, and cried: "Have we, men, become the cattle of this lord?" Indignation was aroused in every breast, and, in the darkness of the night, they swore to put an end to the misery of the valley, or to perish together.

But, in the early morning, Adam the Camogaster led his beautiful daughter, in her holiday dress, as a bride, to Gardovall. Some of the conspirators followed, as a train of honor; others had placed themselves in ambush, near the castle, awaiting the moment for action: all were armed.

When the castellan saw the maiden, he sprang hastily down the castle-steps, to embrace the innocent girl before her father's eyes. Then Adam of Camogast drew his sword, and plunged it into the heart of the tyrant. He and his friends rushed into the castle, slew the servants, gave the signal of liberty from the windows, and were joined by those in ambush. Gardovall was burned. Afterwards (1494) the district below the sources of the Inn loyally bought itself free from the sovereignty of the convent.

The fertile pasture-valley of Schams, smiling pleasantly among the high Alps, and formerly subject to the counts of Werdenberg, was governed by the bailiffs of the bishopric of Coire, dwelling in the castles of Barenberg and Fardun. They practised every thing against the people, even the most humiliating outrages; and the people suffered and were silent. Strong John Chaldar suffered also, but was not silent. When two horses of the lord of Fardun were turned into his wheat, he was angered, and killed them on the spot. He expiated this deed in bonds and chains, until his family were able to free him by the payment of large sums and by many tears.

After Chaldar had returned rejoicing to his family and was seated with them at dinner in his cabin, the lord of Fardun entered. All saluted him respectfully, but he looked contemptuously at them, and spat into their broth. Then Chaldar's anger blazed like lightning; grasping the tyrant by neck and throat: "Now eat the soup which thou hast seasoned!" cried he; plunged the head of the wretched man into the contaminated food, and strangled him. Then he rushed out from his cabin, and roused the people. Fardun and Barenburg crumbled in blood and flames. The bishop was compelled to surrender to the valley his rights over it, for a compensation of thirty-two hundred guilders (1458).

As, in these valleys, the signiors advanced the cause of liberty by their inhumanity and tyranny, so, in other districts of Rhetia, they helped it by their ambition. Bishop Hartmann of Coire was constantly at war with the nobles of the land. Having suffered much damage, and not being himself able to defend the numerous domains of his bishopric, scattered as they were throughout an enemy's country, he granted to his subject-districts the right to form defensive alliances with the neighboring valleys and districts. Thus (as early as 1396) the God's-house people* of the valleys of Domleschg, Avers, Oberhalbstein and Bergun had made a league with the lords of Werdenberg in Schams, Domleschg and Obervatz. This was the first foundation of the subsequent God's-house league.

The counts and lords of the Rhetian highlands had done the same, and in union with the people of the valleys, already leagued together, had concluded with their neighbors of Glarus (in 1400) a perpetual defensive alliance against the offensive pretensions of the bishop of Coire.

But, in these alliances of the valleys, the rights, great and small, of their various lords were always reserved; and these rights were much abused. The lords knew no law but their own will and power. There was neither justice in the courts nor safety on the highways.

Desiring to put an end to these disorders, without violence and without revolt, several loyal, respected and intrepid peasants formed an association in Upper Rhetia. They met every night between the abbey of Disentis and the little city of Ilanz, the first walled place on the Rhine. There, in a wood near the village of Truns, they met and conversed together; and afterwards communicated their resolves, in confidence, to the most estimable men of their respective communes.

Then, on one and the same day, all the communes and valleys of Upper Rhetia sent their most respected and best-informed men as deputies to their several signiors, to demand that justice and security should be guaranteed to all by a solemn agreement to which all should make oath, without injury to the real rights of the greatest or the least.

The signiors were terrified by this demand issuing from the forest of Truns, and they thought of what had taken place in the Swiss Confederacy one hundred years before. The pious and prudent abbot of Disentis, lord Peter of Pultinga, was the first who assented to the just requirements of the people. The counts of Werdenberg, of Sax,

* Subjects of the Convent or God's-house, as all religious establishments were called; or Casa Dei, whence Caddean, the name sometimes given to these Rhetians.

the barons of Rhezuns, and others, followed; either from fear of their own subjects, or from fear of the powerful bishop of Coire, and to strengthen themselves against the latter.

Then these lords, and the deputies of the communes of Upper Rhetia in their modest grey frocks, met in front of the village of Truns, in the open air, under the shade of a maple-tree, and swore by the holy Trinity to a perpetual covenant for the maintenance of justice and security, without injury to the rights of the greatest or the least. This was in May, 1424. Thus was formed the Upper or Grey league (so called from the grey frocks of the deputies). Afterwards it was completed by the accession of the valleys of Misox and Calanca. Soon the name of Grisons (Graubundner: Grey-leaguers) spread over the whole of Rhetia, although the God's house league already existed separately, and although, moreover, there were numerous districts in the mountains, on the side of Tyrol, which belonged, neither to the God's-house nor to the Grey league, but to the extensive sovereignty of the rich count, Frederic of Toggenburg.

But, shortly afterwards, this rich count died childless, and there was great fear of a war for the inheritance. Then assembled the people of the districts, villages and jurisdictions which belonged to the house of Toggenburg, in Rhetia. They came from Davos and Klosters, Kastels, Schiersch and Seewis, even from the prebendary's jurisdiction of Schiersch, from Malans, Maienfeld, Belfort, Churwalden, Outer and Inner Schalfick. They said: "Since we are left free by the death of the count of Toggenburg, let us, like the people of God's-house and the Highlands, make, in these mountains, a league which shall endure forever: for the injury of no one, but for the protection of our hereditary rights; for union in danger and in death. No one shall cite another before a foreign tribunal, nor make alliance with others, but by consent of all. When the estate of Toggenburg shall be settled, we will surrender his property to the recognized heir, but even he shall not be able to dissolve our league. So said they and solemnly swore on the Friday after Corpus-

Christi day in 1436. This was the origin of the League of the Ten Jurisdictions.

A new Confederacy was also formed between the three leagues of the Rhetian Alps. And the Rhetians from that time were called Grisons.

CHAPTER XXIII.

QUARREL RESPECTING THE TOGGENBURG-INHERITANCE.

[A. D. 1436 to 1443.]

VERY different effects did the death of the rich count of Toggenburg produce among the Swiss: here it enkindled the destructive flames of civil war.

As soon as Frederic of Toggenburg closed his eyes in advanced old age, numerous heirs presented themselves. His domains were large; many lay beyond the Rhine; many along the Appenzeller mountains from the lake of Zurich as far as Tyrol. Among them were the Toggenburger-land, the signiory of Uznach, the March, Windegg in Gaster, the Rheinthal and the Ten Jurisdictions in the Grison country. There were others also in Thurgau and elsewhere. Madam Elizabeth, widow of the deceased, thought herself the rightful heiress; but some distant relatives of her husband disputed her right, and advanced their own claims. Zurich, also, believed herself to have some rights over this inheritance, because the count, who died childless, had been her citizen and co-burgher; Schwyz made the same claim, because the count had been co-burgher with that canton likewise.

Madam Elizabeth, to secure a powerful protector, united with the city of Zurich, and made to the latter, under hand and seal, a donation in form of Uznach, the Uznach mountain and Schmerikon. The Schwyzers thereupon requested the count's relatives to forbid his widow to alienate any portion of the estate. Then those of the count's subjects who inhabited Lichtensteig, Neckarthal, Thurthal, St. Johannserthal, Uznach and the lower part of the lake of

Wallenstatt, came and said to Schwyz: "Our late lord, always thoughtful of our happiness during his life, wished that, after his death, we might find protection and security with you. Receive therefore our oath, and number us henceforward forever among your people." And the people of the country of Sargaus, which the count of Toggenburg had only held on mortgage, requested duke Frederic of Austria to ransom them, as his faithful subjects. He did so. But, perceiving that their intentions were not loyal, he gave them up to count Henry of Werdenberg.

When Zurich learned that the people in Uznach and other places had sworn allegiance to Schwyz, the city was angry and made many threats, because Uznach was her domain. But the Schwyzers at once sent troops into the March and to Uznach, to protect their new people by force, denied the right of the Zurichers, and associated Glarus in the sovereignty over the new territory, that they might have her support in case of need.

Since the rulers in the cities and cantons of Switzerland had conquered Aargau and established the common bailiwicks, they had become haughty; they indeed wished to enjoy liberty themselves, but not to confer it on others; they preferred subjects rather than free fellow-citizens, their equals in rights. As formerly they had been unwilling to admit Aargau to a free participation in their confederate bond, so now, their intentions were no better respecting Toggenburg. They wished to be lords; they wished to have serfs.

Hence much discord, hatred and contention. A great Diet, assembled at Zurich, in vain attempted to restore concord. The deputies departed more embittered than they had come. Then, at the head of Zurich was the burgomaster Rudolf Stussi, and at the head of Schwyz the landammann Itel Reding of Bieberegg. Both ambitious, enterprising, talented and eloquent men; but they hated each other, and each was zealous for his own canton, indifferent to the peace and welfare of the common Confederacy.

Then for the first time was seen what an abyss of misery is opened by cantonal egotism and selfishness, when the interests of one canton are preferred to those of the whole Confederacy. During the great famine of 1439, occasioned by continual rains which destroyed the crops in the ground, it had already become evident that the ancient beautiful union no longer existed. One canton meanly prohibited the exportation of provisions into the others, so that the sufferings of all were increased, and with them the hatred. Schwyz and Zurich then threatened each other with the sword.

To prevent greater misfortunes, the Confederates arbitrated at Berne. Schwyz assented to their decision, but Zurich would not listen to it. The latter called the Confederates partial, because they left Uznach to the Schwyzers, although the countess Elizabeth had deeded it to Zurich; and moreover, no mention was made of Gaster and Windegg, although Schwyz had taken possession of these districts before the decision, and in spite of the protest of the Confederates.

Burgomaster Stussi said, "Then the sword must decide." But he first sent to the Schwyzers an open letter, in which he no longer styled them Confederates. And he proposed to them an appeal to the tribunal of the Roman king, as head of the German empire, from which they both held. The Schwyzers replied, "The king's tribunal may be excellent, but it is not that we swore to be ruled by in our perpetual bond as Confederates."

Thereat the Zurichers and Schwyzers marched with their troops against each other on Mount Ezel. The Schwyzers took post above, the Zurichers below, near Pfeffikon. Stussi himself went against the March, but found those of Glarus and Schwyz so well entrenched and fortified that he withdrew without undertaking anything. Envoys from Uri and Unterwalden came to Itel Reding on the Ezel. They besought him, in the name of God and the fatherland, again to attempt a reconciliation, in order to prevent that unheard-of crime—the shedding of Confederate blood by Confederate hands. But at this moment blood had already been shed. For a troop of Zurichers advanced as far as the first posts of the Schwyzers. Many were wounded; eleven Zurichers slain; the rest fled.

The Confederates, however, once more obtained a truce and fresh negotiations. But nothing could be accomplished, because Zurich persisted in preferring the arbitration of the Roman king to that of the Confederates. Then all the Confederates became embittered against Zurich. Zurich armed, and Stussi marched with more than six thousand men towards Mount Ezel, where Schwyz and Glarus awaited him in warlike array; some soldiers from Uri and Unterwalden had also joined the latter.

But in the middle of the night, a strange, unaccountable terror suddenly seized upon the Zurichers posted near Pfeffikon. In their fright, they hastily embarked in fifty-two bateaux, and fled through the darkness to Zurich. The Schwyzers stationed on the upper part of the Ezel immediately marched down, overpowered and occupied the country on the lake, and persuaded all the Confederates to advance against Zurich.

Fear and disorder prevailed in the city, when she saw herself deprived of all assistance; she negotiated anew and submitted to the arbitration of the Confederates. Not only was Zurich compelled to give up all claim upon Toggenburg, but, also, to reïmburse Schwyz and Glarus, by surrendering all property and rights over land and people in Pfeffikon, Wollrau, Hurden, and other places. Thus one canton made conquests from another. In the same year, (1440), Schwyz, in a more honorable manner, acquired the village of Merlischachen from the wealthy lords of Moss, and Uri found opportunity to recover the lost valley of Leventina. It happened in this wise: Either at Airolo or at Bellinzona, the justice stipulated by treaty was refused to some men of Uri. Angered thereby, the banners of Uri, as they returned from mount Ezel, marched straight over the St. Gotthard and took possession of Leventina and Bellinzona without opposition. The old duke of Milan, unprepared for war, was obliged to purchase peace dearly by giving up Leventina to Uri.

In the mean while, duke Frederic of Austria, a grandson of that Leopold who fell near Sempach, had become emperor. He had openly said that he meant to take back from the Swiss all the property of his ancestors. With this object he constantly sounded the disposition of the people, the nobility and the cities of Aargau.

This pleased burgomaster Stussi and the council of Zurich, who were irritated against the Confederates. If Zurich, the vorort of the Swiss Confederacy, had magnanimously forgotten her own causes of resentment, and, in a noble spirit, warned her Confederates of the hostile designs of Austria, with what resplendent honor would her virtue have shone before all the Confederates and their descendants! But Zurich listened only to vengeance, felt only her injuries, joined the emperor, secretly concluded a criminal alliance, and forgot the Confederates. Great souls were wanting. This shameful treaty was made in 1442.

As soon as this became known, all the Confederates cried out against the vorort; she had broken the perpetual bond. They assembled in diet, and summoned Zurich to abandon her alliance with Austria. Numerous useless parleyings took place. Zurich would not separate from the emperor. The latter sent his captain, Thuring of Hallwyl, to the city, which solemnly took, upon his hand, the oath to the empire, and swore to advance the emperor's interests, and to avenge any injury done to him. At the captain's request, the Zurichers even removed the white crosses, distinctive marks of the Confederates in all their former wars, and placed in their hats the red crosses which the Austrians wore. Others assumed the imperial eagle and the Austrian peacock's feather.

This greatly exasperated the Confederates; the breasts of all the peeple were inflamed with anger. Insults, trespasses, assassinations and incendiarisms prevailed everywhere. Finally, all the Confederates declared war against Zurich.

CHAPTER XXIV.

WAR OF ALL THE CONFEDERATES AGAINST ZURICH. THE HEROES-DEATH NEAR ST. JACQUES. PEACE.

[A. D. 1443 to 1450.]

THIS declaration of war by the Confederates did not terrify Zurich: she counted on the emperor's powerful assistance. Already, in fact, on summons of the emperor, besides Thuring of Hallwyl, many other knights and warriors, and even William, margrave of Baden, had hastened to the city's aid. More than five thousand Austrians were there.

Now began the war of Swiss against Swiss. Near Pfeffikon and Freienbach on the lake of Zurich, the Schwyzers fought against double their number of Zurichers; as did Lucerne, Uri and Unterwalden, on the heights of Hirzel, against the Zurichers in the fortifications on the mountain. The fortifications were stormed and destroyed; this cost much noble blood. I cannot enumerate the villages reduced to ashes on the lake, in the territories of Zug and Schwyz, and in the free bailiwicks. Every day blood reddened the earth; every night flames reddened the sky. In vain did the courageous city of Bremgarten defend herself, in behalf of Zurich's share in her government. The fate of Bremgarten terrified Baden, which had preferred to remain neutral. She opened her gates to the Confederates. Neither the town of Rumlang nor the strong castles of Gruningen and Regensberg could withstand the courage of the Confederates.

Finally, the latter, Schwyz, Uri, Unterwalden, Glarus, Zug and Lucerne, about five thousand strong, crossed the Albis, Itel Reding with them, against the city of Zurich itself. And the citizens and Austrians, on foot and on horseback, burgomaster Stussi with them, hastened to meet the invaders: all hurried across the Sihl. In the meadows between the village of Weidikon and the ancient chapel of St. James, against each other rushed the bloodthirsty bands, thousands against thousands, on the 22d

July, 1443. The shock and conflict were frightful. Terror seized upon the Zurichers, who fought without order, as they had come forth without order. Now they fled in confusion over the bridge of the Sihl. There, burgomaster Stussi, venerable in his white hair and his heroism, stopped in the middle of the bridge, brandished his broad battle-axe and shouted: "Halt, citizens, halt!" But a man of Zurich cried: "May God's lightning blast thee! All this evil comes from thee alone," and ran him through with his lance. The burgomaster's armor clattered as he fell. Over his dead body enemies and friends rushed into the suburb. The citizens closed the inner gates; all outside was pillaged by the conquerors. The latter hacked into pieces the corpse of Stussi, tore his heart with their teeth, greased their boots and shoes with the fat of his body, and threw his mutilated remains into the Sihl. Houses and villages burned around. The flames furnished light, while the conquerors sat on the bodies of their slain enemies, and caroused together.

Then the Confederates besieged Rapperswyl, the fortress of which was occupied by Austrians; the Bernese did the same with Laufenberg. Both places held strong. But the fortress of Greifensee was obliged to yield when assaulted. Hans of Breitenlandenberg, surnamed the Savage, had defended it valiantly with a few men for twenty-six days. It cost Itel Reding and his Confederates dear. Therefore they were so exasperated that they demanded the death of the Savage and his heroes, when they yielded at discretion. "All, all must die," shouted the raging soldiery, "and the men of Griefensee also." Captain Holzach, of Menzingen on the Zug mountain, cried out: "Confederates, fear God! Spare innocent blood! Stain not the honor of the Confederacy!" But Itel Reding, the landammann, said: "This man has Austrian sympathies. They must all die, excepting the people of Griefensee." The sanguinary hordes howled approval. In vain did old men and young, fathers and mothers, implore pity. Reding gave the signal; the circle was closed. The executioner of Berne entered it with his sword. The Savage died courageously. After his, fell many other heads. The executioner stopped and looked at Itel Reding, as if to ask for mercy on the rest. Then Reding was exasperated, and said: "Quick! To thy work! If thou dost not thy duty another shall do it on thee!" Then fell the heads of Felix Ott, of Hans Escher of Zurich, and others. When the fiftieth fell, it was already night. Itel Reding caused straw to be brought and kindled. When the sixtieth was dead, Reding withdrew from the shuddering crowd.

After this, the Confederates returned against Zurich with twenty thousand men, and besieged the city for sixty days in the summer of 1444. The Zurichers made a valiant resistance. Sixteen of them, who called themselves the Bucks, formed a military association, and did much damage to the Confederates by a partisan warfare.

The Austrian nobility of Aargau were also active in behalf of Zurich. Thomas of Falkenstein, landgrave in Buchsgau and Sisgau, in order to injure the Bernese, sent two of his people to set fire to the city of Aarau in the night. When this had failed, he rode with the lords of Baldegg through the city of Brugg, and said: "We have come from the camp of Zurich, and are going to Bâle to request the assistance of the lord-bishop in restoring peace." On the second night afterwards, he reäppeared at the city-gates and said: "We bring peace. Here is the lord of Bâle. Open to us." And he showed two of his servants in the colors of Bâle, at his side. When the watchmen, deceived, opened the city-gates, Falkenstein entered with four hundred horsemen, plundered the city, seized and imprisoned the avoyer Effinger, the lords of the council and the principal citizens. He meant to have them all beheaded at break of day. But the news of his deed had already spread through the country. The peasants rose on all sides. Falkenstein set fire to the city and carried off the prisoners. They were to be beheaded in the oak-forest not far from Brugg. But when John of Rechberg, one of his accomplices, begged for their lives, the prisoners were taken to Laufenberg and secretly confined in the tower on the rock over the river, so that no one knew where they where. But Burgi Kuffier let himself down from the tower by a rope of bed-clothes, leaped into the whirlpool of the Rhine, escaped and made all known. Then the wives of Brugg ransomed their husbands from the enemy's power with much gold. The Solothurners and Bernese, in revenge, destroyed Falkenstein's castle of Gosgen; they burnt Farnsburg also and other places.

In the mean while, Zurich, besieged, was in distress. The emperor, engaged in a distant war, could not help her. He called on the king of France for assistance against the Swiss. The king of France, at this time, had his land full of disorderly foreign troops; among them were many English and other people, who had fought against him under the count of Armagnac, until they were conquered. The king collected all these, gave them leaders, and, under the command of his own heir, the dauphin Louis, sent thirty thousand Armagnacs against the Confederates, to the aid of Zurich. They marched to the neighborhood of Bâle, where the Solothurners, with troops from Berne, Lucerne and Bâle, were besieging the high fortress of Farnsburg. These immediately sent messengers to the camp before Zurich, asking for assistance from the Confederates, because the Armagnacs were so numerous. "They are only miserable wretches!" said those before Zurich, and contented themselves with sending six hundred men to reïnforce the besiegers of Farnsburg.

As soon as it was known that the foreign enemy was already encamped in the fields near Munchenstein, not far from Bâle, nine hundred of those before Farnsburg and the newly-arrived six hundred marched towards them. On the 26th of August, 1444, in the early morning, they found several thousand Armagnacs before the village of Prattelen, drove them, in a bloody fight, back into their entrenchments near Muttenz, and out of their entrenchments into the waves of the neighboring Birs.

From the towers of their city, the burghers of Bâle saw the little troop of Swiss advance against the superior forces of the enemy. Three thousand Bâlese came out to persuade the Swiss to take refuge in the city; but they could not succeed. The Confederates crossed the Birs by swimming, and reached the opposite bank in spite of the terrible discharges of the enemy, whose whole force was there drawn up. Like destroying angels they penetrated those numberless hordes. They were soon separated, but still fought, five hundred in an open plain, the rest behind the garden-wall of the hospital near St. Jacques. Terribly, like lions, fought those of the plain, until, man by man, they fell dead upon the dead bodies of numerous enemies; terribly, like lions, fought those behind the wall; thrice they repelled the assault; twice they themselves made the attack; the wall fell, hospital and chapel were burned. All the Confederates here died heroically. Ninety and nine were found suffocated in the cellar vaults. But thousands and thousands of the enemy, with their horses, covered the ground from Prattelen to St. Jacques.

When, at the end of this ten hours' battle, knight Burkhard Munch, lord of Auenstein and Landskrone, an enemy of the Confederates, with other knights, rode over the battle-field and over the bodies of the Swiss, he said, joyfully: "Now I am bathing in roses." Then cried captain Arnold Schik of Uri, rising from under the dead: "Swallow this rose!" and shattered Burkhard's forehead with a deadly stone.

Fifteen hundred Confederates fell with immortal glory at St. Jacques. Only ten men saved their lives by flight. They were despised and proscribed throughout all Switzerland, because they had not shared the glorious courage and the glorious death of the heroes, as Swiss should.

Louis, the dauphin, stopped there, upon the field of the dead, and dared not advance farther. He was informed that the Confederates had left the walls of Zurich to march against him with their whole force. "Upon my honor, a more obstinate people cannot be found!" cried he; "I will attempt no more against them." And, full of respect for their great courage, he concluded peace with them at Ensisheim.

But the internal war against Zurich, Austria and her nobility still continued. Bâle now courageously and openly joined the Confederates, aided them in the field, and drove out from her walls all the nobles who had given advice and assistance to the Armagnacs. Her troops marched with the Bernese and Solothurners to Rheinfelden This city was devoted to the Confederates; but in the fortress on the rock in the Rhine lay John of Falkenstein, Hallwyl, and many nobles and Austrians. These fled in the night; the fortress was destroyed. Rapperswyl had also to undergo a new siege; the city was strong. John of Rechberg and the Zurichers assisted it vigorously. But these were completely defeated by the Schwyzers and Lucerners, near Wollrau, on a clear winter's night (16 December, 1445). Still more bloody, in the following year (6 March, 1446), was the defeat of the Austrians, when, six thousand strong, John Rechberg the heroic warrior being with them, they tried to enter Switzerland near Ragaz. Eleven hundred Confederates, of all the cantons, obtained this decisive victory, of which peace was the result.

The emperor, engaged in other matters, hated this war, from which he derived no glory. Zurich and the Confederates, since Stussi had fallen and Itel Reding was also dead, drew together of their own accord. There were still some fighting and burning here and there, but negotiations proceeded actively, until finally, on the 13th of July, 1450, the decisive arbitration was pronounced by the avoyer Henry of Bubenberg: "Zurich shall renounce her alliance with Austria, and shall reënter into possession of all the territory taken from her by the Confederates, with the exception of the strip of land she had previously lost on the upper lake."* All parties agreed to leave Toggenburg to a relative of the deceased count, the baron of Raron, who shortly afterwards (1469) sold it to the abbot of St. Gallen.

* This now forms part of the canton of Schwyz.

CHAPTER XXV.

RHEINFELDEN IS DEVASTATED. FREIBURG FALLS INTO THE POWER OF SAVOY. THURGAU BECOMES A COMMON BAILIWICK OF THE CONFEDERACY.

[A. D. 1450 to 1468.]

WHILE the Confederates were still negotiating peace, an unheard-of trespass occurred. The imperial-city of Rheinfelden, devoted to the Swiss, and formerly mortgaged to Austria but afterwards restored to the empire, was under the protection of Bâle, Berne and Solothurn. Each of these places had only a guard to represent her in the city. No one feared any evil. But knight William of Grunenberg, to whom Austria had transferred her mortgage-rights over Rheinfelden, as a compensation for his destroyed castle, desired possession of the city. He employed John of Rechberg to take it by surprise. Thomas of Falkenstein, the incendiary of Aarau, and author of the nocturnal massacre of Brugg, was also persuaded to second the enterprise.

One morning (in November, 1448), during divine service, there arrived at Rheinfelden a wood-laden boat, which had come down the Rhine; some men in long grey frocks, who were on board, said that they were returning from a pilgrimage to the gracious Mother of God at Einsiedeln, and wished to stop there for dinner. But, as soon as they were under the gate, they suddenly threw off the frocks which concealed their armor, and killed the guards and toll-gatherers; one hundred and twenty armed men came from beneath the boat-load of wood, and carried carnage into the city; on the land-side, through the opposite gate, which they broke in, came Grunenberg and six hundred, who had been in ambush. They massacred those whom they found in the streets, pillaged the houses and committed all kinds of excesses; drove out men, women and children, who, stripped of every thing, found their way to Bâle, where they were compassionately received and lodged in the hospital and inns.

The Bâlese did still more. Animated by vengeance, they issued from their gates in strong force, entirely routed Rechberg and Falkenstein near Hesingen, and burned many castles of the robber-nobles. But when, shortly afterwards, by the treaty of peace, Rheinfelden was restored to the house of Austria, and the nobles were compelled to evacuate the city, these robbers carried off all the household furniture, destroyed windows, doors and stoves, and left nothing but the bare walls.

A great part of Switzerland was desolated by so long a war. Commerce and the trades languished in the cities, agriculture in the country. This insensate war had cost the Zurichers 1,070,000 guilders. They called in all the money they had lent. As emperor Sigismund had mortgaged to them the county of Kyburg and could not redeem it, Austria gave up the fee of that country, in lieu of payment.

The animosity between Berne and Freiburg was embittered by the war, because Freiburg had always held with Austria against Berne and the Confederates. Freiburg, having passed from the dukes of Zahringen, its founders, to the heirs of Kyburg, was afterwards sold by the latter to the house of Austria. Therefore it was devoted to Austria. And therefore Berne had assisted the duke of Savoy in the many disputes and war between him and Freiburg.

After peace was reëstablished, Austria recompensed the people of Freiburg but poorly for their fidelity: she treated them harshly; arbitrarily deposed their avoyer and council, refused to refund the money advanced, and gave command of the city to marshal Thuring of Hallwyl, with unlimited authority. This alienated the hearts of the citizens. Conspiracies and disturbances took place; the people thought to shake off the Austrian yoke. Berne hoped to profit by these circumstances, and to remove the formidable influence of Austria from her neighborhood. Then came the duke of Savoy and demanded from Freiburg 200,000 guilders, which she owed him. Affairs were in such a bad state, that Austria herself saw she could no longer hold Freiburg; she negotiated with Savoy, and soon came to an agreement. Thereon Austria ordered the marshal of Hallwyl to leave Freiburg. But he told the council-lords that duke Albert himself was coming to the city, that preparations should be made for a solemn reception, and the citizens send to him all their silver-plate, in order that he might welcome the duke with becoming splendor. When he received the silver, he had it packed up and sent off secretly. Then he rode forth, pretending to go to meet the duke. The avoyer and many council-lords accompanied him and his knights. When at a league's distance from the city, he turned, handed to the avoyer the document by which duke Albert renounced his rights over the city, and said: "Your silver-ware is the price of your freedom. Fare you well!" Hallwyl spurred onwards, and the men of Freiburg returned astonished home.

Then fresh disorders and agitations took place. The country-people were against the city. The city, moreover, feared to fall under the dominion of Berne. The duke of Savoy rigidly exacted the payment of the debt. This threw the council of Freiburg into great distress, and they surrendered to the sovereignty and protection of the duke of Savoy. On the 10th of June, 1452, in the cathedral-church of St. Nicholas, the avoyer, the council, the sixty, the bannerets, the two hundred and all the commons of the city took the oath of fealty to the duke of Savoy, who, in return, confirmed the ancient franchises of the city and district.

In the mean while, notwithstanding the peace, the rest of Switzerland was far from quiet. The continual wars had made the hearts of the people savage. The common men preferred to fight and plunder, rather than to plough the earth, herd cattle, or exercise a trade. When their own country was at peace, the sound of the drum drew them abroad. One came and enlisted soldiers for the German, another for the French wars. The lords and rulers sought to gain glory and money and reputation with the princes, because they imagined themselves to be princes over their own subjects.

When the king of France perceived this disposition, he testified much friendship towards the Confederates, made a neighborly compact with them (1453), and many hundreds of valiant Swiss went to join his armies. With the same views, the duke of Milan ceded the Leventina to Uri in perpetuity, and made a treaty or capitulation (1467) with the Confederates, respecting the passage of travellers, the freedom of trade, tolls and different jurisdictions. These were the first treaties of the Confederates with those neighbors, whose fields they were afterwards, for vile hire, to water with so much precious blood.

But other contests were not wanting. When the city of Strassburg complained to the Zurichers that the robber-count of Thengen had plundered the merchants of Strassburg, the banners of Zurich were quickly displayed to avenge her friends. The castles of the robber fell. Zurich took Eglisau and Rheinau, and held Eglisau and the convent of Rheinau under Swiss protection, in payment of her costs (1457). Strassburg invited the stout, valiant young men of Zurich to a festival, in celebration of their victory and friendship. The young men descended the Limmat, the Aar and the Rhine, in boats, to Strassburg. They started in the early morning, and took with them boiling millet-porridge and hot rolls, well covered. In the evening, landing at Strassburg, they presented the porridge and the rolls, still warm, at the joyous festival, to show how quickly friends can reach friends.

On the following year, a shooting-match at Constance had an unfortunate result. There a citizen of Constance refused to receive a Bernese plappart (twenty-nine plapparts make a guilder) from a man of Lucerne, and contemptuously called the Swiss money cow-plapparts. Piqued at this, all the Swiss left the fête. They soon returned in rage, four thousand men from all the cantons, and ravaged the territory of Constance in Thurgau. Constance was compelled to purchase peace with a large sum. This was called the plappart-war.

As the Confederates were returning home from Constance, three hundred of them, men of Uri, Schwyz and Unterwalden, requested passage and a night's lodging from the city of Rapperswyl. The wearied men were received with friendly hospitality. The citizens of Rapperswyl, although faithful servants to the dukes of Austria, constantly suffered much maltreatment from them. Therefore the citizens were well disposed towards the Confederates, treated them most hospitably, and, on that same night, Rapperswyl and the Confederates concluded an everlasting friendship; and, without reference to Austria, Rapperswyl entered into a defensive compact with the three Waldstatten (1458), and afterwards (1464) with Glarus also.

When arch-duke Sigismund heard this, he was much angered. But he was fully occupied with more serious troubles, which left him no time for the Confederates. The pope of Rome, himself, had a quarrel with the duke, excommunicated him and called upon the Swiss to take possession of the remaining Austrian territory in Helvetia. They, knowing very well that not only the pope, but also the emperor, was opposed to the grand-duke, were, excepting Berne, soon under arms, and invaded Thurgau, which was obliged to swear fealty to the seven cantons of the Confederacy, reserving its rights and tribunals. Diessenhofen in vain defended herself valiantly for Austria. All the country-people were for the Swiss. From this time the Confederates (Appenzell and Berne excepted) retained the rights which Austria had possessed over Thurgau.

Berne and Schaffhausen were, however, associated in the protectorate over Diessenhofen. The duke, seeing that all was lost, sold the city of Winterthur also to the Zurichers. Thus broad, beautiful Thurgau became a Swiss domain in 1460.

At the same period, Muhlhausen, an imperial-city in Alsace, was much distressed by the inimical robber-nobles in her vicinity, and could no longer resist them. A master-joiner had cut off six plapparts from his servant's wages; the servant implored the protection of a noble; the noble picked a quarrel with the city. Hence a feud and war. Then Muhlhausen asked assistance from the Confederates. The latter, friendly to the city, showed themselves ready to sustain her. But the nobles secured the aid of duke Sigismund of Austria. After long parleyings without result, the flames of war spread afresh from Schaffhausen to

Waldshut and Muhlhausen. Many castles and villages were destroyed, many men slain. The Confederates, conquerors everywhere, at last laid siege to Waldshut. Berne wished to take this city by assault, and to make of it a fortress of the Confederates against Germany. The rest had no such far-reaching views. Berne, with regret, was silent on seeing her Confederates accept a treaty of peace on conditions of reimbursement of their war-expenses. In vain said the Bernese soldiers: "We did not take up arms that we might carry home gold, but that we might conquer cities and castles." A peace was concluded at Waldshut, by which Muhlhausen and Schaffhausen were secured against Austria and the nobility. This was in 1468, in which year also, duke Sigismund made to the Confederates a solemn cession of his rights over Thurgau.

CHAPTER XXVI.

UNION OF THE THREE LEAGUES IN RHETIA. DISCORD IN BERNE. COMMENCEMENT OF THE BURGUNDIAN WAR.

[A. D. 1469 to 1476.]

THE Grisons in the Rhetian highlands had taken no part in the wars and disturbances which desolated Switzerland, sometimes even for a plappart. They lived then in the first innocent love of liberty and of the everlasting rights which belong to all men. They resembled the Confederates of the earlier times, who sought the noble jewel freedom, not for themselves alone, but for others also; they asked only for independence from the tyranny and caprices of great lords, but desired no subjects or slaves. Many valleys in the Upper and God's-house leagues had freed themselves from tribute and service by heavy payments, never by force and revolt. But when the great lords, regardless of the purchased rights, tried to impose the yoke anew upon men lawfully free, then the people rose, with arms in their hands, and with the force of enraged lions, against the enemies of their rights and happiness, and triumphed, as did the first Confederates. Many haughty nobles, who had sworn to a "black league" against the descendants of John Chaldar (1450), lie slain and buried in Schamserthal.

To strengthen their hands against the attacks of their enemies and to preserve concord among themselves, deputies from all the communes and all the jurisdictions of the three leagues assembled in the little village of Vazerol, in the centre of the country (1471). There they swore, in the name of the three leagues, to remain always bound together for their rights in danger and in death; to stand as a single state against foreigners; to discuss their common affairs and decide their differences every year in general diet. The Diet was to be held alternately at Coire in the God's-house league, at Ilanz in the Upper league, and at Davos in the league of the Ten Jurisdictions. The deputies to the Diet were not, however, to have ultimate legislative authority, but only the right of initiative: the adoption or rejection of what they might propose belonging to the sovereign-people in their communes. In any dispute between two leagues, the third was to be arbitrator; whatever two leagues agreed upon, was obligatory on the third. So with their organization: each commune had its own laws and its own ammann; several communes united had their landammann and their low and high tribunal or jurisdiction; hence such a union of communes was called a high jurisdiction; several high jurisdictions formed a league, and the three leagues composed the republic of Rhetia. The people themselves elected and installed their magistrates, and chose therefor the most estimable persons, in whom they had confidence.

While union was thus strengthening the people in the Grison country, discord and the arrogance of great power brought the commonwealth of the city of Berne into much danger. This city, first built on free soil by the dukes of Zahringen, and peopled by free burghers and industrious mechanics, counted also among her citizens the signiors possessing jurisdiction in her neighborhood; so that the city protected the rights of these signiors over their respective territories, and the signiors, on their side, helped the city as good burghers. Many members of these noble families sat in the city-council, and at all times made themselves useful to the commonwealth by their wisdom, their courage and their riches. They had especially assisted the city to increase the number of her subjects by purchase or conquest, and to obtain great influence in the Confederacy. The common citizens, nevertheless, considered themselves the equals of the noble signioral families, but the latter looked with contempt upon the farriers, the butchers, the bakers and other respectable mechanics, and prided themselves on their noble birth and the long series of their ancestors. This angered the citizens and caused them to seize every opportunity to humble the pride of the nobles.

Such an opportunity was presented at this period when great dissension took place in the council of Berne, in consequence of a constable of the signiory of Worb having exceeded his authority. On the appeal of the condemned constable to the council, two parties were formed: that of the signiors, who were leagued together for the maintenance of their guaranteed prerogatives and demanded a sentence accordingly, and that of the other members of the council, having at their head Peter Kistler, by trade a butcher. The signiors were deprived of their prerogatives. Thereupon they all left the city, with their wives and families, and retired to their hereditary estates in the country. And when Peter Kistler was afterwards elected avoyer of Berne (1470), he took pleasure in bringing the nobles to an equality with the common citizens. The avoyer, councils and burghers of Berne published a severe moral and sumptuary law. When the wives and daughters of the nobles learnt that they must give up the long trains of their dresses, they broke forth into complaints, and persuaded their husbands and fathers not to obey, for the long train was the distinguishing mark of nobility. Hence new troubles arose, so that the Confederacy became anxious and desired to mediate. This determined the council of Berne to put an end to the dispute. They first caused the sumptuary law to be executed, and then banished the nobility, who submitted. But shortly afterwards (8 April and 17

May, 1741), milder laws were adopted and better observed. Thus quiet was once more restored to the Bernese.

Never had internal peace been more necessary. The days had come in which the whole Confederacy required more harmony and vigor than ever before, in order not to become the prey of Charles the Bold, duke of Burgundy. This was a proud prince, loving glory and dominion, but impetuous, passionate against all who opposed him. His territory extended from the Swiss frontier, across the Jura and the Rhine, between the Rhine and France, as far as the North sea. He had driven out duke Réné of Lorraine, and even terrified king Louis XI. of France, in Paris, with his arms. The latter therefore hated bold Charles of Burgundy, and constantly excited fresh enemies against him The king applied, with many flatteries, to the Swiss, whose formidable valor he had become acquainted with, when yet dauphin, on the field of St. Jacques. He spared neither presents nor gold chains for the council-lords in the Swiss cities, to persuade them to help him against the duke. The ejected Réné of Lorraine also earnestly implored their assistance, and the emperor of Germany himself incited them against Burgundy. They had really no cause of complaint against the duke, except that his bailiff, Peter of Hagenbach, had shown himself remiss in protecting Swiss merchants, when, on their journeys through Burgundy, they were maltreated by his people. However, they did not long resist the entreaties and presents of king Louis, especially as the warlike youth of the Swiss cities thirsted for new exploits. Austria, Lorraine, and other sovereignties of German soil had also united against Burgundy.

Thus the Confederates made a compact with France (1474), and, with eight thousand men, invaded Upper Burgundy, pillaging and burning; while the Lorrainers and Austrians did the same, with ten thousand. Bâle, Freiburg, Schaffhausen and St. Gallen also sent troops with the Confederates. They all behaved barbarously, and bore with a heavy hand upon the counts and lords in Vaud who were in favor of Burgundy, and upon the duke of Savoy, who held with Charles the Bold. The Bernese and Freiburgers took Morat, which was obliged to swear allegiance to them. The banners of the Confederates floated victorious far along lake Leman. Many Savoyard and Burgundian castles fell in flames, on the right and left. A garrison was placed in the castle of Grandson, on the lake of Neuchâtel. The Valaisians also joined them against the great power of Savoy.

Now when the Swiss were fully engaged in this war for the French king and the German emperor, they were suddenly and perfidiously deserted by both. First, the emperor made peace with the duke of Burgundy; then, twelve weeks afterwards (1475), the king of France concluded a truce with him for several years. He had promised the Swiss to stand with them against the duke; now, he even granted to the latter a free passage across his territory against the Confederates. For Charles the Bold was most irritated against the Confederates, and wished to humble them and avenge himself. He had an only daughter, sole heiress to all his domains; with her and his riches he dazzled both the king and the emperor. He flattered the one and the other with the expectation that he would bestow his heiress upon the son of each. He intended nothing less.

His hands being thus freed, he raised powerful forces in his own country, in France and Italy. The betrayed Confederates were terrified, and sent two embassadors to him, to offer peace, an exclusive alliance and every satisfaction. But he haughtily rejected their proposals, and marched from Besançon over the Jura against Grandson with sixty thousand men, to sacrifice the Swiss to his vengeance. This was in March, 1476.

CHAPTER XXVII.

RESULT OF THE BURGUNDIAN WAR. FREIBURG BECOMES FREE.

[A. D. 1476 to 1477.]

WHEN duke Charles of Burgundy had passed the Jura, he found the city of Yverdun already in possession of his people, by the aid of treacherous citizens; in the castle alone a weak troop of Bernese still resisted his whole force. And when he appeared before Grandson, the little garrison intrepidly withstood his rage, and was not intimidated; although the castle was assaulted day and night. Irritated at having been uselessly detained for ten days before this miserable place, he ordered a general attack, and threatened to hang all the Swiss if they resisted any longer. This shook the courage of many, especially of the cowardly captain, John Wyler. Thereupon came to them, from the enemy's camp, a Burgundian noble, who spoke German, praised their courage, said that the duke respected it, and, in the name of the prince, promised them a free retreat if they would desist from their fruitless resistance. They allowed themselves to be persuaded, and after having presented a hundred guilders to the Burgundian, in gratitude for his mediation, left the castle without mistrust. But the duke caused them to be seized and hung naked on the trees, by hundreds; others were cruelly dragged about in the water with ropes, until they were drowned.

In the mean while, the Confederates, twenty thousand strong, hurried towards Grandson, without fear of the duke's army, thrice their numbers. In the dawn of the 3d of March, 1476, the soldiers of Lucerne, Schwyz and Bernese Oberland, the vanguard, showed themselves among the vineyards between the lake of Neuchâtel and the Jura mountains. After having made their prayer, they commenced the attack. With firm step, Freiburg and Berne, also, pressed forward, led by the experienced warrior, John of Hallwyl, and the Bernese avoyer, Nicholas of Scharnachtal. And when this vanguard had already, for several hours, maintained a severe combat on the bloody field, then, first, the main body of the advancing Confederates appeared upon the heights, in the bright rays of the noonday sun. From the tops of the hills resounded the spirit-stirring notes of the horn of Unterwalden, and the gloomy bellowing of the bull of Uri.* There, also, waved the banners of Zurich and Schaffhausen. "What people are

* A horn which imitates the voice of this animal.

those?" cried the duke. "Those are the men before whom Austria fled!" replied the lord of Stein. "Alas!" said the duke, "a handful of these men have harassed us the whole day; what will become of us when they come in such numbers!" And terror seized upon his troops, when the bloody work commenced anew. In vain did the duke throw himself before the flyers. He could not stop them; they carried him away with them. The eager Swiss pursued even into the dark night. But when the men of Berne and Freiburg saw the bodies hanging on the trees before Grandson, furiously they stormed the castle. The Burgundian soldiers tremblingly surrendered. But they were all hung without pity in the place of the dead Swiss, whose bodies their friends carried away.

Bold Charles had lost a thousand men and his magnificent camp equipage, valued at more than a million of guilders. Even his ducal robes, ornamented with pearls, diamonds, rubies and other precious stones, fell into the hands of the Confederates. A Swiss found upon the highway a diamond, large as half a nut. He sold this brilliant stone, the value of which he did not know and which he was about to throw away, to a priest for three francs. Afterwards, it passed through many hands, until it finally reached the triple crown of the pope at the price of 20,000 ducats. Another diamond, also found in the camp, through successive purchases and sales, went to ornament the royal crown of France. So valuable was the booty.

Soon, unexpectedly, Charles returned with fresh forces, by Lausanne, into Switzerland. He mustered his large army near Lausanne in April; then he marched to the shores of the lake of Neuchâtel, and thence against Morat (Murten). Here Adrian of Bubenberg, with six hundred braves and the men of the city, maintained a better defence than had formerly been made at Grandson. While the duke was detained here, the Confederates and their friends assembled their troops. Morat was already in danger; the ramparts and tower were breached. The wall was shaken, but not the courage of Adrian of Bubenberg and his Swiss.

He remained firm, until the Confederates arrived from

all sides, with their allies of Bienne, the Alsace cities, Bâle, St. Gallen and Schaffhausen. These came first. After them, in the bad weather, over the bad roads, hurried the men of Zurich, Thurgau, Aargau and Sargans. John Waldmann, the leader of the Zurichers, allowed his tired people only a few hours' rest at Berne, on the evening before the battle; then gave the signal for marching at ten o'clock at night. The whole city was illuminated; before every house stood tables with refreshments for the soldiers. In the darkness, through storm and rain, the main body of the troops marched towards Morat.

The day of battle dawned. The sky was covered with clouds. Rain fell in streams. Then the Burgundians deployed their immense array before the eyes of the Confederates. But the Confederates were barely thirty-four thousand men. John of Hallwyl, before he gave the signal for attack, knelt down with his army. And, while they prayed, the sun broke brightly through the clouds. At once, John of Hallwyl waved his sword and cried: "Up! up! Confederates! See! God will shine upon our victory!" He said. It was the 22d of June. Then thundered the shock of arms; then the smiting and fighting spread from the lake to the heights. On the left fought Hallwyl; on the right, by the lake, the strength of the Swiss army, under John Waldmann; among the trees on the shore, Bubenberg. Hallwyl had a hard fight; but he maintained it until Caspar of Hertenstein, the white-haired general of Lucerne, appeared on the heights behind the enemy. Hallwyl had sent him thither through by-paths. Now death penetrated the ranks of the Burgundians, in front and rear. Thousands fought, thousands fell, thousands fled. The duke saw that all was lost; leaped upon his fleet horse, and, pale and gloomy, with barely thirty knights, escaped to the lake of Geneva. Fifteen thousand of his people lay slain between the lake of Morat and Avenches. Many, seeking for safety, perished in the water and in the swamps of the lake-shore. The rest were dispersed; all the enemy's tents, provisions and treasures became the booty of the victors. The dead bodies were buried in trenches with quicklime and covered with earth. Some years afterwards the people of Morat built an ossuary which they filled with Burgundian bones and skulls, to show foreigners how formidable the Confederates are when united.

Then duke Réné of Lorraine, whom Charles had formerly driven from his country, could triumph. He made active war against his humbled enemy, and re-took the city of Nancy. He also requested a reinforcement of six thousand men from the Swiss; they sent eight thousand, under command of John Waldmann, the victorious hero of Morat. When they joined Réné's army, Charles the Bold also reäppeared with fresh forces, and vigorously attacked Nancy. Thereat Réné hastened with his own troops and the Swiss, to save the hard-pressed city. A battle immediately took place near Nancy, on the 5th of January, 1477. But Charles's army was discouraged. The commander of his vanguard, count Cola Campobasso, instead of attacking, treacherously passed over to Réné. Réné's army was stronger in numbers and in courage than that of Charles. The latter was therefore vanquished and fled; falling with his horse, on a slightly-frozen marsh, he was slain by his pursuers. Five hundred of his nobles and knights lay around him; the bodies of thousands of his soldiers covered the battle-field. Thus died the formidable enemy of the Confederates.

Then Charles's enemies took possession of his country. But the states of Upper Burgundy sent to the Confederates and asked for peace, and even to be admitted into their bond. Berne, politic and magnanimous, was in favor of this admission. "The Jura and the Vosges will be a strong rampart for us Confederates against France," said they. But the others, especially the small cantons, were opposed. They feared that such an extension of the bond would draw them into many foreign wars, or that they would themselves become insignificant from the larger size of so many other cantons. Therefore the Burgundians were compelled to purchase peace from the Confederates for 150,000 guilders. But duke Maximilian of Austria obtained Upper Burgundy with the hand of Maria, daughter of Charles the Bold. And Austria made with Zurich, Berne, Lucerne, Uri and Solothurn, a treaty for mutual defence and perpetual peace, in which Unterwalden, Schwyz, Zug and Glarus shortly after joined. By this treaty Austria renounced her pretensions to every thing that the Confederates had taken from the house of Habsburg, and both parties promised mutual assistance in case of need.

A treaty was also made with the king of France, and he was permitted to enlist soldiers for his army from among the Swiss. For this purpose he lavished much money, many presents and pensions in Switzerland. Then the bailiffs, patricians and council-lords enrolled valiant soldiers for the king; were enriched, as captains and officers, by his gifts and pay; and, for the sake of these, watered foreign soils with noble Swiss blood.

But, at this time, there were in the country many idlers, who, in war, had lost all taste for labor, for a regular and honest life, and preferred to live by fighting and plundering. Many went, at their own cost and risk, to seek fortune in foreign wars, and these emigrations were endless. Many others lived a disorderly life by plunder in their own country. Others committed still other excesses. At Zug, in carnival time, some, over their play and wine, talked of the unequal distribution of the Burgundian booty, and said that the great families of Berne and Freiburg had appropriated much the larger share. They formed a league under oath in order to bring these latter to account, and called themselves "the band of joyous life." Noisily and jovially, all armed, they passed through the cities and cantons of Switzerland, their numbers constantly increasing with wild young men, on their way to demand from Geneva an unpaid contribution for the expenses of the Burgundian war. They did no harm to any one, and paid for whatever they used. At Berne they were seven hundred, at Freiburg two thousand strong. This disorder excited great fear. The authorities exhorted their subjects to take no part in any illegal arming. Diets were held. The young men of the joyous band were appeased by friendly words, but could not be persuaded to return peacefully to their homes until Geneva and Lausanne had paid up their arrears. Then they dispersed.

At the same time, Berne made a peace and compact with

Savoy, restored Vaud, which she had received on mortgage, and kept only Aelen (Aigle); on the other hand she obtained that Freiburg should be declared independent of Savoy, as a free city of the Roman empire (23d August, 1477). For Berne did not like to have a Savoyard garrison so near her. Freiburg, as the price of her liberty, assumed a large portion of the Savoyard debt.

CHAPTER XXVIII.

THE GLORIOUS DAY OF GIORNICO. NICHOLAS VON DER FLUE. FREIBURG AND SOLOTHURN IN THE SWISS CONFEDERACY. DEATH OF JOHN WALDMANN AT ZURICH.

[A. D. 1478 to 1489.]

IN the valleys and in the mountains, in the cities and in the country-communes of Switzerland, the people were full of military pride. Since the duke of Burgundy had lost his treasure in one battle, his army in a second, his life in a third, the Swiss feared no man more. Hence wars without end.

One day some subjects of Milan cut a parcel of wood in a forest of Leventina. At once some young men of Uri passed the St. Gotthard, and, in revenge, robbed and maltreated the subjects of Milan in the neighboring villages. Uri, instead of punishing these young men, took them under her protection, declared war against the Milanese, and called on the Confederates for assistance. The Confederates saw the injustice of Uri, and wished to mediate, but not to desert those of Uri in their danger. Therefore they immediately sent troops to act in case of need.

When the duke of Milan knew of this, he sent count Borelli with a large force along the Ticino. Near the village of Giornico lay the advanced guard of the Swiss. They were only six hundred men of Uri, Lucerne, Schwyz and Zurich; the other Confederates, to the number of ten thousand, were still far behind. Borelli wished to occupy

Giornico with the best of his troops. But it was mid-winter. The Swiss let the waters of the Ticino over the meadows, which were immediately covered with ice; then they fastened ice-nails to their shoes. While the Milanese were ascending the slippery slope with insecure steps, the Swiss rushed upon with firm foothold (28th December, 1478). Their small number had easy work with the multitude of enemies, who could not stand securely on their legs. Frischhans Theilig, the Lucerners' captain, was the angel of death to the Milanese. These fled in terror: fifteen thousand men before six hundred. Their blood dyed the snow as far as Bellinzona; more than fifteen hundred were slain. This almost incredible feat made the name of Swiss celebrated throughout Italy. Milan purchased peace, paid damages, and recognized that the Leventina with the valley of Brugiasco belonged to Uri in perpetual fief, on condition that Uri should yearly send to the Duomo of Milan a wax candle weighing three pounds.

In most of the wars, especially against Burgundy, the cities of Solothurn and Freiburg had fought valiantly for the Confederates. Therefore Berne desired to bring these two cities into the Confederacy. The free country-people in Uri, Schwyz and Unterwalden were, on the contrary, much opposed to this. They feared lest the cities, which were more advanced in civilization and acquirements, and which, moreover, were always striving to increase their territory and subjects, should finally become masters, and rule the whole Confederacy to suit their pleasure and their interests. On account of this jealousy and fear, they were unwilling to admit any more dominant cities. The cities, on their side, entertained quite other suspicions against the free country-cantons. Immediately after the disorders occasioned by the band of joyous life, Zurich, Berne and Lucerne had made with each other and with Solothurn and Freiburg a treaty of coburghership, for mutual support, because they feared lest the free country-people of the small cantons might wish to have all Swiss as free as themselves, and even excite the subjects of the cities, sooner or later, to throw off the yoke of the city-burghers and to introduce an entirely communal government. The city-burghers did not desire this. They had acquired their subjects by conquest or purchase, and wished their rights to remain untouched.

Thus arose a reciprocal mistrust among the Confederates. An occurrence confirmed the suspicions of the cities. At Escholzmatt, in the Lucerne bailiwick of Entlibuch, lived Peter Am Stalden, a valiant warrior; he was often visited by his cousin, the ancient landammann Henry Burgler of Obwalden, and the latter's brother-in-law Kuhnegger; seated over a glass of wine, they liked to talk about liberty. Peter had reason to complain of the bailiff in Entlibuch and of the patricians in Lucerne. The Obwaldeners persuaded him to strike a great blow in the city itself, on the feast of St. Leodegar. Men were to come from Obwalden and help: the avoyer, council and hundred were to be sent to the other world, towers and walls to be thrown down, Lucerne to become a beautiful village, Entlibuch a free state. Such was their plan. The Lucerners heard of it, because Peter betrayed himself by imprudent talk. He was seized and imprisoned; forced to confess everything, and beheaded.

This happened at the time (1481) when all the Confederates and with them deputies from St. Gallen and Appenzell, Solothurn and Freiburg, were assembled in diet at Stanz in Nidwalden. There the suspicions and distrust between all the cantons broke forth, on occasion of the division of the Burgundian booty, the admission of the two cities into the Confederacy, and many other matters. The three primitive cantons, Uri, Schwyz and Unterwalden, uttered such terrible threats against the cities, and Lucerne and the cities were so enraged against the three cantons, that the Freiburgers and Solothurners voluntarily and modestly withdrew their application, and a report was spread through all the land that the sword would be resorted to, and that the Confederacy must be dissolved.

This report terrified the pastor of Stanz, Henry Imgrund, a zealous Confederate. He seized his walking-staff, and hurried to the wilderness of Raufttobel, to announce this misfortune to the pious brother Nicholas Lowenbrugger. This pious man, who was also called "von der Flue" from the rock near Saxeln in Obwalden, on which he dwelt, had already lived several years in the solitude of this wilderness, engaged in prayer and the contemplation of heavenly things. He was revered for his devotion throughout the whole country. It was said of him: that he had lived many years without food or nourishment, except that he partook monthly of the holy supper. He slept in a narrow cell upon hard boards, a stone serving him for a pillow. His wife, with whom he had had five sons and five daughters, lived above on the mountain on his farm. He had formerly shown himself a courageous and humane soldier, in the war of Thurgau.

As soon as Nicholas von der Flue heard of the discord of the Confederates from the pastor of Stanz, he left his hermitage, went to Stanz, and entered the hall where the council-lords were assembled. All rose from their seats at the appearance of the venerable old man, of tall spare form, but still youthful vigor. He spoke to them with the dignity of a divine messenger, and exhorted them to peace and concord in the name of that God who had given so many victories to them and their fathers. "You have become strong," said he, "by the power of your united arms; will you now separate for the sake of vile booty? Beware lest neighboring nations perceive this! Cities! insist not on burgher-rights which wound the old Confederates! Cantons! remember how Freiburg and Solothurn have fought by your side! Receive them into the bond. But, Confederates! enlarge not too much the hedge which encloses you. Have nothing to do with foreign quarrels! Beware of all party-spirit! Far from every one be the thought of accepting gold as the price of his fatherland."

This and more said Nicholas von der Flue, and all hearts were so touched and moved by the words of the holy hermit that in a single hour all was settled. In the same day Solothurn and Freiburg joined in the perpetual bond of the Confederates. This was on Saturday, 20 December, 1481. In the covenant of Stanz, then concluded, they ratified all the ancient compacts, as well as the Pfaffenbrief (an edict of 1381 against the encroachments of the priests) and the convention of Sempach, and accepted the proposition of pious Nicholas to divide among the cantons all territory conquered in war, and all booty among the troops. It was also agreed that, without consent and authorization of his lords and magistrates, no one should assemble the communes and make important propositions. But if the subjects of one canton should rise against their magistrates, all the other cantons were to aid in compelling the discontented to return to their duty.

This done, the hermit returned to his solitude, each deputy to his canton. Joy prevailed everywhere. From all the church-towers the solemn sound of bells announced the general satisfaction, from the Alps to the Jura.

But the concord reëstablished at Stanz did not restore the ancient discipline and habits of the Confederates. Cupidity and haughtiness increased among the city-authorities, venality among the magistrates, rudeness in the communes, dissipation and the taste for robbery among the people. The law was too often but a deceitful web, through which the rich passed unscathed, but in which the poor man was taken. And justice, when she had slumbered too long, frequently woke in bloodthirsty anger. In only three months of the year 1480, nearly fifteen hundred assassins and robbers were condemned by the tribunals of Switzerland. In the diet of Baden it was decided that whoever stole the value of a rope should be hanged without mercy. The emigration to foreign wars was continuous. Young men frequently marched forth, by hundreds and thousands, with musicians at their head, over the Rhine and over the mountains, to follow the standards of kings, and to find booty, or death. Neither was there any lack of wars in the neighborhood. In one single year (1487), there were four wars on the side of Italy: of the Grisons against Milan; of the Grisons and Confederates near Roveredo against Venice; of the Valaisians against Milan; of the Bernese and other western Swiss for the duke of Savoy against the Piedmontese near Saluzzo.

Internal dissensions and troubles, also, were not wanting. The nobles and priests in Zurich, who were mortal enemies of wise and valiant John Waldmann, burgomaster of this city, because he sought to restrain them, excited the burghers and country-people against him by their talk, called him a tyrant who made laws on his own authority and trod under foot the ancient rights. John Waldmann was the son of a peasant of Blikestorf in Zug; he came to Zurich as a tanner, there raised himself by his great talents and courage, acquired glory as the victorious hero of Morat and Nancy, and was highly esteemed by Confederates and princes. But the Confederates complained of his friendship for Austria and Milan, the Zurichers of his haughtiness and abuse of power. This did not restrain the burgomaster; and woe to any one who opposed him in word or deed! When Frischhans Theilig of Lucerne, the heroic warrior of Giornico, who had often blamed Waldmann's partiality for Milan, came to Zurich one day with cloth for sale, Waldmann caused him to be seized and beheaded, though Lucerne begged earnestly for the life of her hero.

Such arrogance excited public indignation against this man so rich in the gifts of nature, and at last occasioned his ruin. His enemies directed against him the discontent of the country-people on the lake of Zurich, when the communes of Maila and Herrliberg rose first and were shortly followed by several of the lake-villages, who complained of the severity of the laws and numerous vexations. The peasants from the lake came with arms to the walls of Zurich and said: "Remember, lords, how you promised in the Wasserkirche, after the war of Zurich, that you would impose no new tax upon us!" Thither came, also, deputies from the Confederates, as mediators, according to the agreement of the recent Diet, and declared that the complaints of the communes should be examined into and the people tranquillized. But Waldmann, who thought that the honor of the city was compromised by this declaration, caused the city-recorder to alter the sentence to the effect that the peasants, having made unfounded complaints, were humbly to ask pardon for their injustice, and to have their grievances examined into at the first fitting opportunity.

As soon as this falsification of the sentence became known, there was a fresh rising against the city and disturbances within the walls, so that the burgomaster no longer went forth without his armor, and slept in the council-house. But woe to that magistrate who requires other arms for his defence than the love of the people. Burgomaster and knight Waldmann was seized in a tumult, with his adherents, carried to the Wellenberg, tortured and beheaded (6th April, 1489). Waldmann was indeed criminal, but the furious party-rage against him was not less so.

On the day of his death, the magistrates and subjects of Zurich, as equal parties, appeared before the tribunal of the Confederates, and the latter succeeded in reconciling both by what was called the convention of Waldmann. It enjoined on the people of the country to submit loyally and sincerely to the burgomaster, councillors and great-council of the city of Zurich, but secured to them the right of carrying their merchandise to what market they pleased; of establishing themselves wherever they chose; of exercising handicrafts in the villages; of cultivating the vine and managing their lands to their liking; of choosing a sub-bailiff for themselves in the lake-communes, and many other privileges. In case the city of Zurich attempted to exercise any illegal power over the people on the lake, then two or three parishes were to assemble and deliberate, and ten or twenty deputies from each parish were to carry their complaints before the Confederates at Zurich, in order to obtain justice.

This convention was sealed by the seven cantons of the Confederacy, as mediators and sureties, on 9th May, 1489.

CHAPTER XXIX.

THE SUABIAN WAR. FORMATION OF THE CONFEDERACY OF THE THIRTEEN CANTONS.

[A. D. 1490 to 1500.]

WHEN, in any country, the spirit of party prevails over truth, and power over justice, then farewell peace! farewell liberty! Such was the lot of Zurich after the execution of John Waldmann. By the convention of Waldmann, the city lost much of the ancient respect of her subjects, and troubles which endured for centuries were originated. The enemies of Waldmann, seated in the council, possessors and dissipators of his wealth, persecutors of his partisans, surpassed him in tyranny and injustice. Their arbitrary government desolated the country. This government was called the "council of horn;" its hardness caused Waldmann to be much regretted.

In St. Gallen, also, discord again prevailed between the city and the abbot. When the latter began to build a new convent on his own estate and territory at Rorschach, the people of St. Gallen were irritated. The Appenzellers, never friends to the abbot, hastened to their assistance; even the abbey-people declared in favor of the citizens. The convent was destroyed. Then the abbot cried for help to the four cantons, protectors of the abbey; Zurich, Lucerne, Schwyz and Glarus came and restored peace by force of arms (1490). This cost St. Gallen a great deal of money, and Appenzell lost, for war-expenses, the Rheinthal and a part of the signiory of Sax, which the protecting cantons retained, and in the government of which they associated Uri, Unterwalden and Zug, afterwards Appenzell (1501) and finally (1712) Berne also. Such conquests of Confederates from Confederates made bad blood.

Fortunately danger and trouble soon appeared from abroad. This united them all anew, and was therefore salutary.

Maximilian I. of Austria was emperor of Germany. He had received from France the country of Lower Burgundy, and, to hold it more securely, incorporated it with the German empire, as a single circle. He wished to make Switzerland, also, such a German imperial circle. The Confederates refused, preferring to remain by themselves as they had been until then. In Suabia, the existing states had formed a league among themselves for the suppression of small wars and feuds. This pleased the politic emperor; by becoming an associate, he placed himself at the head of the league, which he was able to direct for the aggrandisement of his house of Austria. He desired that the Confederates, also, should enter the Suabian league. The Swiss again refused, preferring to remain by themselves as before.

The emperor was irritated at this, and, at Innspruch, he said to the deputies of the Confederates: "You are refractory members of the empire; some day I shall have to pay you a visit, sword in hand." The deputies answered and said: "We humbly beseech your imperial majesty to dispense with such a visit, for our Swiss are rude men, and do not even respect crowns."

The boldness of the Confederates wounded the Suabian league no less. Many provocations and quarrels took place, here and there, between the people on the borders, so that the city of Constance, for her own security, joined the Suabian league. For, one day, a band of valiant men of Thurgau, incited by the bailiff from Uri, had tried to surprise the city, in order to punish her for her bravadoes against the Swiss.

Neither were the Austrians good neighbors to the Grisons. The Tyrol and Engadine were constantly discussing and disputing about markets, privileges and tolls. Once, indeed, (1476) the Tyrolese had marched armed into the valley of Engadine, but were driven back into their own country through the narrow pass of Finstermunz, with bloody heads. Now there was a fresh cause of quarrel. In the division of the Toggenburger-inheritance, the rights of Toggenburg in the Ten Jurisdictions had fallen to the counts of Matsch, Sax and Montfort, and afterwards (1478 and 1489), by purchase, to the ducal house of Austria. Hence much trouble arose.

As the Grisons had equal cause with the Confederates to fear the power and purposes of emperor Maximilian, the Grey league (1497) and that of God's-house (1498) made a friendly and defensive alliance with Zurich, Lucerne, Uri, Schwyz, Unterwalden, Zug and Glarus. The Ten Jurisdictions dared not join them for fear of Austria.

Then the emperor restrained his anger no longer. And, though already burdened with a heavy war in the Netherlands, he sent fresh troops into the Tyrol, and the forces of the Suabian league advanced and hemmed in Switzerland from the Grison pass near Luziensteig (between the Rhetian mountains and Germany) along the lake of Constance and the Rhine, as far as Bâle.

Then Switzerland and Rhetia were in great danger. But the Grisons rose courageously to defend their freedom, as did all the Confederates. The Sargansers, also, and the Appenzellers hastened to the Schollenberg; the banners of Valais, Bâle and Schaffhausen soon floated in view of the enemy. No man stayed at home.

It was in February, 1499, that the strife began. Then eight thousand imperialists entered the Grison territory of Munsterthal and Engadine; Louis of Brandis, the emperor's general, with several thousand men, surprised and held the pass of Luziensteig, and, by the treachery of four burghers, the little city of Maienfeld. But the Grisons retook the Luziensteig; eight hundred Suabians here found their death; the rest fled to Balzers. Then the Confederates passed the Rhine near Azmoos, and, with the Grisons, obtained a great victory near Treisen. The Suabian nobility, with ten thousand soldiers, were posted near St. John's at Hochst and Hard, between Bregenz and Fussach. Eight thousand Confederates killed nearly half of the enemy's army, ascended as far as the forests of Bregenz, and imposed contributions on the country. Ten thousand other Confederates passed victorious over the Hegau, and in eight days, burnt twenty villages, hamlets and castles. Skirmish followed quickly upon skirmish, battle upon battle.

The enemy, indeed, issuing from Constance, succeeded in surprising the Confederate garrison of Ermatingen while asleep, and in murdering, in their beds, sixty-three defenceless men. But they bloodily expiated this in the wood of Schwaderlochs, whence eighteen thousand of them, vanquished by two thousand Confederates, fled in such haste that the city-gates of Constance were too narrow for the fugitives, and the number of their dead exceeded that of the Swiss opposed to them. A body of Confederates, on the upper Rhine, penetrated into Wallgau, where the enemy were entrenched near Frastenz, and, fourteen thousand strong, feared not the valor of the Swiss. But when Henry

Wolleb, the hero of Uri, had passed the Langengasterberg, with two thousand brave men, and turned the strong entrenchment, his heroic death was the signal of victory to the Confederates. They rushed under the thunder of artilley into the ranks of Austria, and dealt their fearful blows. Three thousand dead bodies covered the battlefield of Frastenz. Such Austrians as were left alive fled in terror through woods and waters. Then each Swiss fought as though victory depended on his single arm; for Switzerland and Swiss glory, each flew joyously to meet danger and death, and counted not the number of the enemy. And wherever a Swiss banner floated, there was more than one like John Wala of Glarus, who, near Gams in Rheinthal, measured himself singly with thirty horsemen.

The Grisons, also, fought with no less glory. Witness the Malserhaide in Tyrol, where fifteen thousand men, under Austrian banners, behind strong entrenchments, were attacked by only eight thousand Grisons. The ramparts were turned, the entrenchments stormed. Benedict Fontana was first on the enemy's wall. He had cleared the way. With his left hand holding the wide wound from which his entrails protruded, he fought with his right and cried: "Forward, now, fellow-leaguers! let not my fall stop you! It is but one man the less! To-day you must save your free fatherland and your free leagues. If you are conquered, you leave your children in everlasting slavery." So said Fontana and died. The Malserhaide was full of Austrian dead. Nearly five thousand fell. The Grisons had only two hundred killed and seven hundred wounded.

When emperor Maximilian, in the Netherlands, heard of so many battles lost, he came and reproached his generals, and said to the princes of the German empire: "Send to me auxiliaries against the Swiss, so bold as to have attacked the empire. For these rude peasants, in whom there is neither virtue, nor noble blood, nor magnanimity, but who are full of coarseness, pride, perfidy and hatred of the German nation, have drawn into their party many hitherto faithful subjects of the empire."

But the princes of the empire delayed to send auxiliaries, and the emperor then learnt, with increasing horror, that his army, sent over the Engadine mountains to suppress the Grison league, had been destroyed in midsummer by avalanches, famine, and the masses of rock which the Grisons threw down from the mountains; then, that on the woody height of Bruderholz, not far from Bâle, one thousand Swiss had vanquished more than four thousand of their enemies; that, shortly after, in the same region, near Dornach, six thousand Confederates had obtained a brilliant victory over fifteen thousand Austrians, killing three thousand men, with their general, Henry of Furstenberg. Then the emperor reflected that, within eight months, the Swiss had been eight times victorious in eight battles. And he decided to end a war in which more than twenty thousand men had already fallen, and nearly two thousand villages, hamlets, castles and cities been destroyed.

Peace was negotiated and concluded on 22d September, 1499, in the city of Bâle. The emperor acknowledged the ancient rights and the conquests of the Confederates, and granted to them, moreover, the ordinary jurisdiction over Thurgau, which, with the criminal jurisdiction and other sovereign rights, had, until then, belonged to the city of Constance. Thenceforward the emperors thought no more of dissolving the Confederacy, or of incorporating it with the German empire. In the fields of Frastenz, of Malserhaide and Dornach, were laid the first foundation-stones of Swiss independence of foreign power.

The confederated cantons thankfully acknowledged what Bâle and Schaffhausen had constantly done in these heroic days for the whole Confederacy, and that warlike Appenzell had never been backward at the call of glory and liberty. Therefore, Bâle (9th June, 1501) and flourishing Schaffhausen (9th August, 1501) were received into the perpetual Swiss bond, and finally (1513) Appenzell, already united in perpetual alliance with most of the cantons, was acknowledged as coëqual with all the Confederates.

Thus, in the 205th year after the deed of William Tell,

the Confederacy of the Thirteen Cantons was completed. But Valais and Grisons were considered as cantons allied to the Confederacy, as were St. Gallen, Muhlhausen, Rothweil in Suabia, and other cities: all free places, subject to no prince, united with the Swiss by a defensive alliance.

CHAPTER XXX.

THE SAVAGE MANNERS AND MERCENARY WARS OF THE SWISS; THEY CONQUER VALTELINA AND THE ITALIAN BAILIWICKS.

[A. D. 1500 to 1525.]

At that period, the thirteen cantons of the Swiss Confederacy were not yet, as now, equal in virtue of the bond, nor bound together directly by one and the same covenant. They were properly united only with the three cantons of Uri, Schwyz and Unterwalden, as with a common centre, but among themselves by special treaties. Each canton was attentive to its own interests and glory, seldom to those of the others, or to the welfare of the whole Confederacy. Fear of the ambition and power of neighboring lords and princes had drawn them together more and more. So long as this fear lasted, their union was strong.

As the governments were independent of each other, so far as their covenants allowed, and of foreign princes also, they called themselves free Swiss. But within the country districts there was little freedom for the people. Only in the shepherd-cantons (Uri, Schwyz and Unterwalden, also Zug, Glarus and Appenzell) did the country-people possess equal rights, and in the city-cantons, only the burghers of the cities; and often, even among these latter, only a few rich or ancient families. The rest of the people, dependent on the cities, having been either purchased or conquered, were subjects, often indeed serfs, and enjoyed only the limited rights which they had formerly possessed under the counts and princes. Even the shepherd-cantons held subjects, whom they, like princes, governed by their bailiffs. And the Confederate-cantons and cities would by no means allow their subjects to purchase their freedom, as the old counts and lords had formerly permitted the Confederates themselves to do.

But the people cared little for liberty; made rude and savage by continual wars, they loved only quarrels and combats, revels and debauchery. When there was no war in their own country, the young men, greedy of booty, followed foreign drums, and fought the battles of princes for hire. There were no good schools in the villages, and the clergy cared little for this. Indeed, the morals of the clergy were often no less depraved than those of the citizens and country-people; even in the convents great disorders frequently prevailed with great wealth. Many of the priests were very ignorant; many gambled, drank and blasphemed; many led shameless lives.

In the chief cities of the cantons, debauchery and dissipation were rife. There was much division between citizens and councillors; envy and distrust between the different professions. The lords, when once seated in the great and small councils (legislative and executive), cared more for themselves and their families than for the welfare of the citizens; they endeavored to advance their sons and relatives, and to procure lucrative offices for them. In all the cantons, there were, certainly, some great, patriotic souls, who preferred the interests of their country to their own, but no one listened to them.

As Switzerland had now no foreign wars to fear, and the neighboring kings and princes were pleased to have in their armies Swiss, for whose life and death they cared much less than for the life and death of their own subjects: the principal families of the city- and country-cantons took advantage of these circumstances to open fountains of wealth for themselves. The desire of the kings to enlist valiant Swiss favored the avidity of the council-lords, as did the wish of the young men to get booty. In spite of the positive prohibition of the magistrates, thousands of young men often enlisted in foreign service, where most of them perished miserably, because no one cared for them. Therefore the governments judged it best to make treaties with the kings for the raising of Swiss regiments, commanded by national officers, subject to their own laws and regularly paid, so that each government could take care of its subjects when abroad. "Confederates! you require a vent for your energies," had Rudolf Reding of Schwyz already said, when, years before, he saw the free life of the young men after the Burgundian war.

Now began the letting out of Swiss, Grisons and Valaisians, to foreign military service, by their governments. The first treaty of this nature was made by the king of France (1479 and 1480) with the Confederates in Lucerne. Next the house of Austria hired mercenaries (1499); the princes of Italy did the same, as did others afterwards. Even the popes themselves wanted a life-guard of Swiss; the first (1503) was pope Julius II., who was often engaged in war.

Switzerland suffered much from this course. Many a field remained untilled, many a plough stood still, because the husbandman had taken mercenary arms. And, if he returned alive, he brought back foreign diseases and vices, and corrupted the innocent by evil example, for he had acquired but little virtue in the wars. Only the sons of the patricians and council-lords obtained captaincies, commands and riches, by which they increased their influence and consideration in the land, and could oppress others. They prided themselves on the titles of nobility and decorations conferred by kings, and imagined these to be of value, and that they themselves were more than other Swiss.

When the kings perceived the cupidity and folly of the Swiss, they took advantage of them for their own profit, sent embassadors into Switzerland, distributed presents, granted gratifications and pensions to their partisans in the councils, and for these the council-lords became willing servants of foreign princes. Then one canton was French, another Milanese; one Venetian, another Spanish; but rarely was one Swiss. This redounded greatly to the shame of the Swiss. When the German emperor and the king of France were, at the same time, canvassing the favor of the cantons and bargaining in competition for troops, so great was the contempt or insolence of the French embassador at Berne (1516), that he distributed the royal pensions to the lords by sound of trumpet; at Freiburg, he poured out silver crowns upon the ground, and, while he heaped them up with a shovel, said to the bystanders: "Does not this silver jingle better than the emperor's empty words?" So much had love of money debased the Swiss.

The twelve cantons, Appenzell being the only exception, were at one moment allied with Milan against France, at the next, with France against Milan. Milan was rightly called the Schwyzer's grave. It was not unusual for Confederates to fight against Confederates on foreign soil, and to kill each other for hire. The ecclesiastical lord, Matthew Schinner, bishop of Sion in Valais, a very deceitful man, helped greatly to occasion this. According as he was hired, he intrigued in Switzerland, sometimes for the king of France, sometimes against France for the pope, who, in payment, even made him cardinal and embassador to the Confederacy.

The mercenary wars of the Swiss upon foreign battlefields were not wars for liberty or for honor; but these hirelings of princes maintained their reputation for valor even there. With the aid of several thousand Confederates the king of France subjected the whole of Lombardy in the space of twenty days. But the expelled duke of the country soon returned with five thousand Swiss, whom he had enlisted contrary to the will of the magistracy, to drive out the French. Then the king of France received twenty thousand men from the cantons with whom he was allied; maintained himself in Italy, and gave to the three cantons, Uri, Schwyz and Unterwalden (1502 and 1503), the districts of Palenza, Riviera and Bellenz. But, as soon as the king thought he could do without the Swiss, he paid them badly and irregularly. Cardinal Schinner, pleased at this, immediately shook a bag of gold, with 53,000 guilders, in favor of the pope and of Venice. At once (1512) twenty thousand Swiss and Grisons crossed the high Alps, and joined the Venetians against the French. The Grisons took possession of Valtelina, Chiavenna and

Bormio. They asserted that, a century before, an ejected duke of Milan had ceded these valleys to the bishopric of Coire. The Confederates of the twelve cantons subjected Lugano, Locarno and Valmaggia. The French were driven out of Lombardy, and the young duke, Maximilian Sforza, son of him who had been dispossessed by them, was reinstated in his father's inheritance at Milan. Victorious for him, the Confederates beat the French near Novara (6th June 1513); two thousand Swiss fell, it is true, but ten thousand of the enemy. Still more murderous was the two days' battle of Marignano (14th Sept. 1515), in which barely ten thousand Swiss fought against fifty thousand French. They lost the battle-field, indeed, but not their honor. They sadly retreated to Milan, with their field-pieces on their backs, their wounded in the centre of their army. The enemy lost the flower of their troops, and called this action "the battle of the giants."

Then the king of France, Francis I., terrified by a victory which resembled a defeat, made, in the next year, a perpetual peace with the Confederates, and, by money and promises, persuaded some to furnish him with troops, the others, that they would allow no enrolling by his enemies. Thus the Confederates once more helped him against the emperor and pope, and against Milan, and the king concluded a friendly alliance with them in 1521. During many years, they shed their blood for him on the battle-fields of Italy, without good result, without advantage, except that the Confederacy stood godmother to his new-born son. Each canton sent to Paris, for the fête, a deputy with a baptismal present of fifty ducats. More agreeable to the king than this present, was the promptitude with which the Swiss sent sixteen thousand of their troops to his assistance in Italy. However, as they had lost (20th April, 1522) three thousand men near Bicocca; as of nearly fifteen thousand who entered Lombardy (1524) hardly four thousand came back; as, finally, in the battle near Pavia (24th Feb. 1525) in which the king himself became prisoner to the emperor, the Swiss experienced a fresh loss of seven thousand men, they, by degrees, lost all taste for Italian wars.

CHAPTER XXXI.

BEGINNING OF THE RELIGIOUS SCHISM IN SWITZERLAND.

[A. D. 1519 to 1527.]

THE mercenary wars in Lombardy, Naples, France, Piedmont, and wherever else they were undertaken for hire and presents, had also some good results. The military glory acquired was, indeed, of little advantage to the country, and the conquest of the Italian bailiwicks of more prejudice than profit. For the Confederacy gained no strength or security against foreign powers by the acquisition of this small territory or the increased number of her subjects, but was made weaker by internal dissensions respecting this perilous property, while the sale of offices, the bad government, the corruption of justice, made her despicable in the eyes of Europe. The avaricious military leaders and bailiffs were the only gainers. A few families were made rich; the subjects poor and savage.

The good results of these campaigns were, that, after so many losses and sacrifices, the Confederates at last discovered that it was not good for them to mix in foreign quarrels, to allow foreign embassadors to acquire so much influence over the cantons, or to permit the magistrates to receive presents and pensions from princes. Therefore several cantons forbade the open or secret reception of such money, and decreed that no member of a free government should be the hireling of a foreign lord. Even the common people, several times, gave way to their anger against those who, for the silver crowns of kings, carried on a slave-trade for foreign service, and betrayed kings and fatherland equally. Thus there was a great rising at Lucerne (1513) to obtain the punishment of such dealers in human flesh. The ominous excitement of the people at last became so general, that Lucerne, Berne and Zurich expelled from their councils these hated eaters of men, and punished them pecuniarily and capitally, or by banishment. After thousands and thousands of valiant young men had fallen in distant lands, Switzerland found a respite from her disorders, the governments administered the laws better, moderation and good conduct replaced vicious excesses. Many cantons undertook this reform with much earnestness.

At this time there were many learned men in Switzerland, particularly among the clergy. In the cities were very good schools. But the country-people lived in the deepest ignorance, and hardly one in a thousand could read or write. Hence the greater part of the people had no knowledge of religion, especially where the pastors neglected to give them truly Christian instruction. This occasioned great evils; still more, when the clergy preferred to keep the people subservient by ignorance, rather than to make them enlightened and pious; and when, more devoted to the pleasures of the world than to heavenly things, they unblushingly gave to their flocks an example of cupidity, debauchery, drunkenness and gambling, instead of warning them from such vices.

These things disgusted all persons of sound mind and good heart, especially when they saw that the most vicious and licentious priests and monks were absolved by their superiors, themselves not free from blame, and remained unpunished. And the indignation of many, both laymen and ecclesiastics, was excited when the Dominicans, at Berne, having recourse to the vilest fraud for the vilest purposes, played upon credulity by pretended apparitions and miracles, so that a poor unfortunate, named Jetzer, became almost crazed in consequence.

At this period Leo X., pope of Rome, wishing to embellish his capital with palaces and the most magnificent of all churches, required a great deal of money, and therefore instituted the sale of indulgences. He leased this traffic in Switzerland to a Franciscan monk, Bernardin Samson. But as much money was thereby taken from the country, the civil authorities were displeased, and not unwillingly saw an opposition excited against this trade. When the pastor of Einsiedeln, a secular ecclesiastic, by name Ulrich Zwingli, a native of Wildhaus in Toggenburg, preached publicly against the pretence of offering forgiveness of sins for money, even the bishop of Constance displayed no anger.

But Zwingli did not rest here; he warmly attacked the sins and vices of both laymen and clergy. Then many opposed him, tried to reduce him to silence. But he, instead of being frightened, became bolder, and drew his arguments from the word of God. And he began to teach that a pure life and religious mind were more pleasing to the Heavenly Father than pilgrimages and macerations of the flesh, and that the bread and wine in the holy supper were symbols of the life and blood of Jesus. He also repudiated the mass, the doctrine of purgatory, the worship of saints, the celibacy of priests, and many other things.

Other ecclesiastics, among whom were many learned and pious men, thought like Zwingli. Especially had he many followers in the cities of Zurich, Berne, Bâle, Schaffhausen, St. Gallen, Bienne, Coire and others, where good schools and solid information prevailed. And when Zwingli, called to Zurich, on the 1st January 1519, preached there publicly as pastor, the people embraced his doctrine and the government gave him their approbation and protection. Many monastic and secular ecclesiastics in Switzerland followed his example, and taught and preached to the people as he did, without fear of man. The adherents to his opinions were numerous everywhere.

These opinions spread, not only in Switzerland but far over Germany also. At the same period, a learned Augustine monk of Wittenberg, Martin Luther, without knowing any thing of Zwingli, preached nearly the same doctrine as the latter. And, as in Switzerland many magistrates became followers of Zwingli, so in Germany and Sweden and Denmark and England, kings and princes, with a large portion of their people, embraced Luther's doctrines. Hence his followers were called Lutherans. In Switzerland, however, the new church-party adopted no man's name, but was called "evangelical-reformed;" that is: the church of Christ restored to its primitive purity according to the word of God.

In fact, the pope himself had not denied, at the imperial Diet of Nuremberg (1522), that many abuses had crept into the catholic church; "But," said he, "the cure must be slow and gradual, lest a total destruction should ensue from the endeavor to remedy all at once." So thought, also, the good catholics of Switzerland, and they were frightened at innovations, and at the idea of abandoning the ancient holy faith of their fathers. And many pious and respectable men among them said warningly: "Beware of what you are doing! You accuse us of error; are not you, fallible men like ourselves, also subject to error? We follow the traditions of pious men who lived a thousand years, and more, nearer to the time of Jesus; why should we rather believe you, who are but of to-day? Beware then! while with your lips you invoke the love of God, you are bringing bloody hatred, discord and desolation into the fatherland."

Loud and long were the talks and negotiations on these matters; each party thought itself right, and accused the other of error and heresy. All hearts were filled with bitterness and anger. Public conferences on religion, at which the magistrates presided, were held between learned men of both church-parties, to put an end to the schism; but, as is almost always the case, each remained attached to his own ideas with more obstinacy than before.

The new doctrine of the reëstablishment of the ancient Christian faith spread further every day. As Zwingli contributed most to this in Zurich, so, at Berne, Berchtold Haller, Lupulus, Nicholas Manuel; and in Bâle, Œcolampadius; among the Grisons, Henry Spreiter at St. Anthony's, John Comander at Coire, John Blasius at Malans; on the lakes of Geneva and Neuchâtel, Nicholas Farel; in Bienne, Thomas Wyttenbach; and numerous others in other places. As in Zurich and Berne, the new worship was also soon adopted in Schaffhausen, Bâle and St. Gallen; the mass, the adoration of saints, the convents, were abolished; the laity received wine, as well as bread, in the holy supper; priests were allowed to marry, and the reformed service was introduced among the country-people by sovereign decree, and sometimes by force, even against the wishes and convictions of many of the subjects.

If the authorities and pastors went too far in their zeal, the rude people often went still further; they profaned the long-adored images of saints, insulted the cross, and mocked those who wished to remain faithful to their ancient belief.

This embittered the minds of the catholics, so that they were filled with hatred against the reformed Confederates. Lucerne, Uri, Schwyz and Unterwalden held fast to the old faith, burned the writings of Luther by order of the pope (1521), and forbade all persons to preach the new doctrine in their territory, under penalty of death. In the cantons of Glarus and Appenzell, the people were divided (1524) so that catholics and reformed lived in the greatest discord. But in Solothurn and Freiburg the governments forbade all innovation.

Finally, when the evangelical doctrines penetrated into the common bailiwicks of the Confederacy; into Rheinthal and Thurgau, into Toggenburg, into the free bailiwicks, into the county of Baden and other places, those who remained catholic were alarmed. The small cantons feared lest the reform of the common bailiwicks would not only restrict their rights of sovereignty, but also render the reformed cities too powerful. The ambition of the cities to extend their territory was well known to them. They saw, moreover, the violent conduct of the evangelicals in several cantons, and how they prevented the catholics from following the worship of their fathers. And the ill-will became still stronger on the part of the catholics, when they perceived that the new teachers did not agree among themselves; that, in the reformed cantons, violent sectaries occasioned all kinds of disorders, and resisted the laws and authorities. The anabaptists, especially, caused great trouble and scandal; preaching in the woods and fields, they announced the near coming of the Messiah, and the abolition of all spiritual and temporal subjection. Such was the excitement of these enthusiasts, that the cities of Zurich, Berne, St. Gallen, Schaffhausen and Bâle were compelled to put a stop to its consequences by the severest penalties. For these people introduced among themselves community of property and wives; young girls assumed the character of the Messiah; and Thomas Schmucker, with an axe, beheaded his own brother Lienhard on the Muhlegg, as an expiatory sacrifice for the sins of the world.

CHAPTER XXXII.

PROGRESS OF THE DISCORD IN CHURCH-MATTERS.

[A. D. 1527 to 1530.]

FROM year to year, from day to day, the disorders, agitations and enmities, occasioned by the church-schism, increased in Switzerland. Each party, to prove its possession of true Christianity, pursued the other with most unchristian hatred. The greatest misfortunes were anticipated. There were, however, many wise and well-intentioned Confederates, among both catholics and reformed, who said: "If our faith be the true one, if it come from God, let us show it to be such by works of love towards each other: for love is of God, but hate and enmity are of the devil." But that which is generally the case occurred now. The voice of the wise was drowned by the cries and uproar of those who were zealous from religious presumption, or from pride and selfishness.

Among those who raised their voices against either the old or the new worship, were thousands and thousands who cried out and made an uproar, not for the sake of religion and the love of goodness and truth, but to advance their own interests under pretext of piety. Among the country-people, many expected more freedom and privileges from the adoption of the new faith; and, when they found themselves disappointed, returned at once to the catholic church. Thus when the council of Berne suppressed the convent of Interlaken, and established reformed preachers, the peasants were greatly delighted. "No more convent," said they, "no more tithes, no more taxes!" But as the city exacted tithes and taxes in her own behalf, the angry peasants became catholics again, drove away the reformed preachers, and advanced in arms as far as Thun. Then the city called upon her other subjects to arbitrate in this matter; Berne wished for peace, because she could not expect prompt or hearty aid from the neighboring cantons, all catholics. The subjects did honor to the confidence of the government, decided justly and said: "The temporal rights of the convent pass to the temporal authority, and in no way become the property of the peasants." The insurgents of Grindelwald dispersed, still dissatisfied, although the city had remitted many of the former charges for the benefit of their poor.

But quiet was not restored. For the dispossessed monks of Interlaken travelled about and secretly excited the people. The abbot of Engelberg, fearing for his own ancient rights and revenues in Bernese Oberland, did the same, particularly in Oberhasli. Oberhasli had enjoyed great freedom from the oldest times: she had her special seal, her banner, a landammann of her own choice, and was not so much under the immediate sovereignty as under the protection of the city of Berne. Now, when the communes of Oberhasli, excited by the monks of Engelberg and the Unterwaldeners, their neighbors, abolished the reformed worship (1528), and introduced catholic priests from Uri and Unterwalden, the Grindelwaldeners did the same; Aeschi, Frutigen, Obersimmen and other valley-districts followed the example, and the Unterwaldeners even sent auxiliaries over the Brunig to act in case of need. Berne armed hastily, and sent her troops to prevent the spread of the rebellion. The insurgents, losing courage, dispersed, and the Unterwaldeners recrossed the Brunig. Berne punished Oberhasli severely: took away the banner and seal of the valley for a long time; deprived the inhabitants of the right to choose a landammann forever; put to death the leaders of the insurrection, and compelled the rest to beg for pardon on their knees, within a circle formed by the troops. In Frutigen, Simmenthal and the other places, the reformed worship was reëstablished by force.

Whenever the reformed governments undertook to change the church-service in their own and subject districts, they generally met with little opposition. For the people were either desirous of a pure faith, or ignorant and full of servile fear of the lords and magistrates in the cities. They often adopted the new worship less from conviction than in blind submission. But in the common bailiwicks, where the catholic and reformed cantons held equal sover-

M*

eignty, great difficulties prevailed and violent disturbances. In the free bailiwicks and in the county of Baden, some communes changed their worship in one and the same year, according as the influence of the catholic or of the reformed cantons preponderated. The city-council of Bremgarten, urged by the catholic cantons, drove from their employ the pastor Henry Bullinger, who had spread the new faith through the free bailiwicks, while the people, encouraged by Zurich and Berne, maintained the reformed worship. Even the abbey of Wettingen adopted the latter, and Toggenburg, in spite of her sovereign, the abbot of St. Gallen, decreed the abolition of the mass and of the adoration of saints.

The exasperation of the catholic and reformed cantons against each other grew more savage from day to day. As the catholic avoyer Werli had acted zealously against the evangelical worship in Frauenfeld, the Zurichers seized him on his passage, although he wore the colors of Unterwalden on his cloak, and publicly executed him. On their side, the Schwyzers laid hands on the reformed pastor Kaiser, of Uznach, and burnt him at the stake as a heretic. At last every one feared for his life, when compelled to pass through a canton of different faith. When bailiff Anthony Abacker had to go from Unterwalden to his office in the free bailiwicks, he was unwilling to do so without an armed escort. So great was the distrust, the fear and the hatred! When this catholic bailiff reached the free bailiwicks, the reformed subjects therein trembled. For their safety, Zurich sent eight hundred infantry to Bremgarten and to the abbey of Muri (1529), and several thousand men into Gasterland, into Thurgau, and toward the canton of Zug. Berne also armed ten thousand men, to be ready for the fight, in case of need.

The catholic cantons, on their side, armed no less. Uri, Schwyz, Unterwalden, Zug and Lucerne marched their troops together towards the frontiers; fifteen hundred Valaisians were with them. They had made a league with the Roman king for the defence of the ancient faith.

Now, when the other cantons saw that Confederates stood ready to draw the sword against Confederates, they interfered as mediators, and exhorted to peace. The noble spirit of the best days of the Swiss bond still prevailed, and the Confederate on the Limmat had not forgotten that the man in the Waldstatten was his brother. Thus it was with the officers and soldiers of the opposed armies, who took their dinners amicably together on the frontiers, set their milk-porridge on the boundary-stones of their cantons, and fought playfully with their wooden spoons, whenever any one passed the border in fishing for a good morsel in the common bowl. This time, also, the landammann Aebli of Glarus and the syndic Sturm of Strassburg succeeded in establishing an equality of religious rights between the discordant parties on the 26th of June, 1529. The troops returned to their homes.

But hardly were they there, when the old quarrel was renewed, and the reformed were moreover very active in spreading their doctrines everywhere. In consequence of the zeal of Berne the evangelical worship was adopted in the principality of Neuchâtel, and the learned Berchtold Haller opened a way for it in the canton of Solothurn. The activity of Zurich gained over to the new faith many communes in Sarganserland and Thurgau and in the county of Baden, as well as Kaiserstuhl and Zurzach. And when, at this time, the abbot of St. Gallen, Francis Geisberger, died, Zurich, with the reformed portion of Glarus, undertook to suppress the abbey of St. Gallen, and to secularise all there belonging to the chapter. The burghers of St. Gallen did, in fact, introduce the reformed service into the abbey-church. A large part of the riches of the abbey was devoted to the support of the poor; the reformed subjects of the abbey were relieved from many charges, and their communes received the privilege of choosing their own pastors.

This offended the catholic cantons. For Zurich and Glarus were not the sole protectors of the abbey of St. Gallen, but Lucerne and Schwyz also. And, although the former, in the changes, had reserved the rights of the two catholic protecting cantons, they nevertheless made continually fresh innovations; and, moreover, though the reformed always asserted liberty of conscience among the subjects in the common bailiwicks, as a principle, they rarely allowed it as a fact. Even Rapperswyl at last fell from the ancient faith, and Toggenburg entertained the hope of purchasing herself entirely free from the rights of the abbey.

Then Uri, Unterwalden and Zug, also, joined with Schwyz and Lucerne, for they found that the last agreement respecting religion was by no means for their advantage. And they said: "This is a hard knot, which the sword only can loose."

CHAPTER XXXIII.

THE WAR OF KAPPEL. DEATH OF ZWINGLI. AVOYER WENGI OF SOLOTHURN.

[A. D. 1531 to 1533.]

THE citizens of Zurich were violently excited. All wished for war, but not all from the same motive. Some desired it from an overweening zeal for the new faith, persuaded that they ought to sacrifice property and life for their religion, and risk every thing to spread it over Switzerland. Others looked to conquest, and wished to obtain the exclusive sovereignty of the common bailiwicks by destroying the authority of the catholic cantons therein. A third party desired war, in the hope of crushing the catholic citizens. For many in Zurich were still secretly true to the faith of their fathers, either from conviction or from dislike to the austerity of the evangelical preachers, who without forbearance censured the licentiousness of manners, and inveighed against the venality and pensions of the great lords.

Berne, on the contrary, desired peace. For Berne was not sure of quiet in her own territory, and would derive no advantage from the secularization of the distant abbey of St. Gallen. Therefore Berne said to the Zurichers: "Why shed the blood of your compatriots? Prohibit all trade in grain with the Waldstatten, until they fulfil all the articles of the treaty of religion, and give you satisfaction." Thereto Zurich replied: "Such a measure is quite as hateful as war, and does not bring about a decision so promptly as a brisk fight." They therefore prepared for war: Zurich eagerly, hurriedly; Berne slowly, unwillingly; this was of disadvantage to both.

But the five catholic cantons, Lucerne, Uri, Schwyz, Unterwalden and Zug, said to Zurich and Berne: "You spread your innovations every day by fraud and by force; shall we allow the holy faith of our fathers to be entirely banished from the country of our fathers? You make our subjects unfaithful, and encourage the rebels. You have permitted the insurgents of Rheinthal to seize the Unterwaldener bailiff, Kretz, and to keep him prisoner in the council-house at Alstetten. You have stripped the abbot of St. Gallen of his rights and property. We have asked for Confederate justice, and you have denied it to us. We wish for a reconciliation, and you drive us from free fields and markets. Therefore, since you will have it so, let the sword decide. God be the judge!"

Thus said the five cantons, and their banners marched at once with eight thousand men towards Zug and into the free bailiwicks. There was already a troop of Zurichers encamped near Kappel; it was weak. But the headquarters of Zurich were to follow. The Bernese were stationed near Lenzburg, and knew not what to do, as they had received no orders. The banners of the five cantons advanced (12th Oct., 1531) as far as Kappel; three hundred of the bravest immediately precipitated themselves into the ranks of the Zurichers. The rest rushed after. The combat was terrible. Too late and too fatigued came the chief banner of Zurich over the Albis. With it was Ulric Zwingli. There fought Swiss against Swiss with the ancient heroism. Over six hundred Zurichers were slain. Under the dead lay the body of Zwingli. The rest fled, pursued until night. The victors returned late to the battle-field, thanked God, according to the custom of their fathers, for the bloody defeat of their vanquished brothers, and plundered the deserted camp of Zurich.

A few days afterwards, however, the heights of Albis were again covered with reformed auxiliaries. The Bernese took post in numbers near Bremgarten, and pillaged the convent of Muri; on the other side, the evangelicals advanced as far as Zug mountain. Several troops of them were sent to plunder the convent of Einsiedeln. But John Hug, son of the avoyer of Lucerne, with six hundred chosen men, surprised them before break of day (24th October) on Mount Gubel, near Menzigen, and put them to flight after a short battle.

These defeats spread mourning and terror through the city of Zurich; twenty-six members of the great and little councils had lost their lives on the field of battle. The reformed Grisons, already on the march, stopped near Uznach. The evangelicals of Glarus wished to remain neutral. The Toggenburgers desired to treat with the catholic cantons, protectors of the abbey of St. Gallen. Then Zurich thought: "We stand alone; peace is necessary."

The five cantons, without arrogance, offered peace on equitable conditions. It was concluded with Zurich on the 16th of November, at the farm of Teynikon, below the Breitholz, in the open field. Arbitrators were to decide afterwards respecting the expenses of the war; but both religious parties were to have equal rights in the common bailiwicks. When the Bernese heard this, they marched home, and willingly accepted the peace. Many of them were still faithful in their hearts to the Roman-catholic church. Even the Bernese general, Sebastian of Diesbach, returned to the catholic faith a few years afterwards and went to Freiburg in Uechtland.

After the five victorious cantons had made peace with Zurich and Berne, they demanded satisfaction from Solothurn, which had sent auxiliaries to the Bernese. Most of the communes of the canton of Solothurn had already embraced the evangelical faith, and were therefore willing to aid the Bernese. In the capital city, however, the council and citizens were divided, and this gave rise to many quarrels and persecutions about doctrine. But when the five catholic cantons required an indemnity of a thousand guilders, or that the Solothurners should return to the faith of their fathers, few were willing to pay. Most of them again called themselves catholics. In the city itself, the catholics took up arms against the reformed, to compel them to abjure the evangelical faith, and came with a loaded cannon in front of the house where the latter were even then deliberating. The crashing shot was about to be fired. Suddenly a venerable man advanced from the furious crowd, placed his breast, full of true patriotism, before the cannon's mouth, and said: "If citizens' blood must flow, let my blood flow first!" All drew back trembling when they saw the act of this great Christian hero: it was the avoyer Wengi of Solothurn. No blood flowed. But the evangelicals of the city, willing to leave every thing rather than their beloved faith, sacrificed their property and estates, and went into other cities and lands. The Roman-catholic worship was reëstablished (1533) in forty-four communes of the district, thirty-four of which had embraced the evangelical doctrine.

These were the results of the fratricidal victory near Kappel; but not all: the abbot of St. Gallen was restored to all his rights, and the further spread of the evangelical doctrine in the common bailiwicks stopped forever. Furthermore, the influence of the victors was so preponderating, that the catholic worship was reinstated by force in several places in the common domain.

CHAPTER XXXIV.

GENEVA SEPARATES FROM SAVOY. BERNE SUBDUES VAUD.

[A. D. 1533 to 1558.]

Not less violent, at this time, was the excitement respecting church-matters among the people in other districts of the Helvetian mountains. In the valleys of the Grisons, where no restraint was exercised, some communes embraced the new faith, others retained the old. In Valais, where Thomas Plater preached reform most zealously, the evangelical worship had numerous adherents at Sion and Leuk. In Vaud, along the shores of lake Leman, Lausanne, with the other cities and most of the village districts, separated from the Roman church. Geneva did the same; but with great troubles and commotion. For religious discord was then added to the civil disorders which had long prevailed in that city.

Geneva was already renowned as a beautiful and populous city, flourishing by the arts, the science, the industry and activity of her inhabitants. Twice had this very ancient city of the Allobroges been destroyed in the time of the Roman emperors; twice had she risen from her ruins. Even at this day, two street-pavements are found, one under another. After the Romans, the Burgundian kings often resided there; afterwards, under the Franks, the Burgundian free-men there held their diet. From unremembered times, a bishop thence exercised spiritual dominion over a large territory. He enjoyed a princely title, great estates and prerogatives, as well as the right of supremacy over the city. This had formerly belonged to the French kings, who conferred it on the bishop. The other rights of the kings were exercised by the counts of Geneva as bailiffs. By degrees, these counts had made their offices hereditary in their families. Not only did they consider the whole district of Geneva, excepting what belonged to the bishop, as theirs, but they were also the deputies or stadtholders of the bishop in the management of his temporal rights. Hence arose endless disputes between the bishop of Geneva and the counts of Geneva. The citizens gained by this dissension. Supporting by turns the cause of one or of the other, they obtained new privileges and franchises from both. Finally, three parties contended for preëminence in that narrow corner of the earth: the bishop, the count of Geneva and the burghers of the city. A fourth soon made his appearance: the neighboring, powerful count of Savoy. The citizens first called him to their aid against the count of Geneva, and granted to him many of the rights of the latter; but he therefore wished to have them all. He tried to supplant the counts of Geneva, and, when this family died out, he bought all their estates. Thus he acquired great influence in the city-commonwealth.

Becoming more and more powerful, so much so as to assume the title of dukes, the counts of Savoy became more and more dangerous to the citizens. They soon appropriated all the power of the bishop, by always, as was easy, placing a son of their house in the episcopal chair. But, when one of these bishops, after the war of the Swiss with Charles the Bold of Burgundy, made (1493), for himself and the city, a treaty of coburghership or defensive alliance with the cities of Freiburg and Berne,* the citizens unexpectedly acquired in these neighboring Confederates new sureties for their threatened rights, against the powerful dukes and bishops. This had important consequences.

One day (in 1517) an evil-disposed student at Geneva maliciously cut off the leg of a mule belonging to the episcopal judge Grossi. Then he and a troop of wild comrades, who bore ill-will to the judge, caused the mule's leg to be carried through all the streets by an idiot, and told him to cry: "Who'll buy, who'll buy a piece of the gross beast?" Grossi felt doubly angry at this allusion to his name and insult to his person. He cited the offenders before the bishop's court. The bishop pardoned them all, excepting one Pecolat, whom he imprisoned, and another, named Berthelier, who fled to Freiburg. Now arose a dispute as to the jurisdiction to which Pecolat belonged. The city of Geneva succeeded in having him brought before her tribunal. The affair was lengthened out, and carried before duke, bishop, archbishop and pope.

In the mean while, Berthelier was not idle at Freiburg. Clothed with full powers by his fellow-citizens, he strengthened the bonds of union between Freiburg and Geneva. When, to complete his work, he came back to Geneva under a safe-conduct (6th February, 1519), and brought the compact with Freiburg to the city, the duke was so enraged thereat, that he put to death at Turin some Genevese who were travelling through his country. This act of vengeance increased the bitterness and open division be-

* The close compact of Geneva with Freiburg was formed in 1519· with Berne, in 1526.

tween the partisans of the Confederates and those of the duke of Savoy. The latter, few in number, were called Mamelukes; the others, Eidsgenossen, or, as they said in their French idiom, Huguenots.

The dispute respecting the compact was carried before several Swiss diets, but without result. The duke so cruelly maltreated the Huguenots, whom he termed rebellious subjects, that many fled to Berne and Freiburg. He even seized and executed Berthelier. The Savoyard nobility were ordered to harass the city in all possible ways. Then, to these troubles, was added the dispute about the new church-doctrine. Most of the Huguenots were evangelical-reformed. Even the prior of St. Victor, named Bonnivard, was one of the first who preached against the pope.* Thereat the duke and bishop redoubled their severity against the Genevese, so that Berne and Freiburg could no longer leave their allies without protection. With twelve thousand men, they marched through Vaud to Geneva, ravaging as they went (10th Oct., 1530). Then deputies from Valais and the ten cantons interposed as mediators, persuaded the troops to retire, and peace was concluded at St. Julian (1530). The duke promised to respect the rights of Geneva, under penalty of losing the whole of Vaud; on her side, Geneva agreed to respect the rights of the duke, under penalty of forfeiting her alliance with the Confederates.

Peace was reëstablished, friendship was not. The exasperated duke secretly continued his persecutions. In the city, the parties of catholics and protestants hated one another. They made onslaughts against each other; assassinations followed. But the Huguenots had the upper hand. The bishop, frightened by the people, left the city, and fixed his seat at Gex. He and the duke of Savoy made a sudden assault, to surprise the city with an armed force. They were repulsed by the vigilance and courage of the excited citizens (1534). The latter immediately established the evangelical worship, declared that the

* He was seized by the duke's emissaries, and carried to the castle of Chillon, at the east end of the lake of Geneva, where he was confined for six years in a dungeon on a level with the lake.

bishop's sovereignty had ceased and that their city was an independent republic (1536).

This was a bold and momentous step. It was, however, a successful one. At this period John Calvin, a French ecclesiastic from Royon, joined the Genevese. He was a wise man, skilled in affairs of church and state, a zealous and often cruel partisan of the evangelical faith. He not only established the new worship which William Farrell and Anthony Saunier had introduced, but he also repressed the extreme corruption of manners by severe discipline, and helped to consolidate the new commonwealth by stringent laws. Such was Calvin's influence, that at last nothing was done contrary to his will; such his reputation for insight into spiritual things, that, in Switzerland, France and Germany, the reformed were called Calvinists, after his name.

In the mean while, as the exiled Mamelukes and the Savoyard nobility of Vaud pressed the city sore, the Bernese declared war against the duke of Savoy, because he had not observed the treaty of St. Julian. They sent seven thousand troops into Vaud (January, 1536); within eleven days they conquered all from Morat to Geneva, and relieved this city, which received them joyfully; drove the bishop away from Lausanne, took possession of his property and rights, and made themselves sovereigns of the whole of Vaud, much more easily than they had formerly done of Aargau. For the duke of Savoy could make but slight resistance, being also engaged in war with the king of France, and in great need. The cities and communes of Vaud submitted willingly to the Bernese, because the yoke of the dukes of Savoy had often borne heavily upon them, and because the magistrates of the country had cared more for themselves than for the people.

But Valais and Freiburg looked with jealous eyes upon the conquest of Vaud by Berne. They wished to have a share in it. The Valaisians took possession of the territory between their frontiers and the Dranse; the Freiburgers took the districts of Rue and Romont. Berne willingly allowed this, that she might hold the main part of the country undisturbed and establish herself firmly therein. With this purpose, she immediately introduced the reformed service everywhere, placed eight bailiffs over the conquered districts, and appointed for her newly-acquired territory a separate treasurer, to collect the revenue of the state. Only a few places retained their former franchises. The city of Lausanne, however, preserved her old important privileges, so that she was like a protected city. Twice already, in earlier times, had Berne conquered Vaud: once in the Burgundian war, when she kept Bex and Aigle; the second time, before the peace of St. Julian, when she kept nothing. But now, the third time, she did not give back her fine booty.

For a long while, the rich and powerful counts of Gruyeres, who held much land in Vaud, steadfastly refused to render homage for their estates to the cities of Berne and Freiburg. But, as these counts were burdened with debt and in want of money, the cities prudently bought up the claims of their creditors (1554). Thus Freiburg acquired the signiory of Gruyeres; Berne, the valleys of Rougemont and Oron.*

Thus Berne doubled the extent of her territory, and by her skilful policy in seizing auspicious moments, by the public spirit, the resolution and determined valor of her citizens, became the most powerful city of the whole Confederacy in lands and people.

CHAPTER XXXV.

RELIGIOUS HATRED IN THE ITALIAN BAILIWICKS, IN GRISONS AND EVERYWHERE. DISPUTE ABOUT THE CALENDAR. THE BORROMEAN LEAGUE.

[A. D. 1558 to 1586.]

THE city of Geneva, with a little territory outside her walls, flourished thenceforward as a republic, and became

* These form part of the present canton of Vaud.

one of the most celebrated cities of Switzerland by her industry and science. Nevertheless, the Confederates long hesitated to admit her as an allied canton, on account of her continual disturbances. Those disturbances were the fruits, partly of the new freedom itself, partly of the inflexible severity and ardent religious zeal of John Calvin. Calvin pursued with exile, the sword or the stake, every one who opposed his doctrine and measures.

Berne alone held true to Geneva, Geneva to Berne; in 1558, they renewed their coburghership or mutually defensive alliance for all time. Geneva found in Berne her surest protection against outward and inward troubles; Berne, on her side, found in Geneva a strong fortress against Savoy, for holding Vaud in awe, and for reducing the Vaudois themselves, in case they wished to reclaim ancient franchises which the confederate city was not inclined to allow.

The religious discord among the Confederates and their subjects had, in the mean while, affected many hearts in the Italian bailiwicks beyond the St. Gotthard. The number of evangelical-reformed was especially great in the bailiwick of Locarno; among them were many of the richest and most respected families; Lelius and Faustus Sozzini (Socinius) had there spread a much freer doctrine in matters of faith than even Zwingli in Zurich or Calvin in Geneva. But the Sozzini were driven away, and their adherents banished or punished with death. In Locarno itself, Beccaria afterwards became the principal teacher of the evangelicals. The catholic bailiff imprisoned him, but a troop of the reformed assailed the castle and released Beccaria by force. The bailiff, invested with full powers by the seven catholic cantons participating in the government, at last ordered all the evangelicals to attend the catholic worship, and banished many from the country. "That is contrary to our agreement respecting religious equality!" said the evangelical participating cantons. "No," replied the catholic cantons, "that agreement does not extend to the Italian bailiwicks; here the majority of votes decide." And so the persecutions continued. The papal nuncio or embassador did his best to increase them.

Finally the general banishment of the reformed from Locarno was decided upon and put in execution (March, 1555). One hundred and fifty persons were compelled to assemble in the council-house and listen to their sentence in submissive silence. Suddenly the papal nuncio entered the hall, and angrily cried out: "This is too lenient! The exiles must be deprived of their property and estates, and of their children also!" But even the deputies of the catholic Confederates shuddered at the idea of such barbarity. Much more humanity dwelt in their hearts than in the heart of the priest of God. And they said: "We never revoke our once pronounced sentence."

Then the exiles, with their wives and little children, went far away from the homes of their fathers, in the rigorous season of the year, over inhospitable mountains. The evangelical Confederates receïved them with Christian charity. More than a hundred found an asylum in Zurich. Among them were several rich and learned men: the Orelli, the Muralte, and others, whose families still flourish at Zurich. They carried to that city the art of weaving silk, established mills and dye-houses, and so enriched her by their industry, that the prosperity of Zurich soon became celebrated even beyond the limits of Switzerland.

In spite of the church-dissensions, the Confederates would probably have returned to their ancient concord, had they not lent too ready an ear to the insinuations of foreign embassadors. At this same period, religious wars desolated France and Germany also; the envoys of the sovereigns engaged in these wars sought favor and assistance from the cantons of their own faith, and excited them against the others, and the clergy on both sides did their best to inflame the minds of the people. Some of the reformed cantons did, indeed, prudently avoid all intermingling in foreign quarrels; but not all, and not the catholic cantons. These last were influenced by the advice of the papal nuncio, and not less by the gold which the French embassador lavished in order to procure Swiss mercenaries for the service of his king. In 1553 they made, with king Henry II. of France, the first formal agreement (called Capitulation) respecting Swiss regiments to be sent into the French service, supplied ten thousand men in one year, and considerable reinforcements annually. The Swiss have always fought with glory upon foreign soil, though but the mercenaries of foreign masters. Their blood did not flow for their fatherland, their deeds do not belong to the history of that fatherland. Let foreigners praise the exploits they paid for.

The papal nuncio especially labored without relaxation to injure the reformed cantons. He sowed discord everywhere in the name of religion. He even attempted to reëstablish the dominion of Savoy in Geneva, and perhaps in Vaud also. Some of the reformed cantons, jealous of the preponderance of Berne, would willingly have seconded him in this. But the design failed. For when the duke of Savoy did, in fact, reclaim Vaud, in 1564, Berne, prudently avoiding an encounter with a too powerful enemy, prevented greater losses by the voluntary surrender of the little district of Gex, and of all the territory beyond the lake of Geneva. In exchange, duke Emanuel Philibert, by the treaty of Lausanne, renounced his pretensions upon Vaud, and the king of France guaranteed this treaty, but with the express reserve of the ancient franchises which Vaud had enjoyed under Savoy. Geneva, however, remained long exposed to the attacks of Savoy. But the necessity of constantly defending her political existence against the intrigues and great power of her enemy, developed new strength in this small but courageous republic, always manfully supported by Berne. At last (1581), Zurich also entered into perpetual coburghership with the Genevese.

Of all the defenders of the Roman See, none ever exercised so great an ascendancy in the Confederacy as cardinal Charles Borromeo. Seldom also do we see a man more capable, by his talents and his virtues, of executing great enterprises, than this young prelate, active, pious, burning with zeal for his faith. To arrest, by eternal barriers, the spreading of the new doctrine, to strengthen against the storms of time the ancient catholic church, already deeply shaken, was the task to which he devoted his life. With this object he abolished many abuses in Italy, reformed the manners of the clergy, and made numerous journeys. He came into Switzerland also. But what he did here was not all for the advantage of the Confederates.

When in Valtelina, where the Grisons wished to establish reformed schools, he labored secretly, but assiduously against them. In Grisons he would willingly have armed catholics against evangelicals; but, excepting the court of the bishop of Coire, the free sons of the highlands received him coldly. They were wearied of religious disputes, in which, as among the Swiss, the selfish interests of the rich families were mixed up. Thereby the noble and innocent baron John Planta of Rhezuns was brought to the scaffold (1572) and many an honest man lost honor and country, property and life. Even in our day men talk in the Grison mountains of the formidable tribunals of Thusis and Coire, of the armed assemblages of the people, and of the venality so common in those days of corruption. A law passed (1570) at last put a stop to that impudent ambition which obtained honors by money and intrigues, and another (1574) forbade armed assemblages in the country. For the love of justice, among the Grisons, was allied to the love of unshackled liberty. A small number only of noble and ambitious families cared little for liberty or justice.

When cardinal Charles Borromeo came to the Confederates in Switzerland, he received a most hearty welcome from the catholic cantons. As they did but little for scholastic instruction, he established a priests'-school, or seminary, for young Swiss, at Milan. He also decided that a papal nuncio should always reside in Switzerland. This justly displeased the evangelicals; they feared that such a representative of the Roman court would constantly interfere in civil matters by spiritual means, produce discord, and attempt to tyrannize. Once, when a nuncio came to Berne in the winter of 1580, the government ordered him out of the city, and the boys in the streets pelted him with snow-balls.

The strife between catholics and protestants, at this time, occupied nearly the whole world. Spain, Savoy and the emperor were the most zealous partisans of the pope.

But the Huguenots, or reformed, almost triumphed in France. The Roman court attempted to persuade the whole catholic world to undertake a war for life and death against the evangelicals. They called this a holy war. In Switzerland, cardinal Borromeo earnestly urged the catholics to form a strong league among themselves for the support of their church. This increased the anger and animosity of the evangelicals. Men's minds were embittered against each other. Excesses were committed on both sides. It went so far that the reformed refused to receive the newly-improved calendar which then appeared (1582), because it had been perfected by order of a pope. The evangelicals were so distrustful of every thing, even of what was good, which came from Rome, that they preferred to adhere to the defective reckoning of the old calendar. This almost occasioned a bloody civil war.

The dispute about the old and new calendars induced the seven catholic cantons to favor the cardinal's projected league for the support of the Roman church. On the 10th of October, 1586, deputies from Lucerne, Uri, Schwyz, Unterwalden, Zug, Solothurn and Freiburg assembled in the city of Lucerne, and there swore to the league, which was called the Golden or Borromean. It had better have been called the Bloody. It separated Confederates from Confederates still further.

CHAPTER XXXVI.

INSURRECTION AT MUHLHAUSEN. THE RHODES OF APPENZELL SEPARATE. THE DUKE OF SAVOY TRIES TO SURPRISE GENEVA.

[A. D. 1587 to 1603.]

From this period, the catholic cantons were more closely united with foreigners than with the Swiss of evangelical faith. The foreign powers were pleased with this, because they knew how to take advantage of the division. Then came the embassador of Spain and scattered gold, and made a treaty for his king (1587) with Lucerne, Uri,

Schwyz, Unterwalden, Zug and Freiburg. Then came the papal nuncio and preached war against the reformed or Huguenots in France; and more than eight thousand catholic Swiss marched to take part in that foreign civil strife. Then came messengers from the Huguenots and preached war in defence of the evangelical faith in France; and thousands of reformed Swiss and Grisons marched to the bloody French battle-fields, while the cantonal governments pretended to know nothing about the matter. On foreign soil, for vile hire, Swiss murdered their own brothers in honor of God, as followers of Jesus. Such was the result of religious hate.

Thisevil spirit spread its poison every where. Even the most insignificant quarrels became the cause of great misfortunes, as was the case at Muhlhausen (Mulhouse).

The city of Muhlhausen, in Alsace, is of very ancient origin. For about five centuries it was, like most of the cities of Switzerland, a free city of the German empire; for one or two hundred years it had had a defensive alliance with Bâle, then with Berne, Freiburg and Solothurn, finally (since 1515) it had been an ally of the Confederates, with seat and voice in the diets. Now it happened that the Finninger family of this city had and lost a law-suit with other citizens respecting a piece of wood-land. In their anger, the Finningers appealed to the Austrian government at Ensisheim, then to the Diet of the Confederates. And, as the Catholic Swiss were told that this was a good opportunity to bring Muhlhausen back to the old faith, they embraced the cause of the Finningers and threatened the city-council of Muhlhausen with the disruption of the ancient alliance. The city-council thereupon applied to the evangelical cantons, who decided in their favor. At once, the catholic cantons and Appenzell sent to Muhlhausen the treaty of alliance with the seals torn off. The Finninger party made a disturbance at this, gained over the people, and deposed the city-council as having occasioned the rupture with the Confederates. The evangelical cantons wished to mediate and settle the matter amicably, but were not listened to; and when they threatened to restore the old order of things by force, the citizens armed, and obtained reinforcements of Austrian soldiers. The reformed Confederates immediately sent troops, under the lead of general d'Erlach; six hundred Bâlese in advance. Heavy artillery thundered from the city walls. In the middle of the night, the Swiss assailed and forced the gate. There were combats and massacres in all the streets; the citizens were conquered; the foreign garrison was disarmed and sent away, and quiet restored by the decapitation of the principal insurgents. But from that year (1587) Muhlhausen lost her alliance with the catholic Confederates, and never again recovered the right of voting in the Diet.

Shortly afterwards the canton of Appenzell was threatened with no less serious calamities. Here, evangelicals and catholics had hitherto lived with one another; the evangelicals being more numerous in the Outer Rhodes, the catholics in the Inner and in the chief town Appenzell. Now, the capuchins came into the country, and secretly preached that the reformed must be brought back to the catholic church by force; the landammann Meggelin, a zealous partisan of the ancient faith, wished to make a beginning. He cited twenty-seven reformed young men to answer before the assembly of the two councils, and caused the council-hall to be surrounded by catholic peasants. In case the twenty-seven would not submit, he was to give a signal from the windows, the council were to retire immediately, and the peasants to fall upon the young recusants. But he had not managed well. When the men would not submit, and he was hastening to the window, the lords of the council to the door, the seven and twenty produced the arms they had concealed under their cloaks, and so terrified the landammann that he shouted from the window: "Peace; disperse!" So the peasants dispersed, and the twenty-seven retired without injury. That day (14 May, 1587), was the beginning of many disturbances.

From that time the parties harassed and persecuted each other bitterly. The reformed were oppressed in the Inner, the catholics in the Outer Rhodes. Prisoners were made, more than once the tocsin was sounded; more than once arms were seized. Enlightened patriots, however, happily prevented a civil war. Finally, when concord could not be reëstablished in the councils, nor in the parishes or meetings of the communes, nor in the general assemblies, the intervention of the Confederates was invoked. But the Confederates, unhappily, were rather partisans than judges. The catholics supported the catholics, the reformed supported the reformed. At last, the Appenzellers said: "This will not restore peace; the country must be divided and each division have its own faith, its own magistrates, and its own tribunal."

This did in fact take place after ten years of troubles, and the act of division was signed on the 8th of September, 1597. The land and rights, the banners and seals, even the arms in the arsenal, were divided between the Outer and Inner Rhodes. The evangelicals established themselves in the Outer Rhodes, and altogether numbered 6322 persons; the catholics dwelt in the Inner Rhodes, and altogether numbered 2782 persons. But the two, although divided, as were Ob- and Nid-walden, remained one single canton, in the circle of the Confederates, as did Unterwalden.

This satisfied everybody, except landammann Tanner of the Inner Rhodes. He was an irreconcilable enemy of the evangelicals of the Outer Rhodes, and did not wish to be at peace with them; he constantly excited fresh troubles and disorders, and hoped to persuade the catholic cantons to compel the Outer Rhodes to yield all their prerogatives to the six or seven catholics living there. Tanner did not succeed in this, and finally became so odious to his fellow-citizens on account of his actions and opinions, that he lost all his property, estates and dignities, begged his bread from place to place, and died miserably in a cow-house in Thurgau.

It was indeed fortunate for Switzerland that the kings and princes, busied with constant wars, could not interfere in the domestic troubles of the Swiss. Otherwise, her independence would probably have been endangered more than once. But Spain and Milan were at war with France and the German emperor with the Turks. Each desired aux iliaries from the Swiss. But the Confederates, either because they would not trust each other, or because one part preferred one prince and the other part another, held themselves aloof. They frequently endeavored, by friendly intervention, to reconcile the king of France and the king of Spain. Zurich besought the emperor, Lucerne besought the pope, to turn their hearts to thoughts of peace. These attempts had small success.

Thereat, and because Henry IV. of France was beloved for his virtues and valor by both catholics and protestants, and because he promised to pay to Switzerland 400,000 crowns annually in settlement of outstanding debts, and, moreover, sent a million of ready money by his embassador, all hearts were turned to him. And they made a new league with him in 1602.

This displeased the Spaniards, as well as the pope and the duke of Savoy. All three hated the valiant king Henry IV. And the duke of Savoy thought this the best time to get possession of the beautiful city of Geneva. So he secretly sent his general Brunaulieu and his soldiers, with some Spaniards, to surprise the city in the midst of peace. In a dark night (between the 11th and 12th of December, 1602), they advanced to the walls, applied their scaling ladders, clambered up and thought themselves the winners. But a Genevese sentinel heard the noise and discharged his musket. The watchman dropped the port-cullis; the citizens were awakened, ran to the walls in arms, with shouts of: "The enemy! the enemy!" killed those who had entered the city, and threw down the scaling ladders. The Savoyards retired with considerable loss. Thirteen of their nobles were made prisoners and executed the next day.

Berne and Zurich immediately sent auxiliaries into the city, and compelled the duke to make a treaty of peace (11th July, 1603), by which he agreed never more to station troops within four miles of Geneva, to build no fortress there, and never again to attack the city. Since that time the Genevese annually celebrate the night of the Escalade as a festival of joy and triumph.

CHAPTER XXXVII.

TROUBLES IN BIENNE. CONSPIRACY AGAINST GENEVA. THE BLACK DEATH. COMMENCEMENT OF CIVIL WAR IN GRISONS.

[A. D. 1603 to 1618.]

At the same time that the Genevese were successfully defending their youthful liberty against the attempts of the duke of Savoy, the people in Valais fought their last bitter fight about religious matters. Here the reformed were inferior in numbers; therefore they succumbed. They had already been merely tolerated for more than fifty years, in virtue of an agreement made in 1551, but at last were no longer allowed. The bishop and council ordered them to sell their property and to leave their country. In vain did the evangelical cantons intercede (1603). The catholic cantons, Lucerne at their head, with much expenditure of money, but behind all the nuncio of the Roman court, insisted, on the other hand, that the reformed and their clergy should be driven out. And they were driven out and saw the land of their fathers no more.

So the citizens of Bienne had a strife with their bishop. Bienne is an old city, pleasantly situated on her lake. She had long been subject to the counts of Neuchâtel with peculiar privileges; later (in 1274), she had been transferred to the bishop of Bâle,* who, in order to gain her affection, had conferred on her the franchises of a free imperial city. With these franchises, the city soon became flourishing; her arms were victorious in many a feud, and the dwellers in the valley of Erguel followed her banner. To protect her rights, she early (1279) entered into alliance and coburghership with Berne, then with Solothurn also (1382), and a century later (1496) with Freiburg. She had a good understanding with all the Confederates, and was therefore honored as an allied city. At last (1554) she tried to purchase all the bishop's rights over

* The territory subject to the bishop of Bâle was entirely distinct from that subject to the city of Bâle.

her citizens and over the district of Erguel, so that she might become the capital of a fine territory. But the project failed and occasioned many calamities and a quarrel between Bienne and the bishop of Bâle. Finally (1610) the dispute was settled by Confederate arbitrators: Bienne, continuing to render homage to the bishop as prince of the country, was to form no new alliance without his consent and that of the Confederates; the bishop, retaining his rights over the city, was compelled again to confirm the franchises of Bienne and to permit the troops of Erguel to march under the banner of the city, in war, as before.

We should speak of many other disturbances and discords in those times; of the conspiracy of two Frenchmen, Du Terreil and La Basside, who wished to surprise the city of Geneva by treachery (1609) and deliver her to the duke of Savoy, but were betrayed and executed; of the troubles in Thurgau (1610) where drunken peasants at a wedding in Gachnang maltreated the signior Hector of Beroldingen, demolished his chapel, and stoned the bailiff's lieutenant, which occasioned so serious and wide-spread a dispute between the evangelical and catholic cantons, that the latter would no longer sit in Diet with the Zurichers, and both parties threatened war, until the successful intervention of the other Confederates. But greater and more terrible misfortunes claim our attention.

The plague broke out in Switzerland. This horrid disease was called the "black death." It came from distant countries to Bâle (1610), where it killed nearly four thousand persons. On the next year, it penetrated deeper into the land: to Berne and Solothurn and Freiburg. In Zurich, five thousand persons died; nearly two thousand in the country of Glarus; even more in Toggenburg and Appenzell. At Sarnen in Obwalden, two hundred and eighty bodies were buried in one grave. In Thurgau the black death depopulated whole villages, and the fields remained untilled, because there were no hands to cultivate them. When the dead were counted in Thurgau, the number was 33,584. Nearly one-fourth of the people were buried, everywhere.

The hand of the black death reached as far as the high

valleys of Grisons. But other scourges, the work of man himself, then desolated those valleys.

Since the king of Spain had become master of Milan and of Lombardy, he had secretly tried to obtain also Valtelina, a country subject to Grisons, that he might border on Austria by Tyrol. For Austria was the best ally of Spain, and could send no aid to Milan except through the territory of Venice or Grisons. Therefore the governor of Milan, following his king's instructions, constantly interfered in the affairs of Valtelina, where many disputes existed among the people, especially on matters of religion. For since Grisons (1552) had allowed to the Valteliners the free exercise of the evangelical worship, the inhabitants of many communes had adopted it, and there was enmity against them on the part of the catholics.

The king of France, being inimical to Austria and Spain, warned the Grisons of the designs of Spain. The republic of Venice, which feared the union of the Austrian and Spanish forces, did the same. Venice, as well as France and Spain, sent embassadors to Grisons, to gain the chiefs and principal men by promises and presents. This gratified the lords; some of them were interested for France, others for Spain, few for their own country. At the head of the Spanish party was Rudolf Planta; at the head of the French, Hercules of Salis. The former, in the beginning, had the power and most of the catholic communes on his side. The Spanish governor of Milan built a fortress on a hill by the lake of Como, and called it Fuentes, from his own name (1604). Thence he looked far into the valleys of Chiavemra and Valtelina; he thus held in his hand the key of the principal Grison pass.*

This terrified the Grison people and occasioned much excitement. Each party blamed the other. The communes raised their banners and established a criminal court at Coire, to try the traitors. As happens in popular disturbances, the innocent and guilty were imprisoned, banished and stripped of their property; George Beeli, the

* The pass of the Splugenberg. The road over the Bernardin, the other important pass from the Grison territory into Italy, was construoted more recently.

Austrian bailiff at Castels, and Caspar Baselga, formerly captain for the prince-bishop at Furstenberg, were beheaded on the common place of execution in the city of Coire (1607). They had served the Spaniards more faithfully than their fatherland. The Confederacy asked in vain for their lives. Beeli acknowledged his guilt on the scaffold and said: "The citizen of a free country ceases to be a freeman, when he attaches much value to the favor of foreign princes!"

A new criminal court at Ilanz shortly afterwards mitigated many of the sentences. But party hate was not mitigated. Spanish and French gold fomented it. One recruited in favor of Venice and France, another in favor of Milan. Each wished for vengeance, for foreign pensions and presents, and to become great. New tribunals were assembled, new injustices committed, new enmities excited; at last the Spanish, as well as the Venetian, alliance was rejected. Finally, communes stood against communes, brothers against brothers. In the valley of Engadine, the divided people marched with arms into the field; at the head of the Spanish party was Augustin Travers, Rudolf Planta's brother-in-law; at the head of the Venetian party, Anthony Travers, Augustin's brother. Some men were already killed on both sides by cannon shot, when the wives and sisters rushed wailing between their brothers and husbands, and pacified the raging combatants.

But the flame thus quenched by the love of tender women was soon rekindled by the fanaticism of hard-hearted priests. At Bergun, in a wild mountain-valley among glaciers, the evangelical clergy of the country assembled for church business (1618). Some of them said that the governor of Milan had sent large sums into the land to procure the acceptance of the Spanish treaty, and that, if he did not succeed, he meant to excite a rebellion in Valtelina, that he might overwhelm all the evangelicals in one fearful pool of blood.

When this was reported through the country, the frightened people rose; first in Engadine, whence Rudolf Planta was compelled to flee into Tyrol. A reformed pastor, George Jenatsch, marched against him with an armed force from Samaden. A criminal court was assembled at Thusis, and conducted with great cruelty by reformed pastors. Rudolf Planta was there declared an outlaw, as was his brother Pompey. There John Flugi, bishop of Coire, who had fled, was sentenced to lose property and life; Augustin Travers was banished in perpetuity; many others were proscribed and punished; most severely Nicholas Rusca, arch-priest of Badano and Valtelina, and John Baptist Prevost, surnamed Zambra, landammann of Pregall. Rusca, a pious catholic priest, although on the rack he steadfastly asserted his innocence of any Spanish conspiracy, died in prison, poisoned, as was said. His body was buried by the executioner. And the landammann Zambra, an infirm old man of seventy-four, was beheaded with the sword, because he acknowledged, under torture, that he had received pay and presents from Spain as well as from France.

The blood of Zambra and Rusca cried to Heaven. Now came days of terror and lamentation over Rhetia. Woe to the people who pretend to execute justice with arms in their hands!

CHAPTER XXXVIII.

TERRIBLE DESTRUCTION OF PLURS. MASSACRE IN VALTELINA. CIVIL WAR AMONG THE GRISONS.

[A. D. 1618 to 1621.]

NATURAL calamities preceded those which the passions of men soon occasioned.

In the valley of Chiavenna, which Grisons governed by bailiffs, as she did Valtelina and Bormio, at the foot of the mountain of Conto, lay the rich town of Plurs, with many churches, palaces and pleasure-gardens, like a beautiful city. Many trades were there pursued, and, among other things, more than twenty thousand pounds of silk were manufactured there yearly.

But it happened that, on the 4th of September, 1618,

after many days of heavy rain, a portion of the soil of mount Conto slid and covered several vineyards. The shepherds hastened to Plurs to warn the inhabitants, and said: "The mountain has shown large cracks for many years; the cows often run from it with loud lowings." Others came and said: "In the neighboring villages, the bees have deserted their hives in swarms, and have fallen dead from the air to the ground." The people of Plurs did not regard these warnings.

Suddenly, at nightfall, the earth resounded dismally and to a great distance. Then ensued the silence of death. The bed of the Maira was dry for two hours. When the morning came, the sky was seen to be wonderfully obscured by dust and vapor. The rich town of Plurs and the village of Cilano were buried beneath the fallen summit of mount Conto. Heaps of rocks are piled hundreds of feet above the dwellings, and form a vast tomb, in which lie the bodies of twenty-five hundred victims.

This filled neighboring Valtelina with horror. But men quickly forgot the misfortunes of their fellows; sedition and the desire to avenge the death of pious priest Rusca, soon displaced all their feelings. The whole of the Grison country, likewise, shuddered at the destruction of Plurs. But party-hate forgot it as quickly. Here, the relatives of the unfortunates condemned by the tribunal of Thusis, cried for vengeance against the injustice of the French party; there, the catholic communes loudly accused the reformed with wishing to extirpate the ancient faith from the mountains of their fatherland; the banished called for assistance to the Confederates, to the house of Austria and to the Spaniards in Milan.

Many of the Grey league, especially the Lugnetzers, once more raised their banners and marched upon Coire, to obtain justice; the Engadiners, Brettigauers and others of the French party, stood in arms against them. When they came hand to hand, and some had been slain, the people of the other high-jurisdictions forcibly intervened and instituted at Coire an impartial tribunal (June, 1619), which mitigated the severe sentences of Thusis, and recalled the banished of Planta's party.

This moderation again embittered the people of Engadine, Munsterthal and Davos. They marched once more with their banners to Coire, and declared the sentences of the court void. In vain did Thomas of Schauenstein, baron of Haldestein, go amicably to their camp, exhort them to abstain from violence, and propose: "That, to pacify the country, the chiefs of both the Planta and of the Salis parties should be excluded from all offices for twenty or thirty years." This pleased no one. The armed men decided rather to expel from the country the embassadors of foreign powers, as the authors of all the troubles. They drove away the judges at Coire, as well as their troops entrenched near Reichenau, and established a new criminal court at Davos. The sentences of Coire were not only confirmed, but even aggravated, and the recently-returned exiles were again banished. Here, as at Thusis, it was the reformed ecclesiastics who principally instigated this pernicious severity.

Thereat the banished brothers, Rudolf and Pompey Planta, went to the archduke of Austria to invite an armed invasion of their country. They enlisted unemployed soldiers in Etschland; and their brother-in-law, Jacob Robustelli, stirred up the Valteliners, and got under his banners many vagabonds from the Milanese.

In the night of 19th July, 1620, Jacob Robustelli, with his bloodthirsty hordes, descended into the valley of Valtelina. There the conspiracy for the murderous destruction of all the reformed in the country was ripe. The village of Tirano, chief place of the valley, was silently surrounded. Four musket-shots gave the signal. The massacre began. The tocsins howled. From village to village, the reformed were beaten down, strangled, shot, stoned to death, and their bodies thrown into the waves of the Adda. Neither women, nor infants, nor old men were spared. Some had their noses, their ears, their cheeks cut away; the bowels of some were torn out; gunpowder was forced into the throats of others and fired. A butcher boasted that he had killed eighteen persons. The head of the reformed pastor of Tirano was stuck on a pike and placed in his pulpit. No sacred thing remained unprofaned.

After several days of massacre, Jacob Robustelli assumed the chief command in Valtelina; Bormio united with him; Chiavenna, alone, remained faithful to the Grisons. But the latter, divided among themselves, were still more so after these doings. The catholic communes of the Grey league, persuaded by their priests and the heads of the Spanish party, refused to send troops against the insurgents in Valtelina. On the other hand, from several high-jurisdictions of the leagues of God's-house and the Ten Jurisdictions, nearly two thousand men passed the mountains under command of Ulysses Salis, Hercules' son, and John Guler. While these were advancing, the Plantas led Austrian troops, under General Baldiron, from Tyrol into the Grison district of Munsterthal, and threatened to keep possession until the exiles were recalled; and over Chiavenna came Milanese soldiers in aid of the Valteliners. The Grison troops, already in possession of half of Valtelina, were compelled to retire before superior forces and await the assistance of the Confederates, which had been called for.

But as the Grisons, so were the Swiss divided. When Berne sent general Nicholas of Mullinen with two thousand men towards Rhetia, the catholic cantons closed the way against him, near Mellingen in Aargau. By a circuit, he reached Zurich, where colonel Jacob Steiner joined him with a thousand men. When they wished to cross the March, the Schwyzers rose in a body against them. By another circuit they reached Grisons. Thence, united with the Grison troops, they marched upon Bormio and arrived victorious at Tirano; but the catholic banners of the Grey league would not go with them. Before Tirano they had a bloody fight with the Spanish troops and the Valteliner insurgents (11th Sept., 1620). There the valiant Nicholas of Mullinen died the death of a hero, and all the Bernese officers, excepting one, fell with him under the walls of Tirano. Fluri Sprecher, one of the Grison colonels, also fell, as did many others. But Tirano remained unconquered. And as the powder, lead and matches of the army began to fail, it marched back over the mountains into Grisons.

Here Pompey Planta had in the mean while put in movement the Grey league, for the protection of which fifteen hundred men had come from the catholic cantons under lead of colonel John Conrad Beroldingen of Uri, and encamped near Reichenau, two leagues from Coire. They talked of making the Grey league a fourteenth canton of the Confederacy, of giving Valtelina to it alone and separating it from the rest of Grisons. Such a rupture of old friendly relations greatly disturbed all well-meaning people. They unitedly demanded a reconciliation, obtained the recall of the foreign embassadors who had been expelled, and even submission to the Confederates. But the French embassador, when he came again into the country, renewed his former intrigues and made a party for France. The Spanish governor of Milan, on his side, sent emissaries with gold, to stir up the great lords and the communes against France. The papal nuncio, also, excited the catholic communes against the evangelical. The deputies of the Confederates, instead of restoring peace, quarrelled bitterly among themselves, so that they returned home without settling any thing. The Bernese army followed them.

Thereat discord and hatred increased in the land. George Jenatsch, formerly a reformed pastor, now a man of war, with some soldiers, surprised Pompey Planta in the castle of Rietberg and slew him. Then he assembled the banners of Engadine, Bergun and Munsterthal, with them vanquished the troops of the catholic cantons in the Grey league, and after a seven hours' fight, drove them over the mountains back into Uri (11th April, 1621). With defeated Conrad Beroldingen fled also the abbot of Disentis, Sebastian of Castelberg, conscience-stricken on account of the Valtelina massacre. The Grey league, surprised and overpowered, was compelled to give up its alliance with Milan.

Fresh negotiations were opened with Spain and Austria for the restitution of Valtelina. But neither Spain nor Austria was in earnest. They wished to hold Valtelina, Chiavenna and Bormio, and even Lower Engadine in addition, that they might always in future have an open communication between Tyrol and Milan, for mutual help against the French. At last the people of several communes, wearied by these lengthened negotiations, seized their arms in wild disorder, and marched against Bormio and Valtelina, to subdue the country by their own power. They did not succeed, and, beaten by the Spaniards, returned home again with loss and shame.

This ill-advised expedition of the people, undertaken while their deputies were still negotiating with the archduke of Austria, greatly excited the anger of this prince. "Since you wish for war, you shall have war!" said he, and ordered his troops to march against Grisons.

CHAPTER XXXIX.

THE GRISONS ARE BROUGHT UNDER THE AUSTRIAN YOKE.

[A. D. 1621 to 1630.]

On an autumn-day (1621) powerful forces penetrated from all sides into the land of the Grisons. Over the mountains and through the valleys of Tyrol came many thousands of Austrians, whom Rudolf Planta guided into his own fatherland. The imperial general Baldiron put to the sword all who opposed him; slaying and burning, he subjugated the whole league of the Ten jurisdictions, disarmed the people, and compelled them, surrounded by his troops, to swear fealty to the house of Austria on their knees. With more than seven thousand Spaniards and foreigners, the duke of Feria came over from Italy, drove out the valiant garrison at Chiavenna, and took possession of the country. When the soldiers of Zurich, who were posted near Maienfeld, saw this overpowering force, they went home.

Then general Baldiron practised unprecedented cruelties in the league of the Ten jurisdictions. He was called the new Holofernes. No life or property remained safe from his soldiers. The peasants were treated like cattle. An imperial ensign rode up a mountain on the back of a respectable countryman, whom a soldier drove from behind. "This is the way to tame these wild peasants!" said the ensign. Many capuchins came with the troops, and tried to make the people catholics. The reformed clergy were ejected by the soldiers. Seventy-five churches were soon without pastors. The bishop of Coire was greatly pleased thereat.

Then said the valiant people in Brettigau, when the soldiers tried to force them to attend the worship of the capuchins: "This is too much! If we must lose our country and our liberty, let us at least save our souls!" And they fled into the woods, which became their arsenals. There they cut clubs, into which they drove large nails; of their knives they made daggers, of their scythes spears. Then, on Palm Sunday (1622) they rushed forth with loud shouts, surprised the garrison and camp of the Austrians, and slew about four hundred men, took many prisoners, and drove the rest out of the land. They marched in force to the city of Maienfeld and besieged the Austrians who had taken refuge there. They also besieged Baldiron with his Spaniards and Austrians in Coire. At the success of the valiant Brettigauers, all the Grisons of the Ten juris dictions boldly rose, with warlike Rudolf of Salis, landammann Peter Guler of Davos, and Thuring Enderli of Maienfeld at their head. To them hastened the friends of liberty from the rest of Grisons and from Switzerland, especially the valiant Appenzellers. Other Swiss sent money. Baldiron retired with shame. The Grisons said to the Diet of the Confederates: "Stand by us, when the enemy returns!" But the Confederates, as usual, quarrelled among themselves and sent no help.

Cruel Baldiron did in fact return with fresh forces (July, 1622). He led ten thousand soldiers over the mountains. Old men, women and children were massacred by the furious enemy. There was fighting in the valleys, there was fighting above the clouds on the highest Alps. But the overpowering forces of the enemy conquered. The last combat took place (5 Sept.) in Brettigau itself, near Raschnals, on Aquasana plain. Here, when after a bloody fight, the little troop of Grisons was broken and yielded, thirty men of Brettigau stood firm; unwilling to survive their country's precious liberty, they devoted themselves to a glorious death. They raised their clubs, with bowed heads they rushed impetuously into the ranks of the Austrians, fought terribly in the thick crowd and fell, man after man, like heroes, surrounded by the bodies of numerous enemies. The banners of the city of Coire and of the Grey league arrived too late to help. When from a distance they saw the flames of so many villages and that all was lost, they sadly turned away.

Woe to the conquered! Now they suffered the greatest misery. Now were they pillaged, robbed and murdered. The soldiers put trembling old men to the sword, outraged the women, and when there was nothing more to plunder, carried off and sold even the bells of the churches. Many hundred unfortunates wandered away; many hundreds died of starvation and of the Hungarian plague. This was a fatal pain in the head.

The God's-house and Grey leagues sent supplicating messengers to the plenipotentiary of the Archduke of Austria, at Lindau (Sept). The Confederates also, moved by compassion, interceded. But the Archduke obstinately persisted in his determination: The Ten-jurisdictions must be subject to his ducal house, and the two other Leagues must always allow a passage to the Austrians and Spaniards. The catholic Confederates, well pleased in their hearts, aggravated by their reproaches the misfortunes of the Grisons and said: "We have often warned you." But the burgomaster of Zurich, John Henry Holzhalb, said: "Dear allies, place no reliance on any help from us at present. We have too much to do at home. We see that you must undergo a great deal. Our Lord God will send you better help in time. For the present, do your best to save your country from utter destruction."

When the Grisons saw that they were deserted by the Confederates, they resigned themselves to drink the bitter cup. Eight jurisdictions and Lower Engadine were separated from the Rhetian league and became completely subject to Austria. There was great suffering. The disorders of the soldiery, the violence of the Austrian officers, the encroachments of the bishop of Coire were unrestrained.

Then God touched the heart of the king of France. He made a treaty (1623) with the pope, with Venice and Savoy. He could not allow the Austrians always to have a free passage over the Grison Alps, and thus to become all-powerful in Italy. When the emperor at Vienna and the king of Spain heard of the preparations of France, they at once accepted the proposition of the pope that he should provisorily occupy and hold Valtelina, Chiavenna and Bormio, until the settlement of matters between the kings. And this was done.

But the king of France, not pleased with this, sent his troops through Switzerland to Grisons (1624). Berne and Zurich gave him passage. All the exiled Grisons formed the vanguard of the army. The hero Rudolf of Salis led them, with valiant colonel George Jenatsch and many others. Zurich also sent troops under colonel Caspar Schmied; as did Berne, under brave Nicholas of Diesbach. The bands of Valais came likewise. When all these drew near, the whole of Grisons rose joyfully in arms. The garrisons of Austria and their cruel officers were driven from the Ten-jurisdictions by the united forces (1625); Chiavenna, Bormio and Valtelina were reconquered.

As soon as the league of the Ten-jurisdictions was reünited to the others, the Rhetians expected that their French auxiliaries would restore to them all their subject countries. But the French general the count of Coeuvres said: "Not so! Valtelina, Chiavenna and Bormio shall pay to you an annual tribute of 25,000 crowns; but, in return, these countries shall choose their own magistrates; you shall not send to them either governors or garrisons."

The Grisons were aggrieved at this, and still more so when the kings of France and Spain made a peace at Monzona in Arragon (5 March, 1626) and solemnly confirmed nearly all that the count of Coeuvres had said The treaty of Monzona was executed in full. The foreign troops left Grisons, and, for security, the pope's soldiers occupied Valtelina (1627). The emperor in Germany having a good understanding with Spain, was quiet for the time.

However, as soon as Spain and France broke their peace, and began a fresh war in Italy, the emperor marched a force of forty thousand men into the Grison country, so suddenly that no resistance was possible (1629). A part of the troops went to help the Spaniards in Lombardy; the rest subjected the Grisons in their own country. The Ten-jurisdictions again became subject to Austria; Lower Engadine the same. The emperor's sword was law to the whole of Grisons.

Such was the misery of the people at this time, that all hope of better days was lost. The passages and cantonments of foreign troops increased from day to day; barns and stables were emptied. The peasants had to build fortifications for the soldiers. Pestilential diseases spread, so that nearly twelve thousand men died thereof. Then came the bishop of Coire and added to their misery by compelling all who had formerly been subject and tributary to his bishopric, again to become subject and tributary, in perpetuity. There was no justice, no mercy.

CHAPTER XL.

THE GRISONS RECOVER THEIR LIBERTY.

[A. D. 1630 to 1640.]

BUT so long as a people do not lose their desire for freedom, and faith in themselves, nothing is irretrievably lost. Then God always sends a day of salvation. Such was the experience of the men in the Grison country.

When all were bowed under misery and oppression, the emperor made peace with the French at Cherasco in Italy (June, 1630), and agreed to withdraw his garrisons from the Grison valleys. The emperor, at this time, was sore pressed by war in Germany, and the great Swedish king, Gustavus Adolphus, had crossed the sea against him with his army.

As soon as the Austrians left the Leagues, and their

fortresses had been blown up, all the people joyfully renewed their oath to the ancient compact for liberty, and stationed six thousand men under arms to defend the frontiers of their fatherland. And as, at the same time, there came to Coire the renowned warrior, duke Henry of Rohan, embassador from the king of France to the Confederates and Grisons, they made him their general (1631), and gave him great power. He was a wise and loyal as well as a valiant lord, who loved the free Grisons. He fortified all the defiles towards Germany and Tyrol, brought a reinforcement of French troops into the country (1632), and put every thing on the best footing. While his king was at peace with the emperor, he could not, as the Grisons wished, enter Valtelina with an armed force. Thus passed nearly three years.

When France finally joined Sweden against the emperor, and a fresh war broke out, the French king notified the duke of Rohan that he need no longer delay to gratify the wishes of the Grisons. Rohan secretly opened negotiations with the evangelical cantons, Berne, Bâle and Zurich. Having an understanding with them, he brought a strong force through their territories, to the great displeasure of the catholic cantons, and from Grisons marched over the Alps into Valtelina (1635). The whole of the Grison country resounded with arms. Six thousand valiant men marched with the French to the conquest of the subject territory. Colonels George Jenatsch, Florin and Peter Guler raised three fresh troops in the pay of France.

Then bloody and terrible battles were fought with the Austrians and Spaniards in the valleys of Chiavenna, in savage Freelthal, near Morbegno in Valtelina, and near Mazzo in Bormio. Everywhere Rohan and the bold warrior Jenatsch were in advance, everywhere victorious.

After the conquest was completed, the Grisons hoped, from one day to another, to reënter into possession of the territory formerly subject to them. But the king of France still made difficulties, and wished every thing to remain as arranged at the peace of Monzona. The Grisons were very indignant at this. But France was too powerful for them, and they were compelled to be silent. Many and fruitless negotiations took place; the people were harassed by the cantonment of French soldiers, but could do nothing. Almost all that Rohan had promised remained unfulfilled, but not by his fault. He was powerless against the orders of his king, who had sent Lanier, as his envoy, to Coire. Now Lanier was a haughty, irascible man. When most of the Grison troops in the pay of France threatened to quit the king's service because they were not punctually paid, Lanier cried out angrily: "I will plant my spear in Coire, and set my foot on the necks of the mutinous leaders!"

Then the Grisons came together and said: "Austria has oppressed us; France has deceived us. Let us trust no foreign power."

And, on the 6th of February, 1637, thirty-one of the principal men of the whole republic met at the house of burgomaster George Meier in Coire, and swore to risk life and property in order to free their fatherland from the foreign yoke. Then they went into all the valleys and made the necessary preparations with the greatest unanimity.

Colonel Jenatsch was to negotiate with Austria at Innspruch, for the reëstablishment of the ancient friendly relations, but at the same time to keep the duke of Rohan quiet and unsuspicious by manifestations of great friendship. The Grisons armed. There were then but few French troops in the land. The Zuricher colonel, Caspar Schmied, was still, however, stationed near Luziensteig. But the Grisons had already sent to Zurich, so that he received orders, at least not to oppose them.

The duke of Rohan noticed the agitation and secret arming. He strengthened his garrison in the Rhine-fortress on the Landquart (near Pfeffers). Then came Jenatsch and successfully combatted his suspicions. Suddenly the whole people rose in the mountains. Jenatsch with six battalions of his countrymen surrounded the French in the Rhine-fortress. By agreement with Grisons, a German force appeared in a threatening attitude near Lindau; a Spanish on the lake of Como. Rohan, surprised on all sides, was obliged to consent to withdraw his troops at once from Grisons and Valtelina. He also answered for marshal Lecques and all the French, who were five thousand strong. So they went over the Rhine, out of the Grison territory. Duke Rohan took a friendly leave of the chiefs of the republic (May, 1637), as did marshal Lecques. When the latter, however, on his departure, saw colonel Jenatsch, growing pale with anger, he aimed a pistol at him and cried: "Thus I take my leave of a traitor!" But the pistol missed fire.

Jenatsch did not lose his life till two years afterwards, when he was enjoying himself with other colonels and officers at an entertainment in Coire. About midnight (January 14, 1639) Rudolf Planta, Pompey's son, with other conspirators, entered the ball-room. A bullet passed through the colonel's cheek; he defended himself with a candlestick. Six blows of a hatchet deprived him of life. His body was interred in the cathedral with military honors. This was the end of a man who loved and saved his country, but was not ashamed to employ therefor the most dishonorable means. Rudolf Planta, his murderer, died a violent death a year afterwards, during a popular tumult in Engadine.

After the Grisons were by these means freed from foreign power and again masters of their subject territory, they sent envoys to the kings of Spain and France to request that they might hold their conquests in peace. At Milan (September 3, 1639) a perpetual peace was negotiated and concluded between the Spaniards and Grisons, and the Grison sovereignty in Bormio, Valtelina and Chiavenna was completely acknowledged, but on condition that the catholic church should remain alone dominant in these bailiwicks. Such was also the wish of the catholic communes in Grisons.

Friendly relations were reëstablished with the ducal house of Austria by the renewal of the ancient treaties (at Feldkirch, August 9, 1641). Austria was overburdened with war in Germany, and was glad to retain her former rights in Engadine and the Ten-jurisdictions. But, before ten years had elapsed, the communes of this League purchased all the rights of the duke over them at a great price. So did the communes of Lower Engadine. Thus, from this time, Austria retained nothing but a few signioral rights at Rhezuns and Tarasp.

By these means the league of the Ten-jurisdictions became free and independent, like the two others in the Rhetian highlands. Davos remained, as formerly, the chief place of the League, although the other high-jurisdictions, incited by colonel Peter Guler and other leaders, made so violent an opposition to this that Zurich, Berne, and Glarus had to interfere to prevent misfortune. By the decision of the recorder of Zurich, John Henry Wasser (January 11, 1644), Davos retained most of her ancient honors: the assembling of the diet, the guardianship of the banner and archives of the League, and the right to name the banneret, subject to the League's approval.

CHAPTER XLI.

OF THE TROUBLES AMONG THE CONFEDERATES DURING THE THIRTY YEARS' RELIGIOUS WAR IN GERMANY, AND HOW SWITZERLAND'S INDEPENDENCE OF THE GERMAN EMPIRE WAS ESTABLISHED.

[A. D. 1618 to 1648.]

THE negotiations and warlike movements about the Grison territory had occasioned much anxiety in the cities and communes of Switzerland, much talk in diets and councils, much expense for embassies and armaments, but no Confederate achievement by which the freedom and independence of the Rhetian highlands or the ancient glory of Switzerland were upheld. This resulted from the fact that the Confederate cantons lived in no less discord among themselves than did the Grisons. When the reformed cantons wished to aid, the catholics opposed. When the catholics wished to do anything, the reformed withstood them. Those held with Spain and Austria, these with France and Venice. One party received money from the former, the other from the latter, and each made treaties and furnished troops to the foreign power which it favored. This made a few lords in the land rich, many families poor and destitute.

In the common bailiwicks, where the catholic and reformed cantons shared the government, they quarrelled as before. Although, according to agreement, both religious parties had equal rights in the bailiwicks, the catholic were harassed by the reformed bailiffs, the reformed by the catholic. In Thurgau and Rheinthal, the sovereign cantons disputed: as to whether the majority of votes should decide in religious as well as in civil matters. The ecclesiastical lords, as usual, took part in the quarrel to embitter it. The bishop of Bâle, sustained by the emperor, so long as the latter was victorious in the German war, required Muhlhausen and Bâle to restore to his see the property which it had lost long before. The abbot of St. Gallen claimed in Thurgau and Rheinthal more rights than justly belonged to him; the abbot of Einsiedeln attempted to make the foresters of Schwyz tributary to him; the abbot of Fischingen wished to build a catholic altar in the reformed church at Lastorf. These ecclesiastical lords always found supporters as well as opponents. And, more than once, Swiss stood ready to draw the fratricidal sword against Swiss, in civil war. The fear of foreign powers alone restrained them.

At this period a long and terrible war desolated Germany. It began, between catholics and protestants, in Bohemia (1618), then spread over Germany, and, finally, drew Sweden and Italy, Spain, Hungary and France, into one common misfortune. It was begun for religious matters, it was continued for the acquisition of crowns and lands. Therefore, sometimes the Venetians and French, sometimes the Spaniards and Austrians, earnestly endeavored to secure the assistance of the Confederates, or a passage across the Grison mountains.

The armies of the contending powers, as they followed each other on German soil from battle-field to battle-field, often approached close to the frontiers of the Confederates But the latter, conscious of their division and weakness, wished not to see the foreign sword in their valleys, adding to the calamities they already endured. Therefore they prudently maintained their neutrality in all foreign warfare and the inviolability of the Swiss soil. But so great was the continued discord among themselves that they often hindered the legitimate defence of their territory and of their allies.

Thus, for instance, when Muhlhausen was in danger from the passage of Swedish and imperial troops, Zurich and Berne sent soldiers to protect her (1632). But when the Bernese wished to cross by the defile of Solothurn, the guard barred the passage and sounded the tocsin. The bailiffs, Philip Roll of Bechburg and Ursus Brunner of Falkenstein, with captain Suri, surrounded the Bernese soldiers, shot, sabred and killed several, and disarmed all. Solothurn was obliged to suffer severely for this outrage: some of the perpetrators were punished by death, some by banishment; but hatred and distrust were not appeased.

On another occasion, when the Swedish general Horn (1633), to surprise the Austrian city of Constance, had passed with his force through the Zuricher city of Stein in Hegau, the catholic Confederates accused the reformed with favoring the Swedes to the prejudice of the emperor. Uri, Schwyz, Unterwalden and Zug, claiming an equal right on the emperor's side, sent three thousand men towards the lake of Constance. But Zurich armed at once and threatened to join the Swedes, if the catholic Confederates made common cause with the Austrians against them. Peace was preserved, but not without difficult arbitration.

As the Swedes had done at Stein, so, shortly afterwards, near Schaffhausen, did the imperialists violate the soil of Switzerland. Too late, feebly and without union, the people of Schaffhausen seized their arms, and some troops of Zurichers came into Thurgau to support them. The villages of Bargen, Altdorf, Beggingen, Barzheim and Schleitheim were partly pillaged, partly burnt by the soldiery. The vigorous peasants fought bravely against the foreign plunderers and killed many, while the frightened government of Schaffhausen exchanged polite notes with the imperial general.

Austrian soldiers and camp-followers more than once pillaged the territory of the city of Bâle, and laughed at the weak half-measures of the Confederates. As these could not cause their own territory to be respected, still less could they defend the territory of their allies from encroachment. They entirely abandoned Rothweil, an imperial city in Suabia, their ally, because she had received an Austrian garrison against the Swedes. And when the guaranteed neutrality of the free county of Upper Burgundy, as well as her hereditary union with Austria, was disregarded, sometimes by the French, sometimes by the Swedes, the Confederates opposed the enemy's arms, not with the sword, but with suppliant envoys and letters; it was the same when duke Bernard of Weimar encamped with the Swedes in the bishopric of Bâle (1638). He remained as long as he pleased, in spite of all remonstrances, and impoverished the already poor people.

It was indeed often said in the Diets that an army ought to be stationed on the frontiers to maintain the sacred rights of the Swiss soil, and to defend the honor of the fatherland, not with paper, but with arms. But central Switzerland said: "The frontier cantons may protect themselves." And others said: "The expenses of an army are too great." Each expected sacrifices from his Confederates, but no one was willing to make sacrifices himself. The old, magnanimous, Swiss, manly heart beat no longer. The envoys of foreign powers also interfered, as usual, either to command as masters, or to make parties. Even in the most just or the most trivial matters, the Confederates had not always courage enough to resist the overbearing spirit of the foreign embassadors. In 1642, when the French embassador was passing through Mellingen, a little city on the Reuss, and the people of his train had a quarrel with the burghers about the bridge-toll, so that the burghers seized their arms and closed the gates, the anger of the embassador was not appeased by the Diet's ordering the avoyer, recorder and toll-gatherer to go to Solothurn, ask his pardon on their knees and return the twelve batzen that had been paid; and the cowardly Diet went so far, at his demand, as to keep these men in prison at Baden, until he was satisfied.

In consequence of so many negotiations, quarrels and armaments, several of the governments wanted money, and imposed taxes and contributions. But when the council of Berne (1641) decreed a tax of one in the thousand on property, without stating how long it should last, the country-people were afraid it would be permanent. They complained loudly in Aargau and Emmenthal, and nothing could remove their mistrust. Thereat the council adopted severe measures, and caused some of the principal persons who opposed the tax to be seized. This occasioned such a rising of the people in Emmenthal, that the city of Berne was garrisoned, and troops sent to Thun, Burgdorf and Lenzburg. The malcontents held open council at Langnau. The disturbance was allayed by moderation, with the aid of deputies from the Confederate diet. The tax was paid. Berne promised a removal of each and all the abuses of which the people had complained.

Shortly afterwards (1645) disturbances also took place in the canton of Zurich respecting an extraordinary real-estate tax. Happily, by gentleness and prudence, the council of Zurich so calmed the insurgents, that they voluntarily begged pardon for their disobedience. Only in Knonau and Wadenschwyl did they remain obstinate, threaten an armed opposition, and fail in respect to their magistrates and officers. At once, these communes were occupied by troops and disarmed. Men, women and children were compelled to ask for mercy on their knees within a circle of soldiers. Seven ringleaders and authors of the revolt were executed with the sword. Wadenschwyl paid a fine of 26,163 guilders, Knonau 12,170. This was the result of the rebellion.

Many foreign vagabonds were at that time scattered through Switzerland. They came from Italy and Germany, desolated by the war.* Deserters and marauders excited the people against the magistracy, either to curry favor with the peasants, or to profit by disturbances.

* Such is the origin of the *heimathlosen* (homeless people, having no fixed abode and no claim upon any commune or canton), the presence and maintenance of whom have ever been a source of great trouble to Switzerland, always an asylum for refugees from other nations.

Idlers and strollers were so numerous, that in a single day (1639) one hundred were counted at Schwyz, and sixty-three hundred and seventy in the county of Baden. The country was unsafe on account of them, until very severe measures were adopted. At Bremgarten, two hundred and thirty-six malefactors suffered death in one single year. This so terrified the vagabonds that they all fled.

The peace which the great powers of Europe finally concluded, after the thirty years' war, was more serviceable to Switzerland than the sword of justice. While negotiations were going on in Westphalia, at Munster and Osnabruch, the Confederates also sent their embassador, John Rudolf Wettstein, burgomaster of Bâle. He managed the affairs of the Confederates like a firm and skilful man. And, as the Germans had always held the Swiss to be subjects of the German empire, and the imperial tribunal had pronounced sentences against Confederates instead of citing them before their own courts, burgomaster Wettstein declared the steadfast resolve of the whole Confederacy to maintain their complete independence of the empire. There the independence and self-sovereignty of the Swiss Confederacy was solemnly recognized and acknowledged by the emperor, kings and princes unitedly, in the Westphalian treaty of peace.

CHAPTER XLII.

HOW THE PEASANTS IN THE CANTONS OF LUCERNE, BERNE, SOLOTHURN AND BALE UNDERTAKE TO REVOLT, AND LOSE THEREBY.

[A. D. 1648 to 1655.]

THE magistrates in city and country were well pleased when the emperor no longer addressed them as "Beloved and faithful to ourselves and the empire," but styled them: "Strong, steadfast, honored and especially dear." And the Swiss might indeed have been called a happy people, had they been united among themselves. But the religious discord between catholics and reformed did not cease, and to this old trouble was added a new one.

In most of the cantons, great dissatisfaction prevailed among the country-people, who, in many valleys, were still serfs, or, at least, bore all the old burdens of servitude. Seeing that the people in Schwyz, Uri and Unterwalden were free, that they had no magistrates or laws but such as they themselves voted for, and paid no taxes or contributions but such as they themselves decreed, the peasants in other cantons lamented that they remained serfs and subject to the city-burghers, without hope of ransom; that they were compelled to pay taxes and contributions respecting which they had not been consulted; that obligations and laws were imposed upon them without reference to their wishes. But it was still more grievous that they were forced to yield servile obedience to avaricious governors and haughty bailiffs; that they were beaten, maltreated and imprisoned for the most trivial fault, or reduced to poverty by law-suits and arbitrary fines. Complaints against governors and nobles did little good, and often aggravated their sufferings; for relatives of the bailiffs usually formed part of the government. Even the recorders, under-bailiffs and constables, as they were all from the cities, thought they could, with impunity, harass any peasant who opposed their will. However, as the evil was not equally great everywhere, and there were many good and upright officers over the country, all remained quiet for a long while.

But when (August, 1652) the government of Berne, for the better regulation of their coinage, refused to receive the small change of other cantons, and reduced the value of their own batzen* by one half, general discontent was manifested. For he who thought he had ten batzen, found that he had but five; and the poor man suffered most, the rich man least. Thereat the people assembled in the villages, and, to the common grievance, each added his own special complaint: one against the bailiff, another against the constable; one against the government-trade in salt,

* In 1852, when the old Swiss money was called in, and a coinage identical with the French adopted, the batz was worth about three sous.

another against the same in gunpowder; one against the trades-corporations and the imposts, another against the labor-dues and the disregard of ancient rights. The more the people talked, the more excited they became.

Now it happened that the government of Lucerne, also, after the example of Berne, reduced the value of their batzen. Then the communes of Entlibuch sent deputies to the government and requested, either that the money should be taken for dues at its old value, or the products of the soil received in payment in lieu of money. But they were so harshly answered that they went back very sad. Thereat the country-people were angered, and when the collectors came among them, maltreated them and drove them away. On this, the avoyer Dulliker, with civil and ecclesiastical lords, went to Entlibuch (February, 1653) to bring the elders of the communes to reason. But the people came out from all the villages with spears and clubs: in front a white flag; then three young men who blew Alpine horns; then the leaders, and behind three others in the ancient Swiss costume, representing the men of Rutli; a great crowd, fourteen hundred strong, followed them. Thus they marched into the village where the envoys of the city were assembled. Then arose a great tumult, and cries against the depreciation of the coin, against the toll near Wollhausen, against the high interest on money, against the bailiffs' fines, against the arbitrary imposts on sales, and such things; and the people gave utterance to such threats and insults, that the envoys could do nothing with the excited multitude, but returned home to the city. The country-people held meetings; stationed guards; examined travellers; exhorted the neighboring subjects of Berne to make common cause with them; and the ten bailiwicks of the district made and swore to a league among themselves, at Wollhausen.

As the matter was becoming serious, the six catholic cantons sent deputies to mediate amicably. But when these deputies met at Willisau with the delegates of the ten bailiwicks, who had put in writing twenty-seven causes of complaint, the assembled peasants renewed their tumult and even seized the deputies, set a guard over them, occupied the main passes to the city and threatened to attack Lucerne. Immediately, four hundred men marched from the small cantons to garrison and defend the city. Zurich and Berne armed. When the country-people in the ten bailiwicks heard this, their courage failed them; they released the imprisoned deputies and besought them to mediate. The deputies did so justly, and pronounced this sentence (19th March): "The government shall retain its sovereignty and the people their rights; the imposts on sales shall be equalized throughout the whole land; the avoyer of Willisau shall be chosen from among its burghers alone; there shall be no appeal from Entlibuch to Lucerne in matters under one hundred guilders; the league of the ten bailiwicks at Wollhausen is annulled; no such league can hereafter be allowed under severe penalties, but no damages shall be required from the country for the expenses of the present difficulty."

When all was thought to be settled, the storm broke forth anew in the canton of Berne, from Thun as far as the city of Brugg. For when the government here had wished to send troops against the peasants in the canton of Lucerne, the people said: "No! we will not march against our brothers; we have as good cause of complaint as they." In all the villages, tumults, uproar and disorder prevailed. No one wished to obey, every one to command. The cities of Thun, Aarburg, Zofingen, Aarau, Brugg and Lenzburg alone remained quiet; the clergy in the country were also faithful to the government.

Berne at once called for Confederate assistance to put down the revolt. Schaffhausen, Bâle and Muhlhausen immediately sent troops. But Zurich and Lucerne advised an amicable settlement. The government of Berne was at last inclined to this. However, before the parties could come to an understanding, the troops of Schaffhausen had already entered the country in the neighborhood of Brugg, those of Bâle and Muhlhausen near Aarau. This enraged the people in Aargau and they rose in a body (18th March, 1653) throughout the whole county of Lenzburg. Thereat the Schaffhausen troops retreated, and those of Bâle and Muhlhausen retired from Aarau to the left bank of the

Aar into the bailiwicks of Biberstein and Schenkenburg. But here the people rose also as far as into the territory of Solothurn, so that the men of Bâle and Muhlhausen were compelled to return home. At Erlisbach, the country-people of Solothurn and Aargau stood in arms; between their ranks, as through a street, the troops of Bâle and Muhlhausen marched back to their own country.

Then the tumult increased. The peasants held general assemblies at Langenthal, besieged the castles of the bailiffs, sent deputies to the government at Berne and even applied secretly to the French embassador, La Barde, for foreign assistance. This was a great mistake. For the French embassador betrayed them, and many well-intentioned persons abandoned their cause, because they had asked for foreign interference in the affairs of their fatherland.

In the mean while, deputies from six reformed cantons appeared at Berne, to terminate peacefully the quarrel between magistrates and subjects. The delegates of the communes came also, and it was agreed: "That the salt-trade belongs to the government; to the subjects, the right to purchase salt for their own consumption freely, wherever they please; the duty on sales and the obligation to enter a trades-corporation cease; the batzen remain at the value last determined, but the capital and interest of debts shall be reckoned no higher than in 1613; money lent on sufficient security and at fair interest shall not be reclaimed under six years; the fees of the constables shall be diminished." When these and other matters were thus equitably agreed upon, the delegates of the communes knelt before the council of the city of Berne to ask for pardon, and everything seemed well settled.

But the country-people in the canton of Lucerne again made a disturbance on their side, complained of the sentence which had been rendered and said: "We cannot see any such wrong in our league at Wollhausen, as the sentence declares." And they sent messengers to the subjects of other cantons saying: "We wish to be no longer slaves of the cities, but free people, as are those in the small cantons." The people in Aargau and in Emmenthal joined their voices to theirs. They blamed the delegates who had knelt before the seated council at Berne and accepted the agreement. Even in the cantons of Solothurn and Bâle, many of the country-people were excited and joined those of Lucerne, Emmenthal and Aargau. They held a general assembly at Sumiswald (13th April, 1653) and chose Nicholas Leuenberger, a countryman of Schœnholz, to be their leader and chief of the leaguers of the four cantons of Lucerne, Berne, Solothurn and Bâle. They decreed: "The people shall respect the rights of the magistrates, and the magistrates the rights of the people; no subject shall take arms against the governments, but if the latter send troops, they shall be repelled by force." They invited the subjects of all the Confederates, in writing, to meet at Hutwyl on a certain day, for the discussion of the rights and liberties of all, and the formation of a people's-league in opposition to the master's-league, that all Swiss might be free Swiss. This displeased the masters in the cities. An important and decisive moment was at hand.

As, formerly, the counts and signiors had freed themselves from the emperors and acquired an hereditary dominion over their districts; as, afterwards, the larger cities of Switzerland, favored by fortune and circumstances, had enfranchised themselves from the dominion of the counts and signiors by purchase or by force of arms; so, now, the subject country-people wished to reduce the power of the cities and to become free. But their enterprise was not well calculated.

In fact, these tumultuous hordes did not bring to their work either the pious loyalty or firm union anciently manifested by the men of the Waldstatten, or the prudence and considerate strength exercised by the cities. They were rude, ignorant people, without experience in civil concerns, badly taught, distrusting one another, each thinking more of his own advantage than of the common good. They listened more willingly to the cries of violent men than to the counsels of the wise; all wished to command, none to obey. Therefore they were at variance among themselves, and ready for all excesses. They maltreated all who were not of their opinion. Some they threatened with fire and sword; some they mutilated.

In the mean while, the cities armed to put down the rebels, but opened negotiations in order to gain time. Berne, as well as the Diet at Baden, was more frank with the people. Many conferences were appointed or held with the delegates of the insurgents; but with such disorderly bands, each of whom contradicted the other and changed its mind every day, no business could be brought to a conclusion.

After all attempts at conciliation had proved vain, the Vorort, Zurich, ordered the whole Confederacy to arm (11th May, 1653). Berne assembled the troops of Vaud, which, in consequence of the difference of language, had remained foreign to the affairs of her German subjects, and named Sigismund of Erlach as her general. He had about ten thousand men. About five thousand came from the catholic cantons, led by colonel Zweier; the other Confederates, eight thousand in all, were commanded by general Wertmuller of Zurich. The free country-people of the small cantons held true to the cities, and adopted their cause against the insurgents, partly from love of justice and neighborly friendship, and partly because they themselves had subjects, whose rebellion or freedom they did not desire. They garrisoned and protected Lucerne.

The insurgents were as prompt to arm. They occupied the defile near Gumminen towards Vaud, those near Windisch and Mellingen towards Zurich. They assaulted Aarburg and Aarau, Zofingen and Lenzburg, but without success. For they had no heavy artillery nor a sufficiency of other arms, nor discipline among themselves, nor experienced leaders, because until then all officers had been taken from among the burghers of the cities.

As soon as Leuenberger, the chief of the leagued peasants, and Schybi and Ulli Galli and other leaders of the revolt, saw that there was a serious opposition, they tried to ensure the success of their perilous undertaking by boldness and by new negotiations. Leuenberger, who was encamped a league from Berne-city at Ostermundigen, where his soldiers robbed and plundered the neighborhood, wrote once more to Berne for an amicable settlement of the dispute. The city-council, to avoid effusion of blood and to gain time, sent deputies to the rebels; conceded many things and even to pay 50,000 livres to the country-people, not, however, as a compensation for their war-expenses, but as a relief to their poor. The delegates of the peasants finally subscribed the before rejected agreement, and promised submission and fealty. But hardly had they reached their camp, when all was again nullified. For, as the Confederates were advancing, the rebels refused to disperse until all the troops had returned to their homes.

In the mean while, Wertmuller and Zweier, with united forces, marched over the Heitersberg as far as Mellingen. Thence they sent to Leuenberger, and granted another conference at his own request. At this moment, Leuenberger, who had written to the council of Berne to complain of the advance of the Confederate auxiliaries while his own peasants were besieging the cities in Aargau, unexpectedly saw his force increased to twenty thousand men. Then his courage also increased. He was no longer afraid, and replied that the sword must decide.

But the attempts of the rebels upon Wohlenschwyl and Mellingen as well as upon Zofingen having proved unsuccessful, they again lost heart, and once more sent messengers to the Confederate council of war, to obtain favorable conditions. But now the council answered: "Peasants cannot propose conditions. Dissolve your league. Return to your homes. Your chiefs must await the sentence of their magistrates. Do this and we will leave you in peace."

The terrified envoys of the country-people of Berne, Bâle and Solothurn immediately swore to these conditions. Not so the Lucerners. They excused themselves, for want of authority. There was no longer any plan, any coherence or coöperation among the people. Wertmuller advanced. From Berne and Mangen, on the other side, came general Erlach towards Langenthal. On his passage he dispersed a troop of two thousand peasants. In the field before Herzogenbuchsee (28th May) he found a post of six peasants armed with halberds. They assured him that the rebels had entirely dispersed. But, as he rode towards the town with his followers, shot after shot was fired at him. Quickly discovering the forces of the insurgents, which had taken possession of the neighboring wood, he attacked them on three sides at once.

Then ensued a desperate conflict. The insurgents, overpowered, retreated towards the town, defending their ground foot by foot. While a part of the town was in flames, they fought from the houses; then from behind the walls of the church. At last they fled and dispersed through the woods.

Erlach and Wertmuller joined forces near Langenthal. All rebellion was put down in that region. Wertmuller, desirous to observe the peace already promised to the country-people by the council of war at Mellingen, blamed the Bernese leader for the massacre at Herzogenbuchsee. But when the latter explained the circumstances to him, it was agreed that the covenant of Mellingen should apply only to Lower Aargau; and that, in the districts above Aarburg, Berne should have full power by right of conquest.

Suddenly, in all the villages, to cries of rebellion and bold bravadoes, succeeded the stillness of death and the repentance of terror. The people were disarmed, the leaders of the revolt imprisoned. The Confederate council of war sat in judgment at Zofingen. Schybi was brought there from Entlibuch and beheaded with the sword. Leuenberger, betrayed in his own house by a neighbor and accomplice, was thrown into prison at Berne. There he was executed, and his bloody head was nailed to the gallows by the side of the insurgents' written league. In the same way died his secretary Brommer. Ulli Galli was hung on the gallows. At Bâle, seven old men were condemned to death, as partakers in the revolt; all had snow-white beards. Many others were also punished, some by death, some by banishment, more by fines. The people of the free bailiwicks were compelled to pay 10,000 florins, those of the county of Lenzburg 20,000, the Solothurners 30,000; others, other sums. And the emperor, Ferdinand III., declared the insurgents who had fled to be outlaws throughout the whole Roman empire.

But the insurgent country-people in the canton of Lucerne, when they saw their affairs separated from those of the rest at Mellingen, decided to come to an agreement with their government. Uri, Schwyz, Unterwalden and Zug sent deputies to Stanz to arbitrate between magistrates and subjects (7th June). The Entlibuchers alone resisted the settlement; for there were several burghers in Lucerne who privately encouraged them, and hoped by their means to bring about a change in the city government. But these burghers were betrayed and imprisoned, and the Entlibuchers reduced to obedience by the superiority of the forces sent against them.

Such was the result of the insurrection. That which rises lawlessly must fall lawlessly. For a long while the cantons quarrelled with each other about the war-expenses: Berne especially with Zurich, Solothurn with Berne, until (1654) they came to an agreement on this matter in the Confederate Diet, where it was decided: That, for the future, each canton should, at its own expense, assist and support the others in case of need.

CHAPTER XLIII.

ANOTHER RELIGIOUS WAR. THE BATTLE NEAR VILLMERGEN. COMMOTION IN BALE. THE PESTILENCE.

[A. D. 1656 to 1699.]

Hardly was the quarrel about the war-expenses happily settled, when another, more serious than the first, arose between the cantons.

It was again occasioned by unchristian hate between reformed and catholics. The clergy of both church-parties, instead of quenching the hell-fire of discord, did their best to fan it by talk and preaching. The governments already had many subjects of dispute, especially in the common bailiwicks, where all had rights and each wished to be master. No one trusted the others, while each attributed evil intentions to the rest. The catholics said: "The

Bernese and Zurichers are fortifying their cities and making alliances with Holland and England! They must have some purpose! It is against us!" The reformed said: "The catholics confirm the Borromean league, renew their treaties with Savoy and the bishop of Bâle, and show themselves over-friendly to the king of Spain! This is not without a motive! They aim at our religion!"

Then it happened that, in 1655, six families of Arth, in the canton of Schwyz, were obliged to flee, because they were of the evangelical faith. Their lives were not safe in Arth. With prayers and tears, they presented themselves before the council of Zurich, beseeching them to intercede that they might at least obtain the free exit of their household property. The council of Zurich, moved with compassion, wrote to Schwyz and asked permission to remove the property of these fugitives. But Schwyz refused the request, and demanded the surrender of the persons. When the reformed cantons appealed thereat to the Confederate right, the Schwyzers said: "We are accountable only to God and ourselves for the management of our affairs." And they confiscated the property of the fugitives, cast their relatives, who were also of the evangelical faith, into prison and chains, tortured them and even condemned some to death.

Then Zurich seized her arms, after the mediation and entreaties of the neutral cantons had proved useless in the Diet. As quickly did Schwyz and the catholic cantons raise their banners. Zurich, supported by Muhlhausen and Schaffhausen, entered the field with ten thousand men, over-ran the whole of Thurgau, and besieged Rapperswyl. But the catholic cantons held Rapperswyl and the Albis, and also occupied Bremgarten, Mellingen and Baden, and the Brunig against Berne. The Bernese stationed troops to defend their frontiers against Freiburg, Solothurn and Unterwalden, and marched with forty banners towards Lenzburg, to assist the Zurichers.

There was no discipline among the reformed troops. They pillaged and burned, wherever they went; devastated the convent of Rheinau, plundered villages and churches, and drove off the cattle. Among the Bernese there was so little order, that they encamped in the territory of Villmergen, without thought of the enemy, without sending forward scouts, and without sufficient ammunition for their artillery. And, although two young men of Aargau had discovered the enemy near the village of Wohlen and hastened back with the alarm, no attention was paid to their warning, because some young lords of Berne returned from a ride with the assurance that there was no danger.

But on the height of Wohlen, behind the wood, there were, in fact, more than four thousand Lucerners. Colonel Pfyffer of Lucerne led them on. And, from within a sunken way on the height, which hid half their bodies, they suddenly fired upon the surprised Bernese. It was two o'clock in the afternoon of the 14th of January, 1656. The Bernese were thrown into such confusion and terror that they could hardly be brought to stand. As powder and balls were wanting, they discharged their field-pieces but twice. All fled. Ten fresh banners came to their assistance, but were dragged away by the fugitives. During the combat, colonel Pfyffer received a letter from Lucerne, ordering him not to attack, because there were hopes of a friendly settlement. But he, guessing the contents of the letter, put it, with seal unbroken, into his pocket, and pursued the flying Bernese, large numbers of whom were slaughtered. They lost about eight hundred men and eleven field-pieces. At a short distance, among the hill-vineyards, were stationed several Bernese battalions: they saw the flight towards Lenzburg and the massacre of their fellow-soldiers, but did not move, because they had no orders.

The troops of Aargau, alone, when they learned the defeat of the Bernese, became excited and wished to advance and renew the battle. But the council of war forbade this and had much difficulty in restraining their impetuosity. Such was the battle of Villmergen. For three days, the victors remained exulting on the field of combat. Then they returned home with much booty, and shortly afterwards (26th January, 1656), a truce and then peace was concluded. As no provisions were allowed to pass into the small cantons, and as neither the Lucerners nor the Ber nese could trust their own discontented peasantry, it was for the interest of all to put an end to this war, which lasted only nine weeks and had already cost Zurich alone more than 414,000 florins. The treaty of peace left every thing about as before. In religious matters and in all relating to emigration from one canton to another, each had power to do as it pleased within its own territory.

The catholic cantons might have derived much greater advantage from the faulty military organization of the reformed, had their own troops been on a better footing. Dissatisfied at the little they had gained, they threw all the blame on colonel Zweier of Evenbach, chief of the forces of Uri, and said that he must have had an understanding with the Zurichers and Bernese, that he had hindered the pursuit of the flying enemy at Etzel, and the raising of the siege of Rapperswyl. And a monk of Einsiedeln boldly declared that the Zurichers had sent to the colonel fourteen hundred ducats concealed in a capon. This gave rise to long disputes and interminable suits before the Diet.

Now, there was once more a false peace in the land. This was seen to be the case everywhere, and especially in the common bailiwicks. Whatever injured one party pleased the other; and the common people imitated the masters in their unchristian fanaticism. Little was wanting to cause a fresh outbreak of the war.

A Lucerner, who had enlisted soldiers for the Spanish service, was travelling on the day of Pentecost (1664) with forty-three recruits, through by-paths in Thurgau; in the village of Lipperswyl they entered the reformed church with drawn sabres, and made much noise and disturbance. A woman, seized with affright, fled to the village of Wigoldingen, uttering loud shrieks and calling for help. The Wigoldingeners rushed forth, fell upon the Spanish soldiers, killed five, wounded others, and made some prisoners. This occurrence again brought the reformed and catholic cantons into arms against each other. They called out troops. The five catholic cantons immediately occupied Kaiserstuhl, Mellingen and Bremgarten. Many diets and conferences were held. The catholic cantons could only be appeased by blood. Two men of Wigoldingen were condemned to death (5th Sept., 1665) by a majority of the cantons governing Thurgau, in spite of the intercessions of Zurich for mercy on the unfortunates. When the commune of Wigoldingen was sentenced to defray all the expenses of this long quarrel, collections were made in all the churches of Zurich on their behalf.

Shortly afterwards, information was received that the king of France intended to build a strong fortress at Huningen, near Bâle, as a means of defence for France, of offence against the Swiss. This made the Confederates anxious, and they sent messengers to Paris to the king (1679). But when their attempts to prevent the building of the fortress proved vain, the excitement increased, especially at Bâle. Here the citizens complained against the little, or executive, council, accusing many of its members with having received French gold, and with having exceeded their authority in matters of election and legislation, to the detriment of the state. The corporations were assembled. Many abuses came to light. Lords of the council and their wives, who had influenced the council elections, were deprived of their honors, or cast into prison and heavily fined. The council yielded, for the exasperated citizens seized their arms. The Confederates sent mediators to settle the quarrel (1691). Too much space would be required to detail the divisions, disturbances and acts of violence which took place. Finally, after the mediators, with delegates from the council and the citizens, had come to a settlement of the rights of the great and little councils in matters of police, legislation and administration and in nominations to office, and the approving majority of the citizens had sanctioned it by an oath, the peace was broken in the most bloody manner.

When John Fatio, one of the advocates of the citizens, was imprisoned over the Rhine-gate, on accusation of having done much on his own motion, and without authority from the citizens, an armed band, distinguished by white scarfs on their arms, assembled at night and demanded the release of the prisoner. The alarm was given. The friends of the government rushed forth. Citizens stood in arms against citizens; two of Fatio's partisans were shot (23d Sept., 1691); about fifty others were imprisoned the next day; armed peasants were brought into the city to maintain order. A severe tribunal sat in judgment on the authors of the revolt. John Fatio, John Muller and Conrad Moyses were beheaded (28th Sept.) on the square before the council-house; others were punished by the galleys by banishment, or fines.

Thus sometimes here, sometimes there, numerous civil discords and disputes were added to the quarrel about creeds and churches, so that it seemed as if Switzerland would never find rest, only she was no longer disturbed by foreign powers. Affliction and distress were in many households. At last, to all their miseries was superadded a contagious pestilence, which swept away many persons (1697), especially in the city of Bâle and in Aargau. It manifested itself by plague-boils on the lower-stomach. The temperature was unwholesome, and the preceding winter had been very warm. Venomous worms and caterpillars devastated trees, grass and fruits; and never before had so many water-mice and moles been seen. This lasted until the year drew towards its close, and a more severe winter appeared.

CHAPTER XLIV.

HOW THE TOGGENBURGERS WERE DEPRIVED OF THEIR ANCIENT LIBERTIES BY THE ABBOT OF ST. GALLEN, AND WHAT HAPPENED IN CONSEQUENCE.

[A. D. 1700 to 1712.]

THE ancient Swiss became independent, and thus remained so long as they did not fear foreign powers, nor flatter them from motives of interest or vanity. And they were esteemed by other nations, so long as they themselves esteemed eternal justice more than life. But when from cupidity or cowardice they preferred prudence to right, when it became usual for them to sell flesh and blood into foreign service, when the principal men allowed themselves to be bound by the gold chains and decorations of princes, then ruin fell on the fatherland. Men abased themselves abroad, in order to stand high at home; they preferred their own canton to the Confederacy, their own family to their canton; they were small in great things, and great in small; they sought employments from selfish interest; they sold offices at auction, or disposed of them as marriage-dowers; the Swiss were called free, but most of them were wretched subjects and had less freedom and fewer rights than the serfs of kings; craft and violence were constantly employed to diminish more and more the few franchises of the people, and to increase the absolute power of the masters.

Such was especially the lot of the country of Toggenburg. There the communes, by favor of the old counts of Toggenburg, had formerly acquired great privileges: a voice in the appointment of the higher and lower tribunals, in the disbursement of fines and other communal moneys; a right through their general and other assemblies over the administration of the public revenue and over the military force. No man, except one of themselves, could be appointed bailiff over them.

But when the abbot of St. Gallen (1468), for 14,500 Rhenish florins, purchased from a baron of Raron those rights over the land which the latter had inherited from the old counts of Toggenburg, the abbot desired also to appropriate rights which he had not purchased, but had solemnly confirmed to the people. And as the Toggenburgers had (1436) made an alliance with the cantons of Glarus and Schwyz for the protection of their own privileges, so later (1469), the abbot made another defensive alliance with the same cantons for the protection of his rights. As his abbey was an ally of the Confederacy, but he himself a titular prince of the holy German empire, he took advantage of this double character to become, or to appear, more than he really was. When interest dictated, he acted against the emperor as a free Confederate, or against the Confederates as a prince of the empire and a vassal of the imperial throne.

He behaved with moderation at first; he began by questioning the freedom of the Toggenburgers, and by calling the people his serfs (1510) that they might insensibly become accustomed to the name. Finally he attacked their franchises. This occasioned many lawsuits before the protecting cantons. But the protecting cantons were favorable to the abbot. So he first (1539) secured an appeal to his tribunal from all the courts in the land; then (1540) he assumed the exclusive right of appointing all judges and of disbursing the confiscated property of criminals; also the right to select a foreigner as bailiff, and to manage without question the estates of all churches and curacies; the right of hunting and fishing; afterwards (1543), the appointment of pastors to all the churches, of recorders and constables (1555), and the power to grant the right of citizenship (1596). Finally all general and other assemblies of the people were forbidden, and the military power passed entirely into the hands of the bishop (1654). Then he ruled as he pleased; allowed forced recruiting for foreign service; filled all offices with his own creatures; looked on with indifference when magistrates and convents, by craft and intrigues, obtained possession of the best estates, or when the public fines were raised to exorbitant sums.

At last abbot Leodegar Burgisser thought himself absolute master in the land. He ordered the people to build and maintain, at their own expense, a new highway through the Hummelwald. And when the delegates of the people represented to him that this was a more grievous burden on the Toggenburgers than the old labor-dues and day-service from which they had twice ransomed themselves, he condemned these men to a fine of 1540 crowns, compelled them to recant in open court, and deprived them of civil rights.

Then (1701) the oppressed Toggenburgers laid their complaints before Schwyz and Glarus. Glarus was touched by the sufferings of the poor country-people; as was Schwyz, although the Toggenburgers were of the reformed faith. "Even if the Toggenburgers were Turks and Heathens," said the Schwyzers in general assembly, "they are nevertheless our Confederates and fellow-countrymen, and we will see justice done to them." This displeased the abbot and he appealed to all the cantons, invoking the Confederate right. This occasioned many fruitless Diets from year to year. Zurich and Lucerne, who were also protectors of the abbot, took part in the angry quarrel. Many supported the Toggenburgers, because they also were reformed and were persecuted for their religion; many opposed the bishop, because he had recently made a defensive alliance with Austria and treated the country of Toggenburg as if it were a fief of the emperor and empire. The longer the quarrel continued, the greater, as usual, became the confusion of the matter. Finally the ancient religious hate added its poison also.

For when Schwyz and the catholic cantons saw that Zurich and Berne supported the Toggenburgers, and encouraged them to maintain their ancient rights, principally from religious sympathy, Schwyz adopted the party of the abbot of St. Gallen and declared (1703): "The newer rights of the abbot, his deeds and charters supersede the old franchises of the country, and without consent of Glarus and Schwyz no new reformed church shall be established in Toggenburg." But this did not deter Zurich and Berne, and the Toggenburgers still asserted their ancient franchises. Now came the imperial envoy and brought a document from his master which said: "The emperor must decide, because the country of Toggenburg is incontestibly an original imperial fief." But Zurich and Berne replied: "Toggenburg lies within the Confederate borders, and the abbot of St. Gallen has for many years recognized us as arbiters." The embassadors of Holland and of the kings of Prussia and England also encouraged the Zurichers and Bernese to resist the emperor.

As the quarrel extended more and more, and discord, feuds and assassinations prevailed in Toggenburg, because the abbot of St. Gallen himself designedly sowed dissension between the catholic and reformed inhabitants, a wise man of Zurich, named Nabholz, attempted, by his counsels, to restore peace and order. His efforts were fruitless. The abbot obstinately insisted on all his claims to power. The Toggenburgers, however, disregarded them, and would not obey him, but drove his governors, officers and soldiers out of the castles. Thereupon the abbot occupied with troops all the bridges, roads and passes of the ancient territory of St. Gallen. The Toggenburgers armed. Avoyer Durler of Lucerne, a zealous friend to the abbot, called on the catholic cantons to put down the insurgents. Avoyer Willading of Berne opposed him, and called upon the reformed cantons to draw the sword without delay against the catholics, in order to protect the ancient rights of the Toggenburgers and to defend the reformed church. Twelve years had this quarrel lasted, and it became more and more bitter every day.

As soon as the Toggenburgers saw that Zurich and Berne would protect them, and learned that inspector Bodmer was coming to defend them with nearly three thousand Zurichers, they declared war against the abbot (April 12, 1712) for the maintenance of their franchises. Nabholz, hitherto their friend and counsellor, now became their leader, called out the landsturm, and fought for them against the abbot's people as faithfully with the sword as he had done with the pen. The convent and castles of the abbot were seized, but he threw sixteen companies of infantry into the city of Wyl for its defence. In the mean while the troops of Zurich pillaged and sacked the territory of St. Gallen without hindrance.

Now Lucerne, Uri, Schwyz, Unterwalden and Zug also seized their arms, covered their frontiers, marched upon Toggenburg and occupied the county of Baden. The nuncio counted out to them 26,000 crowns from the papal treasure, and at Rome prayers were offered to the saints in their behalf. The priests distributed consecrated bullets and amulets to the soldiers.

Thereupon Berne drew 10,000 crowns from her treasury and sent fifteen thousand men into the field. She stationed troops on all her frontiers, and even in the county of Lenzburg, near Othmarfingen, against Baden and the free bailiwicks. A Bernese battalion marched towards the Stilli; under cover of twelve field-pieces they crossed the Aar, and joined the troops of Zurich near Wurelingen. The latter had, by this time, made themselves masters of all Thurgau. Thus war and cries of war prevailed throughout the land. Even the Valaisians were in full march to support the catholic cantons.

Glarus remained neutral in this disturbance, as did Solothurn and the bishop of Constance. Bâle and Freiburg lamented this war of Swiss against Swiss, and exhorted them to an amicable settlement, but too late. The abbot of St. Gallen sent his valuables for safety to Lindau (a Suabian city on an island in the lake of Constance); he himself retired to Rorschach, and called upon the cities of St. Gallen and the cantons of Appenzell and Glarus for assistance; they did not help him, but maintained their neutrality. Thereat the emperor, from Presburg in Hungary, ordered the Suabian circle to support the abbot of St. Gallen.

CHAPTER XLV.

THE TOGGENBURGER WAR. SECOND BATTLE NEAR VILLMERGEN. PEACE CONCLUDED AT AARAU.

[A. D. 1712 to 1718.]

THE Zurichers and Bernese had marched with ten thousand men against the little city of Wyl to besiege the bishop's troops therein. Thither came Nabholz also, with two thousand Toggenburgers and a body of men from Thurgau. The little city was cannonaded and bombarded, the country and villages were ravaged. But the abbot's soldiers defended themselves very valiantly under major Felber, and made several bloody sallies. And when the men of Thurgau withdrew from the besiegers, by whom they were held in little esteem, Felber extended his forays as far as Braunau and Summeri. So cruel were his people, that they killed two defenceless men, and cut off a woman's hands and feet. Then the cry for vengeance against such cruelty arose throughout all Thurgau; the raging landsturm marched once more on Weinfelden; among them were seen women, and children twelve years old. And they were as cruel to the catholics as these had been to the reformed.

Then said Nabholz to the generals of Berne and Zurich: "Let us invade the abbot's ancient states, whence come many of the defenders of Wyl. When they see their huts and villages burning in the distance, they will quit the others, and the city will be weakened." So with one thousand men he entered the abbot's ancient country, near Oberglatt. And when those in the city saw their dwellings burning in the distance, they hastily left their ranks to fight for their huts. Thereupon the city was distracted with fear and surrendered to her enemies (22 May). The abbot's soldiers dispersed and were so angry with their leader Felber, that his life was not safe, and he was obliged to seek protection of the besiegers, in order to escape to Bernardszell. But the furious people pursued him there, dragged him from the curate's house, set him on a sorry horse, led him with shouts and insults to the bridge over the Sitter, and killed him with four gun-shots through the body. Then they hacked his corpse with their knives, and threw it into the waters of the Sitter (24 May).

In the mean while valiant Nabholz had penetrated still further into the ancient territory of the abbot of St. Gallen. There the inhabitants of Gossau surrendered to him, after having, in their anger, assassinated their own general. Two days before they had repulsed a thousand Toggenburgers, who had been sent against them with fire and sword, and who, in their flight, had strangled the defenceless catholic priest of Niederglatt in a stable. The banners of Zurich and Berne advanced victorious through the whole of Thurgau as far as the city of St. Gallen. Here they placed a garrison in the city and at Rorschach. The abbot, full of fear, had already fled to Augsburg with his valuables.

When the Toggenburgers saw that their cause was successful, they condemned to death several of the abbot's people who had betrayed them. They entirely threw off the abbot's sovereignty, annulled also their alliance with Schwyz and Glarus, and said to the people of Gaster, Uznach, Gams and other places: "Let us form a single republic, which shall be like the free cantons of the Confederates." And they drew up a constitution, which they carried to Aarau, where the cantons were holding a Diet. But this plan displeased the lords of Zurich and Berne, because they preferred to have the Toggenburgers as subjects rather than as free fellow-confederates. Even Nabholz, the zealous defender of the Toggenburgers' cause, refused to support their petition, though they offered him much money.

In the mean while, also, two thousand Bernese had passed the Aar near Stilli and united with three thousand Zurichers, led by colonel Hans Caspar Wertmuller. They crossed the Hasenberg to bring the county of Baden into complete subjection, drove out the scattered forces of the catholic cantons and advanced as far as the city of Mellingen. On the opposite side, from the county of Lenzburg, came seven thousand Bernese over the Bunz. The catholic garrisons fled to Baden. Mellingen was taken without a blow. All the inhabited places of the county of Baden were compelled to render homage to the conquerors, as did the city of Bremgarten. Then the army marched to Baden to besiege the fortress. Wertmuller encamped among the vineyards on the Lagerberg and awaited the arrival of the Bernese, who had made a circuit from Mellingen to Fahrwindisch, along the Reuss, to attack Baden on the opposite side. The besieged kept up a heavy fire from the city, from the square of the capuchin-church and from the lofty castle, upon Wertmuller's camp. The Zurichers replied with forty cannons and mortars. The churches, the tower and many houses were greatly injured. The parapet of the castle fell with a crash upon the rocks below. Then on the other side, near the great baths, over against the castle, appeared the Bernese also, with twenty field-pieces, howitzers and mortars. This so terrified the besieged, that they surrendered on hard conditions (31 May). The commander of the fortress, Crivelli of Uri, marched out with his garrison, but without artillery.

This event and the fact that the Rheinthal, also, was obliged to render homage to Berne and Zurich, occasioned great trouble, discord and disorder among the catholic cantons. Some wished for peace, others for war. The embassadors of Austria and France promised assistance; the pope sent money; Freiburg and Solothurn took up arms for them; so did Valais and all the catholics in the common bailiwicks. But thereat those reformed cantons which had hitherto been quiet, threatened to arm also, and the evangelicals in the common bailiwicks prepared to support Zurich and Berne. Thus, at this time, one hundred and fifty thousand Swiss stood in arms for bloody conflict with each other; never had the Confederacy raised so many troops to repel a foreign enemy. But one sword kept the others in the scabbard. France and Austria did, indeed, march their troops towards the frontiers; but the English, Dutch and Prussians, on the other side, held them also in check.

While the deputies of the Confederates were assembled at Aarau and negotiating for peace, bailiff and knight Ackermann of Unterwalden marched with five thousand men against the bridge of Sins, where lay some Bernese troops: three hundred entrenched in the church-yard of Sins, seven hundred near the village of Auw. These latter were surprised, so that they saved themselves with difficulty. Many Bernese were slain. Colonel Monier of Berne, who fought valiantly, first in the church-yard, then in the church, was compelled to surrender with his soldiers. They would have been massacred without pity by the troops of Unterwalden, Schwyz and Zug, had not Ackermann, who was himself wounded, withstood the bloodthirsty men with noble heroism (20 July). On the other side, also, the Schwyzers advanced (22 July) against the lake of Zurich, near Hutten and Bellenschanz. But here they encountered the valiant Zuricher leader John Caspar Wertmuller. Seven hours long fought the Schwyzers; they lost two hundred men; but they were forced to give way before the Zurichers. On their slain were found consecrated letters, with numbers, crosses and promises of certain victory.

An army of the catholics, over nine thousand strong, crossed the country above Muri to Villmergen, where the Bernese were posted with eight thousand men. Here, close to the same place where the Bernese had once already (24

Jan., 1656) experienced a bloody defeat from the catholic cantons, below Dintikon and Hembrunn, the earth was again to be reddened with the blood of Swiss, shed by Swiss. It was the 25th of July, 1712. The thunder of artillery opened the fight. It lasted four hours. Then the Bernese spread terror and confusion among the people of the catholic cantons, broke their array and slew them in their flight. Two thousand and more of the catholics covered the field with their bodies.

When, after this, the Toggenburgers subdued Uznach and Gaster, the city of Rapperswyl yielded to the Zurichers, and the victors entered from all sides into the territory of the catholics, the latter became alarmed and sued for peace.

Lucerne and Uri had already signed a treaty of peace at the Diet of Aarau (18 July); but the Lucerner peasants, urged, in the name of God and of religion, by the papal nuncio and by their priests and monks, who were opposed to peace, marched against the city to force their government to renew the war, then finally against the Bernese at Villmergen. Here they found their ruin, as has been related. Even after the battle of Villmergen, some two thousand men of Willisau rose against the government of Lucerne; but they were soon reduced to obedience by Bernese troops and compelled to pay heavy costs. The Bernese soldiers were the best in the Confederacy, in equipment, discipline, the quality and management of their arms.

Finally (9th and 11th August, 1712) a general peace was concluded at Aarau, greatly to the advantage of the conquerors. The five catholic cantons were obliged, not only to yield to Zurich and Berne their rights over Baden, Rapperswyl and the lower free bailiwicks, but also to associate Berne in the sovereignty over Thurgau and Rheinthal, whereby the votes and rights of the two religious parties were equalized therein. Glarus also participated, with Berne and Zurich.

The humbled abbot Leodegar of St. Gallen would not accept the peace, but remained obstinate and self-exiled until he died. In the mean while, Zurich and Berne held possession of his territory. But when the new abbot Joseph subscribed the peace at Rorschach (1718), his estates were restored to him; even the Toggenburgers were again subject to him, but with greater privileges and rights, under the protection of Zurich and Berne. Only the pope and his nuncio rejected the treaty of Aarau and declared it null. But the reconciled Confederates cared little for this, and when the people of some bailiwicks of the canton of Lucerne were again excited by the priests against their government, the latter introduced into the city a garrison from Entlibuch, demanded of the pope the imposition of a tax upon the convents for the costs of the war and also the recall of the nuncio Caraccioli, whom they called the originator of all the trouble. The catholic cantons long felt the bitter effects of this war; for they had incurred great expenses. Schwyz levied a tax of five crowns on each household; Lucerne was obliged to exercise force to raise her share of the costs; Uri to appease her subjects in Leventina by important franchises (1713), and thenceforth to call them "dear and faithful compatriots."

CHAPTER XLVI.

CONDITION OF THE SWISS AT THE COMMENCEMENT OF THE EIGHTEENTH CENTURY. THOMAS MASSNER'S QUARREL.

[A. D. 1701 to 1714.]

After the fratricidal battle of Villmergen, the Confederates were engaged in no foreign or domestic war for the space of eighty-six years. But this period was not one of happiness, of quiet or of glory; it passed in constant differences, sometimes of one canton with the others, sometimes of the magistrates with their subjects. During every ten years there were, now here, now there, fresh intrigues. fresh conspiracies, fresh revolts, until the rotten edifice of the old Confederacy crumbled at the first blow given to it by the hostile hand of France.

The first wars of the ancient Confederates were undertaken on their own account and for their protection against the oppressors of their rights and liberties. Thereby they obtained an imperishable glory among the nations of the earth. Then the cantons and cities, which had become free, undertook numerous wars to acquire sovereignties and subjects and to extend their limited territories. They reaped internal discord and an equivocal reputation. The deeds of the greatest conquerors finally fall into oblivion or contempt, as they are seldom for the benefit of humanity. Afterwards, they sold their soldiers for hire to foreign countries and foreign wars, and with the blood of their brave men purchased for the sons of noble families large pay, annual pensions, golden chains, decorations and titles, such as kings are accustomed to confer on their servants. Therewith despotism and pride and a shameless luxury entered into a few great families, foreign manners and foreign vices into the cabins of the people; Switzerland became the theatre of the scandalous intrigues of foreign embassadors and of the ambition of the home governments for unlimited power over their subjects. Then the Confederates showed more friendship for foreign kings than for each other; they forbade free emigration between the cantons, and even prohibited the purchase and sale of the most necessary articles. Their Diets were heartless ceremonials and their mean deeds contradicted their imposing words. Finally, the Swiss drew the sword, no longer against foreign potentates but, urged by sectarian hate, by envy, ambition or party spirit, against each other only. Thereby they more than once sullied the glory of their forefathers, and impelled each other to the brink of a common abyss.

In vain did wise patriots urge that the Confederate bond should be ameliorated and strengthened before it was entirely loosed. In vain, also, in the Diet itself, did the evangelical cantons propose a new Confederate constitution; the selfishness of the majority caused it to be rejected. And when Sarasin, a Genevese, suggested that a supreme federal authority should be created, by means of which the divided Confederacy would secure more consolidation and unity, he was laughed at.

As an offset, Uri, Schwyz and Unterwalden assembled (24th June, 1713) with great pomp at the Rutli, where, four hundred years before, their fathers had sworn together the first oath of freedom. There, with solemn oath, they renewed their most ancient bond, but with the saddening remembrance of their misfortune at Villmergen and with inimical feelings towards the large cantons in their hearts. And two years afterwards (9th May, 1715), the catholic cantons made a treaty at Solothurn with France, whose king was then the most bitter enemy of the evangelicals. This one-sided treaty frightened the reformed cantons, and made them distrustful. They suspected that it contained some dangerous secret articles, that foreign troops were to be called into the country, the smaller cantons strengthened at the expense of the larger, Geneva and Vaud restored to the duke of Savoy, Thurgau and the county of Kyburg to the emperor. To the honor of the Confederates, the future did not justify these suspicions, but the suspicions themselves showed the reciprocal animosity and distrust which existed.

Parties were constantly formed, not for the glory and happinéss of the whole Confederacy against foreign powers, but for the benefit of some small territory, or for the benefit of foreigners, against fellow-confederates. Some were attached to the emperor, others to France, a very few, only, to Switzerland. Hence crafty embassadors of foreign princes obtained a constantly increasing power in the land, to the constantly increasing dishonor of the Confederates and to the misery of many a family, as shown by the following instance.

A young man from Grisons, who was pursuing his studies at Geneva, took a ride for pleasure into the neighboring territory of Savoy. There the French embassador caused him to be secretly seized (1710) and confined in a fortress, because the young man's father, Thomas Massner, a lord of the council of Coire, was a partisan of Austria. When the father learnt the imprisonment of his innocent son, and had in vain demanded justice and sought assistance, he became very angry, and, with an armed band, seized the brother of Merveilleux, the French chargé at Coire, that he might hold him as a hostage. An accommodation was made; the councillor gave up his prisoner and asked pardon of the French embassador at Solothurn. But, as he did not thereby obtain his son's release, he sought fresh vengeance. And he lay in wait for the duke of Vendome, grand prior of France, as he was passing through Sargansland, took him prisoner and carried him to the Austrians at Feldkirch. The government of the Grison republic petitioned both France and Austria, to obtain the simultaneous release of the innocent prisoners; but without success. The foreign embassadors rather embittered the quarrel. It was in consequence of this dispute that the English embassador, who sided with the Austrians, was assassinated at the baths of Pfeffers; that the league of the Ten-jurisdictions took part for Thomas Massner, and a majority of the corporations of Coire appointed him bailiff of Maienfeld; that the Confederate cantons outlawed this same man, as a violater of the rights of nations, and set a price of two hundred crowns on his head; that, finally, the Grisons themselves, in a criminal court held at Ilanz (17th Aug., 1711), deprived him of civil rights, confiscated his property, condemned him to an ignominious death, and offered a thousand ducats as a reward to any one who would deliver him up.

To prevent greater misfortunes, Thomas Massner had already obtained the release of the duke of Vendome, and had himself fled to the protection of the emperor at Vienna. Here he lived for a long while, an exile; while his unhappy son languished, a prisoner, in a French fortress, and his deserted wife, a widow, in the Rhetian mountains. And, as his life was heavy, far from his home, he one day undertook to return. He could also perceive that the emperor's favor diminished daily. The favor of the people and of great lords is like April weather and thin vapor.

In his own country the sentence of the criminal court of Ilanz and the outlawry of the Confederacy still hung over his head. He wandered among the Alps of Glarus. He was betrayed, and, by order of the French embassador, pursued. One day, when he was trying to escape from his pursuers and had regained the Austrian territory on the right bank of the Rhine, his wagon was upset. Old Massner died of the fall.

When afterwards (1714) peace was negotiated at Baden between France and Austria, a nephew of Thomas Massner was among the emperor's plenipotentiaries. By his cousin's intercession, young Massner was finally freed from imprisonment, after long negotiations with the French. And when he returned home after so many years, he was received by his people with joy, as a triumphant martyr, and repaid for his sufferings by honors and dignities.

Thus did foreign embassadors trifle with the Swiss upon Swiss soil, after having divided them by courtier-like artifices.

CHAPTER XLVII.

DISTURBANCES IN ZURICH, SCHAFFHAUSEN AND THE BISHOPRIC OF BALE.

[A. D. 1714 to 1740.]

It has often been said: "War is the greatest of the evils of life." But so said not the ancient heroic Confederates, who first glorified the name of Swiss before God and man. They marched to battle for their holy right; they knew that there was something better than comfort and effeminate ease, and they thought: "The greatest of the evils of life is slavery under the sceptre of pride and injustice."

And it is a fact that from the time of the last battle of Villmergen until the destructive invasion of the French, though less than a century and in the midst of peace, Switzerland suffered greater calamities than in all her previous wars with Austria and Burgundy. For, while rust corroded the swords of the Winkelrieds, the Fontanas, the Waldmanns, the Hallwyls, the Erlachs, contemptible selfishness and poisonous luxury corroded still more completely the glorious bond of the ancients, and the Confederacy became decomposed like a putrefying corpse. And the children bedecked the corpse with the glittering trophies of their fathers, that no one might know the soul had departed from it.

Nothing great was done. Greatness seemed to all, or to most, to consist in acquiring riches, not virtues; in being lords and subjects, not free citizens. Some purchased the office of bailiff, and sold justice and injustice, like common wares. Some begged for pensions, orders and titles from foreign courts. Some sought to obtain places in the magistrature, not by services to their country but by marriage with the daughters of council-lords. Others sought other advantages; few, laudable occupations. The people of the subject-districts had barely more rights than that of sharing with their cattle the labors of the field, and the governments were so blind that they feared the enlightenment of the country-people. The sovereign cities and cantons undermined the liberties of the subjects; the ruling families in the cities, those of the burghers. From time to time, those whose rights were encroached upon, awoke from their slumber, armed themselves with courage, recovered their rights, or at least prevented further encroachments. But all these petty disputes do not deserve the attention of posterity; in their time they hardly excited that of the other Confederates.

In Zurich, where the citizens had always preserved a free spirit, a trifling question between two trades unexpectedly caused the reformation of several abuses in the commonwealth. Two parchment-makers accused a currier with encroaching on their trade (October, 1712). This personal dispute soon extended to the two trades and then to all the citizens. The ordinances and prerogatives of the industrial corporations were examined and regulated, the legislative functions of the citizens determined, the statutes of the ancient constitutional compact revised to accord with the spirit of the times, and all these useful reforms embodied in a new fundamental law, which was approved and sworn to by the citizens (17th Dec., 1713).

The burghers of the city of Schaffhausen had already, after a long struggle, obtained the same advantages by a revision and amelioration of their constitution (1689). For at Schaffhausen the little council had insensibly usurped arbitrary power, first by specious goodness and fraud, which had been successful through the inattention of the corporations, and then by the bold abuse of authority. The rights of the citizens had been disregarded, and the state-property managed wilfully and selfishly. This is always the case when those who administer the law hold themselves above the law, and think that their will is to take the place of law.

But though the abuses of arbitrary power were put an end to within the walls of the city of Schaffhausen, this was not by any means the case as regarded the rights of the country-people. Hence, when the government once established a new excise in the village of Wilchingen (1717), the village refused to submit, and, when the government recognized its error and removed the excise, brought forward other complaints, also well founded. Foreign lords and powers, as usual, did not neglect this opportunity to meddle in a petty domestic difficulty; pretexts were never wanting. Thus the people of Wilchingen were induced to refuse the usual homage, though Schaffhausen sent troops and offered a ready hearing of all their complaints, because the deputies of the village were encouraged by flattering promises from the imperial court at Vienna. But, afterwards, when Austria feared a rupture with France on more important questions, and wished to secure the good will of the Confederacy, the Wilchingeners were dismissed from Vienna (1726). Many of the rebels were punished by confiscation of their property; others were banished. Wearied by this dispute of many years, the village rendered the long refused homage (1729).

Wilfulness always occasions disasters; and the war of a government against its own subjects, even when successful, confers but small glory. Such was the experience of the bishop of Bâle also, at this period.

He was lord of a fine territory, stretching from the lake of Bienne to the city of Bâle, through the valleys of the Jura, with many cities, castles and towns. Therein were the cities of Bienne and Neustadt, Pruntrut, Delsperg, St. Ursits and Lauffen, as well as Erguel or St. Immerthal, the Freiberg, and the signiories of Esch, Birseck and Zwingen.

When John Conrad of Reinach became prince-bishop (1705) and received the homage of the country, the banneret of the peasants, Wisard, in the name of the people, made a reservation of their chartered franchises and of their defensive treaty with Berne. The bishop would acknowledge nothing of the kind, required an oath without reservation, deprived the banneret of his dignities and offices, and thought that, where might was there also was right. So thought not the Munsterthalers. The banneret went to Berne, reminded the city of her anciently-granted protectorate and demanded assistance. Berne acknowledged the justice of the claim; and, as the bishop persisted in his wilfulness and continued to make innovations and to harass those who opposed him, she sent a thousand men to the borders for their protection, restored to the country its former privileges and to the banneret his office. Thereat the bishop was much incensed. He called on the catholic cantons, and they thought to interfere with the aid of France. But Berne relied on the support of the evangelical cantons and of England. When the bishop saw that he could do nothing, he made a friendly settlement with Berne (30th March, 1706) and confirmed the Munsterthalers in their rights. But he did this with unwilling heart and occasioned them vexation after vexation, especially about the reformed worship in the country. Berne once more clashed her arms (1711). The first threat was sufficient.

Then the bishop again confirmed the franchises of the Munsterthalers, at Aarberg, and consented to the bitter condition that, in case of any future complaint, if he did not satisfactorily reply, within three months, to the second and third summons of Berne, he should forfeit the sum of 20,000 crowns, for which the prevostship of Munster was pledged. Although pope Clement XI. at Rome was very indignant at this stipulation, by which heretics acquired a great advantage over catholics, the treaty was thenceforward respected.

Frequently afterwards the bishops of Bâle attempted to

increase their sovereign power by arbitrary decisions and acts of violence. When the council of the city of Neustadt on the lake of Bienne banished a burgher of that city (1711) and his relatives appealed to the bishop against the council, the prince attempted, without right, to compel the council to revoke its sentence and to pay the costs of the suit. He arbitrarily deposed the burgomaster and five members of the council who would not submit, punished them by fines, outlawed them, pronounced sentence of death on burgomaster Celier, who had fled (1714), and broke up the whole council. Berne finally interfered, restored quiet in concert with the bishop, and secured the infringed freedom of the city.

The bishop treated the city of Pruntrut also with the same harshness. This city held from the old emperors and lords many important franchises which had always been confirmed by the bishops. But when lord Jacob Sigismund of Reinach sat in the bishop's chair, he encroached in many ways on the municipal rights. Influenced by the advice of his civil officer, the signior of Ramschwag, he would listen to no complaints, but treated the district assemblies and their delegates as rebels. Then Pruntrut rose in defence of her established franchises. The bishop called on the catholic cantons for assistance. But their deputies, when they had carefully examined the whole matter, like honest men, said to the prince (1734): "If princely prerogatives are to be maintained, the franchises of the subjects must also be respected." This quarrel remained unsettled for seven years. The hearts of the people were embittered against their signior. And when he, angry with the Confederates, finally introduced French troops into his territory (1741) and arbitrarily punished his subjects in property, honor and life, they bowed in silence beneath the yoke. But they awaited the hour for vengeance, and it struck at last.

CHAPTER XLVIII.

INSURRECTION OF THE WERDENBERGERS AGAINST GLARUS.

[A. D. 1714 to 1740.]

ABOUT the same time there was much trouble and distress in the little district of Werdenberg. After Glarus bought this country in 1517 from the barons of Heuwen, it was peacefully governed by bailiffs, who were replaced every three years. The Werdenbergers had, indeed, viewed with dissatisfaction their subjection to the Confederacy, because they thereby lost all hope of purchasing or otherwise obtaining their freedom. Already, in 1525, they had once been in full insurrection against their new masters, but since then quiet had been undisturbed. The four thousand inhabitants of the three parishes possessed very excellent alps in the Toggenburg mountains, fine lands and orchards in the valleys, and gloried in many franchises. They preserved, as a sacred treasure, the charter of these franchises, according to which the governing bailiff had no right to interfere in their communal affairs or to derive any benefit from the common pastures and woods. The bailiffs did not always respect these franchises, but assumed the management of the communal property, woods and alps; increased the fines on the sale of mountain lands; exercised arbitrary power respecting the right to the best chattels, the choice of officers and other things. This made bad blood among the people, and they appealed to the guarantee of their sealed charter.

But one day (1705) when the fifteen parishes of the free land of Glarus were met in general assembly before their chief magistrates, some said: "The charter was granted by the council without assent of the parishes, and is therefore invalid as well as derogatory to their sovereign rights." Then the assembly decided that the charter must be produced for examination.

Werdenberg unwillingly surrendered her treasure to the bailiff, Caspar Trumpi, for inspection and never received it back again. As the country made bitter but always respectful complaints concerning the abstracted charter, a triple council, assembled at Glarus, promised that all the rights possessed by the Werdenbergers from the earliest times should be recognized in a single document, to be deposited with them. But they, distrustful on account of what had already occurred, demanded the original charter as their property; and then, after fifteen years of useless complaint, refused the usual homage to the new bailiff (1719). The charter was promised to them, if they would do homage, and the landammann of Glarus said to the people assembled in the church of Grabs: "I am an old man with one foot already in the grave; I hope the other may follow, if the promise be not kept!" But the confidence of the people, so often deceived, was not restored.

Concerned at this, Glarus had recourse to the Vorort and to the Confederates assembled in Diet at Frauenfeld. Werdenberg, also, did the same. The delegates of the county were sent away unheard, with orders to submit to their government and to render the homage. They obeyed (July, 1720) but without desisting from their claims. Then Glarus sent for the delegates of Werdenberg to come and examine the documents and negotiate about the charter, under a safe-conduct to which her honor was pledged by oath. When they arrived, they were subjected to threats of violence, because they would not yield in their demands, and thrown into prison, where one of the firmest died suddenly. The Werdenbergers were the more afflicted because they saw that the rights of subjects and the rights of governments were not held equally holy by the Confederates. And forty men of the three parishes swore together to sacrifice property and life rather than the franchises of their country. The agitation continued. The people became excited. The bailiff from Glarus was more like a prisoner than a governor, in his castle. He introduced seventy-five armed men from Glarus into it, as a garrison, in the dead of night.

When the people heard this, they rang the alarm-bells, and crowds rushed in tumult from the communes to attack the castle; they were without discipline and without experienced officers. As soon as the heavy artillery thundered against them from the walls of the castle, they were all terrified and took to flight (21 Oct., 1721). Five days afterwards appeared the general of Glarus, Bartholemeo Paravicini, with two thousand men. Deputies also came from the vorort Zurich.

Then the Werdenbergers saw that their cause was lost, and, persuaded more by the sight of the superior force than by the eloquence of the envoys from Zurich, they brought their arms to the castle and gave them up. Then Glarus, advised by Berne and Zurich to treat with lenity the error of the misguided people, withdrew her troops on the very day the arms were surrendered, and marched them back to Azmoos, through storm and rain.

But an ignorant people think neither of the past nor of the future, and, when a danger has passed, become as bold as they were before faint-hearted at its prospect. Not one of the insurgents appeared at the castle to answer, as they had all agreed to do. Each played the hero anew; they held open general assemblies, swore to maintain their rights, and built a bridge over the Rhine to have a way for escape in the last extremity.

As soon as the troops of Glarus entered a second time into the revolted district, the unarmed crowd of inhabitants fled over the Rhine, persuaded that poverty and exile were better than home with extinguished franchises. But it was winter; and the moans of the children, half dead with cold, and the bitter lamentations of the women broke the spirit of the men. They sent messengers to the castle of Werdenberg and sued for mercy, and, after a few days, resigned to every fate, wandered back to their deserted cabins. A few, only, preferred voluntary exile to the serfdom to which the rest submitted by oath (31 Dec., 1721).

Now Glarus passed sentence on the insurgents. The names of Leinhard Bensch of Rasis, of Hans Bensch, Jacob Vorburger, Hans Rauw and Hans Senn, who had spoken for the people, were nailed to the gallows. Fines and confiscations, of more than 70,000 florins, deprivations of civil rights and banishment punished those who had shared in the insurrection. But no one was deprived of life. The blood which, in civil troubles, flows from the scaffold upon a free soil, falls as the seed of curses and vengeance, which future generations must often reap in terror.

Glarus, it is true, destroyed all the Werdenberger's claims to freedom; but, a few years later, the shepherd-people on the Linth, impelled by a generous feeling, relieved their subjects from many of the ancient burdens, by wisely restricting the power of the bailiffs; finally restored to the Werdenbergers their arms and honors, and never had reason to regret this generosity.

CHAPTER XLIX.

PARTY-RAGE AND DISTURBANCES IN ZUG. POWER AND MISFORTUNES OF LANDAMMANN SCHUMACHER.

[A. D. 1714 to 1740.]

AT the period when peace was restored to Glarus, it was driven away from the canton of Zug by party-rage.

On the shore of a beautiful lake among the mountains lies the little city of Zug, not very secure on the soft bank, which has already twice (1435 and 1594) given way in parts and carried houses and gardens into the flood. The small district dependent on the city was early (1350 to 1484) bought from various knights and convents by savings of the municipal income, and governed by bailiffs. And the bailiwick of Hunenberg, which had ransomed itself from its lords (1414), voluntarily acknowledged the sovereignty of Zug, under reservation of its franchises. In the city itself all the burghers had equal rights. Some noble families, however, who had lived there from very ancient times, generally secured the first offices to themselves, either as heirs of great riches or of great names, by their merit or the influence of party. They often occasioned serious disturbances, sometimes among the citizens, sometimes by their rivalry, sometimes by selling their own and their country's services to foreign powers for gold and titles.

The free communes of Aegeri, Menzingen and Baar, under their own constitutions and laws, independent of the city, formed with it the whole canton. The ammann, or chief of the republic, was chosen alternately from these four districts. The few prerogatives which the city enjoyed, and sometimes abused, served only to excite jealousy and hate in the country against the city. Not a century passed without tumultuous, sometimes bloody, quarrels between the two. Once (1702) it even went so far that Aegeri, Menzingen and Baar were on the point of separating from the city of Zug, and forming a canton apart, had they not been prevented by the Confederates.

The Zurlaubens, barons of Thurm and Gestelenburg, were among the richest families of the land. For two hundred years, they had almost always been in possession of the highest state-offices, and in the favor and party of the French king, who extended to them the distribution of the French pensions, whether gratuitous or stipulated by treaty, and the office of purchasing adherents and votes for France. They had obtained from the city and communal councils the lucrative privilege of the government trade in salt, of which they annually imported six hundred casks from Upper Burgundy. The opponents of the Zurlaubens were looked upon as opponents of France and, consequently, as partisans of Austria.

Among these was Anthony Schumacher, member of the council, a talented but violent man, who carried on a trade in the salt of Hall (a small Tyrolean town on the Inn, where are salt mines). He and other opponents of the ammann Fidelis Zurlauben complained, not without good reason, of the quality of the Burgundian salt; then questioned the faithful management of that business, and finally found fault with the partisan distribution of the French pensions and gratuities. At that time foreign powers freely distributed presents in money to those Swiss whose venal fidelity had been proved, and by such gifts enlisted and purchased fresh hirelings and dependants. The communes of Baar and Menzingen countenanced these complaints and said: "The money should be equally divided among all the citizens. Is not each of us, the least as well as the greatest, an ally of the king?" When ammann Fidelis heard this, he distributed money and presents to a great many people, and kept open tables at the eating-houses, in order to secure to himself friends and partisans against the Harten (Hards) as his opponents were called.

But when Josias Schicker of Baar, an enemy of Zurlauben, and one of the Harten, was ammann of the canton (1728) it was decided that there should be an equal distribution of the French gratuities and stipulated pensions. And, as France would not consent to this, the Harten became angry and persecuted the partisans of the French king, who were called Linden (Softs). They were maltreated, and their places given to the partisans of Austria. Ammann Fidelis, accused of malpractice in appointments to civil and ecclesiastical offices and of having taken excessive profit and usury, was condemned to restore his wrongly-acquired gains, and, when he fled to Lucerne, his property was confiscated and himself banished for one hundred and one years. He never saw his home again. Others of the Linden fled like him, and, like him, were punished. Even the ammanns Weber and Christopher Andermatt shared this fate, because they had once (1715) at Solothurn, in the name of Zug, signed a treaty with France, in which report said there was a secret article respecting the division of Switzerland among foreign powers.

When the general assembly, two years afterwards (1731), conferred the dignity of ammann upon Anthony Schumacher, the alliance with the king of France, who had sent neither pensions nor presents, was broken. Only one man, the council-lord Beat Caspar Utiger, was bold enough to warn the people of the dangers of such a proceeding: but he had to fly in haste from the country in order to save his life.

Ammann Schumacher now established a new tribunal composed of nine of his most devoted adherents, which was invested with the greatest powers by the sovereign people. Fresh prosecutions were begun against the partisans of France. The prisons were filled with them. If any one escaped chains by flight, his name and effigy were hung on the gallows. Whoever pitied the banished or blamed the Harten, was compelled to stand in the pillory, or, for a whole year, to wear a red knit cap, the object of public derision. Schumacher even endeavored to detach Uri, Schwyz and Unterwalden from the French alliance. He did all this, perhaps with the upright intention to free his country from the influence of foreign gold and foreign intrigues, perhaps with the hope that France would consent to the equal distribution of the gratuities and stipulated pensions and thus the credit of the Zurlaubens be destroyed.

Two years long continued these doings of the well-intentioned but violent ammann. But many of the Harten, when they saw that their expectations were not realized, were softened and longed for quiet and their old friends. At this unexpected inconstancy of the people, Schumacher adopted unusual measures to prevent any union between the inhabitants and the exiles and any revolt against his authority. The communes were compelled to arm, to send captains into all the bailiwicks; Baar and Menzingen to establish special guards. The gates of the city of Zug were repaired; closed early and opened late. This occasioned astonishment, as no enemy was seen; and gave rise to murmurs at the expense.

When Schumacher's term of office expired, John Peter Staub was chosen ammann in his stead, and as none of Schumacher's promises to the people had been fulfilled, the Lindens increased greatly in favor. The new ammann himself took part with them, and followed the rushing torrent. Hence, when Schumacher, after several months, gave in his accounts of the state-money, and was found to have had considerable sums in hand without knowledge or permission of the council, he was dragged from the council-chamber and thrown into prison with his friends and followers.

As soon as this was known in the land, the Harten were everywhere deposed from office, and complaints upon complaints were made against their severe government; the banished were recalled from exile and received in all the cabins with tears of joy. Anthony Schumacher, the victim of party-hate rather than of justice, was led ignominiously to the gallows (9th March, 1735), where hung the names and effigies of the exiles. The executioner took them down. The humbled ammann was compelled to carry them on his back to the council-house. He asked only for life. On ten serious accusations, the judges condemned him to perpetual banishment from the Confederacy and to three years of the galleys. But the people, who had before prized him so highly, demanded his blood. For fear of a riot, he was brought to the lake-shore, with irons on his hands and feet, before break of day in the morning of 18th May, 1735. There his daughter shed upon his neck the tears of an everlasting farewell.. The crowd stood by in silence and saw him, surrounded by a strong guard, enter the boat which was to bear him from a land, every league of which had for him only tears or curses. Popular favor is a false harlot; she repays her lovers' faith with affliction. Seven weeks after his expatriation, death freed him, in the prison of Turin, from the miseries of the Sardinian galleys.

But the old troubles were not banished from the land with him; dissension and discontent lasted many years. When Zug renewed her alliance with France, the latter immediately sent presents to her adherents. But when the people learned this, a fresh storm burst forth (1746); those who had received the money were compelled to pay it into the treasury, and were, moreover, punished by heavy fines and banishment. Another outbreak was with difficulty prevented by the Confederates in 1768, and by their mediation, France was induced to furnish the people with Burgundian salt, as before, or with a compensation in money, which last, like the stipulated pensions, was to be equally divided among all the burghers in city and country.

CHAPTER L.

QUARREL OF THE HARTEN AND LINDEN IN THE OUTER RHODES OF APPENZELL.

[A. D. 1714 to 1740.]

It is very unfortunate when magistrates forget that they are but the servants of the state, and wish to make the commonwealth serve their selfish interests, their vengeance or their pride. This had occasioned great trouble in the canton of Zug, and about the same time almost produced a civil war in that of Appenzell.

Since the twelve old Rhodes or districts of Appenzell had separated in consequence of difference in faith, so that the Inner Rhodes at the foot of the high mountains remained catholic, and the Outer, on both banks of the Sitter, reformed, they had indeed counted in the Confederacy as a single canton, but, as regarded themselves, they were two communities, independent of each other in faith, customs and laws.

The old borough-town of Appenzell remained the chief town of the Inner Rhodes. But the Outer Rhodes, which were unequally divided by the Sitter, had long disputes with each other, sometimes about the location of their chief-place, sometimes about the choice of magistrates. The people east of the Sitter were more numerous than those on the west, and were jealous of their rights. Finally, each portion chose its own magistrates, and Trogen became the chief place of the former, Herisau that of the latter. The jealousy on both sides was not thereby diminished, but rather increased.

At Trogen lived the influential family of the Zellwegers, enriched by commerce and manufactures. In Herisau flourished the family of the Wetters. One of the latter held the office of landammann in the year that the city of St. Gallen had a fresh dispute with the Appenzell ers respecting tolls (1732). St. Gallen said: "Let the dis pute be referred to two Confederate cantons as arbitrators, agreeably to the 83d article of the Rorschach treaty of peace, made after the Toggenburg war."

Landammann Wetter declined and said: "The treaty of Rorschach is not obligatory on our people, because it was not confirmed by any assembly of the communes, but concealed from them and signed by a few chief men only, on their own responsibility. If they were still alive they would be punished as traitors to justice and liberty, and for having given to the city of St. Gallen the power to increase her tolls at her option."

Of all the magistrates of Appenzell who had witnessed the treaty at Rorschach, none were living but some relatives of the Zellweger family at Trogen. Landammann Wetter was no friend to these; their riches gave them too much influence in the country. And he said: "They had acted interestedly and on some secret understanding with St. Gallen to the detriment of their own country."

Thereupon the Zellwegers retorted: "Were not the chief men from both sides of the Sitter present at the treaty of Rorschach? Did not the principal men and the judges of all the Rhodes approve it? Has not the treaty been already acted upon and carried out in a previous dispute respecting tolls with St. Gallen, in 1720? Why do you so strenuously oppose it now, but from bad faith?"

The people west of the Sitter paid no attention to this, but believed landammann Wetter and blamed the Zellwegers and their friends in the other district. And, one day, when the heads of all the rhodes were assembled at Herisau, the excited country-people, who were called Harten, rushed into the council-house and into the council-hall. There, with great roughness, they maltreated those councillors who respected the treaty of Rorschach, called them Linden, and dragged the Zellwegers to the window, in order to throw them out to the violent and raging mob. Quiet was not restored until each council-lord had cried from the window: "The government did wrong in not submitting the treaty of Rorschach to a general assembly."

When the parishes east of the Sitter heard how their chief men had been maltreated, they wished to rise and avenge them. But the Zellwegers and other well-meaning persons dissuaded them, and induced them to await the coming general assembly.

When the people from these rhodes came afterwards to the general assembly at Teufen, (20 November, 1732,) they found the men from the other rhodes armed with old swords, and gathered in unusual numbers around the chair of the landammann. By the majority of their votes, these latter overpowered all opposition, deprived of offices and honors all those magistrates who favored the party of the Linden, and declared innocent every one who had been condemned for resistance to the treaty of Rorschach.

Now bitterness and hate prevailed throughout the land, quarrels and disputes between the Harten and the Linden, the partisans of Wetter and of the Zellwegers. Both parties appealed to the reformed Confederates. While the latter, as usual, sat irresolutely in diet at Frauenfeld (January, 1733), the people of the rhodes became so excited that the men seized their arms, and the women and children fled from Trogen to the neighboring Rheinthal. Thereupon a deputation from the Diet hastened to Herisau to restore peace. When Escher, the stadtholder of Zurich and head of the deputation, had with wise words appeased the council, and declared that the Confederates had not the least intention to impose conditions displeasing to their fellow confederates, delegates from the ten parishes of the country were announced as desirous to confer with the deputies. These delegates were so numerous that the market-place of Herisau could not contain them, being four or five thousand men. And they shouted and threatened, and cried: "Have you come here to uphold the traitorous Linden, and to force a free people to observe an agreement to which they never assented. Are we slaves or are we still free men?"

This discussion lasted far into the night. By the light of torches and lanterns, the confederate deputies were compelled, in a severe winter's night (19 February, 1733), to go to a plain near Herisau, and there give to the people a written assurance that the treaty of Rorschach should never be forced upon them. On the next day, a crowd of people again rushed into Herisau and required the mediators to exhort the opposing Linden to submit to the decree of the general assembly. The deputies from Berne and Zurich said: "Our cantons are the originators and guarantors of the disputed article in the Rorschach treaty; shall we act against those who wish faithfully to observe that treaty? This people shall never compel us to decide unjustly." But the other deputies, in cowardly fear and anxiety, decided that it was necessary to appease the people. And the deputation declared in writing, that the Linden must submit to the decree of the general assembly. The Harten themselves had not desired more, so they dispersed satisfied.

This conduct of the Appenzellers, this unworthy treatment of the Confederate deputies, justly excited the indignation of the mediating cantons, especially of Zurich and Berne. But the wounds of the Toggenburg war were still too fresh to permit an armed interference. The matter was frequently discussed in diet at Frauenfeld and Aarau, but without vigor, consequently without result. Moreover, the Linden were thereby encouraged in their resistance to the Harten.

The irritation of both parties at last broke forth in the town of Gaiss, and the people, coming to blows, called on the neighboring villages for assistance. They fought with clubs and sticks. The Harten were victorious this time also, and plundered the barns and cellars of the Linden. These latter, breathing vengeance, assembled the next day in arms at Trogen and Speicher; the forces of the Harten rallied under their banners at Teufen with artillery. Citizen-blood was about to flow. But the government of Appenzell, supported by the Confederate mediators who were at St. Gallen, succeeded this time also, by firmness and prudence, in separating the furious opponents and restoring peace.

In the mean while the Linden had learned by these encounters that they were the weaker party in the land. Therefore they gave up their cause in despair. The general assembly at Hundwyl confirmed the decision of that which had met at Teufen the year before. The leaders of the Linden party were deprived of honors and offices, and punished by heavy fines for the hopes they had entertained of the support of cantons and diets.

CHAPTER LI.

HENZI'S CONSPIRACY AT BERNE.

[A. D. 1740 to 1749.]

THE Confederates were silent respecting the justice or injustice of the measures adopted on the Sitter, because all had enough to do to keep peace at home. Every canton had more or less trouble, and Berne the most of all.

At first the sovereign power of the city of Berne was vested in all the citizens, by virtue of the charter granted to them by duke Berchthold of Zahringen, under the emperor Frederick II. (1218). And the burghers chose their magistrates each year mostly from the noble families established in the city, whose riches, leisure and education rendered them more capable than the common citizens to rule a state with dignity. But as, in course of time, the nobles became haughty and ambitious of absolute power, the citizens, assembled in the preacher's church (1384), made a statement of their liberties in a fundamental law, intended to prevent all abuses. Thenceforward, yearly, sixteen citizens and four bannerets were to choose the two hundred of the great council (as since 1294) from among the artisans: they thought it easier to find twenty men who would not be corrupted by the rich families, than to prevent gold and intrigues from influencing a great crowd. The commons reserved to themselves the passing of important laws and the declaration of war and peace; even the country-district was to be called into council on important matters, as had formerly been and was still for some time the case.

But, by degrees, the powerful bannerets chose for the great council only their friends and relatives; by degrees, these families perpetuated their possession of the government; the great council, in concert with the bannerets and the sixteen, renewed itself annually; by degrees, the commons were assembled more rarely; finally not at all. In 1531, the first law was passed without vote of the burghers, and, in 1536, when war was to be declared against Savoy, the commons were assembled for the last time. After this, not again. The sovereign power became exclusively hereditary in the families of the great council. All the citizens were indeed eligible, nominally; but the ruling families were only a small number, who divided all places and offices among themselves.

An unjustly acquired sovereignty, however good and wise it may be, never effaces by its virtues the stain of the original injustice, and always trembles for its power. Berchthold's old grant and the citizens' fundamental law still lay in their golden chests; but the ruling families of the great council desired neither to enforce nor to revoke them. Nothing was said of the rights of the commons of Berne, but the inscription still remained on the city-seal.

Several times the burghers murmured against the hereditary power of a few families. The yet unrevoked grants and charters gave to the dissatisfied a pretext and color of right. But the ruling power imposed silence on free voices. When, in 1710, several burghers demanded the restoration of the old constitution, in a memorial to the great council, and even formed a conspiracy, prisons and banishment disposed of the malcontents. When, afterwards, in 1744, twenty-four burghers of the city presented a respectful petition that in future the council should no longer be chosen arbitrarily and by favor, but selected by lot from among all who were eligible, they were punished as rebels, some by confinement to their own houses, others by banishment.

Among these was captain Samuel Henzi, a man of noble mind and uncommon acquirements. The time of his banishment, which he passed at Neuchâtel, was shortened by pardon. When he returned to Berne, but found that he was ruined, and, on application, that he was excluded from all lucrative employment, his heart became filled with bitterness and he could not restrain his indignation.

At that same time there lived in the city many upright and wealthy men of respectable citizen-families, such as the Fueters, Werniers, Kupfers, Bondelys, Lerbers, Knechts, Herborts, Wyses and others. These men mourned in silence over the down-trodden rights of the commons, and lamented that the chartered prerogatives of the citizens could not be maintained against the power of those who now sat, like hereditary lords, in the council-hall. Henzi joined them, as did Michael Ducrest, the surveyor, who lived at Berne under arrest, on account of his participation in the disturbances of his native city, Geneva. By mutual complaints of the usurpation of the government and of the haughty harshness of some of its members, the feelings of these men became excited; and in conversations in which the abuses of the commonwealth were vividly presented to all their minds, bold resolutions were formed. No one can say who had the first thought of a new conspiracy. But captain Henzi, whom his recent disgrace impelled to the zealous adoption of energetic measures, soon became the soul of the whole, in consequence of his eloquence and superior acquirements.

They met in the evenings; formed plans for the restoration of the ancient order of things agreeably to the charter and fundamental law, and bound themselves to fidelity and silence by a fearful oath. Henzi desired to act with energy, but also with moderation. Such was also the wish of Daniel Fueter, the goldsmith. All the best informed and most upright men agreed with them: they aimed simply at the destruction of existing abuses. Force was only to be employed in the last resort to resist force. But when the circle of the conspirators was enlarged, and men were admitted of ill-regulated minds, fiery ambition and ruined fortunes, the original moderation no longer prevailed. This is proved by the secret document they drew up to justify their enterprise, in which a deadly hatred depicts in the blackest colors all the faults of the governing families. "The sword, not the pen," said they, "is the weapon by which the lost chaplet of liberty must be regained."

It was agreed that, on the 13th of June, 1749, the arsenal was to be taken by storm, liberty proclaimed, the commons assembled, a new government installed, and the great council of the reigning families dissolved.

The government, unsuspicious of the threatening danger ruled with dignity and wisdom. All the Confederates honored their extended views and noble institutions. Even foreigners admired the good results of their rule. Their virtues had caused most of the citizens to forget the ancient prerogatives of the commons, and the subjects congratulated themselves on the mildness and justice of their lords and masters. But the day intended to ruin all approached.

The number of conspirators already amounted to sixty. But Henzi, who had been most earnest in the cause before the later evil designs were revealed to him, abhorred it, as did many of the others, when he learned that a large portion of the conspirators concealed the worst intentions under the mask of patriotism. Then Henzi withdrew his countenance from those whom imprudence and disunion were leading to the brink of ruin. He meditated flight. Before he could succeed in this, every thing was betrayed by an ecclesiastic, himself an accomplice, bound by the oath. Henzi was seized on a party of pleasure and thrown into prison; as were lieutenant Emanuel Fueter and the merchant Samuel Wernier. The others fled in great terror, and, when at a distance, learnt with horror that those who remained had confessed, under fear of chains and torture, their intention of assassinating the principal citizens, of burning the city, of pillaging the public treasury; or that these things were at least believed by the public. Few felt themselves capable of such crimes.

When these things came to light, Henzi appeared the most guilty of all. He had repaid with ingratitude the kindness of the government which had shortened his term of exile. Sentence of death was passed upon all three. The others implored mercy; Henzi did not; he disdained a life of disgrace.

On the 16th of June, 1749, Henzi, heart-broken but fearless, took leave of his wife and children; saw the heads of Wernier and Fueter, his accomplices, fall beneath the sword of the executioner; then presented himself without trembling to the death-stroke. He knew how to die with more dignity than he had lived.

The rest were banished from the country. When Henzi's widow stood on the bank of the Rhine with her two young sons, she cast on her native land a last despairing look, and said to the bystanders: "Did I not know that these children would one day avenge the blood of their slaughtered father, dear as they are to me, I would gladly see them swallowed by these waves."

But the sons, when arrived at manly years, were more magnanimous than their mother. One of them, governor of the noble youths in the service of the hereditary stadtholder of the Netherlands, repaid his own undeserved misfortunes by benefits to the burghers of his native city.

However, these events were not unattended with good results to Berne. The wants of the state were discussed more freely. Many members of the council, worthy descendants of their renowned ancestors, urged the reform of abuses. Afterwards (1780), the sentence pronounced on all the criminals was revoked, and the banished were allowed to return. So much had public opinion changed, that those who had been carried too far by their noble desires to benefit the commonwealth were received with pity or respect; while contempt was the lot of those who, instead of dissuading the malcontents from their perilous designs, had entered the conspiracy only to become cowardly traitors.

CHAPTER LII.

OF THE REBELLION IN THE VALLEY OF LEVENTINA.

[A. D. 1750 to 1755.]

SHORTLY after these distressing events at Berne, others, even more melancholy, occurred in the valley of Leventina. Here, in a district extending eleven leagues from the snow-clad heights of the St. Gotthard to the mountain-torrent of the Abiasca, on both sides of the Ticino and in the wild side-valleys, dwelt a people content with the small returns of their herds upon the Alps, their woods upon the mountains, and their pack-horses upon the St Gotthard pass. The ancient franchises with which they had passed from the dominion of the Visconti family to that of Uri remained unimpaired. Uri derived but a small revenue from the tolls, and a trifling impost.

Therefore Uri thought that neither pay nor other compensation was due from her when the men of the valley followed her banners in the Toggenburg war. "For," said Uri, "we have protected you, and maintained your franchises during nearly two centuries and a half, almost without compensation; why do you now ask pay from your sovereign?" Hereto the people of Leventina answered, and said: "You are obliged to protect us and to maintain our franchises by the old agreement you made, but no agreement obliges us to go to war for you at our own cost." And, as Uri still refused to pay the wages for their faithful service, and as the people of Leventina thereupon seized the bailiff of Uri and appropriated the tolls, deputies from the five catholic cantons came to Altdorf and said: "Uri owes the money."

So peace was restored, and no bad feeling remained in any heart. Uri acknowledged her error and she loved justice.

But in the valleys of Leventina dwelt some men who were unjust towards their fellow-citizens, and especially towards the widows and orphans whose property they managed. The widows and orphans complained to Uri, and the government decided that all guardianship accounts should be settled according to the ancient custom. This frightened many of the rich men of the valley. They said: "This is an innovation. Uri will again attempt to deprive us of our liberties." And they went into the villages round about, where they had many debtors, and excited the people and said: "Let us be united and we can easily stand against Uri. If you are courageous, we will throw off the impost and collect the tolls for ourselves." Thus said they, and wished to cover up their own crime with the crime of the whole people. It was in the beginning of 1755, when all the country lay under the snow and the unemployed peasants had much leisure on their hands. They held meetings in their villages, and formed all sorts of resolutions. Each wished to appear bolder than the others. They seized Gamma, the bailiff of Uri, as well as the collector of the tolls, and empowered the tribunal of the valley to sit in judgment on important cases.

When the government of Uri heard of these disorders they earnestly entreated the valley-people to return to their allegiance. Two men of Leventina, Wela and Bull, appeared before the general assembly to answer; they spoke boldly, not as subjects, but as masters; there were fully two thousand men in arms on the other side of the St. Gotthard to support them.

Immediately, the horn of Uri was heard along the Reuss. Through storm and rain, nearly a thousand Urners, with six pieces of heavy artillery, ascended the rocky paths of the St. Gotthard and showed themselves above the sources of the Ticino. The watchmen of the rebels fled in terror and spread fear through the whole valley.

The chiefs of the insurrection, Urs, captain of the country, Furno, banneret of the valley, Sartori, council-lord, and others, their adherents, met together and held a council of war. They decided: to draw Uri into the valley as far as the foot of the high Platifer, where the Ticino, with frightful rush, breaks through a cleft in the rock, and where a handful of men can hold at bay a whole army on the rock-hewn path. When the enemy were entangled in the pass, the men of Leventina would come forth in numbers from all the lateral valleys, in the recesses of which they were till then to be concealed, surround and annihilate the forces of Uri.

Unfavorable weather covered the St. Gotthard with deep snow, even after the lower valleys began to grow green. Therefore the Urners stopped in the valley of Urseren. But, in the mean while, the notified Confederates of Zurich, Lucerne, Schwyz, Zug and Unterwalden hastened with auxiliaries over the lake of the Waldstatten. Valais, Berne and Glarus occupied the frontiers of Leventina.

At last the battalions of Uri, reinforced by eight hundred warlike Unterwaldeners, passed the heights of the St. Gotthard (21st May, 1755). But when the rebels, instead of the small force of Uri, saw the banners of the Confederates, their country completely surrounded, and the Lucerners in the valley of Ronca, all their courage failed. They fled, throwing away their arms, back into their villages; many into the forests. In vain did signal-fires on the heights give notice of the danger and call for a general rising.

The Urners and Unterwaldeners advanced cautiously from village to village, leaving guards at every defile, as far as the last hamlet on the Abiasca. All yielded and were disarmed; the other Confederates received notice not to advance further with their auxiliaries; good discipline was maintained; the chiefs of the rebels seized, one after the other; and Urs, the captain of the country, himself dragged from the capuchin-convent, where he had hoped to find a safe asylum.

Then began the judgment of a whole people; an imposing and fearful spectacle, such as Switzerland has seldom seen.

Near Faido, where the St. Gotthard road passes through a small valley, surrounded by wooded mountains, is an open, even space, to which the people were accustomed to resort for deliberation. Here they were now assembled from all the villages. Nearly three thousand men appeared on the day of judgment (2d June), awaiting their sentence. The Confederates, in arms, surrounded the criminals. Among the multitude reigned the silence of death, broken only by the monotonous thunder of the waterfall on the neighboring rock.

When all was ready, sentence was passed on the people. The forfeited rights of their ancestors, their honors and guarantees were taken from them. Then they were condemned, bareheaded and on their knees, to witness the execution of their chiefs and to swear obedience to Uri.

Within the circle of bayonets, the thousands swore the bitter oath which annihilated the liberty inherited from their fathers, and with the guilty living punished their guiltless posterity. Then, at a signal, the crowd of penitents sank shuddering to their knees, and, with brows uncovered, saw fall beneath the sword of the executioner the banneret Furno, the captain of the country Urs, whose bloody heads were nailed to the scaffold, and the councillord Sartori.

After this terrible solemnity, all the people returned to their cabins, with deep fear in their hearts, and on the next day the avenging army of the Confederates marched back over the St. Gotthard. Eight men of the subjugated valley, more guilty than the rest of the rebels, walked in chains before the banners, and received the death-stroke in Uri.

CHAPTER LIII.

HOW THE ANCIENT CONFEDERACY FELL INTO STILL GREATER DECAY. THE HELVETIAN SOCIETY.

[A. D. 1755 to 1761.]

At this same time there were many upright and well-informed men in the Confederate land, and their hearts were heavy when they heard of all these troubles and disorders. They saw therein presages of the general ruin and destruction which drew near; but no one listened to their warnings. There was certainly a great deal of good, but evil began to obtain the ascendancy.

True patriotism dwells side by side with true liberty. Hence there was more patriotism in the capital cities than in the country districts; more in the shepherd-cantons than in the bailiwicks. The burghers of the sovereign cities, jealous of their prerogatives, disliked to see a subject rise to eminence by learning or riches. All paths by which he might attain distinction as statesman, scholar, soldier or clergyman were designedly closed to the peasant. In many places even commerce and the mechanic arts were forbidden to him. Bound to the plough and to service, he saw in the city-burgher his born lord, general, judge and priest. The subjects of kings enjoyed more rights than the subjects of the Swiss. Even the growth of the small cities, flourishing by means of commerce and good schools, was viewed with secret dissatisfaction by the capitals.

Hence that holy love which willingly sacrifices to the fatherland whatever is dearest disappeared from among the people; mean selfishness filled the empty place. Hence there was obedience; not the obedience of freemen but of slaves, not from conviction but from fear, full of distrust of the nobles and the cities, full of obstinacy against the introduction of improvements. For the common people were brought up in blindness of mind; the young men, often without instruction or in schools worse for the intellect than the wildest impulses of nature. It was thought that a blind people could be more easily led. But the blind, also, more easily smite their own masters when evil advisers place a sword in their hands against them. No one thought of this.

At home the governments were satisfied with being good managers. The highest as well as the lowest offices in each canton were paid moderately, often meanly; fortunes were made in foreign service or in the bailiwicks. Order prevailed in public affairs; love of justice in spite of unfavorable laws; and the rights, even of the meanest, were generally respected and enforced. In consequence of the trifling state expenses, imposts were rare and never burdensome. In the capital cities, science and taste flourished by the side of wealth, especially among the reformed. Zurich and Geneva were distinguished among all for their eminent scholars and artists. At Bâle, on the other hand, a narrow and calculating spirit caused the decline of her time honored university, so that it had nearly as many teachers as scholars, and became an establishment rather for the support of the former than for the education of the latter.

In the capital cities of catholic Switzerland, where the clergy opposed free inquiry, science attained no distinguished honor. The monkish spirit drove the young men away from living knowledge to the coffins of dead erudition.

The shepherd-cantons cared not for culture or information. Personal liberty and freedom from taxes supplied the place of all. The peasant in his hut, fed by his flocks, choosing his own magistrates, knowing no laws but such as he had helped to make, thought himself the freest son of earth. Poor, rude and superstitious, he allowed himself to be led by the priests and rich families of his district; but he was led, not imperiously governed.

In many cantons, the governments accomplished good things. Berne built palaces for the commonwealth, constructed highways, and amassed treasures by economy. Zurich encouraged commerce, science and agriculture. Lucerne struggled gloriously against the nuncio and the papal court of Rome (from 1725 to 1748), when they tried to make the spiritual power superior to the temporal rights of the government.

All Switzerland indeed, to the eyes of foreigners, seemed a paradise, the abode of happy and peaceful men. But they saw only the beautiful verdure of the plains, not the barren rocks; the majesty of the snow-mountains, not their destructive avalanches. They saw the pomp of the Diets, not their bickerings; the images of William Tell, not the slavery of the subjects; the illumination of the cities, not the spiritual darkness of the villages. Everywhere great names and words, small sentiments and actions.

The consciousness of their weakness, which forbade manly enterprises, was called moderation, and cowardice was called love of peace. Men sought for pensions, titles, chains of gold from foreign kings, and boasted of their country's independence. They praised the peaceful happiness of the Swiss, when to centuries of civil and religious wars had succeeded a century of mutinies, conspiracies and insurrections.

A mean-spirited, small city-policy, without the dignity of virtue, thought to secure respect by the darkness of mystery. Freedom of the press was forbidden. Hardly six years after the establishment of the first Swiss press, an official inspection of books (called censorship) was introduced into Zurich and other cities. The gazettes were compelled to be silent respecting the affairs of the country. It was more easy to learn the doings of the Grand Turk or of the

Great Mogul than those of Zurich, Berne or Schaffhausen. This diminished the attachment of the Confederates for their Confederacy, as seemed to be the wish of the governments.

Entirely to destroy this holy and powerful feeling, the old hate between the small communities, originating in former religious wars and feuds, was carefully cherished. Freiburg celebrated the fratricidal day of Villmergen as a religious festival. ' Coldness and distrust separated the valleys of the same mountains. They no longer fought against each other with the sword, for fear of foreign nations; but more bitterly with tongue and pen. They reciprocally forbade the supply of the most necessary provisions; and even, on the frontiers and highways, stationed soldiers and constables, who, with revolting harshness, prevented the transport of garden-produce, eggs, fowls and fish from one little corner of Switzerland to another.

"Without the advice and consent of the others, no canton shall enter into alliance with foreign nations." So says the ancient, perpetual bond. Nevertheless, without the advice and consent of the others, the cantons, one and all, made special treaties with France or Austria, with Spain or Venice. "No judge shall be acknowledged who has bought the office." So declares the perpetual bond. But the sale of offices was public, in the forest-cantons and elsewhere.

Such had the Confederacy become; everywhere more or less openly corrupt. Here, some villages and small cities boasted of their insignificant privileges and opposed their badly-understood rights to all improvement in the laws; there, the cities strove for more authority over the country; now, the ancient families of the cities claimed precedence of the more recent; then, those families who sat in the places of government demanded that their authority should be perpetuated by law. Everywhere prevailed mean disputes, selfishness, vanity and self-importance. The Swiss were more friendly with foreign nations than with each other; and it was easier for them to settle in any other part of the world, than to change their abode from one village to another, or from one canton to another, within their own fatherland. A Swiss, when he had passed the limits of his own little district, was no less a foreigner in the Confederacy, than was an Indian, a Persian or a Russian.

While the monarchies were perfecting their organization and increasing their power, nothing was done in Switzerland, either to ameliorate her constitutions, or to strengthen her bond. While France and Austria grew to colossal powers and improved their military systems, the careless Swiss allowed their arms to rust. They boasted of the victories of their ancestors, and thought not how to secure victory in the day of danger. Their means of defence dated from the Thirty Years' War; their latest military tactics were nearly a century old. They forgot to provide the means by which a force was to be armed; there was no uniformity in their weapons or in their management of them. Some few, indeed, as Berne, Zurich and Lucerne, had introduced more improvements into their military systems than had the others; but what these cities did seemed intended rather to put down an insurrection of their own subjects than to repel an invasion of foreign forces.

Such a condition of things greatly saddened the hearts of many right-thinking and far-seeing men in the land of the Confederates. Some of the noblest met together at the baths of Schinznach on the Aar: Iselin, the philanthropist of Bâle, Hirzel, the sage of Zurich, the independent Urs Balthazar of Lucerne, the valiant Zellweger of Appenzell and others. They founded (1761) a fraternal association of patriotic Swiss, a Helvetian society, for the increase of information, of public spirit, of Confederate brotherly love. They met every year; every year their number was increased from all the cantons and allied places. Here, the most worthy men of the fatherland learned to love one another. Here, friendships were formed for the public good. In these holy meetings, the flame of the ancient Confederacy once more blazed pure and noble. But the governments of the cantons viewed these assemblages with suspicion and permitted them unwillingly.

CHAPTER LIV.

KING FREDERICK THE GREAT, AS PRINCE OF NEUCHATEL, BEHAVES NOBLY TOWARDS HIS SUBJECTS.

[A. D. 1762 to 1770.]

FOR the chiefs and councils of the cantons were afraid lest, by such societies, the doings of the governments should be unfavorably criticised, their authority diminished, information disseminated among the people, and their subjects imbued with a greater love of liberty.

The king of Prussia, who was lord and prince of Neuchâtel, showed himself much less fearful of the enlightenment of his people. He even increased and extended their privileges, instead of diminishing or restricting them.

Neuchâtel and Valengin, with the fertile valleys along the lake and among the Jura mountains, had belonged to the kingdom of Burgundy in the earlier times, and afterwards passed to the German empire. In the castle on the lake-shore dwelt the barons of Neuchâtel. They granted great privileges to all who would settle on their savage mountains and clear their impenetrable forests. Thus the country became peopled, and about the castle grew the city, which received from count Ulrich and his nephew Berthold (1214) the same rights as Besançon, the principal city of Upper Burgundy.

Afterwards, when lord Rolin of Neuchâtel transferred his sovereignty and property to emperor Rudolf of Habsburg (1288), the country passed by turns into several hands. First, Rudolf of Habsburg ceded it to the powerful Burgundian house of Chalons; then, nearly three centuries afterwards (1505), it came into possession of the family of Longueville; and when the last daughter of that house, Mary, duchess of Nemours, died (1707), full twenty heirs claimed this fine principality. But the estates of the country, composed of the twelve judges of the principality of Neuchâtel, met together, examined the titles of the claimants, and recognized king Frederick I. of Prussia as next heir to the house of Chalons.

Thus the king of Prussia became prince of Neuchâtel, subscribed to the constitution and franchises of the country, and exercised his rights over it by a royal governor, and a state-council which he chose from among the natives. Thenceforward, he also was considered an ally of the Confederacy, because the principality was numbered among the districts allied to Switzerland. For the ancient lords of Neuchâtel, as well as the cities and many of the free communes, had successively, during many centuries, enjoyed the right of perpetual coburghership with the cantons of Berne, Solothurn, Lucerne and Freiburg, and thereby the protection of the whole Confederacy.

The people of Neuchâtel were very jealous of their rights, and would permit no encroachment on the part of the king of Prussia. In 1748, when he leased the revenues which he derived from the country, the people were opposed to the innovation, and in 1766, when he wished to renew the lease, there was much more disturbance. The king, through his chargé, Gaudot, laid his complaints before the canton of Berne, as the umpire appointed by compact; and Berne decided almost every thing in favor of the prince. Thereat the people of Neuchâtel were so enraged, that they followed Gaudot when he returned from Berne and attacked his house (25th April, 1768). In vain did the magistrates try to restrain them; in vain were the troops called out. Gaudot and his nephew, when they saw their danger, tried to frighten the people by firing from a window upon the crowd. They did wrong. A carpenter who had almost forced his way into the house was killed. The people rushed furiously over his dead body, and Gaudot fell, pierced by three bullets.

Urged by the envoys of the king and by the council of the city of Neuchâtel, Berne, Lucerne, Solothurn and Freiburg, after long deliberation, sent a garrison into the disturbed city, to preserve the public peace. Then tedious inquests and interminable parleyings took place. The king's plenipotentiaries thought this a good opportunity for the exercise of arbitrary power, that the country might in future be held in more submission and fear. But the Confederates were unwilling to be the tools of foreign ambition, and the banneret Osterwald spoke energetically and courageously in defence of the laws and franchises of his fatherland against the foreign servants of the prince. Finally, the matter was judged and decided. The city of Neuchâtel was compelled to give up her arms, to bear all costs, to indemnify the family of the unfortunate Gaudot, and, in the persons of the city-council, to ask pardon of the king's plenipotentiaries at the castle. The more guilty insurgents, most of whom had fled, were banished, fined or hung in effigy. Then the garrison of the Confederates returned home.

But the king of Prussia, after all this, instead of restricting or diminishing the privileges of the people of Neuchâtel, as Uri had done in Leventina, consolidated and even increased them by new grants. This won back to the house of Prussia the hearts of all the people. Not only did he soon restore their arms, but he allowed a yearly just valuation of the ground-rents, which might be paid in fruits and wine, or in money. He disclaimed the right of arbitrary removal from office; and furthermore, gave to the united communes the privilege of an independent general council, without whose assent the prince could make no change in the management of the state. Many things which were doubtful or obscure in the ancient laws were corrected and elucidated, and always to the advantage and gain of the people. Thus did the king, what no government of the Swiss republic had ever done. But he was one of the most excellent and wisest princes of that century. He was Frederick the Great.

CHAPTER LV.

PARTY-QUARRELS IN THE CITY OF LUCERNE. HISTORY OF LAND AMMANN SUTER OF THE INNER-RHODES OF APPENZELL.

[A. D. 1770 to 1784.]

ABOUT the same time, the city of Lucerne also was the scene of still more afflicting troubles and disturbances. Here, as in some other cities of Switzerland, the principal and noble families had long since taken possession of the government as an inheritance, and almost entirely annihilated the ancient influence of the rest of the citizens in the commonwealth. More than one person, raised to the magistracy, not by talents or virtues but by the favor of influential relatives, thought he had a right to live at the expense of the state without doing much for the state. Sometimes an excessive indulgence, sometimes an ambitious jealousy, on the part of the rulers towards each other, brought great evils on the commonwealth and on themselves. Such was the increasing corruption of morals, that unfaithfulness in the management of the public property was not unusual. Magistrates absconded with government-money; the granary and arsenal were plundered; even the state-treasury was broken into and robbed.

Already the amtmann, Leodegar Meyer, had been obliged to expiate in exile his excessive luxury, to supply which he had abstracted a large sum from the state-money. Shortly after him, the state-treasurer, Jost Nicholas Joachim Schumacher, wasted in prodigal expenses 32,000 florins belonging to the country and was forever banished from the territory of the whole Confederacy (1762). His son, Placidus Schumacher, was not deterred by his father's warning example from a most disorderly life. He first spent all his own property; sank in debt; then, as amtmann, mismanaged the signiory of Heidegg; entered the Austrian military service; left it; wandered about the territory of his native city and in the neighborhood; associated with discontented men, and made himself beloved by or of importance among them by his extravagant speeches. Although there was no appearance of sedition, the suspicions of the government were aroused, because they were too well aware of their own arbitrary conduct and weakness to have any confidence in the people. Schumacher and some of his loose companions were imprisoned under charge of seditious designs, though he had merely drawn up a petition expressing the complaints of the malcontents in the ordinary and legal manner. He was accused of high treason, and, although nothing was proved, was beheaded (1764), to the terror of the citizens and country-people. Others, who had been with him, were sentenced to banishment.

Some years afterwards, when those who had decreed Schumacher's death became sensible of their own unfounded fear and injustice, each wished to throw off the burden of guilt. The council-lord, Valentine Meyer, who conducted the trial, had contributed most, it was now said, to the severity of the sentence. The family of the victim at first privately then publicly, accused him. Then it was remembered that he was the son of Leodegar Meyer, and might, probably, have been actuated by bloodthirsty revenge. Even those who had joined with him in the trial, judgment and sentence, and had signed the latter, meanly declared against him. Then general Pfyffer, head of the French party, who was Meyer's enemy because the latter had often spoken zealously against the injurious influence of France, rose triumphant against him; then every one who feared or envied his talents or acquirements accused him. To him, as a clear-thinking man, was attributed the authorship of a pamphlet which had been published at Zurich with this title: "Would not the catholic Confederates be benefitted by the complete suppression or the restriction of the regular monastic orders?" This added the convents, clergy and nuncio to the crowd of his enemies. An ironical refutation of the pamphlet, not without satire against the monks, which he read to a circle of confidential friends, was, when it appeared in print, burned with ridiculous solemnity by the hangman of Lucerne, a false friend having betrayed the name of the author

This was enough to condemn him. He was to be made a victim. In order to find grounds of accusation, his enemies used every means, violated the faith of the state, the secresy of the post-office, broke into his house and ransacked his papers. When all these high-handed measures had failed to discover any crime, he was arrested at his country-place where, knowing his innocence, he dwelt freely and fearlessly. Forty-three days he lay in prison and had no hearing. In vain did the upright and brave avoyer Keller, the wise patriot Felix Balthasar and many other impartial men address the council in his behalf. In vain did Meyer himself send a justificatory petition: they decided not even to open it. In vain did honest Casimer Kruss advise reconciliation and peace. Meyer was sentenced to fifteen years of banishment; while on the other hand, each of those who had been condemned to exile or the galleys as accomplices of Placidus Schumacher, received a pardon (1770). Then, for the first time, did the divided principal families make peace among themselves, agreeing that the troubles in Lucerne arose, not from injustice, but from the too severe application of the laws to the members of the government and of the ruling families; and that mutual forbearance and a firm alliance could alone prevent the prerogatives of the nobility from passing into the hands of the citizens.

Shortly after these events, the bloody end of Joseph Anthony Suter, landammann of the Inner-rhodes of Appenzell, made it evident that the freedom and rights of the citizen are no safer with a whole people than under the sovereignty of a few noble and patrician families, when the spirit of moderation and justice has given place to the intrigues of selfish ambition and revenge.

Suter was innkeeper at Gonten; a man of little education, but of cheerful mother-wit, charitable to the poor, kindly to all. For these qualities, the Appenzellers made him bailiff of Rheinthal, preferring him to John Jacob Geiger. The latter had sought the office, as it was lucrative, to compensate him for the sacrifices he had previously made. Two years afterwards, the nine rhodes of the country chose the amiable Suter governing landammann, and again preferred him to his rival Geiger.

This enraged the latter and many others in the country who thought themselves of importance. They secretly formed a party against Suter. Many rich people, also, were his enemies, because he had zealously opposed an unjust law which gave to home creditors the preference over foreign ones against insolvent debtors. "For," said Suter, "it is unjust, destroys the confidence of foreigners and prevents them from loaning money in our country." But the rich men said: "Suter favors foreigners; he is not a friend to his own people."

Suter did not care for these calumnies, but used all the means in his power to benefit the country. He obtained for his canton from the commune of Oberried in Rheinthal the refusal of one of the finest alps on the upper Santisberg, in case it should be sold. The Appenzellers, when once in great want of money, had sold this alp to the Oberrieders. Afterwards, when it was reported that large portions of the great Santis-alp had been mortgaged to foreigners, landammann Suter persuaded the members of the council to have the alp appraised and the money appropriated, and to take immediate possession.

Herein his zeal carried him too far. Oberried justly complained to the Diet against the Inner-rhodes, and the council, repenting their precipitancy, withdrew their pretensions. Suter, however, obstinate and made proud by his dignities, would not yield, but carried on the suit at his own expense. After he had lost it before the Diet (1775) and came home, he was ashamed to acknowledge the truth. When it became known that the canton of Appenzell had been sentenced in the costs and that all her real estate in Rheinthal was held as security for their payment, although Suter declared that he would pay the whole, the enemies of the landammann raised a great outcry, and his colleague, landammann Geiger, and the council said: "Suter has deceived the government by misrepresentations, and has brought shame and disgrace on the Inner-rhodes before all the Confederates." And the council, without a hearing, though he was chief of the canton, took from him the seal of state, deprived him of all his honors and dignities, and declared him incapable of filling any office in future.

Then said Suter: "You, my enemies, have neither authority nor right to pass such a sentence; the general assembly shall judge between you and me."

But before the meeting of the general assembly, many reports, unfavorable to Suter, were spread among the people. The capuchins, who were also his enemies, wen from house to house, and preached and spoke of Suter's secret sins and misdemeanors. When the general assembly was held, loud cries were raised among the people for and against the accused, and he was dragged by force from the landammann's seat, in spite of hundreds of voices proclaiming his innocence.

Then, while this deserted and ruined man was making a pilgrimage to the miraculous image at Einsiedeln, he was, during his absence, banished forever by the council from the whole Confederacy, as an enemy to religion, liberty and peace; his name nailed to the gallows; his property, real and personal, sold at a very low price to pay the costs and his debts; every one of his friends deposed from the council, and even his own true wife forbidden, under penalty of deprivation of civil rights, to call him husband any longer. No one knew the reasons for so severe a punishment. So far as the judicial sentence expressed any, it mentioned only trivial faults, but hinted mysteriously at secret crimes, which could not be made public for fear of scandal. It was uncertain whether this mystery was intended to veil the iniquity of the banished man or that of his judges.

The outlawed old man dwelt thenceforth, much commiserated, at Constance, on the lake. Some years after, he demanded an impartial tribunal and a safe-conduct. Seventy men of Appenzell voluntarily united to serve him as an escort. But Suter's petition was refused, and four of the most resolute of the seventy were condemned to death and led to the place of execution, but pardoned after being whipped by the hangman.

Now silence and terror prevailed. The banished man

remained at Constance. Sometimes he went into the Outer-rhodes to see his friends. After a long while, there came into the country a person named Baptista Ross, who, when considered a partisan of Suter, had been declared infamous. When now again arrested he said, in order to make himself of consequence: "Old Suter is raising a force in the Outer-rhodes to attack the town of Appenzell, and to rouse the people to revolt against Geiger's party." He even cited some honest men as witnesses. But the honest men said: "He tells a falsehood."

He was believed nevertheless; the people were excited against the exile by atrocious calumnies; then they determined to get possession of his person. This was done in a shameful manner. They went as friends to his own daughter, who was married at Appenzell, and deceitfully persuaded her to write to him to come to the Crown-inn at Wald, a commune of the Outer-rhodes, where he would hear important and agreeable news.

Unsuspectingly the old man obeyed the call of his deceived daughter. He was decoyed, under various pretexts, as far as Oberegg, a hamlet of the Inner-rhodes. There he was seized, bound and carried on an open sled to Appenzell (9th Feb., 1784). It was a rough winter's day. While his guards refreshed themselves at the inn of Alstatten, the old landammann lay praying upon the sled. The stormy wind shook the new-fallen snow from his grey locks.

Before the criminal court he renewed the oath of his innocence. Thrice in a single day subjected to torture, he would acknowledge no guilt. Nevertheless sentence of death was pronounced against him. Twenty of the judges would not give their votes thereto, and solemnly protested in the records of the court against participation in the sentence. But it was carried into effect that same day (9th March, 1784). Old Suter heard his doom with all the calmness of innocence; with all the calmness of innocence he went to the place of execution. There his head fell.

CHAPTER LVI.

DISTURBANCES AND INSURRECTIONS IN THE CANTON OF FREIBURG.

[A. D. 1781 to 1790.]

WHILE party-hate occasioned fermentation in the land of Appenzell, it showed itself still more dangerous in the canton of Freiburg. Dissatisfaction had long prevailed in city and country.

Here, in the earliest times, the avoyers and a few judges had managed the affairs of the city and of the territory immediately surrounding it, which is still called the ancient district. Important matters were decided by the assembled people. When the people became too numerous for this, the supreme power was confided to a committee of wise men, called the great council. At first this council was composed of burghers of city and country, as representatives of a free people; then of nobles and patricians only; finally, of none but the members of certain families.

Then, between the great and little councils (the legislative and executive), the council of sixty, an intermediary authority, was established, and from this council of sixty proceeded yet another authority with greater power, the secret chamber (1553), which could nominate to and exclude from all offices. For a long while, an equal number of burghers from the four districts or banners of the city were chosen for the sixty and great council, but at last only the members of certain families, which were called the secret families. Finally (1784) all the other burghers were thenceforward forever excluded from entrance into the number of the secret families.

Hence arose dissatisfaction among the city-burghers against the governing or secret families who held all the offices. And there was latterly a division among the secret families themselves, because the nobles among them claimed precedence over those who were not noble. With the decline of the liberty of the commons, industry lost its strength and life. Before the institution of the secret chamber, numerous weavers brought prosperity to the land; every year more than twenty thousand pieces of white cloth were sold to Venice alone. The number of working tanners in a single quarter of the city was nearly two thousand. But now there was an end to all this. The people of the ancient district also regretted the free old time; for now they were nearly on a par with common subjects.

Although the government had already, several times, repressed with severity, as criminal innovations, the respectful petitions of individual burghers and even of whole communes, some persons thought it a duty to renew their complaints, in consequence of the continued dissatisfaction of the people.

In the pretty village, La Tour de Treme, upon his own extensive estate, lived a man well versed in the sciences and in the history of his country. His name was Peter Nicholas Chenaur, and he was much esteemed for his uprightness and magnanimity. He and his friends, John Peter Raccaud and the lawyer Castellaz of Greyerz, saw that all petitions to the government would be useless without an earnest demonstration on the part of the whole people. They sent confidential messengers into the valleys, and found all ready to sustain them.

Then Chenaur ventured to go to the city of Freiburg (3d May, 1781), to lay the complaints of the country before the council. Fifty or sixty armed men escorted him. But the council, already informed of the popular movement, had closed the gates against him, strengthened the troops and armed the citizens. Thereat wild cries of revolt resounded from village to village. The alarm-bells were rung. When Chenaur saw the movement so general, he became bolder, organized the people into battalions with officers, and breathed courage into them. Once again but in vain, did Castellaz send a petition to the council of Freiburg, requesting them to listen to the complaints of the people or to submit the difference to the mediating cantons. This proving fruitless, Chenaur (4th May), with more than twenty-five hundred peasants, for the most part badly armed, marched against Freiburg, as far as St.

James's chapel. With six or eight hundred men, he advanced close to the city; others went by the way of the gate of Bourgillon; five hundred lay in the woods of Schonenburg on the right bank of the Saanen. From distant parts of the canton many others were hastening.

The garrison of the city marched out with great military pomp. By the side of the banners of Freiburg floated the standard of Berne. For Berne, called upon for help, had at once sent three hundred dragoons, then under drill. Colonel Froideville, a prudent and humane officer, commanded them.

Froideville spoke kindly to the insurgents, required them to lay down their arms, promised forgiveness of the past and a hearing of all their complaints by the government and mediating cantons. More the peasants had not asked. They were ready to lay down their arms on Froideville's word of honor. But when he demanded the surrender of their leaders, they became suspicious, and refused.

During these parleyings, the crowd of peasants had been surrounded and the heavy artillery brought up. When the insurgents saw this, they were terrified and threw down their arms. Those who could, fled. This flight struck terror into the bands behind. They hastily dispersed.

Among the fugitives was Chenaur. But one of his own people, Henry Rossier, either from anger at the failure of the enterprise or to curry favor with the victors, treacherously murdered him from behind. The dead body of Chenaur, given up to the executioner, was cut into pieces, and the head exposed on a pike from the Romont gatetower. Castellaz and Raccaud, condemned to be quartered, happily escaped by flight. Others of the leaders were punished by deprivation of life, property or honor.

In the mean while, Berne, Solothurn and Lucerne had sent more troops, and mediators, to Freiburg. But the government gave notice that, from its own innate goodness, it would listen to the complaints of the communes; then allowed the whole country no more than three days time to draw up in writing and submit a statement of grievances. Notwithstanding this short space, and notwithstanding the soldiers with whom the city swarmed, numerous delegates of the communes hastened to Freiburg from far and near.

The examination of the complaints dragged on from month to month, without result. Then the people thought of their disappointed expectations, and lamented the death of the man whose life had been a sacrifice. Every day Chenaur's grave was surrounded by praying multitudes. Pilgrims thronged to it with hymns and crosses and banners. In vain did the government station sentinels with loaded arms; in vain did the bishop condemn pilgrimages to Chenaur's remains; nothing could prevent the people's grateful remembrance of the dead.

The common burghers of the capital city and the twenty-four parishes of the ancient district had also hoped, with better prospect of success under the circumstances, to secure a recognition of their rights from the governing families. They asked only for access to the chamber of archives. There still lay the charters, sanctioned by oath, of the years 1404 and 1553, which guaranteed to the burghers and inhabitants of the city a share in the elections and in the fundamental legislation. But the government said: "The rules of your corporations and guilds are sufficient to inform you of your rights." Thus repulsed, the burghers and peasants could hope for justice only from the mediating cantons. After long attempts at conciliation, the following declaration from Berne, Lucerne and Solothurn at last suddenly appeared: "We will maintain the present constitution of Freiburg with all our force; the pretensions of the burghers are groundless and unconstitutional; we however recommend to the government that no precedence be allowed to the nobles over the patricians of the secret families, that the burdens on the country-people be diminished, and any abuses that may have crept in be corrected."

The burghers, with consternation, heard this proclaimed from the pulpit (28th July, 1782). On the evening of the same day, all the four banners of the city assembled in front of avoyer Gady's house. The lawyer Rey, the notary Guisolan, the merchant Ignatius Girard, spoke in behalf of the citizens. The avoyer listened calmly, with apparent assent.

But, a few days afterwards, Rey was banished with his family for forty years, Guisolan for twenty, Girard for ten; even Emanuel of Maillardon, son of one of the ruling families, was exiled for six years, because he had said in an assembly of the banners: "It is desirable that the burghers be reinstated in their ancient rights." Many others suffered in like manner.

Nevertheless, the government wisely lightened many of the burdens of the peasants, increased the number of secret citizens by the addition of sixteen families, and promised that, in future, when one of these families became extinct, it should be replaced by three new ones.

CHAPTER LVII.

DISTURBANCES IN THE BISHOPRIC OF BALE, IN VAUD AND GRISONS.

[A. D. 1790 to 1794.]

BUT about this time also, there arose in the vicinity of Switzerland a storm which threatened misfortune to the Confederates and to all the thrones and countries of Europe. France, in consequence of the continued extravagance of her former kings, was sunk in hopeless debt and misery. In spite of constant increase, the heavy taxes and imposts did not produce sufficient to pay the enormous interest and the expenses of the state, but there was an annual deficit of 140,000,000 of francs. The rich convents, nobles and princes would bear no portion of the burden, and the exhausted people could endure no more. In the courts of the king and princes, in the castles of the nobles, in the abbeys and great cities were still magnificence and abundance, feastings and pleasures, while the country-people lay steeped in wretchedness and misery. Law did not govern, but arbitrary will; there was no religion, but mockery and unbelief among the great, ignorance and su perstition among the lower classes. This must needs bring a curse upon the country. And it came.

As soon as the dissipated court could no longer meet its expenses, and the people could no longer pay taxes, the whole came to the ground. When the king assembled the states-general for advice and assistance, they abolished the privileges of the nobles and clergy. The people rose and destroyed the prisons. The castles of the signiors disappeared in flames. The property of the clergy was converted to the uses of the state; its value was three thousand millions of francs. Then the princes, nobles and clergy fled, terrified, into foreign lands; many into Switzerland; many to the kings of other countries, whose help they asked. And when the kings armed and threatened, the French also seized the sword and said: "We are masters on our own soil."

There was a great difference of opinion in the minds of the whole world respecting these events. The rulers and privileged classes in other countries said: "The French are very wrong." But those who felt aggrieved by their own rulers and lords said: "The French are very right."

So reasoned also in those days the people of the bishopric of Bâle,* especially when their ruler and prince, bishop Joseph of Roggenbach, wished to prevent the communes of the bishopric from holding their customary and lawful assemblies. As the people insisted on their right, the bishop called on the Confederate cantons to uphold him; and when they showed a disinclination to be mixed up in his disputes, he requested the emperor (1791) to send troops for a garrison. Bâle and the other Confederates were at first unwilling to allow the Austrians a passage through the Swiss territory, but finally consented. They thought this of little consequence, although the advocate of the states-general of the bishopric, court-councillor Von Rengger, had declared that the states-general had a right, under the treaty of 1781 with France, to introduce as many French troops as there were Austrians. Thenceforth the bishop had the power in his own hands; Rengger was

* An allied district, not a Confederate state.

obliged to fly, and others who were of the same opinion with him were mercilessly condemned to the pillory and perpetual imprisonment.

But about a year afterwards (April, 1792) war suddenly broke forth between France and Austria; then French troops entered the bishopric and drove out the Austrian garrisons. The bishop, terrified, fled to Bienne; soon, still further. No one helped him. It would have been better for him had he not exasperated his people.

The French wisely respected Erguel and Munsterthal, which had long been in defensive alliance with Berne and Bienne; but they occupied Pruntrut and those districts of the bishopric which were nearest to Germany. And court-councillor Von Rengger came back. With his partisans, he roused the whole land. The bishop's officers were driven away and the prince's revenues sequestrated. But when Louis XVI., king of France, was dethroned by his own people, and his kingdom made a free republic, Rengger also planted at Pruntrut a liberty-tree, as it is called; which is a high pole surmounted by a red cap, in token of the country's freedom. The delegates of the communes assembled around. There they abjured forever all connection with the bishop and also with the emperor and German empire (Nov., 1792). They formed their little state into a republic, which they baptised Rauracia.

But great disturbances arose therefrom. For every one wished to command, no one to obey. The parties persecuted each other. Finally, many demanded the incorporation of their country with France. When Rengger and his party saw that they could no longer maintain their authority, they gave up the life of their three-months old republic, and on the 7th of March, 1793, the assembled people decreed the union of the bishopric of Bâle with France. And this was effected. Only Erguel and Munsterthal still remained independent, in consequence of their alliances with Berne.

Probably, the Confederates would willingly have protested against this dismemberment, for they were inimical to the French in their hearts, but, feeling their weakness, without union among themselves and distrusting their subjects and serfs, they dared do nothing. The Bernese patricians, moreover, by their incautious hospitality to French refugees, had incurred the suspicion of France. Therefore they were silent respecting the division of the bishopric of Bâle, and dismissed the bishop with polite and consolatory speeches when, before the Diet at Frauenfeld, he claimed the right of Swiss neutrality against the French. Even when the people of the great city of Paris stormed the royal palace, and after a bloody fight (10th Aug., 1792) overpowered and slew the Swiss life-guards who were in the king's pay, not a man of the Confederates dared to make public complaint.

The world rang with arms and cries of war, with revolutions, battles and defeats. The French promised fraternity and assistance to every people who wished to make themselves free. They beheaded their own king, Louis XVI. Their arms advanced victorious through Savoy and the Netherlands and over the Rhine. Nearer and nearer drew the danger around the country of the Alpine people.

But the government of the Confederate states showed no foresight in view of the danger. They thought themselves safe behind the shield of their innocence and their neutrality between the contending parties. They had no arms and prepared none; they had no strength and did not draw closer the bands of their everlasting compact. Each canton, timidly and in silence, cared for its own safety, but little for that of the others. Freiburg, Berne and Solothurn did, indeed, unite for mutual defence, not so much against violence and danger from without as against dissatisfaction in their own territories.

Since 1782, Berne had an unsettled dispute with Vaud respecting contributions for the repair of highways to the capital city. The commune of Morsee had brought forward documents (1790) to show that the whole of Vaud should be exempted from contributions. Others now claimed other rights which Berne had allowed to fall into disuse in the course of centuries. All kinds of pamphlets stirred up the people. At Lausanne, Vevey, Rolle and other places, fiery young men, in noisy assemblages, drank success to the arms of emancipated France. Although public order was nowhere disturbed by such proceedings, the government of Berne thought it necessary to put a stop to them by severe measures and to compel silence by wholesome fear. They sent plenipotentiaries supported by an armed force. The guilty and even the innocent were punished. More fled. This silenced Vaud, but did not quell her indignation. The fugitives breathed vengeance. By letters and pamphlets they excited the hearts of their fellow-citizens against the long-revered government. To be merciful at the right moment, to be firm at the right moment, not to be haughty in the possession of overpowering strength, not to appear cowardly in desperate circumstances; this is the highest and hardest task of those in authority.

This was often forgotten among the free Grisons also, where the old popular parties still quarrelled, not to the loss but to the abuse of freedom. Here the principal families, among whom that of the lords of Salis was preëminent, had long been in possession of the most lucrative offices and of the revenues of the country; thus, at a low rate, they bought the most important magistracies in Valtelina, which the Grison communes were accustomed to sell every two years at auction to the highest bidder, and in which the purchasers usually enriched themselves by selling right and justice to the subjects; also, the offices of captains and colonels in the Grison troops on foreign service, and the Grison tolls, which were the only revenue of the state.

But when other respectable families of the country, among them the distinguished Tscharners, Bawiers and Plantas, united to resist the exclusive possession of such great advantages; when (1787) they raised the rate of the tolls-purchase from 16,000 to 60,000 florins; when they demanded that the officers in the pay of France should no longer be appointed by favor but according to length of service; when shortly afterwards, the oppressed subjects in Valtelina brought forward complaints against the injustice of their venal magistrates and the violation of their long acknowledged rights; both parties became inflamed with irreconcilable rancor against each other. They appealed to the people.

When any evil occurred, each blamed the other. When a French embassador, named Semonville, going to Venice through Valtelina, was seized and delivered to the Austrians (1793), the Salis party were accused of this treachery. When there was a scarcity of corn in the land, the Planta party were accused of selling grain to the French; and the people, excited against them, rose (1794).

Each of the three leagues sent thirty-two men to Coire. They formed a general states-assembly for the examination of the complaints. The Planta party justified themselves, then skilfully turned public indignation against their adversaries and demanded their punishment, together with the reform of abuses. An impartial tribunal condemned many of the original complainants to fines and restitution, others to banishment from their fatherland.

CHAPTER LVIII.

HISTORY OF PARTIES AND EXCESSES IN GENEVA.

[A. D. 1707 to 1797.]

In the mean time the violent war-storm had shaken half the world, and human blood, shed by the sword of battles, had reddened land and sea. The allied kings had sworn to tame France; France, to dethrone the kings. The Confederacy still stood unattacked, between the contending powers, and with armed men on her borders, more to mark the limits of her territory than to defend it. But every patriot trembled for the future. Never were internal union and confidence between people and governments more necessary or less prevalent.

In Geneva the spirit of discontent had prevailed for nearly a hundred years. The grasping ambition of the noble families displeased the people. More than once the city had witnessed scenes of tumult and blood. First, when the dissatisfied citizens complained (1707) that a few families were constantly in possession of the highest offices, that the council did not regard the laws, but governed arbitrarily and no longer consulted the commons on important matters. The executive council called for Confederate intervention, then for a garrison from Berne and Zurich, and, under the protection of foreign arms, caused the prominent defenders of the citizens' rights to be hung, shot, degraded or banished.

The blood thus shed terrified and embittered the citizens, and, on the other hand, so increased the self-confident boldness of the council, that they felt no hesitation in trampling under foot the ancient constitution of the republic, or even in arbitrarily increasing the taxes for the purpose of strengthening the city-fortifications. Michael Ducrest, one of the great council, protested against this, and carried all the citizens with him. The council condemned him to perpetual imprisonment (1731) and Berne, under whose protection Geneva had placed herself, executed the sentence on him at Aarburg. More than once insurrections took place; more than once Zurich and Berne interfered. Peace was not restored. The rancor and bitterness of parties increased. There were even bloody conflicts between them in the streets (1737). Finally (1738), delegates from France, Berne and Zurich having limited the pretensions of the executive council and of the principal families, and wisely regulated many other matters, in an edict which was approved by the council and citizens, peace seemed to be reëstablished.

But, when (1762) the executive council ordered two books written by Jean Jacques Rousseau, a philosopher of Geneva, to be torn by the hangman, and some of the citizens presented a remonstrance which the council refused to receive, fresh hate showed itself in fresh parties. One party called themselves Representatives and said: "The executive council ought to receive all complaints against their own proceedings, and submit them to the general assembly of the citizens for their decision;" the others called themselves Negatives, were supporters of the government, and said: "No, the citizens' assembly have no right of control over the council." The dispute on these matters gave rise to disputes on a hundred others, and there was no end to the disorders and riotous meetings, until Berne, Zurich and France proposed to intervene once more. In order to prevent foreign interference, the council and citizens quickly came to an agreement (1768), and the government granted to the citizens the right of choosing one half of the new members at each renewal of the great council, and of yearly deposing four members of the little council, who should not be reëligible; and many other rights also. A reform in the code of laws was also promised; and additional freedom in the exercise of their trades granted to those native-born inhabitants whose fathers had been long established in Geneva, and had always been zealous in support of the citizens' party, while some of them might yearly be elevated to the rights of citizenship by the government.

This agreement, however, was of short duration, because it had its origin in fear only, not in good feeling. The anger of the governing families was excited at having yielded so much. They wished again to become all-powerful; delayed the reform of the laws; sought the assistance of the French court, and half withdrew the promise made to the native inhabitants. And the French minister Vergennes, who was jealous of the thriving industry of Geneva and wished to draw it, by emigration, into France, took part in the quarrel. By fine promises, he stirred up the Negatives and those numerous inhabitants who deeming themselves entitled to citizenship by right of birth thought they were defrauded of their privileges by the old citizens, against the Representative and people's-party, and persuaded them to make riots in hopes of getting the mastery. When the Representative-party perceived this, they seized their arms, secured the gates, and disarmed the Negatives. But they were so prudent that, in order to gain over all the native inhabitants, they renewed the promises formerly made respecting new citizenship, and granted to the new citizens nearly the same privileges with the old. This agreement was confirmed by an edict passed 10th February, 1781.

This stroke of policy vexed the governing families and their party, the Negatives, as well as the French court.

The latter, in order to produce fear, sent six hundred men to Versoy, in the neighborhood of the city. But Zurich and Berne were offended thereat; for the armed guaranty of the treaty of 1738 did not belong to France. The Confederates declared themselves relieved from that guaranty. When France knew this, she also would have no more to do with it. Thus the Genevese were left free to settle their quarrels among themselves.

As all parties were equally accusers and judges, and the government pertinaciously strove to win back their former authority by force and fraud, the hatred of the old and new citizens broke forth into fresh flame. The government secretly distributed grenades among the soldiers of the garrison. But the citizens, old and new, stormed the city-gates; many soldiers were killed; the little and great councils deposed and a new one chosen from the Representative-party. Many members of the old government fled. But France and Berne said: "We will not allow a government to be deposed by rebels." The king of Sardinia was also persuaded to assist in restoring the old government. Then French, Savoyard and Bernese troops, twelve thousand strong, appeared before the city (May, 1782). Zurich did not interfere. Geneva, divided against herself, soon opened her gates.

Now France, supported by Berne, gave the law; the old government was reinstated with full power; the party of the Negatives triumphed and the common citizens lost many of their long-enjoyed privileges. When the citizens were required to confirm this, barely six hundred were allowed to vote; the rest were excluded because they had taken part in the last insurrection. But, even of the voters, there were one hundred and thirteen men who refused to assent to this extinction of Genevese liberty.

The government, protected by Berne, Sardinia and France, at once forbade all close societies, all military exercises on the part of the citizens, all books and pamphlets on recent events, and, on the departure of the foreign troops, increased the garrison to twelve hundred men, commanded by foreign officers. Thus were the Genevese reduced to subjection. Many emigrated with hearts full of vengeance against their oppressors. Five and twenty of the vanquished Representative-party were banished forever or for limited times; those clergy who had taken part in the matter were deposed from their cures.

Injustice never thrives, and the love of precious liberty is not extinguished by condemnations of books or by bayonets. When the government raised the price of bread on the oppressed citizens (Jan., 1789), the long-restrained hatred of the people burst forth. The citizens armed themselves as well as they could against the hireling garrison, filled the fire engines with boiling water and put to flight the satellites of the government. Thereat the rulers were terrified, reëstablished the previous price of bread, promised to improve the constitution, to diminish the garrison, to restore arms to the citizens, to remove the most onerous taxes, and to raise to the privileges of old citizenship such families of new citizens as had been established in Geneva for four generations. All this was done. Berne and Zurich were persuaded to renew their ancient confederate alliance with Geneva, and joy prevailed.

The government united the more firmly and willingly with the citizens, because they could hope for no help from France, where the people had risen against their king. But fresh disturbances took place. These were occasioned by the peasants in the villages which were dependent on Geneva and subject to the city, as well as by the native vassals and foreign inhabitants of the city, who demanded an equality of rights (Feb., 1791). They more than once came to blows on this quarrel, but the citizens firmly upheld the government. Nevertheless the excitement increased. Some of the former emigrants or exiled burghers of the city who were established in France, wished to avenge themselves and effect the union of Geneva with France. The French resident minister at Geneva, Chateauneuf, also made a party with this object, and underhandedly persuaded the peasants and subject-inhabitants to rise against the government and privileged citizens. All must have equal rights. The people were also told that the rich should be plundered.

At this very time, the French army, intended for Savoy and Italy, approached the city (Sept., 1792), and Geneva, in great terror, implored the assistance of Berne and Zurich, according to treaty. They immediately sent auxiliaries, but quickly withdrew them, when the French army retired and the government of France uttered threats. As soon as the troops were withdrawn, the non-privileged new citizens and inhabitants and the peasants armed themselves and seized the arsenal (Dec., 1792). There were many dissatisfied old citizens with them. In a forced general assembly of the commons, they deposed the great and little councils, and instead of these elected a committee of public safety, a committee of government and a national convention, like the French, with legislative powers. Then all order was at an end. Rioters and brawlers ruled. Whoever held not with them was called an aristocrat. Right and justice disappeared. Party-hate raged. And, as in France, the populace, greedy of blood and plunder, at last obtained the ascendancy, so they were masters also in the unhappy city of Geneva, and committed the greatest excesses. There was no more quiet or safety.

The party of the so-called Revolutionists, entirely to destroy the party of the aristocrats, finally, on a summer's night (July, 1794), took possession of the heavy artillery and of the whole city ; cast into prison many of the formerly most respected citizens, magistrates and men of letters; organised a court by which sixty of these were sentenced to be executed, others to be banished, the property of many to be confiscated and the rest punished in various ways. These persecutions lasted, with some intervals, for two years, during which those who had seized the government wasted and consumed a large portion of the property of the state and of the plundered citizens.

When, however, the people in France had become more quiet and the republican government itself more humane, in Geneva also an intolerable fear of anarchy took possession of both parties. This united all honest men who desired order. Then disorder ceased. The exiles came back. A new constitution, with recognition of state-citizenship and the sovereignty of the people, was established (1795), according to which all old and new citizens, all old and new inhabitants of city and country, born on Genevan territory, enjoyed equal rights. Peace and harmony once more prevailed. Geneva found some quiet after long storms, but only for a short time.

CHAPTER LIX.

OF THE ANCIENT DISTRICT OF ST. GALLEN AND THE WISE ABBOT BEDA; HOW DISTURBANCES ALSO BROKE FORTH ON THE LAKE OF ZURICH.

[A. D. 1794 to 1797.]

THE general war of the kings and princes against the French people grew in the mean while ever more furious, ever more near. Among the Swiss mountains could be heard the thunder of cannon from Italy, from Suabia, from the Rhine. But the rulers of the Confederates seemed not to apprehend the danger which always threatens the weak placed between powerful neighbors.

The banners of France waved victorious through Savoy and the Netherlands, through Lorraine and Holland, and over the soil of Germany. Wherever they appeared, princes, counts and nobles fled in terror, and liberty was proclaimed to the subject-people. The magistrates of the cantons barely restrained their hatred and contempt of the conquerors; they sat in proud security, although the agitation grew more violent about them day by day, and many of their people desired more freedom.

In the ancient district of the abbot of St. Gallen, also, the people rose against the domination of the convent. For they could no longer bear to be deprived of their rights, and to be oppressed by new and extraordinary charges, duties and burdens of the severest servitude, by means of which the monastery grew constantly richer and increased its domains, while the ecclesiastics and officers of the abbey contributed nothing towards the imposts.

Five communes of the district took courage and deliberated together respecting the just complaints they should lay before the abbot. Soon the whole bailiwick of Oberberg joined them. The crowd of those who, with or without reason, had complaints to make, increased daily, so that the number of public grievances amounted to sixty. Thereon the communes assembled, chose committees, and held council at Gossau (March, 1795). At their head was a talented, eloquent and courageous man, John Kunzli. He conducted every thing with great prudence. All the communes signed the paper in which their grievances were detailed and presented it to the abbot.

The abbot and prince, Beda Angehrn, was a wise and good man. He well knew the misery of the poor people, for he was himself the son of a subject of the abbey, from the village of Hagenwyl in Thurgau. He would gladly have relieved the oppressed people; but of all the ecclesiastics of the abbey only two thought like him. The others were angry with the people and said: "This is the French freedom-madness! If the people will not be silent, we must call for assistance on the governments of the Confederates, who have already frequently helped us against our subjects." And they opposed the wise Beda, and so troubled his life, that he had already, at an earlier time (1788), determined to abdicate. But then pope Pius VI. refused his permission, and in a severe letter (16th Aug., 1788) commanded the chapter to desist. The ecclesiastical lords designedly prolonged the discussion in order to tire out the people.

When the prince-abbot perceived their subtlety, he said to the monks: "This is not the time for rulers and subjects to be at variance; they should be united when danger and misery threaten from abroad. Therefore, if you persist in repelling the people, I will throw myself alone into their arms."

And he did so, gave to the people great privileges (Nov., 1795), the right to choose the land- and war-councils, to hold assemblies of the communes, to nominate their municipal officers, and to buy themselves free from the charges to which they had hitherto been subject. He abolished servitude, and decreed that the ecclesiastics and officers should also bear their share of the imposts, and that the abbey should purchase no more real estate. This brought great joy into the land, and blessings were showered on the wise Beda. Soon, the monks of the abbey assented to the agreement which had been sworn to by the people and prince; but only in appearance. So deceitful were they, that almost in the same hour (20th January, 1796) they drew up and signed a secret reservation of rights against their rebellious subjects, as they called the people. They thought they could thereby annul their official act, and, under more favorable circumstances, take back all they had granted. The Confederates, also, protectors of the abbey, in their hearts disapproved the kindness of the pious prince towards his subjects. However, they finally (August, 1797) ratified his doings, because they could not prevent them.

About the same time similar movements took place among the peasants on both sides of the lake of Zurich, as they were anxious to revive their ancient rights. But this undertaking resulted in great suffering and ruin.

Zurich had indeed always governed with justice and prudence the subject-communes of her territory, held them in respectful submission, and by a wise administration caused the country to flourish. Seldom had the subjects to complain of acts of severity or violence, or of injustice on the part of venal magistrates. Since two virtuous burghers of the city, John Caspar Lavater and Henry Fussli, had once (1762) publicly accused Felix Grebel, the wicked bailiff of Gruningen, of injustice, and he had been compelled to leave his country in disgrace, no one had dared to follow in his footsteps.

But other grievances distressed the country, and especially the industrious inhabitants on the borders of the lake; these were the severe restraints of the trades-corporations and the monopoly of commerce by the capital-city. For only the most indispensable handiwork could be exercised by the peasants in the villages, and no commerce was allowed except in wine and grain; the numerous cotton-weavers were obliged to buy their raw material in the city and there to sell their cloth when manufactured. Even what they wove for the use of their own families must first be sold to the citizens and again purchased after it had been bleached and printed. Ecclesiastical and civil offices were closed to the country-people and filled by citizens' sons only. The son of the country-man, confined to the plough and the pruning-hook, or to day-labor in the city, could never raise himself from the dust.

But when the French people, triumphant in their freedom, no longer acknowledged any distinction between peasant and noble, between city and country; many of the people on lake Zurich were excited by this example, and said among themselves: "Why is it not so with us? While we are called free Swiss, we are in subjection to the city. We are like the slaves in many countries." And their excitement was increased by such talk. Some men of the village of Stafa on the lake disseminated their opinions respecting the eternal rights of mankind and respecting the subjection of the country-people to the city, and thought that Zurich ought at last to yield greater freedom to her subjects. They drew up a memorial to be presented to the government, in which they asked for freedom of trade and commerce, equal rights to employment and office for the country-man as well as the citizen, permission to purchase ground-rents and many other things (1794). But what they requested could not be granted without the abolition of centuries-old guilds and corporations, and the abrogation of the ancient constitution of Zurich as an imperial city, to maintain which an oath was taken every year.

When this memorial was sent from commune to commune for approval, and received everywhere with acclamation, the city learnt the proceedings of the people on the lake. Immediately all those who had shown themselves most active were seized and punished with the greatest rigor, as fomenters of a revolt, some by banishment from the Confederacy, many others by fines and deprivation of civil rights (13th January, 1795).

The punishment of so many malcontents did not diminish, but rather increased, the number. Then some lords of the council in Zurich promised them: "If you can show charters and seals to prove your right to privileges which you do not enjoy, we will gladly help you."

Thereat, in the annual general assembly of Stafa (May, 1795) four of the oldest men came forward and said: "It was told us by our fathers that in the archives of the commune existed documents and charters which assured to the people privileges that have been neglected in the lapse of ages. Let us search for and examine them." Although the secretary and bailiff forbade every one even to speak of such documents and charters, the people would not be prevented. And they found in a mill the perpetual covenant made in 1489, on the day of burgomaster Waldmann's execution, between city and country, before the tribunal of the Confederates. This covenant, which had never been annulled, and which was solemnly guaranteed by seven confederate cantons, established general freedom of trade and commerce. They also found a document executed by the burgomaster, council and Two-hundred of Zurich in favor of the country, after the troubles of the war of Kappel (1532). Thereby all former privileges were reäffirmed and even a participation in the government granted.

Then the communes of Stafa and Kussnacht, Horgen, Thalwyl, Ehrlibach and others, sent their deputies to the bailiffs and magistrates, respectfully asking: "If these documents had been annulled by later ordinances, or were still in force?" But the deputies were sent back, and the government of Zurich would neither confess nor deny the validity of the ancient documents, because both courses seemed equally dangerous. The proceedings of the lake-communes were treated as culpably seditious, and they were summoned to the city to answer.

But when those who were summoned did not appear. and, to excuse their disobedience, the communes, especially Stafa, declared: "We have given to no one authority to treat for us in these matters: but we request that these public interests of the country may be discussed with ourselves," the city became very angry. She armed her troops. All communication with Stafa was cut off. Many natives of that place were driven from the capital. And one Sunday morning (5th July, 1795) when the people of Stafa were assembled in church to worship God, the Zurichers with twenty-five hundred men and heavy artillery, entered the peaceful village.

Then Zurich published this declaration: "All your documents and charters are null and void. For one of them was granted at a period when all lawful authority was suspended, and was assented to by the seven confederate cantons only to prevent greater evils. The other was intended merely for peculiar times and circumstances, and was completed and ended with them. We do not find that a single provision of either document has been fulfilled during the space of three hundred years, or that such non-fulfilment has given rise to any complaint on the part of the country."

So said Zurich. The seven confederate cantons, witnesses and guarantors of the thus annulled covenant, were appealed to by the lake-communes. They were all silent. Glarus alone, faithful to the engagement of her fathers, exhorted Zurich to trust to justice rather than force, as no other security can be so great for a state as the confidence felt by every part in the enjoyment of just rights.

Stafa, disarmed and surrounded by bayonets, was obliged solemnly to swear the old oath of submission. All who had taken an active part in the matter of communal rights were punished in various ways: some with perpetual, others with ten or twenty years' imprisonment; some with the house of correction, others with banishment; some with stripes, others with heavy fines. The commune of Stafa, although it had borne for several months the expenses of a military occupation, was still obliged to pay 78,000 florins for costs. One of the oldest and most respected citizens, the grey-haired treasurer Bodmer, was led to the scaffold in Zurich and the sword of the executioner brandished over his head, in token that he deserved death, because he had first insisted on the search after the documents. Then he was carried back to prison, being sentenced to remain there during his life.

Thenceforward the silence of terror prevailed in the country, and the thirst for vengeance in all hearts.

CHAPTER LX.

DESTRUCTION OF THE OLD CONFEDERACY. ENTRANCE OF THE FRENCH INTO THE LAND.

[A. D. 1797 and 1798.]

IN foreign countries dwelt sadly many of those who, at various times, had been banished from the Confederacy because they had, by word or deed, too boldly or importunately defended the rights and freedom of their fellow-citizens. Several of these addressed the chiefs of the French republic, and, with vengeance in their hearts, said: "Those who now rule the thirteen cantons of the Confederacy have driven us from our fatherland; they are your enemies, as well as ours, in the cause of freedom. They prefer to have subjects rather than fellow-citizens, and think themselves little kings and princes. Therefore they secretly assist kings and princes against you. Help the Swiss people to recover their lost liberty; they call you, and await you with open arms. Free men are the truest allies of the free."

Such addresses pleased the chiefs of France. They thought in their hearts that Switzerland would be an excellent bulwark for France, and a desirable gate, through which the way would be always open to Italy and Germany. They also knew of and longed for the treasures of the Swiss cities. And they endeavored to find cause of quarrel with the magistrates of the Confederates. But the latter warily avoided giving offence, acknowledged the free French constitution, and drove away from their territory the unfortunate princes, priests and nobles who had fled from the rage of the French people and found shelter in the Swiss valleys.

Shortly afterwards, came the great general Napoleon Buonaparte, and marched through Savoy into Italy against the forces of the emperor. At this time, only the emperor, with the German empire and the English, struggled against France, as the kings of Spain and Prussia had already made peace with her. And in a very few months, though in many battles, Buonaparte vanquished the whole power of Austria, conquered and terrified Italy from one end to the other, took the whole of Lombardy and compelled the emperor to make peace. He made Lombardy a republic, called the Cisalpine.

When the subjects of Grisons in Valtelina, Chiavenna and Bormio saw this, they preferred to be citizens of the neighboring Cisalpine republic, rather than poor subjects of Grisons. For their many grievances and complaints were rarely listened to. But Buonaparte said to Grisons: "If you will give freedom and equal rights to these people, they may be your fellow-citizens, and still remain with you. I give you time; decide and send word to me at Milan."

But the parties of masters in Grisons could not agree, and many of the Salis faction said: "Let the people of Valtelina remain with us as subjects, or not at all." Now when the last period for decision had passed, Buonaparte became indignant and impatient, and united Valtelina, Chiavenna and Bormio to the Cisalpine republic (22d Oct., 1797). All the property of the Grisons in those countries was immediately seized and confiscated. Thus many rich families in Grisons were made poor.

So the old limits of Switzerland were unjustly contracted; four weeks afterwards also, that part of the bishopric of Bâle which had hitherto been respected on account of its alliance with the Swiss, was added to France. Thereat great fear fell on the Confederates. But still greater misfortunes awaited them. For the country-people in the canton of Bâle murmured loudly against the city; in Aargau several cities reclaimed their old acknowledged privileges from Berne, and Vaud demanded her lost rights with more energy than ever. Then the rumor spread that a French army was approaching the frontiers of Switzerland to protect the people of Vaud. They had called for the intervention of France in virtue of ancient treaties. But report said that the French intended to overthrow the Confederate authorities and to make themselves masters of the country.

Berne and Freiburg immediately raised troops to terrify Vaud and Aargau, and reduce them to silence by force of arms. A Diet hastily assembled at Aarau. There was a great deal of talk, but no decision, because the Confederate cantons could not trust each other or their own people. This was a great misfortune, but did not date from that day. With a presentiment of the general ruin, the lords of the Diet at Aarau once more renewed the old oath of union (25th Jan., 1798), but without the confidence or enthusiasm of their heroic ancestors. Hardly had they sworn when a messenger came from Bâle and said: "Six hundred men from the country have entered our city; the castles of the bailiffs are in flames; all subjects are declared free." Then terror seized the lords of the Diet; they dispersed immediately and in fear.

Then there was great agitation throughout Switzerland, when men saw the fear and weakness of the magistrates, and with these, their opposition to the wishes of the people. In Schaffhausen and in Rheinthal, in Toggenburg, in the March, in Wesen and Uznach, committees of the peasants met, to help themselves. The Italian bailiwicks beyond the Alps planted a tree of liberty on the bank of the Ticino, with rebellious hands. Almost the whole Confederacy was in a state of confusion and dissolution. The governments of the cantons, powerless, distrustful and divided, acted each for itself, without concert. The people of each district acted also for themselves, but with various wishes and intentions. Some, ignorant and rude, could not comprehend the spirit of the age, and wished to maintain the accustomed order of things. Others, with more information and insight, desired equality of rights between city and country. Others claimed only the restoration of privileges formerly guaranteed. Many thought that nothing could be secured without the assistance of France; but the majority of all the people justly deprecated the interference of a foreign power in the affairs of their fatherland.

In the mean while a large army of French advanced. Under their generals Brune and Schauenberg, they entered the territory of the Confederates, and Vaud, accepting foreign protection, declared herself independent of Berne.

Then the governments of Switzerland felt that they could no longer maintain their former dominion. Lucerne and Schaffhausen declared their subjects free and united to themselves. Zurich released the prisoners of Stafa, and promised to ameliorate her constitution to the advantage of the people. A thousand bonfires blazed on hill and valley along the lake of Zurich, when grey-haired Bodmer, with his fellow-sufferers, returned home from the city-prisons. Never in Switzerland was living man received with such solemn honors by his people. Even Freiburg now felt that the change must come for which Chenaur had bled. And the council of Berne received into their number fifty-two representatives of the country, and said: "Let us hold together in the common danger."

All these reforms and revolutions were the work of four weeks; all too late. Berne, indeed, with Freiburg and Solothurn, opposed her troops to the advancing French army. Courage was not wanting; but discipline, skill in arms and experienced officers. From Glarus, Lucerne, the Waldstatten and other cantons came feeble help; also the landsturm, variously armed, in tumultuous hordes, telling their beads. But this troop fled at the first bad news, without having seen an enemy. Then the Swiss and their rulers, in their inmost hearts, regretted that they had unlearned the art of arms and war, and in the days of peace had believed that it must last forever. Now neither the gold of their treasure-chambers, nor pomp, nor pride in long titles of nobility availed them; nor prayer nor rosary. Heaven helps only those who march joyously to battle and to death in a just cause; but rejects those who sit sluggishly in arrogant security.

On the very first day of the war (2d March, 1798), the enemy's light troops took Freiburg and Solothurn, and on the fourth (5th March), Berne itself. In vain did the Bernese make a victorious resistance near Neuenegg under their colonel Grafenried; in vain did they fight valiantly on the Grauholz. Now that all was lost, the armed bands of peasants dispersed in despair, but cried treason and killed many of their own officers.

The day of darkest fate had dawned on the Confederacy;

but the spirit of the ancient bond had long since disappeared. Even on the brink of the abyss, in the near prospect of general ruin, the small states did not unite for the common defence. Each cared and armed for itself alone; negotiated for itself alone with the invading enemy, having no understanding with its neighbors and confederates. Weak when divided, all must needs perish. In vain did they invoke the remembrance of the heroic deeds of their ancestors; these sought a freedom which was worth dying for on the field of battle. With cowardly despair, grudgingly, and in some cases with secret reservation of future withdrawal, the liberty of the subjects was promised, sworn to, signed and sealed. Too late. The battalions of the French army already swarmed over the whole country from the Jura to the base of the Alps.

France now authoritatively decided the future fate of Switzerland and said: "The Confederacy is no more. Henceforward the whole of Switzerland shall form a free state, one and indivisible, under the name of the Helvetian republic. All the inhabitants, in country as well as city, shall have equal rights of citizenship. The citizens in general assembly shall choose their magistrates, officers, judges and legislative council; the legislative council shall elect the general government; the government shall appoint the cantonal prefects and officers." The whole Swiss territory was divided into eighteen cantons of about equal size. For this purpose the district of Berne was parcelled into the cantons of Vaud, Oberland, Berne and Aargau; several small cantons were united in one; as Uri, Schwyz, Unterwalden and Zug in the canton of Waldstatten; St. Gallen district, Rheinthal and Appenzell in the canton of Santis; several countries subject to the Confederacy, as Baden, Thurgau, Lugano and Bellinzona, formed new cantons. Valais was also added as one; Grisons was invited to join; but Geneva, Muhlhausen and other districts formerly parts of Switzerland, were separated from her and incorporated with France.

So decreed the foreign conquerors. They levied heavy war-taxes and contributions. They carried off the tons of gold which Berne, Zurich and other cities had accumulated in their treasure-chambers during their dominion, and had been unwilling to use either for the benefit of their own people or for that of the Confederacy. They sent into France members of the governing or most distinguished families as hostages for the payment of oppressive imports, or for the maintenance of public peace. They diminished, they exhausted the resources of the richest communes and of the poorest huts by the quartering of troops, by forced supplies for their support, and other exactions. In fact, Switzerland, self-sustained, could, with less cost and more honor, have better borne the burden of a year's war, than this occupation by a foreign army, than this fruit of the neglect and surrender of the old Confederacy.

But the mountaineers of Uri, Nidwalden, Schwyz and Glarus, original confederates in liberty, said: "In battle and in blood, our fathers won the glorious jewel of our independence; we will not lose it but in battle and in blood." And, posted at their borders on the Schindellegi and on the Etzel, in view of the French troops, they took the oath of fidelity till death with their general Aloys Reding. Then they fought valiantly near Wollrau and on the Schindellegi, but unsuccessfully; for the curate of Einsiedeln, Marianus Herzog, who commanded the Einsiedelners on the Etzel, fled disheartened from that mountain. But Aloys Reding reässembled his troops on the Rothenthurm, near the Morgarten field of victory. There a long and bloody battle took place. The shepherds fought in a manner worthy of their ancestors, and, like them, victoriously. Thrice did the French troops renew the combat: thrice were they defeated and driven back to Aegeri in Zug. It was the second of May. Nearly two thousand of the enemy lay slain upon that glorious field. Gloriously also fought the Waldstatten on the next day near Arth. But the strength of the heroes bled away in their very victories. They made a treaty, and, with sorrow in their hearts, entered the Helvetian republic.

Thus ended the old Bond of the Confederates. Four hundred and ninety years had it lasted; in seventy-four days it was dissolved. It fell in consequence of internal weakness, but did not deserve so ignominious a fall. Its struggle against the power of the French, then overwhelming the world, was like the final struggle of an old man, who, with stiffening hand, seizes the sword, not to defend the flickering sparks of life, but merely to save his honor.

Say, son of Switzerland: What levelled your high rocky walls, opened your impenetrable mountain-gorges, bridged your broad lakes and your raging torrents, blunted the arms of your arsenals and rendered useless the gold of your city-treasures? Reflect and be warned!

CHAPTER LXI.

HOW THE SWISS SUFFERED GREAT CALAMITIES, UNTIL A NEW CONFEDERACY WAS FORMED.

[A. D. 1798 to 1803.]

Now, when throughout the whole country between the Jura and the Alps, the customary order of things was changed, whether voluntarily or compulsorily, the enlightened citizens of the land said: "A great misfortune has befallen us. Let us improve it for the benefit of our fatherland. So long as we were divided into many small states, we were foreign and inimical among ourselves; each canton was powerless for its own defence, poor in useful institutions, opposed to great public works. Now the old form is broken. The body is consigned to the dust. But nations are immortal, and called to a more glorious resurrection, as soon as their spirit hopefully strives for a higher destiny. Let the Swiss people form one family with equal rights; let us labor with single aim for the maintenance of liberty within and of independence without; so shall we once more be honored among the nations of the earth."

But the uneducated mass of the people did not understand such words, and did nothing but lament their lost quiet and customs. They desired independence and freedom, but not union into one great whole; they would have preferred, on the contrary, that each small district, each valley even, should be an independent, self-governing little canton, ruling itself in general assembly according to its will, and united with the others in a Confederacy.

Every thing that occurred increased their regret for the past, their desire for such a hundred-faced Confederacy, and their dislike to the present or future order of affairs. The new general government, established at Aarau under the name of Executive-directory, commanded neither respect nor confidence, was strange to itself and to the people, dependent on and degraded by its protectors, the French authorities. In the senate and in the great council of the representatives of all the cantons, contentions took place between all parties, between the ideas of the people and of the schoolmen. In the country, the same parties showed their enmity, often with arms in their hands. New and old institutions and laws clashed most disastrously. While the state was in want of the most necessary supplies, and the officers and clergy of their pay, the French commissioners, generals and soldiers lived in shameless extravagance at the cost of the country and sent to France the treasures they amassed by plunder.

Thereat the people said: "This must not be!" And the magistrates of olden time, who had been deprived of their offices, and the monks, who feared the suppression of all convents, and the clergy, who had lost their salaries, and the traders and mechanics, who no longer enjoyed the privileges of guilds and corporations in the cities, travelled about and increased the popular dissatisfaction by their complaints. They dwelt on the prospect of a war between France and Austria, and exhorted the people to help the German emperor with all their power to dispossess the French.

Therefore, when all the districts were summoned to take an oath to support the new constitution (July, 1798), disturbances and risings took place in Rheinthal, Oberland, Appenzell and other places. They were put down by force, and most fearfully in Nidwalden. There a capuchin,

Paul Styger, with other ecclesiastics, had excited the people to wild revolt, by preaching that the constitution imposed by the French was the work of hell. They armed against the French army advancing under Schauenburg. Terribly on the lake, terribly among the mountains, did a handful of shepherds fight for three days against the overpowering force. Three or four thousand French were killed before the rest could penetrate the country. But then, in their rage, they burnt Stanstaad, Ennenmoos and Stanz, and pitilessly butchered men, women, children and priests who could not flee. Nearly four hundred Nidwaldeners thus lost their lives in the midst of horrors (9th September, 1798).

And shortly afterwards, when the government, which had removed its seat from Aarau to Lucerne (4th Oct.), because the former city was too small, ordered a tax and enrolling of the young men for military service, fresh disturbances took place in the cantons of Berne and Lucerne, and in other places. Many young men fled abroad that they might not be compelled to serve in the Helvetian militia, nor in the contingent of eighteen thousand soldiers which was to be furnished for the French army.

At last the German emperor renewed the war against France. Already (19th Oct.) a body of his troops had occupied Grisons, whence all had been obliged to flee who had recommended a union with Helvetia. Afterwards, near Stockach in Suabia, the French received a severe defeat (21st March, 1799), and when the Austrian forces, victorious in numerous conflicts, advanced into Switzerland; when, terrified by the enemy's near approach, the Helvetian government thought themselves no longer safe at Lucerne, and removed their seat to Berne (31st May); then the various parties in the land acquired fresh life and fresh animosity. Swiss fought against Swiss under the banners of France and Austria. Insurrections and rebellions took place in many districts; sometimes on account of the forced enrollment of the young men; sometimes in favor of Austria; at Flawyl and Mosnang in Santis, at Menzingen and Rynach in Aargau, at Ruswyl in the canton of Lucerne, at Morat and other districts in Freiburg; at Schwyz, where the French were either killed or driven out; at Lugarno and in Uri, in Valais and at Aarberg, and in many other places. In the valleys and on the summits of the mountains, on the lakes and above the clouds, the French and Austrians fought; battle-field touched battle-field. Horse and man passed over the mountain-tops, which the chamois-hunter alone had reached before. By turns, the Germans and French took and lost Grisons and the mountains which enclose the sources of the Rhine. As far as the city of Zurich and thence to the St. Gotthard on the left, and to the Rhine on the right, advanced victorious the banners of the arch-duke of Austria (in June); with them were Russians and Asiatic hordes. Such a calamity had not befallen the inhabitants of Switzerland since the days of the Romans, Allemanni and Burgundians.

Many of the old deposed rulers hoped now for a speedy resumption of all their former authority. They even attempted it here and there, under the protection of the Austrian arms. The new abbot of St. Gallen, Pancratius Forster, himself came; reduced his people to a severer servitude than they had before known; took away from them, with the help of dragoons, the charters of freedom which had been granted three years before, and broke into and rifled the archives of the ancient district. But he soon suffered for trusting to might without right. The cities of Zurich and Schaffhausen also learned that the people would not return to their former servitude on any terms.

Shortly afterwards, when the brave French general Massena proved victorious in a terrible battle near Zurich (25th Sept.), and destroyed in the mountains the Russians, whom Suwarrow, their commander-in-chief, had brought from Italy over the Alps, all was again subjected to the Helvetian constitution, even Grisons (July, 1800).

At last the heads of the central government at Berne saw that such a state of things could not continue to advantage. Therefore they undertook to make reforms. But they could not agree among themselves. Regarding persons more than facts, the parties alternately overthrew each other, so that no one remained long in power, and no one benefitted the country.

First the legislative council at Berne deposed the Executive-directory (7th Jan., 1800), and established a new constitution and a new government, which took the name of Executive-commission; then, seven months later, the Executive-commission, by a stroke of authority, deposed the legislative council (7th Aug., 1800) and summoned a new council, and the government called itself Executive-council. Then, after one year, a general Helvetian Diet was assembled at Berne (7th Sept., 1801), to form a better constitution for Switzerland. But as no agreement could be attained, the Diet was arbitrarily dissolved by a part of the legislative and executive councils, who introduced a constitution with a senate and little-council (28th Oct., 1801). At the head of the little-council was placed Aloys Reding, the victor at Rothenthurm, because his name was honored before all others by the Swiss people. But, as he did not possess the confidence of the French government and could not obtain the favor of those who hated to return to the old order of things, the senate was again arbitrarily dissolved by the little-council (17th April, 1802), and Aloys Reding deposed. Men of note were summoned from all the cantons to construct yet another new constitution. It was adopted, with a senate and executive-council, at the head of which, as landammann of Switzerland, Dolder, an adroit politician, was installed.

The Swiss people looked with indifference upon these continual changes and overturnings of the ruling powers, by which laws and authority were shaken rather than strengthened. They lamented the endless disturbances, the taxes and contributions, the troubles occasioned by the French troops in the country. Riots and risings took place continually. Valais especially suffered under the plundering domination of the French generals and soldiers, to whom it was given as a prey. In order to hold a road over the Alps into Italy, the French wished to separate Valais from Switzerland.

A single desire invariably possessed all the districts of Switzerland: that each canton should organize its internal affairs according to its will; each be free, in a new Bond and Confederacy, independent of French power, and relieved alike of foreign troops and former servitude.

When a treaty of peace was finally concluded at Amiens between France and the other contending parties, and the French garrisons subsequently returned home from Switzerland (Aug., 1802), the spirit of parties and districts fearlessly broke forth with fresh violence. Valais formed itself into a separate republic. Uri, Schwyz and Unterwalden armed against the Helvetian government. The city of Zurich, also, separated from it. Bâle and Schaffhausen followed the example. From Aargau, the landsturm marched against Berne. The Helvetian government, though not entirely defenceless, fled to Lausanne, while a Diet assembled at Schwyz to reëstablish the old Confederacy (Sept., 1803). The weak Helvetian army, in the pay of the government, driven from the interior of Switzerland, followed it to Vaud. Everywhere the parties armed; the cities armed to overthrow the general government; the country-people armed to protect their liberty against the pretensions of the cities; Vaud armed in defence of Helvetian unity and freedom. A general civil war was on the eve of breaking out. Blood already flowed. Then the powerful leader of the French people, Napoleon Buonaparte, turned his eyes towards Switzerland. He commanded peace. On the reäppearance of his formidable army (21st Oct.), all parties laid down their arms and requested him to mediate between them; Swiss trusted Swiss no longer.

CHAPTER LXII.

NAPOLEON BUONAPARTE GIVES TO THE SWISS AN "ACT OF MEDIATION."

[A. D. 1803 to 1813.]

He summoned delegates from all the cantons and parties to come to him at the city of Paris; there he heard them. And after he had well understood them, his mighty word put an end to their disputes; because he cared not for persons but for facts. He did not listen to the city-families, who wished for the restoration of their dominion and of servitude; nor to those who desired that the whole of Switzerland should be an undivided community, with a single code of laws and a general government for all; but he listened to the majority of the people, who wished each canton to be self-governing, and city and country to be equal in right and privileges. Napoleon Buonaparte was a shrewd ruler, and he said to himself: "If I grant this to the people they will be satisfied; but Switzerland will be divided against herself, always without unity, weak and subject to my control."

Accordingly he intervened and gave to the Swiss an "Act of mediation," (19 Feb., 1803), which was to be a fundamental law for all. Each canton received therein its constitution. And he said: "Henceforth there shall be a new confederacy of nineteen cantons, viz.: the thirteen old ones with those of Grisons (including Rhezuns and Tarasp, but excluding Valtelina), Aargau (with Baden and Frickthal), Vaud, St. Gallen, Thurgau and Ticino (the former Italian-bailiwicks). No city, no family, shall have exclusive privileges; no canton, subjects; but every Swiss in city and country shall have equal rights, freedom in trade and industry, and liberty to establish himself wherever he may please, without hindrance from any one. The common interests of the Confederacy shall be managed by an annual Diet, held alternately at Freiburg, Berne, Solothurn, Bâle, Zurich and Lucerne. The chief magistrate of the vorort of each year, entitled landammann of Switzerland, shall have the general supervision, and shall communicate with the ambassadors of foreign powers. Each canton, on the other hand, shall be self-governing, with its own laws and magistrates."

As soon as the nineteen cantons were organized and the Helvetian general government, which had returned from Lausanne to Berne, had dissolved itself, Buonaparte withdrew his troops from Switzerland.

Nearly everywhere the districts of Switzerland joyfully arranged their internal affairs according to the new order of things, and gave in their adhesion. In the canton of Zurich only, several communes obstinately refused to take the oath, especially in the districts of Horgen and Meilen; they complained about the burden of the forced redemption from tithes, ground-rents and other charges. They would listen to no representations, but maltreated innocent officers, burnt the castle of Wadenschwyl (24 March, 1804) and seized their arms. The long disorders of past years had accustomed men to right themselves without regard to law. But auxiliaries from the neighboring cantons, joined with those who remained faithful in the canton of Zurich, quickly put down the rebellion after short skirmishes near Oberrieden, Horgen and on the Bocken. The leader John Jacob Willi, a shoemaker of Horgen, and some of his principal partisans, were punished by death, others by imprisonment, and forty-two culpable communes by a war-tax of more than 200,000 florins.

It was fortunate, however, that this spark was so speedily extinguished, before it became a flame, as it might have spread over all Switzerland. For parties were still unreconciled in all the cantons and districts; each thought: "If this new organization can be put down, we may rise above the others." The friends of Swiss unity murmured because they were displeased with the fresh division of their fatherland into nineteen cantons; the convents, because their existence became uncertain; and Pancratius Forster, abbot of the former convent of St. Gallen, openly reviled the St. Gallen districts as rebellious vassals of the German empire, and thought he could more easily reestablish his authority by arrogance and violence than by just means. Many country districts were dissatisfied because they did not have general assemblies to themselves, like the original cantons; many patricians and city-families, because they had lost their privileges and the country-people were no longer subjects.

The majority of the people, however, earnestly desired quiet and peace, held fast to the new organization and to the free state-citizenship which they had obtained. They overpowered the dissatisfaction of the few, and all feared to oppose the will of their powerful mediator, before whom even kings quailed. For such were the power and greatness of Napoleon, that he placed the imperial crown on his own head, and held half the world in awe.

Therefore the country was quiet, and a long succession of peaceful and prosperous years followed. The time of rebellions and civil wars had roused the spirit and vigor and self-reliance of the Swiss from their hundred years' slumber. They waked with fresh life, such as had not before been seen. They had become acquainted with each other during the storm, and were no longer strangers, as formerly. All the cantons felt an interest in what occurred in each. Numerous books, pamphlets and journals, formerly suppressed by suspicious governments, enlightened the people on important matters, gave them a general insight into public affairs, and excited and sustained a before-unknown public spirit. Men of all the cantons formed associations for the improvement of public institutions, for the encouragement of the arts and sciences, for the promotion of union and patriotism. The Linth canal is an everlasting monument of this great, never before manifested, public spirit. Almost a million was voluntarily and readily raised to drain the marshy shores of the lake of Wallenstadt, which until then had produced only poverty, misery and fevers. Not less did the Confederate good-feeling show itself, when a portion of the Rossberg above Goldau, in the canton of Schwyz, undermined by autumn-rains, suddenly slid downwards, with horrible destruction, on the evening of 2d Sept., 1806. Goldau, Lowerz and numerous cabins, with hundreds of prosperous inhabitants, were buried deep beneath masses of rock. Now one sees there only a desolate waste, once it was a blooming valley.

The people, everywhere free, and no longer, as formerly, crushed by a domination which kept them in a state of tutelage, were inspired with fresh energy and applied themselves with ardor to commerce, industrial pursuits, agriculture and the care of flocks and herds; no prohibitory laws of one canton against the others trammelled industry or change of domicile, as before. The coöperation of the citizens in public affairs compelled the governments to be humane and just, to reform imperfect laws, and to favor useful undertakings and institutions. The people wished to be free; but without information and strength, no people can be independent. Therefore the schools of the country were multiplied and improved; for the enlightened man alone knows how to help himself and others. Therefore the military organization of the Confederates was placed on a new footing; so that at an hour's notice, a well-trained force could defend the frontiers against a foreign enemy. In the space of ten years, more useful improvements were projected and executed in Switzerland, than in the course of a century previously.

Napoleon, emperor of the French, who, with invincible power, deposed kings from their thrones, dismembered old empires and conferred new crowns, as if he were lord of the world, showed himself friendly to Switzerland. But his continual wars interfered with and destroyed general commerce and trade. To the Confederates they made especially onerous the fulfilment of the treaty by which they were to furnish to him, as formerly to the French kings, sixteen thousand troops on pay, always complete in number. The young men disliked this service because of the mortality of the numerous battle-fields in foreign lands. Many cities were displeased that the French had, by treaty, the same right of free establishment in Switzerland that the Swiss enjoyed in France. Many others, also, were dissatisfied, and especially because the existence or non-existence of Switzerland depended on the will of a single man, before whose wrath the mightiest of the earth trembled.

However, when Napoleon had penetrated with an immense army into the depths and wilds of distant Russia, and saw that great empire lie at his feet, God, the lord of all, withdrew his countenance from him. The frost of a few winter nights vanquished, in snowy deserts, the armies of the invincible. Then, when he fled in terror, the kings and nations of Europe raised their heads and swore the destruction of him before whom they had so long been bowed. But he quickly assembled fresh forces in great numbers, and, with horse and foot, marched against the kings of Europe, over the Rhine into central Germany. There they met him, on the plains near Leipsic, and, in a three-days' battle, smote him with the sword of their wrath (16, 18, 19 Oct., 1813). He fled across the Rhine. But they followed closely.

When the allied armies of the emperors and kings approached the Rhine and the frontiers of Switzerland, the Confederates thought of their obligations to the mediator, but also of the sufferings and afflictions of the nations under his sceptre. And they said: "Let us remain neutral in this strife of the kings, as we have always promised." Thus decided the cantons in their Diet at Zurich, and their banners marched to protect the territory of Switzerland on the border along the Rhine.

CHAPTER LXIII.

THE SWISS ANNUL NAPOLEON'S "ACT OF MEDIATION," AND DIVIDE, UNTIL FOREIGN POWERS ONCE MORE PUT AN END TO THEIR DIVISION BY FOUNDING A NEW CONFEDERACY OF TWENTY-TWO CANTONS.

[A. D. 1814 and 1815.]

WHEN the throne of the great Napoleon sank under the victorious blows of the allied kings, the wise among the Confederates said: "Now the day has come to secure anew the honor and independence of our fatherland. While our young men, fighting on the frontier, conquer or die for the inviolability of Swiss soil, let our deputies, assembled at Zurich, lay the foundation of a new confederacy, a work of patriotic wisdom, suited to the requirements of the age. Then, but not till then, will we annul Napoleon's 'Act of mediation,' the monument of our former division and weakness."

So said they. Not so, many members of the principal families in the before-ruling cities. These wished to introduce foreign troops into Switzerland, and, under their protection and the consequent terror, to reëstablish a Confederacy of thirteen cantons, with domination and servitude, such as came to a bloody end in 1798.

There were rumors of secret intrigues and negotiations at Waldshut, on the part of some members of the noble families of Berne and Grisons with foreign generals. Then, suddenly, almost immediately after the promulgation of the solemn declaration of Swiss neutrality by the Diet, appeared an order for the widely extended troops to retire from along the Rhine. And the Austrian battalions, horse and foot, troop after troop, with drums beating, passed the Rhine (21 Dec., 1813), through Bâle, Aargau, Solothurn, Berne and other districts, into the territory of France. The people looked on with astonishment and indignation. The Confederate troops were at a distance; most of them full of shame, sorrow and anger. This long passage of foreigners brought fevers and contagious diseases. Many a happy home was thus made desolate.

But the city of Berne, when she saw the numbers of the German troops, declared that Napoleon's "Act of mediation" was annulled and all the dominion and authority she had before possessed over the country reëstablished. The people, overawed, and in the belief that this was an order of the German conquerors whose banners they saw in their villages and on the highways, were silent in anxious suspense. The cities of Solothurn and Freiburg followed Berne's example; as shortly did Lucerne. The Diet at Zurich likewise annulled Napoleon's "Act of mediation," in virtue of which it was assembled, and laid the foundation of a new compact of the nineteen Confederate states (29 Dec).

It was not this, but a reëstablishment of the Confederacy of the old thirteen cantons, with the restoration of former privileges and former servitude, that the chiefs and leaders of the disturbance desired. Therefore they stirred up the original mountain-cantons. Therefore the cantons of Vaud and Aargau had been arrogantly summoned in the Bernese declaration (24 Dec.) to submit anew to their formerly sovereign city.

Thus the whole Confederacy was once more falling to pieces by internal dissensions, while the allied emperors and kings entered Paris, banished the defeated Napoleon to the island of Elba, and seated Louis XVIII., as king of

France, on the throne of his fathers. The Diet, in which deputies from the nineteen cantons were newly assembled at Zurich (6th April, 1814), was the sole weak tie which prevented the entire separation of the cantons. Distrust and enmity prevailed; demands for the annihilation or dismemberment of parts of the Confederacy which had been self-governing and free for sixteen years. Zug demanded from Aargau a portion of the former free-bailiwicks; Uri, the Leventina from the canton of Ticino; Glarus, the district of Sargans from the canton of St. Gallen; the former prince-abbot Pancratius, his ancient territories and sovereignties in Thurgau and St. Gallen; Schwyz and Glarus united, the territory of Uznach, Gaster and Wesen, as well as compensation for numerous ancient rights; Unterwalden Uri and Schwyz united, a similar compensation for the sovereign rights they had possessed in Aargau, Thurgau, St. Gallen and Ticino. Others made other demands.

In Grisons, one party insisted that Rhetia should be detached from the Confederacy; another marched with some hundreds of armed men across the mountain to reconquer Chiavenna and Valtelina (4th May), but were driven back by three thousand Austrians.

During these storms, Zurich, Bâle and Schaffhausen distinguished themselves by their impartiality; Vaud and Aargau, by the enthusiastic energy of their people, showed themselves strong and worthy of their acquired freedom. In the districts and cities of Bâle, Zurich and Solothurn, the friends of liberty held themselves ready to follow the banners of Aargau. Here, twelve thousand well-disciplined troops were prepared to march at the first signal, and as many in Vaud. But Berne feared an open feud; she offered to recognise the independence of Vaud on certain conditions. These Vaud refused (24th July). Aargau armed more threateningly. There were dangerous fermentations in Bernese Oberland (August).

Party-jealousy and suspicion gained strength day by day, especially after men began to discuss the future rights of the people and the future limits of the governing power. There were reports of partial risings, of conspiracies, of arrests and banishments at Lucerne, Freiburg and Solothurn. The city of Solothurn called for a Bernese garrison to protect her from her own people. Confederate troops were obliged to hasten over the high Alps to the banks of the Ticino, in order to prevent a murderous civil war (September); others to the canton of St. Gallen to put an end to revolt and dangerous anarchy: for here the abbot Pancratius was doing all in his power to excite his partisans. On the other hand, Schwyz did the same to take Sargans and Uznach. Many districts insisted on their right to general assemblies.

While Switzerland was thus for a long time the prey to constantly increasing disturbances, while blood already flowed in many cantons and arrests filled the prisons of most of the cities, the plenipotentiaries of nearly all the great empires of Europe were assembled at Vienna, the capital city of the emperor of Austria, to fix on solid bases the future peace of the world. The allied conquerors of France had already assented that the republic of Geneva should enter the confederate compact as a self-governing canton; as well as Neuchâtel, the principality under Prussian sovereignty, and Valais. (On the 12th of September, these three cantons, at their own request, were admitted by the Diet into the Swiss Confederacy.) But now, when the kings and their plenipotentiaries at Vienna saw the interminable quarrels of the Confederates, which time, instead of soothing, embittered, they determined to mediate and to put an end to all disputes by their decision. For this purpose, the deputies of the Confederates went willingly to the imperial city on the Danube, as, eleven years before, to Paris.

There, after long consideration of all disputes and grievances, the declaration of the allied powers and their decisive arbitration were finally made (20th March, 1815). They recognised the act of confederation, to which the majority of the cantons had acceded on the 9th September, 1814, and the integral existence of the nineteen cantons, as well as their increase to the number of twenty-two by the addition of Geneva, Neuchâtel and Valais. To the canton of Vaud was restored Dappenthal, which France had taken from her; to the canton of Berne, as indemnity, were assigned Bienne and the bishopric of Bâle, excepting some small portions which were incorporated with Neuchâtel and Bâle; to the abbot Pancratius and his officers, a pension of 8000 florins; to the cantons of Uri, Schwyz, Unterwalden, Zug, Glarus and the Inner-rhodes of Appenzell, for their former rights, a compensation of half a million of francs from the cantons of Aargau, Vaud and St. Gallen.

The settlement of the Helvetian state-debt of more than 3,500,000 francs, of the claims of those Bernese who had signioral rights in Vaud, and of many other matters, was likewise finally determined. Only the complaints of the republic of Grisons remained unheard. For Chiavenna, Valtelina and Bormio, now annexed to Austria, were not restored to them; nor till 1833 was any compensation made to those whose lawful property and possessions in Valtelina had, years before, been unjustly seized and confiscated by the revolted subjects of the republic.

After the Confederates, through their Diet (27th May), had solemnly assented to this declaration and settlement, which was signed by the plenipotentiaries of the crowns of Austria, Spain, France, Great Britain, Portugal, Prussia, Russia and Sweden, these powers, in like manner, declared their recognition and guaranty of the neutrality and inviolability of Switzerland in all future wars of the princes.

Thus the intervention of the united monarchs of Europe generously put an end to the unworthy disputes of the Confederates; and this is the basis of the compact of the twenty-two confederated republics among the mountains of the Alps and the Jura.

CHAPTER LXIV.

RENEWED LOSS OF LIBERTY, AND WEAKNESS OF THE SWISS.

[A. D. 1815 to 1829.]

THE small communities in the high Alps, without instruction, without commerce, with few wants and resources, taking little interest in their own affairs and less in their neighbors', fell back into the position to which their fathers had been so long accustomed. They peacefully fed their flocks upon the mountains, gave their votes every year in general assembly for magistrates and laws, and left other matters to the good pleasure of their spiritual and temporal lords.

But in the districts from the base of the Alps to the Jura, where greater intercourse and comfort, commerce and industry prevailed, far other wants had been developed. Here, many regretted the loss of important popular rights which had been annihilated or diminished by treachery or craft, or threats of violence, to the advantage of grasping cities or families. They were compelled to submit to political institutions imposed on an unwilling people by arbitrary officers. That they might not fall from one evil into a greater, they thought it most prudent to be silent. They feared to irritate by opposition the powerful sovereigns who, after the conquest of France, had formed a "holy alliance" among themselves and given the law to the nations of Europe. What no one dared to claim as a right, each hoped to obtain from the wisdom or good feeling of the newly-appointed magistrates. The warning past was still near. But the men in power did not willingly cast a glance behind; they looked only to the future and to the demands of their ambition, which they had strengthened in each other by the new compact.

By this compact, which with equal solemnity guaranteed the existence of twenty-two cantons and of fifty-nine monasteries and nunneries, the dignity and power of all Switzerland was once more made subordinate to the individual cantons. The letter of the agreement, vague and elastic throughout, was a most commodious instrument to foster the spirit of cantonalism. Although it was declared to be a fundamental principle that no subject-district should exist in the Confederate states, the fact still remained in a milder form almost everywhere, in spite of the abolished name. Even the subject-country of the prince of Neuchâtel was received into the number of cantons, as equal in dignities and rights. And the inhabitants of Reichenburg in Schwyz were allowed to fall again under the sovereignty of the convent of Einsiedeln without any protest on the part of the state-governments.

Thus from the bloody grave of 1798 the spectre of the old Confederacy came back upon the land of the freed Swiss, and gradually brought in its train all the evils by which the ancient union of the states had been destroyed. The Diets again presented the spectacle of vain pomp and fruitless dispute. The deputies brought to them irreconcilable instructions and obstinate reservations. For the glory or prosperity of the common Confederacy the individual cantons wanted strength, the whole wanted unity. The establishment of the military school at Thun (1818) is the only memorial of a federal spirit which once more shone brightly in the first years, and then became extinct. There were indeed long and frequent discussions and disputes respecting uniformity of currency, freedom of trade, unrestrained establishment of the Swiss in every part of their Swiss fatherland, and many other desirable matters; but nothing was done. The complicated tolls, so injurious to the country, remained unabolished; thousands of heimathlosen, the disgrace of the Confederacy, homeless.

Though the chiefs of these small republics quarrelled bitterly with each other when any sacrifice was to be made for the benefit of the whole nation, yet they were subserviently docile to the hints of foreign courts, whenever any advantage was to be gained for themselves or their families. Mercenary troops were willingly hired out to the kings of France (1816), of the Netherlands (1818) and of Naples (1829) to defend them against their own people; but an asylum was refused to those unfortunates who were persecuted and driven from their homes for political causes. When the holy father at Rome, by his own authority, separated a large portion of catholic Switzerland from its original connection with the bishopric of Constance (1815), fourteen full years were lost in attempts to found a new national bishopric. Then, when all hopes of an understanding were at an end, fatigued with the interminable disputes, some cantons joined the diocese of Coire; others the bishopric of Bâle (1828), the seat of which was established in the city of Solothurn. When the kingly members of the "holy alliance" demanded a restriction on the liberty of the press, the governments, with unseemly condescension, hastened to perform the grateful task. Laws and ordinances immediately trammelled and hindered the public interchange of ideas. Judges were appointed under the name of censors to determine what truths should be concealed from the people, what errors should be elucidated. The information of the public was charged with heavy taxes as a superfluous luxury, and the diffusion and circulation of journals burdened with stamp-duties. Valais and Freiburg opened to the Jesuits, not only their territory, but the schools of their youth. The ecclesiastical power raised itself again with new strength by the side of the civil, to protect it, or, according to circumstances, to brave it.

The lies of a cheat, Clara Wendell, and her band, respecting the death of avoyer Keller of Lucerne in the Reuss (1816) occupied for several years the attention of the Confederacy, and disclosed the imperfections of the Swiss administration of justice in many cantons. When a succession of rainy years produced a scarcity and dearness of produce, and thousands fell sick from unwholesome food, or died of hunger (1817), the governments increased the evils of the time by embargoes between canton and canton, or by prohibiting the export of provisions. Division, disputes and discord prevailed everywhere. No Confederacy was perceptible, but only cantons, united by concordats, or separated by reprisals.

In the seats of some of the state-governments magnanimous men, full of intelligence, of love for their country and for popular liberty, were not wanting. But the good seed which they sowed was choked by the tares which the federal compact and the vicious constitutions of the cantons unrestrainedly fostered.

For the unmeasured power which that compact gave to the cantons at the expense of the Confederacy, had for the most part fallen into the hands of a few men, who ruled the country. The feeling of their unlimited authority by degrees produced domineering pride; irresponsibility produced arbitrary government; long-continued office produced familism and favoritism. Not only the tribunals of the country but even the representatives of the people in the great-councils became subject to their influence. The old aristocracies again raised their heads, without the prestige of ancient recollections, but covered with democratic tinsel. This soon fell away. The citizens of the country, seeing the titled display and pomp of their governors, submitted more and more unwillingly to the burden of taxes, of military and road-service; to the impositions on the poor in favor of the rich; to favoritism; to wasteful mismanagement of the public property; to malpractices in office, against which they had seldom the privilege of complaint.

The small republics, travelling in different directions, separated more and more. But the mind and heart of the people remained constant to one desire: that the slavery and impotence of Switzerland should cease. This spirit showed itself whenever the people met in philanthropic or scientific societies in the various cantons. This was the case in the yearly assemblages (after 1819) of Swiss students at Zofingen; in those of the young men who every year (from 1822) met upon one of the glorious fields of the old battles for freedom; in the federal shooting-matches, and especially in the Helvetian society, active as in the memorable days of its first organization. The public prints, although reviled, prosecuted, restricted and forbidden to exist, spoke more boldly and were read with more avidity by the people. Some voices, single at first, but soon more numerous, were raised in the great-councils themselves for the restraint of the governing power within legal limits.

In free republics, the chiefs have no power which does not proceed from the confidence of the people, and no bayonets can protect their dignities but the bayonets of the people. For fifteen years did the Swiss suffer the evil consequences of 1815. First on the banks of the Ticino did the people, exasperated by the squandering of the public property and by the venality of their magistrates, demand and commence a reform of their constitution (1829). The legislative assembly of Vaud, which had already (1825) been vainly entreated thereto by its most distinguished members, soon followed in the same course, as did that of Lucerne, compelled by the common necessity. The great council of Zurich, by a freer admission to its privileges, hoped to put a stop to more serious complaints.

CHAPTER LXV.

THIRTEEN CANTONS RECOVER THEIR LIBERTY. TROUBLES IN SCHWYZ, NEUCHATEL AND BALE.

[A. D. 1830 to 1832.]

THE majority of the Swiss people would gladly have followed the example. But many of the governments preferred the exercise of arbitrary power under the protection of the "holy alliance." They thought themselves more powerful in their reliance on foreign forces than in the strength and favor of free citizens.

Then a most unexpected occurrence took place. A member of the "holy alliance," king Charles X. of France, broke his royal oath to his people. After three days of bloody fighting in the streets and squares of Paris (July, 1830), he was compelled to flee into exile from the kingdom of his fathers. Soon Belgium, soon Poland rose against their princes. Italy and Germany were full of disturbances. Thus the strength of the "holy alliance" was broken.

Delivered now from the fear of foreign power, the Swiss

people determined to recover their rights, the loss of which they had so long mourned. It is easier to extirpate a noble nation from the face of the earth than to extinguish in their breasts the love of freedom and manly dignity. In the days of autumn the citizens, first in small numbers, then by assemblages of thousands and thousands, in the cantons of Aargau, Thurgau, Bâle, Zurich, St. Gallen, Vaud, Lucerne, Freiburg, Solothurn, Berne, Schaffhausen, even in Schwyz and the Outer-rhodes of Appenzell came with respectful petitions to the governments. They demanded the alteration of the illiberal constitutions of their countries to meet the wishes of the people, and by representatives of their own choice.

The governments were filled with fear and turned anxious eyes towards the foreign courts, whence no further help came. Therefore they yielded, willingly or unwillingly, to the loud and general demand; here, with benevolent wisdom; there, grudgingly, with timid hesitation. But crafty delays excited distrust; inimical reservations occasioned popular tumults at Frauenfeld, St. Gallen, Lausanne and Freiburg; or armed outbreaks, as in the cantons of Aargau and Schaffhausen. But, in the midst of the revolutionary storm, property, persons and the dignity of the magistrates were respected. Neither did streams of blood or incendiary conflagrations, such as were seen in those times at Paris, Brussels, Brunswick, Warsaw, Modena and other places, sully the regeneration of Swiss freedom.

Before the dawning of the last day of that eventful year, almost everywhere, constituent-councils, chosen by the people, or, as in Freiburg, Solothurn and Bâle, the great-councils, were busily at work to satisfy the wishes of their country.

Only in Berne, then the Vorort of the Confederacy, did the nobility of the city hesitate to surrender the privileges which they had succeeded in obtaining, sixteen years before, by revolutionary artifices and the assistance of foreign power. They still hoped for some salvation: either through the variance and feuds of the cantons with each other, or a war between neighboring nations, or their interference in the affairs of Switzerland, or, as is always the case with despairing obstinacy, through some miracle of chance. In fact, Austrian troops were then assembling, with threatening aspect, along the frontiers of the Confederacy, in Vorarlberg, Tyrol and Italy.

To secure peace within and safety without, and perhaps, also, for its own protection, the Vorort called a Diet at Berne. But the Diet decreed: "Each canton shall be free to form its own constitution. Sixty or seventy thousand men shall be held ready for the defence of the Confederacy, in case of war." It declared to foreign powers its intention to remain neutral in all their wars. Thus did the Diet. The nation, electrified, prepared soldiers and arms (Grisons, alone, ten thousand men), more than were required. Those who were exempt from service wished to volunteer. But afterwards, when the foreign courts gave to the Confederacy renewed assurances of peace and friendship, the noble families of Berne perceived with despair that their empire was at an end; and when the burghers of the city refused to admit within their walls mercenary soldiers to act against the people, the patricians submitted to their fate with some show of dignity. A constituent-council, demanded by the country with increasing vehemence, was assembled.

To those who had for years been acustomed to domination or servility, or who, secretly honoring in their hearts the dignity of a free people, had betrayed it by unworthy cowardice, nothing now remained but to decry the awakening of the nation with unrestrained though powerless malignity. In taverns, council-halls, churches, pamphlets and gazettes, they relieved their oppressed hearts by contumely and curses. Many who had before been the strongest opponents of the government became now its warmest apologists. Had a God listened to the prayers of their insanity, disturbance, bloody revenge and civil war would have overwhelmed the Confederacy. But they blew only the flames of their party-rage, which blinded their own eyes. The Swiss people went forward in their work with dignified calmness and determination. Their earnest will secured its own fulfilment.

In the beginning of the summer (1831) the free constitutions were accepted by the people in most of the cantons, and put in operation. The same love of freedom, though with varying requirements, had based them all on the same principles: the sovereignty of the united people; equal political rights and duties for every citizen; more decided separation and independence of the legislative, executive and judicial functions; shorter terms of office; protection of private property against official power; freedom of the press, &c.

Thus the cantons of Zurich, Berne, Lucerne, Freiburg, Solothurn, Schaffhausen, St. Gallen, Aargau, Thurgau, Ticino and Vaud determined the rights of the people and the jurisdiction of the country, in a legal manner, without unreasonable disturbance of before-existing ordinances. Governments and magistrates, councils and judges acted under the old constitutions until the new received force and validity.

But not so peacefully was the formation of a better constitution accomplished in Schwyz. For the chiefs of the scant population of the before-ruling Inner district, or old free-land, so called, refused equal rights to the inhabitants of the Outer districts. And yet these had once been promised to them in the days of trouble and war (1798) shortly previous to the fall of the old Confederacy. But, since 1815, the superannuated privileges of the old free-land had been craftily and insensibly resuscitated under promises of a reform in the constitution which had never been fulfilled. Even in the old free-land itself, all the citizens had not equal rights and duties; but those who were called "new folk," though their ancestors had dwelt there for centuries, were inferior in privileges. At last, when neither earnest petitions for infringed rights, nor negotiations, nor the offered mediation of the Confederacy had produced any result, the Outer districts, March, Einsiedeln, Kussnacht and Pfeffikon, determined to form a separate free commonwealth under another constitution (6th May, 1832). Thus this little cantôn was for a while divided into two parts, not without reciprocal animosity, but without the evil of bloody strife. The soils of Neuchâtel and Bâle, only, were thus stained at that period.

Early in 1831, the paternal prince of Neuchâtel, Frederick William, king of Prussia, sent a plenipotentiary to consult the wishes of the people, and graciously relieved a portion of the burdens which occasioned complaint on the part of the communes. No one then wished to withdraw from under his sceptre. But, shortly after the return of the plenipotentiary to his king, voices were raised demanding: "That the principality be made a republic, like the other cantons of Switzerland." Many who were not inclined to revolt thought this object worthy of every sacrifice. But some hundreds of inconsiderate men assembled in arms, surprised and seized the castle of Neuchâtel (12th Sept., 1831). They were driven out by the appearance of the Confederate troops, whose assistance the government had called for in its need (27th Sept.). For according to the compact, the constitution of the canton could not be changed by force, nor without the consent of the prince and of a majority of the citizens. After the castle was restored to the authorities, and an amnesty promised to the rebels, the Confederate troops returned to their homes.

Their ill-success did not discourage the malcontents. Once again, but in smaller numbers, they raised the standard of revolt (27th Dec.). But they were dispersed by the unaided troops of the government, after bloody combats. Those who saved their lives by flight were punished by banishment. The captives expiated their attempt in unhealthy prisons, or by money, or confinement in foreign fortresses, or in other ways. Even the innocent, on bare suspicion, were given up to the maltreatment of their persecutors. The power and tribunals of a cautious government seemed for a while subservient to the rage of a victorious party.

At the same period the canton of Bâle was the theatre of a much more fearful civil war. Here a majority of the country-communes respectfully petitioned for the restoration of privileges once guaranteed by the capital-city herself, and with this view requested the calling of a constituent-council to be chosen by the people. This request, and their continued persistence in it, wounded and embittered the pride and prejudices of the city. The great-council, composed principally of burghers, on its own authority, drew up a constitution in which the privileges enjoyed by the city since 1815 were preserved to her. Thereupon many members from the country-communes, who had likewise been grievously insulted, left the council-hall. They had in vain demanded the restoration of that equality in political rights and duties which was guaranteed to them in 1798. When men in power exhibit a want of good faith, a pernicious example is presented to the oppressed. Dissatisfaction and indignation on the part of the country followed, contempt and threats on that of the city; then arming on both sides. Liberty-trees were planted in the villages. A provisional government for the country was established at Liestal. But the angry authorities sent troops from the city-gates; after small skirmishes of many days (middle of January, 1831) the rebels were dispersed, the liberty-trees cut down, the revolutionary government broken up. The prisoners, bound with ropes, like vile criminals, were led through the streets of Bâle and exposed to the insults of the populace. Then, under the first influence of terror, the new constitution was presented to the communes, accepted by a doubtful vote, proclaimed, and the severest sentences passed upon the prisoners and fugitives. In vain did the other Confederates recommend wise moderation and a general amnesty. In vain were thousands of supplicating voices raised from the humbled country-communes. Bâle, in the feeling of her right, or of her power, forgot that, in civil disturbances, the sword of severe justice heals no wounds, but may deepen them.

The inflexible harshness of Bâle against her fellow-citizens in the country-districts, who asked only for what had once been promised to them, and what was already granted in other cantons, occasioned a great excitement against the city among the people of the other cantons, still under the influence of the first effervescence of liberty. Soon, in the cantons of Aargau, Berne, Solothurn, Zurich, Thurgau and Appenzell, armed multitudes were prepared to defend and avenge the country-districts. The capital-city hastily erected new fortifications and strengthened her garrison with mercenary troops. With the feeling of increased security, insulting contempt increased. To protest against injustice, the citizens acted with injustice. They provoked, mortified and insulted the people from the country, when they came peacefully to the city for purposes of trade or industry; they violated the secrecy of the post; on bare suspicion, they maltreated citizens and strangers in the streets and houses. Thus they wantonly drove the country-people into open opposition. Parties for and against Bâle were formed in every village; lawless disturbance and insecurity prevailed everywhere.

To restore order and submission by the terror of their arms, the troops of the city once more (21st Aug., 1831) marched with heavy artillery against the little city of Liestal, the centre of the rebellious districts. But, from hills and valleys, forth rushed the landsturm of all the people, inflamed with love of freedom and a thirst for vengeance, and, despising wounds and death, drove the trained troops back to the gates of their city, after a long and obstinate fight. This bloody action of Bâle broke the last bond between city and country.

A cry of astonishment and indignation resounded through all Switzerland. The Diet, to preserve peace, sent troops into the canton to protect the oppressed country-people. A majority of the confederated cantons withdrew their unconditional guarantee from a constitution stained with the blood of so many citizens and loaded with the curses of the country. Bâle, on the other hand, irritated by this withdrawal and the defeat she had experienced, stigmatized the Confederacy as faithless and forsworn; expelled from her republic (22 February, 1832) forty-five of the rebellious communes, although the Vorort, in the name of the Confederacy, protested against this unexampled proceeding; and, as soon as the Confederate garrisons had retired, once again sent hired soldiers into the country by night, either in the hope of avenging her defeat near Liestal, or, as she asserted, to protect the still faithful communes. By a circuit over foreign territory, in the depth of the darkness, the mercenary troops reached Gelterkinden (6 April, 1832). Suddenly the landsturm surrounded them with all its horrors: battle, death and fire. The soldiers, after a courageous but useless defence, fled again over the borders, dispersed and harassed, leaving many behind. The news of this clandestine attempt roused afresh the indignation of the neighboring cantons against Bâle. The defeat of the mercenaries alone calmed the excitement. The Diet intervened once more. But Bâle, entrenched behind her walls and ramparts, was saddened, not humbled, by her double misfortune. She closed her gates against the troops of the Confederacy, when they presented themselves for the maintenance of peace; she refused the mediation of the commissioners whom the Diet sent to Zofingen to settle the differences between city and country. Then the Confederates, assembled at Lucerne, finally persuaded of the inflexible obstinacy and pride of the burghers of Bâle, determined on the division of the canton into Bâle-city and Bâle-country. To Bâle-city belonged Bâle herself and sixteen villages which had remained faithful to her in different parts of the country. But Bâle-country, with fifty-three communes, under its own separate constitution, was admitted into the protection and compact of the Confederates; then both sections were commanded to keep the peace, and the troops were once more withdrawn.

CHAPTER LXVI.

THE LEAGUE OF SARNEN. FIVE HUNDRED POLES ENTER SWITZERLAND FROM FRANCE.

[A. D. 1832 to 1833.]

The rich frontier-city, in her unappeasable resentment, which so many reverses had not extinguished but rather inflamed, seemed prepared to adopt the most violent measures, even the dissolution of the Confederacy or her own withdrawal from it. The rest of the cantons, on the other hand, in their timid prudence, hesitated to execute energetically the decrees of the Diet, because they feared a rupture of the whole Confederacy, a general civil war and the armed interference of foreign powers. These and other considerations encouraged the enemies of popular freedom everywhere to new and more audacious hopes. In order to spread their opinions among the multitude they made use of pulpits and schools, pamphlets and lampoons, newspapers and caricatures, confessionals and workshops, in which they disparaged the new political system. But the friends of their country's freedom combatted them with equal bitterness and similar measures; formed defensive unions and held public meetings. So great were the discord and party-animosity, that nothing was honored, no names were respected; even the holy bonds of blood and the oldest friendships were broken.

The old democratic cantons at the foot or in the valleys of the Alps either looked upon these quarrels of the others with indifference, or, persuaded by their ecclesiastical and civil lords, were inclined to favor Bâle, the patricians, and other enemies of political equality. Most of them were so far influenced as to refuse or withhold their Confederate guarantee to the new constitutions in Switzerland. Such a disposition, which certainly bore the appearance of hostility, wounded the people of the other cantons. Seven of these, Zürich, Berne, Lucerne, Solothurn, St. Gallen, Aargau and Thurgau, therefore met together by their deputies in the spring of 1832. They formed an agreement or covenant by which they mutually guaranteed the maintenance of their free constitutions. This covenant, which embraced a majority of all the people of Switzerland and secured their rights, defeated but did not destroy the plans of their opponents.

In Berne, the violent patrician leaders secretly prepared stores of arms, collected 20,000 cartridges in concealed places, and clandestinely enlisted soldiers, principally mercenaries discharged from the French service, or people without bread and conscience, ready for any undertaking. The conspiracy was to break out at any favorable moment, even in blood and flames. But it was betrayed by the imprudence or drunkenness of some of the hired vagabonds (August, 1832). The ringleaders fled; other accomplices in the criminal design were arrested. Thereupon the country-communes, for their safety and the protection of their freedom, were armed and supplied with heavy artillery. These events opened the eyes of all the people to the revengeful ambition of their former masters, desirous to recover their privileges at whatever cost. The formerly honorable, but in the lapse of time self-corrupted, Bernese aristocracy had set the seal of ignominy upon its impotence.

In the mean while the government and burghers of Bâle had conceived a grander but not less inimical project. They formed a closer alliance with the chiefs of Uri, Schwyz, Unterwalden, Neuchâtel and Valais. These, as well as Bâle, had solemnly objected to and protested against the covenant of the seven great cantons to guarantee their constitutions. In consequence of the loud demand which had long been heard throughout the Confederacy for the remodelling of the compact of 1815, as unsuited to the constitutions of most of the cantons and the requirements of a confederated state, Bâle invited those cantons which were friendly to her to assemble for the purpose of adopting important measures in concert. All, except Valais, prevented by internal differences, appeared on the appointed day (14 November, 1832) at Sarnen in Obwalden. There they unanimously resolved: "To hold fast by the compact of 1815, unaltered; consequently, not to recognise Bâle-country or the Outer-districts of Schwyz, as separate commonwealths; and, when deputies from these should be admitted into a Diet, to send no representatives."

When the Diet assembled at Zurich in March, 1833, to continue the discussion upon a project for a new federal compact which had been commenced at Lucerne, no representatives appeared from the cantons of the Sarnen-league. But they met at Schwyz as members of a distinct Confederacy; they called the Diet an illegal assembly, and declared that Bâle-city and Neuchâtel, the cantons of Uri and Unterwalden with Schwyz Inner-district, though but a small minority, would not submit to the decrees of the Confederate majority.

This bold measure, which, under pretext of literally observing the existing compact, virtually dissolved it, excited great indignation among the Confederate deputies assembled at Zurich, but no general determination to reduce the refractory members to obedience. Their attention seemed to be occupied by the important labor of remodelling the compact, as well as by another matter.

The superiority of the Russian arms had overcome a formidable insurrection and struggle for independence on the part of the Poles. Thousands of unfortunate but valiant Poles left their subjugated country covered with dead bodies and ruins, and wandered, flying the vengeance of Russia, from land to land, seeking refuge. The people of Switzerland, full of wonder and commiseration, assisted the brave men who passed through their cities and villages on their way to France, where an asylum was promised to them. But, after a while, the Poles in France found themselves disappointed in the expectations they had entertained from the hospitality of that country. Many of them, dissatisfied, went into Belgium; many enlisted in Portugal under the standard of Don Pedro, who was contending with his brother for the throne of that kingdom, and, at last, about five hundred unexpectedly crossed the French frontier into the canton of Berne, to seek assistance from the Confederacy (early in April, 1833). But here their numbers caused the other cantons to refuse them entrance into their territory, while France forbade all return. In vain did the Poles appeal to the generosity of the Confederates; in vain did Berne entreat her fellow-cantons not to leave upon her alone the burden of so expensive a hospitality. Most of the cantons, pleased with having escaped the lot of Berne, refused all assistance in this great difficulty. Some excused themselves on account of their great poverty; some feared to increase the number of heimathlosen in their territory; others held these suddenly-arrived strangers to be accomplices in the German insurrection, which about that time broke forth at Frankfort on the Main; while some even suspected Berne of having invited the Poles into the country to serve against her troublesome patricians, or against the neighboring cantons who were opposed to the reforms in Switzerland.

CHAPTER LXVII.

BREACH OF THE PEACE. PEACE RESTORED BY THE DIET.

[A. D. 1833.]

In the mean while the project of a new compact was completed. It was published and submitted to the people of Switzerland for their acceptance or rejection. In expectation of their action, the Diet opened its regular session at Zurich (1 July) with the customary solemnity. But at the same time the plenipotentiaries from the Sarnen-league met together at Schwyz. Never were union and a good understanding between all the Confederates more desirable than on the day when they were to lay the foundation of their new compact, and never did the accomplishment of this desire seem more distant. At the instance of Grisons, the Confederates once more extended the hand of brotherhood to the refractory cantons, and proposed a friendly settlement of the differences between the Inner and Outer districts of Schwyz, as well as between Bâle-city and Bâle-country. The day of mediation was in fact agreed upon (5 August). All the cantons promised to send deputies; even the Confederates of the league. But the latter were not in earnest.

Then, when the people of the canton of Lucerne, disturbed and terrified by the extravagance of the intemperate friends of freedom and that of the monks and priests, rejected the proposed compact (7 July), all the enemies of the new order of things suddenly raised their heads with more audacious boldness. The former rulers of the people thought that the latter could be made as subservient as before. Hence fresh hopes, fresh plans for the reëstablishment of supremacy. No conciliation! No compromise! The edifice of liberty must be overwhelmed in ruin! One vigorous blow would be enough. Messengers hastened hither and thither. There was secret arming in Schwyz, redoubled activity in Bâle. The day fixed for the assembling of the great mediating-council was already close at hand.

On a summer's night (30–31st July), at the sounh of the tocsin, six hundred valiant men of Schwyz marched with heavy artillery and took Kussnacht, a village of the Outer-district, on the lake of the Waldstatten. They brought back prisoners, disregarded the admonition of Lucerne, and threatened to follow up their warlike expedition. But a thousand men hastened in arms from Lucerne to the borders and stopped their further advance. On the 1st of August the Diet at Zurich were informed of this audacious breach of the peace. Their long-suffering patience was at an end. They ordered twenty battalions, under the lead of deputed plenipotentiaries and experienced generals, to occupy Schwyz; they deferred the assembling of the mediators, and issued an address to the nation respecting the malicious enterprise. A cry of indignation against Schwyz resounded through all the valleys. The Confederate troops hastened willingly to fulfil the orders of the highest authority of the country.

Three days after this intelligence, came that of a murderous attack of the Bâlese upon the country-districts of the canton which had been declared free. With sixteen hundred men and twelve pieces of artillery, the citizens and garrison had marched by night (3d August) towards Muttenz. Then they had burned Pratteln, killed several defenceless persons, and, from skirmish to skirmish, taken the road to Liestal. But they soon found their defeat in the oak-wood of Oehrli, not far from Frenkendorf. In small numbers and with a heroism worthy of the most glorious days of Swiss battles for freedom, the sons of the country here made a stand and met the soldiers of Bâle with wounds and death. The disordered troops of the city wavered; then gave way; and quickly dispersed in wild flight through the wood. Breathing vengeance, the victorious country-men pursued; neither asking nor giving quarter. More than three hundred of the aggressors fell dead or wounded. The pride of Bâle was broken. Fear and mourning filled the whole city.

On the evening of this unhappy day, the Diet, informed of the breach of the peace but not of the issue of the combat, met at night and ordered the occupation of the canton of Bâle, city and country, by ten thousand soldiers. On the 4th day of August, the troops of the Confederacy were already in Schwyz; on the 10th they entered the gates of Bâle. The league of Sarnen was dissolved; the refractory cantons enjoined to fulfil their duty by sending deputies to the Diet. Neuchâtel alone hesitated; ten thousand men started on their march towards her borders; she hastened to obey.

These energetic measures restored peace to Switzerland. The troops gained honor by their discipline; the whole nation, by their enthusiasm for liberty and order. The mutinous aristocracy of the cities and principal families, with their ecclesiastical and civil followers, were awed by the majesty of the popular will, which manifested itself in a manner entirely different from the expectations of their blindness.

The embassadors of Russia, Austria, Prussia, Bavaria and Sardinia hurried to Zurich (7th August), to intercede in favor of Bâle, while the most violent of the political associations demanded a court-martial on the authors and chief-leaders of the breaches of the peace, their degradation and execution. But the Confederate authorities, with wise firmness, resisted the solicitations of both parties. Justice and magnanimity honor and preserve republics as well as monarchies. In Schwyz, a reünion took place between the old free-land and the outer districts under a common constitution (19th September); Bâle, with some villages on the right bank of the Rhine, was definitively separated from the whole country (17th August); and a mediatorial tribunal at Aarau determined the allotment of the public property to each of the two commonwealths, into which this single canton, like Appenzell and Unterwalden, was now divided. When the share of each canton, as well as of the Confederacy, in the expenses of occupation, was decided, and the troops had returned to their homes with thanks, the Diet was dissolved (16th October).

Thus the Swiss, at this period, secured and preserved the freedom of their country by military energy and magnanimity. Under the protection and power of the law quiet returned to all the districts of the Confederacy. But the freedom of a people must repose with open eyes: to slumber is to die.

CHAPTER LXVIII.

CONCLUSION.

THIS is the history of past times; a glimpse into the secrets of the future.

Neither the arrow of Tell nor the dagger of Camogaster broke the chains of Swiss bondage. Neither at St. Jacques nor on the Malserhaide was the independence of the Confederates secured. No, the combat for internal freedom and external independence has lasted five hundred years. The men at Rutli and those under the maple-tree of Truns gave but the signal for the holy fight.

For, after the innocent simplicity of Uri had been corrupted by the pride of the other Confederates, they no longer blushed to occupy the seats of the banished signiors and bailiffs, but preferred to have subjects and bond-servants rather than free fellow-citizens. At Stanz, where blessed Nicholas von der Flue appeared to them, they gave to each other a guaranty of everlasting dominion over the people and against their struggles for freedom. And when Toggenburg wished to purchase her liberty they refused all offers. They desired liberty to hold subjects, not to grant freedom. Therefore they at last looked upon the virtues, enlightenment and increasing wealth of the people with more dread than upon open revolt.

But the edifice which had been raised by the hand of base selfishness was to be destroyed by the same means. Soon the world saw with wonder that the Swiss despised and weakened the very foundations of their strength and glory: their perpetual bond, and union. The cantons forgot their first love, cherished enmity against each other and courted foreign powers. The heroes of freedom became slaves in the golden chains of princes. The frugal sons of the Alps, for hire and presents, sold the people's blood in unknown battle-fields, and their votes in council. The manly spirit of the ancient leaders of the country was dwarfed to the timidity of aristocratic council-lords. The government of the country was a state-secret to its own people. And when the governments were almost entirely separated from the people, the people separated from the governments. No empire ever yet perished through the virtues of its citizens. The old Confederacy fell into utter ruin.

But God the Father watches with unabated tenderness over his children. And, as the fecundating rain comes forth from the tempestuous thunder-cloud, so from the world-storm came forth the freedom of the whole Swiss people. At this day we see, what was not the case before, in a space of nearly nine hundred square miles, between lakes Leman and Constance, two millions of men, divided into twenty-two commonwealths, all alike Confederates in freedom. The strongest of the twenty-two republics of the Swiss Confederacy is doubtless weak and powerless against the princes of the earth; but the smallest is invincible, in the compact of all, so long as each Confederate fears less a second Grandson, Morat and Frastenz than the craft and gold of a lord Zoppo or a bishop Schinner.

Not from Germany, not from abroad comes the enemy before whom the Swiss heart should quail. The most formidable adversary of our freedom and independence, when he comes, will appear in our midst. But he must bear a mark by which every one may know him: It is he who prefers the honor of his own canton to the everlasting glory of the whole Confederacy; his own personal or family advantage to the public good. It is he who would rend asunder the unity and grandeur of the Confederacy, and with the purple tatters of her divided majesty, bedeck the dwarfed proportions of cantonal self-sovereignty. It is he who trembles at a sword in the hand of a free people and not at the cajoleries and gifts of kings and their embassadors. It is he who says: "Reduce the press to silence and close the mouths of the teachers of youth; put out your money at interest and expend it not in arms and warlike preparations; shut the doors of the council-chambers, so that the people may not hear our deliberations; thus we may again be lords and masters, and subjects shall serve us!" It is he who sows distrust between city and country, religious hate between catholics and protestants, who raises barriers between canton and canton, or encourages that cantonal selfishness, that family ambition, that pride of nobility, or any of those destructive discords by means of which the old Confederacy found a bloody end in spite of Neuenegg and Rothenthurm.

But we have learnt: That right and justice are stronger than all might; that the prosperity of each family is secure under the laws of freedom only; and that the freedom of each is guaranteed solely by the independence of the Swiss Confederacy. But the independence of the Swiss Confederacy is not based on imperial charters or royal promises; it stands on an iron foundation: our swords. The true Swiss nobility must come from the churches and schools of the people. The real state-treasure must be found in the prosperity of all households. The great armory and arsenal of the Confederacy must exist in the chambers of her citizens. The deliberations of the councils and general assemblies must reach the ears of the whole Confederacy. So shall the holy cause of the fatherland be the holy cause of every cabin, and a godlike public spirit, like a celestial fire, consume all personal and cantonal selfishness.

Neither the arrow of Tell nor the dagger of the Camogaster broke the chains of Swiss bondage. Neither at St. Jacques nor on the Malserhaide was the independence of the Swiss Confederacy secured. At Rutli and under the maple-tree of Truns only the signal for the holy fight was given. We must still fight, Confederates! And you, our children, must still fight over our graves! Watch, therefore, that you fall not into temptation! Trust in God! Confederates! All for each, and each for all!

CONTINUATION

OF THE

HISTORY OF SWITZERLAND.

BY EMIL ZSCHOKKE.

CHAPTER LXIX.

EXPEDITION AGAINST SAVOY. OCCURRENCES AT STEINHOLZLEIN.

[A. D. 1834.]

SHORTLY after the internal storm had cleared away, the Confederacy became involved in a no less troublesome dispute with foreign nations. In consequence of the disturbances of Europe, numerous refugees and exiles had, in those days, sought an asylum on Swiss soil. The sight of the popular freedom here enjoyed aroused in many of them a desire to behold the same in their own countries. In hopes to realize this desire, a secret league was formed among them. Unmindful of the hospitality they here received, they wished, from the Swiss republics, to cast the firebrand of revolution into the neighboring monarchies. Savoy, especially, was selected, because the people there seemed determined to get rid of their king. Such, at least, were the reports brought by the Italian refugees. The

Germans, believing what they said, joined them; among those most willing, and most numerous, were the Poles, who still dwelt in Bernese Jura. Tired of long inactivity, they hoped, through the flames of a general war, to open for themselves a path back to their unhappy country. At the head of the undertaking was placed general Romarino, who had won for himself an honorable name in the Polish struggle for independence.

Towards the end of January, 1834, the conspirators, singly, in order to escape the vigilance of the government, made their way towards the shores of lake Leman. Arms were secretly provided for them. But their purpose could no longer be concealed. Vaud and Geneva immediately called out troops to prevent the violation of foreign territory. It was already too late. In the city of Geneva, some stragglers were indeed seized; but the mob, excited by the heroism of the Poles, impetuously rescued them. Thus they were enabled to continue their route, and to cross the frontiers of Savoy near Carouge (1st Feb.). Although but a few hundred strong, they expected that their little band would soon be swelled to an army by a general rising of the people. Several customhouse-officers were disarmed, and some public money confiscated. On all sides, printed addresses were distributed, proclaiming that the hour for casting off the tyrant's yoke had sounded. But the expected joyful welcome was wanting. The Savoyard peasants looked doubtfully upon the array of foreign invaders; no foot entered their ranks, no hand was raised to help them. Soon came a report that the royal troops were advancing by forced marches from Chambery. Then Romarino looked behind. Terrified he fled. His troops, believing themselves betrayed, hastened after him, without having seen an enemy. In two days, they were all back again in Geneva, where the Poles were disarmed and confined in the barracks of Chantepoulet. The rest returned, each to the place whence he had come.

Where the fire still smoulders under the ashes, every breath of wind enkindles it afresh. The hatred between the Confederates was again awakened more furious than before, when those who had been defeated in the previous year, now raising their heads more boldly, attributed to their adversaries the guilt and shame of the invasion of Savoy. Some did not even hesitate to excite the anger of foreign powers against their own people. "See," said they, "how Switzerland has become a rendezvous for all the disturbers of Europe! Public authority is impotent to prevent the breach of the laws. The people are crazed by the excitement of continual insurrection. Unless foreign powers intervene, the security of neighboring states will be incessantly endangered." Such words found only too ready hearers in the monarchs and their councillors. The aspect of the free self-sovereignty of the Swiss people, in the heart of Europe, had been unpleasant to their eyes. Now came the desired opportunity to suppress it. Sardinia first complained. Austria followed her. In the consciousness of overpowering strength, they imperiously demanded from the little republic the expulsion of all disturbers of the peace. Notes of similar purport soon made their appearance, in quick succession, from Wurtemberg. Baden, Bavaria, the German league, Prussia and Naples; finally, even from distant Russia. The whole country was declared accountable to Europe for what a handful of foreign adventurers had attempted. Hereat indignation spread throughout all the cantons. Every one was willing to respect the law of nations, but never to bow to royal dictation. The vorort Zurich, with dignity, repelled this attack on Swiss independence. With the assent of most of the cantons, she had already pronounced the guilty refugees unworthy of asylum. But this did not satisfy the foreign courts. A second and, shortly afterwards, a third shower of diplomatic notes, still more threatening, followed; and already troops were in motion from East and North, towards the frontiers of Switzerland. A thick hedge of bayonets, in a great semicircle, interdicted trade and commerce, as in time of war.

In the mean while, the citizen-king of France, then friendly to the free Confederates, had testified his willingness again to receive the Poles. They departed; with them many of the other refugees. And as, at the same time, the Vorort gave to the foreign powers quieting assurance for the future (24th June), the latter allowed the half-drawn sword to fall back into the scabbard. A general war, doubtful in its results, might easily have been kindled from this dispute.

Throughout Switzerland, however, there was still great indignation at the pretensions of the foreign powers. In public meetings, the dismissal of those foreign embassadors who had shown their insolence too openly was loudly demanded. Even the last reply of the Vorort was stigmatized by many as a cowardly retraction. The deputy from Berne, especially, opposed it in the Diet, and, when it was finally approved, protested solemnly against it; with him was the deputy from Lucerne. Hereby they acquired great favor with a large portion of the people, and Berne was esteemed by these the "true Vorort," to whom they must look for the maintenance of the honor of the Swiss name. Some, on the other hand, feared evil results from her rashness, and Grisons proposed that a council of deputies should be associated with her in her next year's government of the Confederacy. The anger of the monarchs, also, was now turned almost entirely against this largest and most unyielding of the cantons. This was especially the case when another circumstance provoked it afresh. About the end of June, at Steinholzlein, a watering-place near the city of Berne, some journeymen, at a jovial banquet, which the German courts characterized as seditious, raised the black-red-and-golden flag, and toasted a German republic. Rumor spread, and quickly magnified, the report. To many envoys of foreign powers it appeared a conspiracy against the thrones of their sovereigns. They demanded a severe punishment for so criminal a demonstration. But the government of the Bernese republic answered: "With us the free expression of opinion is no crime, and where no law is broken there is no occasion for punishment." Thereupon another long interchange of notes took place. Finally, the German envoys, in anger, left their old residences in Berne and ceased all intercourse with her government. German mechanics were prohibited from entering, first the canton, then all Switzerland, because they were here trained as apostles of insurrection; an order of the diet at Frankfort also forbade German youth to study at the recently established universities of Berne and Zurich, and fresh hindrances to neighborly intercourse were interposed at the frontiers, to the injury of both sides.

Reflection, however, soon convinced both parties that obstinacy was not for the advantage of either. Berne herself, by degrees, modified her tone. This was especially the case when, with the beginning of 1835, she became Vorort of the Confederacy, and had no longer to consider merely her own relations with foreign states. But her leaning to moderation, now severely blamed as weakness by many who had before praised her opposition, did not at once accomplish her object. Even in February, count Bombelles, the Austrian embassador and chief opponent of the canton in the dispute about the refugees, sent notice of the accession of Ferdinand I., his imperial master, to the throne, by a simple letter through the post, contrary to custom. This opportunity was seized upon, nevertheless, in order to renew the interrupted correspondence. In their letter of congratulation, the state-council of Berne expressed their regrets for the occurrence which had occasioned the alienation. But the reconciliation was still delayed. It could only be looked upon as accomplished, when Bombelles returned to Berne, in June. These unpleasant differences had lasted a year and a half. No one gained honor by them: neither the powerful states by their insolence toward the weaker, nor the free by their disregard of the rights of their neighbors.

CHAPTER LXX.

DISPUTE WITH FRANCE.

[A. D. 1835 and 1836.]

At this time the hope of forming a new and stronger bond between the Confederates diminished more and more. With the deputies from the former Sarnen-league, the spirit of division always reäppeared in the meetings of the Diet. Every step towards improvement was only possible after arduous conflicts. Even for the introduction of uniform weights and measures only seven cantons gave their votes. The nation, however, greeted with joy the decree of the Diet that its sittings should thenceforth be public; and when it unanimously rejected the proposition for the separation of the principality of Neuchâtel, it became evident that the old Swiss spirit was not entirely dead.

That spirit showed itself much more living, however, among the people than among their deputies to the Diet. It was apparent in the attempts now made to fortify by improved internal arrangements the popular freedom obtained since 1830. Everywhere, creative life was manifested; everywhere, magistrates, societies, noble-minded individuals zealously aided each other to remove old abuses or to introduce ameliorations. Above all, the education of youth inspired a before unknown enthusiastic activity. To produce a generation worthy of freedom was an object for the noblest efforts, and the scientific institutions of the cities, as well as the poor village-schools, immediately felt the impulse of the new age. The means of defence also were rendered more efficient. The ancient manliness was again strengthened by military exercise and federal shooting-matches. Even the Diet bestowed more attention than ever on the equipment of the federal army. These are the strongest ramparts of a people's independence: enlightenment of the mind and strength in arms. Without these, the best constitutions are but dead parchments, having neither vitality nor force.

The Confederacy looked on approvingly, when even the half-canton, Bâle-country, the youngest child of their troubles, roused herself with determination to effect these great objects. She was obliged to remedy many deficiencies of earlier times, and, by wise management, to propitiate many troublesome opponents. Therefore her task was more difficult than that of any of the others; the long civil disturbances had too much loosened the bonds of public order, and the government was not seldom deprived of the necessary assistance from the people. More than once, in the beginning, seditious risings took place in separate communes; as on the occasion of the choice of clergy in Muttenz and Waldenburg, and afterwards, in Oberwyl and Allschwyl. Only an armed force could here secure due observance of the laws.

At this time another dispute appeared to threaten more serious consequences. Two French Jews, the brothers Wahl, had bought an estate in the village of Reinach. The purchase was already completed in the customary form when the state-council annulled it, on the ground of an old law by which Jews were refused admittance to the territory of Bâle. The Wahls, on the other hand, based their right on the treaty between France and Switzerland, which authorized such acquisitions. As Bâle-country insisted on her position, they claimed the protection of their native land. Long negotiations now took place between the two governments. When these proved fruitless, France broke off all intercourse with the canton. The citizens of the latter were sent out of the kingdom; even the dwellers on the border, who owned farms on French soil, were not permitted to cultivate them. This unfriendly state of things lasted several months. Finally, after much trouble, the Vorort settled the dispute. Bâle-country was obliged to pay a heavy indemnity to the brothers Wahl, and France desisted from further claims.

This was, however, but a foretaste to Switzerland of a more serious difficulty with her powerful neighbor. King Louis Philippe, from this time, cooled more and more in his friendship towards the country which had once given him a hospitable asylum in his misfortunes. His state-policy offered this as a sacrifice to propitiate the court of Austria, which had always been hostile to him. An opportunity for a quarrel, when diligently sought, is easily found. Several of the refugees, dismissed from Switzerland on account of the Savoy-expedition, had returned and again formed societies among themselves. We then heard of a "young Germany," a "young Italy," a "young Poland;" a plan of theirs for an armed invasion of the grand-duchy of Baden was discovered. Then the Vorort determined again to send away these disturbers of the peace, and requested France (June, 1836) to allow them a free passage, as she had before done. This was granted; but the reply of the French embassador, the duke of Montebello, was in the tone of an angry lord towards his dependants. Never before had the governments of Switzerland been addressed so disrespectfully. It was even reported that Montebello, in an evening visit, had threatened the grey-haired president of the Confederacy, Tscharner of Berne, with a strict blockade of the frontiers of Switzerland, in case she did not readily yield to his demands. No free people can endure such arrogance. The whole country was aroused, and a cry of the deepest indignation resounded through all the cantons. Public meetings were called by men of influence: first in Flawyl, canton of St. Gallen; then simultaneously and in unprecedented numbers, the citizens of almost all the respective districts assembled at Wohlenschwyl in Aargau, at Reiden in the canton of Lucerne, at Wiedikon near Zurich, and at Munsingen in the canton of Berne. Many thousands, and among them the noblest of the Confederates, unanimously demanded of the Diet the maintenance of the Swiss honor. The Diet, supported by such a manifestation of public feeling, replied to the French note as became rulers to whom the independence of their fatherland is an inviolably sacred treasure. Only the Sarnen-cantons, who unwillingly acknowledged even the vorortship of Berne, voted for abject submission.

A few days afterwards, another circumstance blew into fresh flame the fire of just indignation against Montebello. He himself had requested the Vorort to banish a Frenchman of the name of Conseil, as an accomplice of the regicide Fieschi and a dangerous refugee. Conseil was therefore arrested at Nidau (10 Aug.). But it was proved, by the papers found and the examinations made, that, in contradiction to Montebello's complaint, he was a secret spy of France, sent to watch the other refugees. In furtherance of this object, he had quite recently received, from the embassador's office, money and a passport under a false name. The tidings of such dishonorable treachery quickly spread. Every one felt that this was a contemptuous disregard of international rights. The Diet itself took the matter in hand. A report, made by Keller of Zurich and Monnard of Lausanne, fearlessly unveiling the deception, was widely circulated in Switzerland as well as in France. It excited indignation in both countries. Even in the chamber of deputies at Paris, the minister was called to account therefor. The Diet decided, by a small majority, to complain of the embassador to his government and to transmit the documents. The Vorort, however, for fear of more seriously irritating the French cabinet, declined to carry out this decision. On its mere publication in the newspapers, actual hostilities were threatened by France. A new note of the embassador (29 Sept.) demanded a signal satisfaction for the insult. Shortly after, the western portion of Switzerland was "hermetically sealed" until such satisfaction should be given. From Bâle to Geneva, no one could pass the line in either direction; even the mails were stopped. French troops, in long array, kept guard.

But the Swiss people were not terrified thereat. The traders of many cantons, of their own accord, ceased all intercourse with France. Popular meetings contributed money in aid of the more injuriously-affected border-inhabitants. There was much more murmuring in France itself against such manifest injustice, and the royal government, feeling that it had gone too far, soon desired an accommodation. The Vorort called together the recently-adjourned Diet, who solemnly declared that they had yielded authority to no foreign state to interfere in Swiss affairs. Then they approved of the non-fulfilment of their decision in the matter of Conseil, and declared that they had no intention to offend the French government thereby. This declaration sent by courier to Paris, was there received as welcome tidings of peace. The blockade was raised after six weeks' duration (from 1 October to middle of November), and in the same winter, Montebello gave a grand reconciliatory entertainment.

A result, worthy of note, followed this dispute, however. In the canton of Berne, the vacillation of the government had awakened in many the desire for a complete return to the old state of things. With this object, several societies had been formed under the name of "Safety-unions," which were tools in the hands of the defunct aristocracy. Their committees met more and more boldly in the Casino of the capital-city. But now, both people and magistrates determined to put a stop to such dangerous movements. After quite stormy discussions, the great council dissolved the safety-unions (8 March, 1837). But their members were not quieted. At Brienzwyler in Oberland, they preached open rebellion. Armed troops of volunteers immediately hastened from Thun, over the lake, to put them down, and public order was once more saved from the danger of subversion.

CHAPTER LXXI.

PROTOCOL OF THE BADEN-CONFERENCE; ITS OCCASION AND CONSEQUENCES.

[A. D. 1834 to 1836.]

THE popular freedom of the Confederates soon had to withstand still more serious aggressions. The most dangerous foreign enemy came not from the borders of Austria or of France, but from the ultramontane Rome, always striving for the empire of the world. Ever since the days when Napoleon Buonaparte's imperial throne had fallen in ruins, the papal court had employed every means to recover its old church-dominion of the middle ages. To secure the thrones and altars of Europe, no method appeared more efficacious than to bring the nations back to blind submission to doctrine. Switzerland was of no small importance in this scheme of conquest. The old church-piety of her mountaineers, her republican forms of government, the division of the country into many small states and their jealousy of each other, must be more favorable to such a design than could be the case in monarchies. From her situation in the centre of Europe, Switzerland would also be very useful as an advanced post against other countries. Therefore the Roman cabinet especially endeavored to obtain a great influence here.

The papal nuncio had already (1814) reöccupied his ancient seat in Lucerne. His aims were directed towards assuring the inviolability of the numerous convents and ecclesiastical establishments, under the twelfth article of the new confederate league. With this object, the old bishoprics were split into smaller ones, that the divisions might be more easily commanded. The desire of the more intelligent of the people for a Swiss archbishop was entirely disregarded. The nuncio filled the office of chief shepherd directly in the name of the holy father. The order of Loyola, also, immediately upon its reëstablishment after its seeming death of seventy years, secured a firm footing in Valais (1814). Four years afterwards, it established a splendid central point of operations at Freiburg. The effects of this upon a wide circle were soon perceptible in the subjugation of the popular mind to the yoke of priestly domination, as well as in the increasing intolerance between catholics and reformed.

But in the beginning of 1830, the rising of the Swiss people for freedom seemed to circumscribe the further advance of the Roman power. Many flattered themselves that it was forever rendered impotent. Vain delusion! The operation of the national constitutions and laws unexpectedly opened to the Romanists a way to greater influence over the masses than before. Popular elections, the right to form associations, the press: freedom's weapons, were cunningly turned into arms against her. With untiring perseverance, church-questions were introduced into party-disputes respecting municipal matters. A great association of co-believers soon spread like a net over the whole land. Around the banner of the church gathered catholic popular-unions, strongly united, with priests as leaders: especially numerous in some districts of St. Gallen, in the free-bailiwicks of Aargau and in Bernese Leberberg. Where, shortly before, "Freedom and the constitution" was the watchword in the mouths of all, now sounded the war-cry: "Religion is in danger." From the foreign Propaganda and the richest convents, money flowed in to support the secret league. Its leading director was the papal nuncio, and with him abbot Celestin of

Einsiedlen. The free spirit of the nation was regarded as a common enemy.

That which had originally been prepared in secret, was now boldly carried into open effect. Persecutions against those who believed differently were soon commenced. When priest Aloys Fuchs, by preaching and writing, endeavored to reform numerous church-abuses in the chapter of Uznach, he was called to account before an ecclesiastical inquisition at St. Gallen. In vain did he defend his course with noble ingenuousness. As he would not retract, the judges condemned his teachings as irreligious, and prohibited him the exercise of his priestly office. The bishop of Coire confirmed the sentence; Fuchs, however, was honored by public opinion as a martyr for the truth.

But when, at last, the pride of some bishops and priests led them to interfere in the management of the state, then the forbearance of the governments came to an end. Absolute necessity called for a general determined action to restrain the pretensions of the church within her proper limits. Deputies from Berne, Lucerne, Solothurn, Bâle-country, Aargau, Thurgau and St. Gallen met immediately in conference at Baden. Here they came to an understanding respecting the rights of the state in church-matters. Those rights which had long existed in part, and which were even affirmed by law in most monarchies, were secured for all: the Placet* respecting the mandates of church-dignitaries, the right of mixed marriages, the priestly-office oath to maintain the constitution. Steps were also taken towards a negotiation with the papal see for the establishment of a Swiss archbishopric and a priest's seminary, as well as respecting the observance of holy days and the holding of synods (14 January, 1834). All well-intentioned men looked more confidingly to the future; but they were most bitterly undeceived.

For, as soon as the protocol of the Baden-conference was published, suddenly and simultaneously from most of the catholic districts arose a cry of indignation on the

* This relates to the form by which the civil authorities approve of church-decrees and assent to their promulgation.

part of the Romanists against it, as against an unprecedented abuse of power. Curses and threats were heard even from consecrated places. And the tumult increased when pope Gregory XVI. himself, in a circular epistle, condemned the several articles as "false, erring, an encroachment on the rights of the holy see, destructive to the government of the church, tending to heresy, and schismatic." (23 October, 1835.) He, who should be a prince of peace, cast thereby the firebrand of long years of civil discord into the Helvetian Alpine land. The dispute blazed high everywhere. In Solothurn, where it was very virulent, the great-council dared not adopt the Baden-articles. In St. Gallen, they were rejected by the people, in prolonged general assemblies, excited thereto by the party of the zealots, contemptuously styled "redstockings." In Lucerne, which accepted them, the people could hardly be pacified by the representations of the government. The solemn declaration of the latter, drawn up by the clever hand of the secretary of state, Constantine Siegwart, was even inserted by the pope, as heretical, in the list of prohibited publications. Shortly afterwards, the nuncio, in anger and without leave-taking, quitted Lucerne in the dusk of early dawn, and retired into Schwyz (29 November, 1835). Thurgau adopted the articles in spite of the opposition of her clergy; but open rebellion took place in Aargau and Berne.

In vain had the great-council of Aargau published a quieting address to the people at the same time with the Baden-articles, which it approved. No quiet resulted. The priests of many of the catholic communes even refused to read the address at the Sunday-service, as they were ordered (May, 1835). When this disobedience was punished by the tribunals with suspension of functions and fines, the bishop of Bâle refused to enforce the judicial sentence. A great dispute arose between the civil and ecclesiastical magistrates. The former were unwilling to have the reins of legal authority wrested from them. "To the church," said they, "belongs that which is of the church; but to the state, no less, that which is of the state." Accordingly, in that same year, the oath of allegiance was required from the beneficed clergy, without prejudice tc the obedience due to their superiors in ecclesiastical matters. The same form of oath had already been allowed by the bishop, in other districts. But the dispute, once commenced, increased in vehemence. About the same time (7th Nov.) appeared the decree of the great-council for a state-supervision of the property of those cantonal monasteries and nunneries which had been mismanaged. Then the signal for open resistance came from the abbey of Muri and its dependencies. The pretence was that the official oath required of the priests threatened the holy ancestral faith. Excited assemblages took place; a second free-bailiwick-invasion of Aargau was already meditated, and the country was shaken from its peace by the anticipated horrors of a religious war. The government once more strenuously exerted itself to restore quiet. When its words remained unheard in the uproar, it called for troops. The neighboring cantons, Bâle-country especially, immediately sent assistance. The free-bailiwicks were occupied, without stroke of sword (26th Nov.). The exciters of the people fled, terrified. Many of them, even some priests, were condemned by the courts, and the catholic unions were dissolved. Thus order was quickly restored. To complete the work of peace, the great-council issued a solemn declaration that the priestly oath of office in no way impugned the catholic faith. Finally, the pastors took it without further opposition. Shortly afterwards, the unfortunate misled people were, with great clemency, relieved from paying the costs of occupation. Notwithstanding all this, discontent still existed in several places, for a long time. Many awaited only a favorable opportunity to rise in fresh opposition.

Not long after these occurrences in Aargau, an outbreak followed in Bernese Jura. These mountain-valleys contain a strongly catholic and excitable population. When the government of the canton had voted in favor of the Baden-articles (Feb., 1836), the same influences were brought to bear here as on the Reuss. Sermons of priests and distributions of miracle-working medals excited the people to raging fanaticism. From the catholic communes, where French is spoken, rose, louder than elsewhere, the cry of "Religion is in danger." Cuttat, the city-priest of Pruntrut, an official of the nuncio, led the movement. From Pruntrut, it spread quickly into the neighboring villages. Here, excited women, bearing banners and crosses, travelled about, calling on the people to resist. Liberty-trees were planted; magistrates insulted; separation from Berne demanded. Vicar Belet even negotiated secretly with the French embassador for the interference of foreign power. Here, also, the government first attempted to avert greater disturbance by sending commissioners; here also, after all other measures had failed, they were finally compelled to restore order by force of arms (10th March). Now, the ringleaders fled, the liberty-trees fell, and the people, once more sobered, acknowledged that lies and fraud, and even high treason towards the state, had been covered by the false cloak of zeal for religion. But, in spite of their victory, the government did not long maintain their advantage. It was proposed to the great-council, by the advice, it is said, of the before-mentioned French embassador, to negotiate with the pope himself respecting the admissibility of the articles he had condemned. In secret session (2d July) the proposition was accepted by the representatives of the people.

This retrograde step on the part of Berne nullified all proceedings since the concordat of Baden, and prepared for its opponents a great and unexpected triumph. The policy of Rome never draws back; where she can introduce a finger, she soon grasps with the whole hand. Now first began the real work of exciting the people against the liberal governments; now first were the hellish seeds of discord sown in the minds of men by a regular system of preachings and publications. And therewithal, those untiring champions of the church, the Jesuits, that they might be nearer to the theatre of operations, were invited to Schwyz, then the residence of the nuncio. Their entrance was solemnized in May. All friends of the fatherland were terrified thereat; but no general assembly, no cantonal government, no Vorort, raised a voice in protest.

CHAPTER LXXII.

CONSTITUTIONAL QUARREL IN GLARUS. CONTEST BETWEEN THE HORNERS AND KLAUENS IN SCHWYZ. LOUIS NAPOLEON.

[A. D. 1837 and 1838.]

No Alpine valley was so secluded, no people's peace so sacred as to prevent an attempt to kindle the fire of religious discord. This Glarus also experienced. Hitherto this little state, poor in consequence of the ruggedness of her soil yet made comfortable by the industry of her inhabitants, had remained almost undisturbed by the excitement of the times. But now, a serious quarrel unexpectedly took place in consequence of a reasonable desire. The anniversary of the battle of Nafels had always been solemnized separately by the two church-parties. Many, however, had long desired to celebrate the hero-day of their fathers in brotherly union. The general assembly voted to that effect (1835). But the catholic clergy violently opposed this measure; especially Tschudi, a priest of Glarus, whom bishop Bossi of Coire supported by his authority. When, notwithstanding this, the anniversary of the battle of Nafels was celebrated in common at the monuments on the election-field, the priestly anger gushed forth over the land in unmeasured condemnation of the proceeding. But the free minds of the free people of Glarus revolted at this, and they said: "The priests are citizens like the rest of us, and subject to the same laws. No foreign bishop shall interfere in our private state-affairs." Thereupon, it was decreed that the priests of the canton should take the oath of allegiance (29th May, 1836), and at the same time a change in the constitution was decided upon in order to abolish every distinction between the church-parties. Hitherto, for a long while, the reformed and the catholics had had separate positions in the general assemblies held in common, and each division had its peculiar officers. Now began a new building upon the foundation-stone of the legal equality of all. The clergy and their partisans did all in their power to hinder this. As the party of catholics in Glarus itself was very weak, for it numbered only an eighth of the population, the assistance of other states, especially of Schwyz and Uri, was called in. The noise of this dispute soon filled all Switzerland. But the people of Glarus, strong in their good right, pursued their legal course undaunted. The new constitution was adopted (2d Oct.) by thousands of votes. But when, the next year, deputies of both religions, chosen by the assembled people, appeared at the Diet, the Urcantons* protested vehemently. They wished to expel the deputies and to annul the constitution. In spite of them the Diet, though by but a small majority, disregarded their proposition and passed to the order of the day. The requirements of Swiss brotherhood achieved a victory over church-party-spirit. But the partisans were not quieted in Glarus, until the government seriously threatened to punish them. Then they finally submitted to necessity.

Still more violently did a civil storm rage shortly afterwards in neighboring Schwyz. Ever since this divided canton had been reunited in 1833 by the armed interference of the Confederates, the wound had been only scarred over, not healed. Those who longed for a restoration of their old domination constantly played an artful game. This was made manifest when (1836) the Confederate government, after unremitting urgings and petitions, had released them from payment of the costs of occupation. Then the chiefs of the "old free-land" with fresh, imperious haughtiness, at once displayed their rancor against the Confederate states, and especially against the formerly subject Outer-district. With them was the abbey Maria Einsiedeln, and the majority of the clergy, most prominently the nuncio and the Jesuits. Manifold intrigues, arbitrary judicial sentences, public insults, even persecution of their opponents, constantly widened the breach. Finally, a strange dispute in the "old land" gave opportunity for an outbreak. There had been, for many years,

* Urcantons—original or primitive cantons—Uri, Schwyz and Unterwalden.

in the Schwyz district, a law-suit respecting the use of certain extensive common pastures (Allmenden). The rich there fed their large herds of horned cattle, and pleaded long-established custom; but the poor, who had only a few sheep and goats, found themselves restricted, and demanded a division of this common property on equal terms. Hateful envy intermingled her poison. When the court decided in favor of the cattle-owners (Horners), the sheep-owners (Klauens) united with the Outer-district. So the matter became a political apple-of-discord. At the anxiously-expected general assembly of 1838, the new choice of magistrates was to determine who should be masters in the land. Nazar Reding was the champion of the Klauens; Theodore Abyberg, formerly leader in the invasion of Kussnacht, of the Horners. Monks and Jesuits, fearful of a diminution of their influence if the former prevailed, used every method to encourage their adherents. The pretensions of the Klauens were declared in chapter of the priests to be injurious to religion, and denounced from the pulpits. Even bribery was frequently attempted. Thus dawned the first Sunday in May. The people assembled on the field near Rothenthurm. The parties took their stands separately in front of the platform on which the magistrates were seated. The storm broke forth immediately on the election of tellers, which seemed to indicate a preponderance in favor of the Klauens. Then, suddenly, on a given signal, the Horners, armed with clubs, rushed upon their opponents. A savage, even bloody, hand to hand conflict took place. The party of the liberals, forced to fly, dispersed in every direction. The general assembly was necessarily dissolved.

That day shook the state to its foundations. The Outer-district once more called for a division of the canton. The Vorort did indeed hastily send mediators; but they returned without accomplishing any thing, mocked by the leaders in Schwyz. These latter, at a second general assembly (17th June), from which the Klauens absented themselves, succeeded in securing the votes. This result was again violently disputed by their opponents. The whole Confederacy took sides, for or against. The Diet was obliged to enjoin peace. A numerous deputation from this body summoned a third general assembly (16th August), and the proceedings took place in their presence. In the mean while, the civil and ecclesiastical authorities had won over a majority of the people, and their victory was complete and decided. When, thereupon, the Diet recommended forgetfulness of all that had occurred, the Outer-district reluctantly submitted, and every thing returned to its old course.

This storm was not yet entirely cleared away, when all eyes in Switzerland were turned towards France, whence threatening clouds arose. A single individual caused the two nations to arm against each other: Louis Napoleon, a nephew of the great dead emperor. With his mother, queen Hortense, he had established himself at the castle of Arenaberg, in beautiful Thurgau, and had become a citizen of the canton. He was welcomed among the vigorous Swiss youth at the school for military exercise in Thun, and at the joyous public festivals. But, notwithstanding the republican tendencies which he seemed to cherish, the prince had not forgotten the brilliant destiny to which his birth had called him. In October, 1837, at Strassburg, with the hope of recovering the throne of France, he entered the country from which his family had been banished. He thought that the magic of his name would quickly bring the garrison and burghers of the city to his standard. But, instead of the expected crown, imprisonment and exile to America were his lot. Soon, without notice, he recrossed the ocean, to be present at his mother's bed of sickness; and, even after her death, he remained in Thurgau. Then France requested the Confederates to expel this dangerous claimant of the crown, complaining that Arenaberg was a nest of conspirators (1st August, 1838). In the newly-assembled Diet, the deputy from Thurgau declared that the prince was a citizen of that canton: he therefore kept quiet, the government would protect him in his rights. With the deputy from Aargau, those of the western cantons most strenuously insisted on the inviolable independence of the nation. They desired that the improper demand of France should be rejected.

But other deputies were less firm. The Diet decided that instructions must first be received from the great-councils of the several cantons. Then the French government, displeased at this delay, threatened force. Troops advanced from Lyons towards the Swiss frontier. General Aymar, in an order of the day, informed his soldiers that they were called out to chastise refractory neighbors. As soon as the report of this spread, Geneva and Vaud, most exposed to attack, rushed suddenly to arms. A great enthusiasm for their fatherland seized upon all the people. In a few days, twenty-five thousand men stood in arms, the frontiers were occupied, and the fortifications of Geneva bristled with cannon. When the enemy's forces reached the little frontier district of Gex, imagining that terror and confusion prevailed beyond the border, they unexpectedly found themselves in presence of a courageous army. Accident might at any moment have produced a collision. One canton after another voted to reject the demand of France; the warlike fire on lake Leman enkindled a like enthusiasm in the minds of all the Swiss people. At this ominous hour, a letter from prince Napoleon was received by the president of the Diet: he would voluntarily depart, in order not to occasion a breach between two friendly nations. At the same time he left Thurgau and Switzerland. France seized the welcome opportunity to renew her professions of friendship. Her politic king, Louis Philippe, who had made so many sacrifices for the peace of Europe, had only wished to intimidate his opponents. At so determined a resistance, the desirability of exposing his kingdom to the chances of war became doubtful. As soon as his troops left the frontier, the Confederates also returned home, joyful in the conviction that the old hero-spirit of the fathers was still to be found in the sons on the day of need.

CHAPTER LXXIII.

EXPLOSION AT ZURICH.

[A. D. 1839.]

WITH the foreign difficulty vanished also the internal union which it had for a short time produced. The always watchful enemies of popular freedom prepared to deal a decisive blow. And they first succeeded where no one expected it, at Zurich.

Here, liberty had diffused her choicest blessings, as in almost no other region of the Confederacy. Industry and comfort prevailed; newly-constructed highways promoted commerce; by means of the public schools, in the improvement of which Thomas Scherr, a naturalized citizen of German birth, was actively efficient, a well educated generation was growing up, and, by her new university, Zurich had become a far-shining star of science and art. The environs of many villages and of the capital-city, especially since the levelling of her old fortification walls, had been greatly embellished; numerous public buildings, of almost regal magnificence and devoted to noble institutions, had been erected. But, in spite of all these creations of the new age, the old aristocracy remained unreconciled. They could not brook the loss of their privileges; they still hoped for a restoration of their old domination. Every fault of the government was eagerly watched for, to be used for its destruction. The desired opportunity was found, shortly after Zurich entered upon the functions of Vorort, with the year 1839.

Then, in the pride of prosperity and under the pressure of increasing demands for progress, the government undertook the work of introducing the science of the age into religious matters also. On motion of the council of education, they invited David Frederic Strauss of Wurtemberg to the chair of professor of theology in the university (26th January). This person had recently excited much controversy among learned men by his work upon the life of Jesus, in which he had declared the occurrences related in the Testament to be mere traditions of the first church. Some few sustained him, many more opposed. Although the invitation was made according to every legal form, a decided protest was immediately raised against it by the clergy. Archdeacon Fussli proposed in the great-council, that the church-council also should have a voice in the choice of theological professors of the university. His proposition was however rejected by a large majority. Then the opposition called upon the people. No means of arousing the masses can be more powerful than the exciting of religious apprehension. In meetings of the citizens, in pamphlets scattered profusely over the country, from the pulpits even, cries of apprehension and of fear immediately sounded. "The government," it was said, "will destroy religion. Our future pastors will be educated by an unbeliever. Alas for our children! They will fall into a new heathenism. Alas for those in distress! Alas for the sick and the dying! All trust in the divine word will henceforth be taken away from them." The system of public schools was the object of like accusations, and, with Strauss and Scherr, was stigmatized as the enemy of the Christian religion. Thereby a strongly despondent feeling was awakened in the people. It began, at once, to ferment in all parts of the country, where cheerful happiness had hitherto prevailed. In vain did the well-informed try to quiet it, as did burgomaster Hirzel in his address "to his fellow-men." Their voices were lost in the tumult of curses against the government. Whoever said a word in defence of the latter was denounced as a follower of Strauss. The strength of the opposition increased in a few days to an avalanche; the movement quickly escaped from the control of its promoters. Early in February, some bold men had formed themselves into a "Committee of Faith," which soon obtained consideration and great influence. Its seat was at Wadenschwyl on the lake. Hurliman-Landis, a manufacturer of Richterschwyl, Dr. Rahn-Escher and Bleuler-Zeller, both of Zurich, were its most efficient leaders. From these issued the word of command: "Strauss must not and shall not come." To give it authority, a bold address to the great-council was prepared by them, to which nearly forty thousand citizens affixed their names. Therein they demanded the dismissal of the abhorred professor, and, moreover, the controlling vote of the church in the choice of the officers of education, as well as in the direction of the school-studies. A demand made by such numbers and with such vehemence could no longer be withstood. On the 23d of February, the great-council reconsidered their invitation to Dr. Strauss; on the 18th of March they voted his dismissal on a retiring pension. The other demands of the people were referred to commissioners for consideration.

Although the principal matter was now settled, the storm it had aroused was not calmed. Political views had mingled with the religious pretext from the beginning, and the success hitherto obtained by the "beautiful demonstration," as it was called, prompted the conception of broader plans. The leaders soon formed a close and strongly bound union, first of individuals, then of the committees already established in the districts and communes, of which they made themselves the ruling directors. Thus, in fact, if not in name, an opposition-government, inimical to the legal magistrates of the state, came into existence. Fresh concessions of the great-council only increased the arrogance of their demands. When the council (27th June) passed a law whereby the popular wish respecting religious tuition in the schools was carried into effect, the Committee of Faith declared that they could no longer be satisfied with this. They demanded for the church a still greater control over the schools, and soon proclaimed more and more loudly that the government no longer possessed the confidence of the people. "For," said they, "how can men without religion be the rulers of a religious nation?" The fire of zeal for the church, which had smouldered during the summer, was rekindled in the autumn. The Committees were roused to new activity, and, in order to make an overpowering demonstration of popular opinion, a great meeting was called at Kloten. But when the leaders, in preparation for this, assumed also the direction in the communal assemblies and announced their will to the district-authorities, this encroachment upon the powers of the state seemed altogether too presumptuous. The government thought it was time to put bounds to the movement. They declared it seditious, and directed the state-attorney to draw up an indictment against the members of the Committee (23d August). At the same time, for their own protection, they called out troops, whom they almost immediately dismissed, when they saw, on all sides, the manifestations of displeasure at this proceeding. It was already too late. The cry of violence intended against the freedom and faith of the people gained the ascendancy. When the appointed day (2d September) came, ten thousand men hastened to the meeting at Kloten, in spite of a violent rain-storm. Here it was decided: that the government's declaration of the movement as seditious must be withdrawn, the legal proceedings against the members of the Committee quashed, and an indictment drawn up against the state-attorney himself. Twenty-two deputies communicated these demands to burgomaster Hess. Now it became evident that the government was weakened by indecision. Their answer was evasive: The great-council must first be consulted. The Committee hastened its preparations. The most influential of its members, Dr. Rahn-Escher, immediately issued a call for insurrection. It was falsely announced that troops were on the march from other cantons to put down the people. This acted like a spark in a powder-barrel. All bonds of legal order were rent asunder and raging fanaticism filled the land. The storm first broke forth from Pfeffikon and along the lake-shores. During the night, horsemen hurried through the neighboring places, calling on the people to rise. And treason was soon rife in the city itself; it penetrated the session-hall of the government. Perplexity crippled all energy. On the morning of 6th September, the landsturm appeared before the gates of Zurich, in numerous, disorderly masses, singing psalms. Most of them had scythes and clubs, many guns. Pastor Bernard Hirzel of Pfeffikon was their leader. After a hasty discussion with mes sengers from the government, the crowd rushed into the city and over the bridge of the Limmat. In the cathedral-square, they were met by a few armed men, who then chanced to be at the exercise-school in Zurich, and who, reinforced by volunteers, were determined to protect the seat of government from violence. When these would not give way before the on-pressing multitude, pastor Hirzel cried: "Then fire, in the name of God!" Shots fell. They were returned, and many of the country-people retreated in confusion. Then state-councillor Hegetschwyler stepped between the exasperated men, to prevent further bloodshed. A shot from behind stretched him dead upon the ground. At this moment it was reported that the government had abdicated, and the troop of their last defenders immediately dispersed. Many were obliged to save themselves by flight from the vengeance of the landsturm; with them most of the deposed magistrates. They were not in safety till they had passed the borders. But burgomaster Hess and several who had remained with him now united openly with the leaders of the insurrection. By them a provisional government was formed, which henceforth assumed the direction of affairs. But the committee of faith joyously announced to its adherents far and near, that God had given the victory to the just cause. To celebrate this victory, men, women and children thronged in numberless crowds to Zurich on the following days; in the church, prayers alternated with carousings; in the open streets, fanatical preachers rejoiced over the new salvation of the country. Therewithal, bloodthirsty threats were uttered against the followers of Strauss's doctrine; but the prison-doors were opened for the incendiaries of the manufactory at Uster. Shortly afterwards, a new election of all cantonal officers and magistrates took place, and a spirit of bitter intolerance ruled.

The evil results of this unprecedented act of violence were not confined to Zurich alone. Wherever the doctrine prevails, that a popular mob, breaking loose from all constitutional restraints, may depose and institute governments, there political wisdom no longer governs, but intrigue. And this evil example soon had its followers. It first showed its effects upon the then assembled Diet. During the earlier occurrences, which took place under their very eyes, they remained fixed in stupid inactivity. Then, when they resumed their labors, it was evident that the seeds of discord, sown broadcast over Zurich, had germinated luxuriantly among them also. In consequence of the Vorort's apostasy from the cause of freedom, many deputies cherished similar desires, and preparations were thenceforth made for a great political revolution in the country of the Confederates.

CHAPTER LXXIV.

BITTER CONSEQUENCES. CONVENT-REBELLION IN AARGAU.

[A. D. 1840 and 1841.]

THE revolution at Zurich, though accomplished in the holy name of religion, occasioned very unholy troubles. From it proceeded a constant succession of disturbances, quarrels and rebellions throughout the cantons. Soon came the news of the overthrow of an unpopular government in Ticino; then of the success of a reaction in Valais; then of plots in Aargau, Solothurn and Bâle-country. Never had there been days of greater distress to the fatherland from discord than these.

In Bâle-country, deficiencies in the management of the new administration had excited frequent dissatisfaction. When, now, the Sixth of September gave the evil watchword from Zurich, a union under the name of "Friends of the fatherland" was formed for open resistance to the government. Its members, some of whom were men of poor reputation, while the majority were enthusiasts for liberty, did not disdain to coalesce with the partisans of Bâle-city. At first, their designs were not considered dangerous. But, when, after their demands had been rejected by the state-council as improper, they preached resistance in the popular assemblies, and incited the communes to rebellion by envoys, it became necessary to put a speedy stop to the disorder. The government commanded the arrest of the ringleaders at Sissach and Gelterkinden, their headquarters. At the latter place, a tumultuous mob resisted the surrender of a prisoner. Troops were ordered there. The rebellious district was occupied without stroke of sword (15 April, 1840), and disorder immediately disappeared before the determination of the law.

Shortly afterwards, a similar seditious movement commenced in neighboring Solothurn. The constitution was then under revision. It was completed by the close of the year. It was then to be accepted or rejected by the people. There was a provision in the old constitution to the effect that, in case the new one was rejected, the former should remain in force ten years longer. This article, especially, was made the pretext for incitement. For the leaders of the catholic communes liked neither the old nor the new constitution. They frightened the people from their quiet by the assertion that religion was not sufficiently protected in either. The excitement increased as the day for voting drew near, especially in the neighborhood of the Benedictine abbey of Mariastein. The discontented attacked the government more and more boldly in their newspapers. A committee of faith was formed here also. In the popular assemblies, got together by means of disquieting reports, the plan of a constitution, drawn up by the committee and favorable to the church, was promulgated and its adoption demanded. But, as is the custom in Solothurn, many liberals freely attended such meetings, and their votes sometimes occasioned an entirely unexpected result. Then the leaders decided to employ force. The people of the communes quickly seized their arms, in some places for, in others against, the government. The latter did not lose their firmness for a moment. Unwilling to be suddenly deposed, as those of Zurich had been, they transferred their sittings to the barracks, called out troops for their protection, and ordered the arrest of the ringleaders. Thus a surprise was prevented. But the government was still more surely protected by the affection of the best of the people than by barracks and bayonets. They were supported faithfully. On the day of voting (10 Jan., 1841), the new constitution was accepted by a large and triumphant majority, and, shortly afterwards, the names of the old, proved magistrates were again deposited in the ballot-boxes.

More serious and more threatening to the whole fatherland did disorder show itself in Aargau about the same time. The brands had not been extinguished in 1836, in the convent-districts on the Reuss and the Limmat. Dissatisfaction still smouldered under the ashes, and was assiduously fanned by the ministers of the Roman see, who wished to preserve a centre of disturbance for the fitting time. The example of Zurich taught them how their objects might be attained. Following that, a strongly cemented union was established here also; communal committees, closely united among themselves, were appointed; the "Bunzner committee" had the supervision of the whole. Soon the time came when a revision of the constitution was discussed in Aargau also (1840). All moderate men of both church-parties wished to retain the Paritat under which the canton had lived happily for many years. The attack of the leaguers was first directed against the maintenance of this article. In a meeting at Mellingen (2 Feb.), they decided upon an address to the great council, in which the separate management of catholic affairs by special magistrates of that faith was asked for, in unseemly and insolent terms. At the same time, they demanded the restoration to the convents of all their former rights, viz.: the private management of their property, and freedom to receive novices. The great council reluctantly rejected these demands, unprecedented in form and tenor: a compliance with them appeared most pernicious to the canton. To pacify the catholic districts, however, they inserted in their draft of a new constitution a guaranty of church-freedom. When this was submitted to the people (5 Oct.), the compromise was rejected by all parties: to some it seemed to yield too much; to others, too little. A second discussion of the constitution followed. The Paritat was now given up by the liberals, and it was voted: That the representatives to the great-council should henceforward be chosen according to the number of electors, and no longer according to their faith. This exasperated the church-leaders: "Alas for us," said they; "instead of granting our just requests, they deprive us of the little we have. The reformed, who are the most numerous, will enslave us now." They proclaimed this in the free-bailiwicks, in the district of Baden, and as far as the Rhine. Under stormy auspices, an excited meeting was held at Baden (29 Nov). Here, with the members of the Bunzner committee, several foreign priestly and laical champions of the catholic church appeared on the platform, and also an official of the papal nuncio. They demanded a second rejection of the draft of the constitution, and threatening voices were even raised, calling for an entire separation of the catholic portion of the country from Aargau. A breach seemed unavoidable. But the rashness of those speakers occasioned greater unity among all prudent persons: the country must be saved from a great calamity. In order to preserve public order from the imminent danger, the majority of the citizens of all districts and faiths now voted decidedly to accept the second draft (5 Jan., 1841). But the hopes entertained of an immediate restoration of quiet proved vain, nevertheless. Soon the threats uttered at Baden began to ripen into deeds. The leaders recruited; they armed; everything was prepared for an onslaught. The emissaries of the convents and of the Bunzner committee were untiring in their efforts to rouse the citizens of the communes in defence of their threatened religion. Finally, the government ordered the arrest of the members of the committee (9 Jan). This was done; but now the flame of rebellion burst forth openly. A raging mob attacked the bailiff's house at Muri, in order to release the prisoners. In vain was a courageous resistance made by Waller, the government-commissioner. He was maltreated and imprisoned, with other faithful ministers of the law. The same thing occurred at Bremgarten, where serious injuries were inflicted on the officials and liberal citizens. At the head of the excited insurgents in both places, were the friends and servants of the convents. But in the district of Zurzach, father Theodosius, guardian of the capuchins at Baden, himself personally commanded the assembling of the country-people and urged them on. The laws were disregarded in the territory of the abbey of Wettingen also. The broad ramifications of the insurrection, even into neighboring cantons, became every day more and more apparent; a general conflagration threatened the whole country. The delay of another day would probably have rendered all remedy useless. But the government, conscious of their high duties, had already adopted preservative measures. Their armed force, hastily called out, under command of colonel Frey-Herose, marched in the night, through snow and wind, to the boundary of the free-bailiwicks; on the following morning (11 Jan.), to Villmergen, whose fields had already, in earlier ages, been twice reddened by citizens' blood, shed in religious wars. Here, the crowds of insurgents, called from a broad circle by the alarm-bells, had assembled for resistance. After a short fight, they dispersed before the thunder of the cannon. And now, without meeting further opposition, the victors marched to Muri. The convent and neighboring territory were occupied. On the next day, the auxiliary troops, which had been summoned from Bâle-country and Berne, entered the other insurgent districts. Many of the misleaders and of the misled escaped in safety over the borders.

Great indignation was felt by all the people when this second breach of the public peace became known. The supporters of the policy of Rome, and the convents especially, whose authority and money had been used to build up a power inimical to freedom, were again regarded as the principal offenders. When the great-council considered the extent of the danger they had averted, they felt how necessary it was to close its source for the future. Augustine Keller gave an eloquent expression to this feeling. He proposed that the convents, as incompatible with the welfare of the canton, should be forever suppressed. Moved by the power of his words and by the urgency of the momentous occasion, the assembly rose in favor of his motion. Only a few did not vote for it (13th January). And thus ended the many-centuried existence of those institutions of the middle ages, which once, in their prime, dispensed manifold blessings, but which had now become injurious to the country. They were: the rich abbeys of Muri and Wettingen, the capuchin-monasteries in Baden and Bremgarten, the nunneries of Hermetschwyl, Fahr, Gnadenthal and Mariakronung. The monks and nuns, dismissed from their convent-walls, received liberal pensions. The remaining property of the convents, added to the resources of the state, was to be used for the benefit of the catholic churches, schools and alms-houses.

As soon as this bold determination was adopted, voices of cheering approval were heard throughout Switzerland, and through almost all Europe. Still louder rose the cry of indignation from the ranks of the opponents. When the suppression of the convents was announced, the superiors protested. Their example was followed by the primitive cantons, especially by Schwyz, whence the nuncio fulminated the shafts of his anger against Aargau. The agitation occasioned by the fall of these ancient religious establishments spread into distant lands. From the imperial house of Austria, even, came a threatening protest, based on the former rights of the family of Habsburg over Muri. An extraordinary Diet was demanded by a majority of the catholic cantons. When they met, the deputies exhibited great bitterness against each other, as formerly, on the day of Stanz. The Urcantons required that the convents should be reëstablished without delay. "For," said they, "the bond of confederation is broken by this arbitrary proceeding. In the twelfth article of the compact the existence of the convents and religious establishments is expressly guaranteed. If Aargau will not yield voluntarily, she must be compelled." To this, the severely blamed canton replied by her deputy, Dr. Wieland: "That twelfth article is not unconditional. The welfare of the state is of more importance than the existence of the convents. We do only what imperious necessity requires. Our convents have repeatedly promoted insurrections against the laws and constitution. Their reëstablishment would be a deathblow to our commonwealth. The question is no longer: 'Aargau and the convents,' but 'Aargau or the convents.

If the one must stand, the other must fall." This serious dispute was settled by the influence of politic Baumgartner of St. Gallen. Formerly an enthusiastic champion of freedom, on that day he openly deserted the cause he had previously maintained and went over to its opponents. His motion prevailed. Twelve cantons declared (2d April): "The act of suppression is inconsistent with the bond of confederation." But Aargau was unwilling to yield her just right. From respect to the decision of the Diet, she did indeed suspend the present fulfilment of her decree respecting the convent-property, but she appealed to the sense of equity in her fellow Confederates, while in a memorial she laid bare the culpability of the suppressed religious establishments in all their proceedings. Her address produced a slow but increasing effect. The regular Diet of the year did indeed reäffirm the previous declaration, but not with the same decision. Now, the vorort Berne sided with the hard-pressed neighbor canton, and her avoyer, Carl Neuhaus, full of the spirit of freedom, opposed himself like a wall to the arrogance of the friends of the convents. It was soon apparent that some concession on the part of Aargau was more desirable than inflexible obstinacy. Thereupon the great-council decided, that, for the sake of national peace, the three nunneries of Fahr, Gnadenthal and Mariakronung, as least implicated in the insurrection, should be reëstablished in their privileges (19th July). Herewith Vaud and Scaffhausen declared themselves satisfied, and when the Diet met for the third time this year on the convent-question, the declaration of April had no longer a majority of votes. Now, the restoration of all the convents was demanded only by Lucerne, the three primitive cantons, Zug, Freiburg, St. Gallen, Grisons, Valais, Neuchâtel, Inner Appenzell and Bâle-city; ten votes and two halves; while Solothurn, Aargau, Ticino, Vaud, Thurgau, Schaffhausen, Outer Appenzell, Bâle-country, Glarus and Berne, eight votes and two halves, declared themselves satisfied with the concessions of Aargau; Zurich and Geneva wished Hermetschwyl to be added, on certain conditions, to the other three. Thus the matter still remained undecided. The dispute continued: every year the dispossessed abbots renewed their demands for the reëstablishment of their convents; every year thousands of petitioners addressed the deputies in their behalf. A constantly-widening gulf was opened between the parties, and the fatherland would ultimately have been rent by it, had not the hand of God mercifully directed otherwise.

CHAPTER LXXV.

REVOLUTION IN LUCERNE, IN TICINO AND GENEVA.

[A. D. 1840 to 1841.]

THE insurrections of the followers of Rome had failed before the firmness of Solothurn and Aargau. They still, however, expected to succeed in their designs upon Lucerne. Here, a large portion of the people were blindly submissive to the priestly rule, and the seed of distrust of the government had long since taken root. Since the government had urged the acceptance of the Baden-articles, many had fallen away from them, in anxiety about the holy church. The success of the onslaught at Zurich had awakened emulation to follow the example thus set, and the suppression of the convents in Aargau had broken all bonds of existing order. With cries of alarm, the banner of "danger to religion" was raised in all the villages, and a daily increasing number of those who were anxious for their faith flocked around it. Joseph Leu of Ebersoll, an energetic but fanatical peasant, made himself the leader of the movement. Already, in the winter of 1839, he had proposed in the great-council: That Lucerne should withdraw from the league of the seven liberal cantons, should invalidate the Baden-articles, and invite the Jesuits to direct public education. At that time, indeed, this proposition was angrily rejected; but Leu, with untiring perseverance, pursued his object, which became the aim of his life. And when he was applauded more and more by the masses, others, distinguished for their determination and mental gifts, soon joined him: among them, Constantine Siegwart, formerly secretary of state, once a zealous champion for the rights of the state in church-matters, now their equally zealous opponent, Bernard Meyer, Christopher Fuchs and others. When men of such force lay the axe to the root of the young tree of freedom, it must soon totter. A committee of faith, as at Zurich, took the reins with strong hands. Popular unions, with incredible activity, roused the country. The whole territory of Lucerne was brought into a state of feverish fermentation. An immediate change in the constitution was demanded; and the government, all at once become powerless, could no longer avert the imminent storm. A constituent-council was decreed. From pulpits and confessionals, as well as in numerous pamphlets, the people were exhorted to choose only church-pious men, that the canton might be saved from the horrors of radicalism. The exhortation had its effect. Under the appearance of extended popular sovereignty, the direction of the council was secured to a few individuals, and a wide door opened for the triumph of the power of the Roman-catholic church. The remonstrances of moderate men were of no avail: popular indignation was more violent against them than against the so-called heretical reformers themselves. On the 1st of May, 1841, the new constitution was accepted by a large majority of the people; hardly a third of the citizens desired to vote against it. Now, the government quitted their seats. Their farewell-address, full of noble regrets over the destruction of the long-established and beneficent constitution, glanced also, with sad forebodings, at the future. Into the places of the ejected entered a new great-council, the larger proportion of whom were noted for incapacity, and a new government, with minds completely subservient to church-domination. Their first work was to lay the constitution at the feet of the pope for his approval. Nevertheless, he did not approve it unconditionally, but, in his reply, expressed the hope: That he might yet, hereafter, see fruitful proofs of the pious inclinations of the people of Lucerne towards the mother-church and the supreme see of St. Peter.

After this disorderly revolution in the catholic Vorort, the reäction was pressed, with still more vigor than before, throughout the whole Swiss Alpine land. But not with equal success in all parts, and with least among the hot-blooded people of Ticino, beyond the St. Gotthard.

This canton had been the first with Lucerne, even before the Parisian days of July, to commence a reform in her internal affairs. But the changes then made were only half-way measures. Instead of the fine crop hoped for, a fresh, luxuriant growth of the weeds of old abuses soon sprung up. Many magistrates shamelessly plundered the commonwealth for their individual advantage, and the numerous clergy obtained an almost unlimited influence in the legislative council. After the triumph of the committee of faith at Zurich, the daring of the men in power in Ticino increased greätly. They now sought to extirpate the last remains of popular freedom, to trammel the press, to restain the right of association. This attempt, however, resulted in their own bitter defeat. For when the dissolution of the cantonal shooting-unions was ordered by a decree of government, because their bold spirit displeased the rulers, the members rose in active opposition. The alarm-drum beat to arms. Colonel Luvini, with a band of faithful men, surprised the arsenal at Lugano, and marched thence, in arms, to Locarno, where he was received joyfully (4th to 7th Dec., 1839). Liberty-trees in cities and villages proclaimed the triumph of the popular cause. When the state-council saw that all was lost, terrified, they fled over the frontiers into Lombardy; with them, many of their devoted clergy. Then ensued a complete overturn of the former state-management, with new laws and new magistrates. Ticino thenceforward ranged herself under the banner of progress, and a ray of hope lightened those days of sore distress to the fatherland. It was but for a moment, however. In the intoxication of their triumph, the new leaders forgot that moderation towards the conquered is always more honorable than victory itself. The banishment of their opponents from their native soil was not enough: they must also be ruined by confiscation of their property, and declared infamous by judicial sentence.

The exiles swore a bitter revenge for this. By constant intercourse with those of their adherents who had remained, they succeeded in fomenting disturbance. Many priests turned their pulpits into political tribunes and declaimed against the government. Soon a fanatical hatred burned between communes and communes, between citizens and citizens of the same district; the dagger, even, was not seldom bared for assassination. As the vorort Lucerne was now thrown open to those who fought for the destruction of Swiss freedom, her example incited to a similar attempt here. In the mountain-valleys of Maggia and Berzasca, where the adherents of the conspirators were numerous, the signal was given for a counter-revolution (1st July, 1841). At the same time, the exiles, with troops they had enlisted, entered the country from Lombardy and marched towards Locarno, the seat of the government. The latter, forewarned from Milan, prepared for defence. Troops hurried to Locarno, and the shooting-unions again proffered enthusiastic support. An encounter took place near the Brolla-bridge, half a league from the capital-city. The insurgents were defeated here, and in a still more destructive battle, the next day, near Tenero. Reduced to despair, throwing away their arms, they fled with their hirelings. One of the leaders, lawyer Joseph Nessi, was given up by his own men; the Lombard authorities sent others, as prisoners, to Ticino. Deputies came from the communes of Maggiathal, imploring mercy. Peace was restored in a short time, and a thanksgiving-festival solemnized the renewed triumph of freedom. But this, also, did not remain unsullied. A drum-head court-martial condemed Nessi to death. Even Luvini, at whose feet the wife of the unfortunate man cast herself with her children, could not save him. He was shot. Great as had been the exultation of many in Switzerland at the failure of the insurrection, their horror at this bloody deed was equally great. Sentences of death, in civil struggles, fix an indelible blot on the cause in which they are issued, and always elevate the sufferers to the dignity of martyrs. The government was more merciful a few months later, when it permitted several of the exiles to return to their homes. Thenceforward, trusting to the love of the people, it secured a firm opposition against all further intrigues of its enemies.

In the same year, the republic of Geneva began also to be a theatre of civil disturbance. The constitution of 1814 had deficiencies arising from the period of its adoption. Long since, but in vain, had enlightened members of the government itself sought to introduce propositions for more open elections, a shorter term of office for members of the council and the right of free petition. They were thwarted by the opposition of those of different views. In spite of these latter, Geneva, though restricted at home, had always sided with the party of progress in Confederate matters and there led in the cause of freedom. But now an association of citizens under the name of the "Third of March," boldly entered the lists for a new regulation of their own cantonal affairs. The people, instructed by writings and speeches, soon pronounced in favor of their object. This caused the state-council, though yielding unwillingly to the general demand, to lay propositions for a reform before the chamber of representatives (22d Nov). That which, if offered of their own accord a few months earlier, would have been accepted with gladness, was now received with cold mistrust and already was no longer satisfactory. A constituent-council, chosen from among the citizens, would alone accomplish the desired object. This demand became the watchword of the day. To give it force, the March-union assembled with crowds in the vicinity of the council-house. The state-council, on its side, summoned troops to protect the magistrates, and ordered the doors of the building to be barricaded. A serious conflict seemed imminent. But of the militia summoned, none appeared from the city and from the country-communes only a very few. These few, also, immediately dispersed. When the council saw themselves thus deserted by their fellow-citizens, they yielded entirely to the loudly-declared popular will. Their decision was announced amid the congratulations of the assembled crowd. The elections of the constituent-council soon followed; on 23d Dec., it began its work. The hitherto chained waves broke forth ragingly.

Though numerous concessions were made in favor of popular sovereignty, there were some who demanded more and greater. Again there were threatening assemblages; again the troops were summoned (Jan., 1842). The work at last came to a conclusion in the midst of an unfavorable party-hatred, and unexpectedly received the approval of the majority of the citizens. The March-union, which had given the first powerful impulse, had fallen in their estimation. This was very evident, when few of its members received votes at the new election of magistrates, and many friendly to the old state of things were chosen. The old spirit was again breathed into the new form; therefore the buds of future discord sprouted into life with the very introduction of the altered constitution.

CHAPTER LXXVI.

TERMINATION OF THE CONVENT-QUESTION. FORMATION OF THE SONDERBUND.

[A. D. 1842 to 1843.]

THIS was a period of constantly increasing party-bitterness. The scales rose and fell, according as one side or the other obtained a momentary preponderance. No longer did the leaders and orators of the people alone take part in the great war of opinion, but all classes showed more and more plainly their sense of its momentous importance. The whole fatherland was soon divided into two great camps. On one side floated the holy banner of religion, calling for a restoration of the institutions of the good old times; on the other, men stood in defence of acquired popular rights and desired a new and stronger bond of confederation. On this side were the inhabitants of those cantons which were rich in enlightenment and industry; on the other, the uneducated shepherds of the mountains, especially of the primitive cantons, with church-led people of other districts. The papal court directed the movement on the part of the latter, furnished them with leaders and war-cries. The struggle had the appearance of relating solely to the catholic faith, while it was really political. Many of the reformed held with the church-party, many of the catholics with the party of freedom, according to their political bias.

The question of the Aargau-convents was always the apple of discord, which excited the combatants. The less a settlement was attempted inside of the council-hall, the more earnestly was the matter discussed outside. So long, however, as Zurich remained under the dark laws of the September storm of 1839, the balance inclined in favor of the reëstablishment of the suppressed convents. But great changes took place in this canton in the course of a few years. Many, who had formerly been zealous for the overthrow of the old government and constitution, now blushed to see their native canton hand in hand with the hereditary foes of popular enlightenment. Thus it happened that, in 1841, their ears were again opened to listen to an address from the unions of Aargau respecting the matter of the convents. This solemnly declared that the people of Aargau did not desire the oppression of their catholic brothers, but only freedom and equal rights for all; that the suppression of the convents, as magazines of incessant disturbance, was not a deed of gratuitous violence but of imperious necessity, and that Aargau expected friendly and neighborly assistance from Zurich in the troubles of the times. This address produced a deep effect. When, shortly afterwards, some members of the deposed government called a meeting of the people at the village of Schwammedingen (29th Aug.), more than twenty thousand citizens were present, and unanimously declared their approval of the proceedings of Aargau. This great manifestation of repentance at once changed the course of things. Public spirit was rejuvenated and demanded a recurrence to the liberal measures of the government of 1830. But it disdained to repay like by like, violence by violence: the popular wish for improvement must be demonstrated by the legal votes of the communes. In vain did the collapsing band of the men of September oppose this wish. In vain did their most clever champion, state-councillor Blanschli, endeavor to raise the credit of his government by ferretting out the communistic tendencies of certain German journeymen, and cause conservative axioms to be embodied in a defensive plea by two Germans, the brothers Rohmer. The fresh stream of the movement swept uninterruptedly onwards. When, in May, 1842, the great-council was chosen anew by the people, the names of the once so-beloved, but afterwards severely calumniated, people's-friends were again deposited in the ballot-boxes, by large majorities. Zurich again retrieved her ancient dignity. But now, made wise by bitter experience, she pursued her course with more enlightened moderation, free from all excess.

While reaction lost one star here, another quite as promising beamed from over the lake of the four cantons. Lucerne, becoming Vorort with the new year 1843, turned her whole influence to secure the preponderance of the catholic cause in the Confederacy. It was an omen full of significance that, on 22d January, the papal nuncio, after seven years' absence, returned from Schwyz to his ancient residence. He was welcomed with solemn pomp. As soon as he was there, the execution of great designs commenced. From the state-council of the Vorort, at once issued an imperious mandate to Aargau to annul all sales of convent-property: in case of refusal, she was threatened with the interference of the Confederacy. As this canton did refuse, the Vorort forwarded an angry circular letter to the several Confederates, requiring the Diet to decide the question respecting the existence or non-existence of the convents. The councils and communes assembled to give instructions. There were still doubts of the result. Finally, every thing depended on the decision of St. Gallen. But here an agreement of opinion was more difficult than elsewhere, as the parties were exactly balanced in the great-council. At last an instruction emanated from that body, by which, in consequence of their inability to agree, the vote for or against was left entirely in the hand of the deputy. In anxious suspense, the nation saw the Diet assemble. At first a decision seemed hardly possible. Then the deputy of Aargau hastened home, to solicit fresh directions, with which to close the last gap in the ranks of the liberal cantons. In a memorable sitting (28th and 29th Aug.), the great council of Aargau now determined to make another peace-offering to the fatherland, and to add Hermetschwyl to the other three restored nunneries. This noble offer accomplished the purpose. Now the deputy of St. Gallen, Fels, heartily gave his deciding vote in favor of Aargau. The required number of twelve votes was complete. The convent-question was dismissed as decided, and a dangerous dispute seemed finally settled.

But this hope was disappointed. Lucerne and the Ur-cantons, with Zug and Freiburg, refused to recognize the validity of this decision, which they termed a breach of the compact on the part of the twelve cantons. They even showed themselves determined to give a formidable stress to their protest. They prepared an opposition which could only end in a final struggle for life or death. Great activity was noticeable everywhere among the church-party. Numerous journeyings, secret appointments and meetings took place. No uninitiated person could unravel their whole meaning. It remained a secret for an entire year, that, in a conference of the deputies held at the baths of Rothen, near Lucerne (13th to 15th Sept.), the basis of that Sonderbund (separate league) of Ur-schweiz was laid, which afterwards proved so eventful in the history of the Confederacy. Like the old Borromean league, it was a formal and solemn offensive and defensive alliance between those six catholic states against the liberal cantons. Lucerne was placed at the head as catholic Vorort. She was even empowered to institute a council of war, to call out troops, and to execute the plans of the league with an armed hand. All this was concluded by the leaders in council; the people were not asked for their approval. The undertaking was therefore a breach of their own cantonal constitution, and even more: a rebellion against the general compact of the Confederates, although under the pretext of wishing to preserve it from infringement. This was loudly proclaimed to the world by a second conference held at Lucerne towards the end of January, 1844, in a public manifest, wherein it was also declared that the six cantons would not rest nor desist until the convents of Aargau were reëstablished and the rights of the catholic church secured. The more intelligent were convinced that other plans lurked in the background: the annulling of the liberal reforms since 1830, and the elevation of the church-party to supreme power in Switzerland. This became more evident, day by day, from the zeal with which the Sonderbunders endeavored to strengthen their party in every direction. They failed, indeed, in their attempts to win over Thurgau and St. Gallen, but all the greater was their triumph when Valais joined them, after a long contest stained with the blood of her citizens.

CHAPTER LXXVII.

PARTY-HATRED IN VALAIS AND FRATRICIDE ON THE TRIENT.

[A. D. 1844.]

In this rugged, highland valley, accessible to its neighbors on the right and left only by mountain-paths covered with glaciers, dwelt a people generally uneducated and subservient to the priesthood. Some families of the old-time nobles ruled them, but without the power or the will to ameliorate their mental or physical condition. After its union with Helvetia, this country remained for fifteen years sunk in dead inaction. The reform-movement of the Vaudois, in 1831, had first excited to emulation the people of Lower-Valais, influenced by the conversation and customs of their lively neighbors. They had, from of old, been subject to the upper portion of the country. But when, in that year, they loudly expressed their wishes for an equality of rights, they were soon again reduced to silence by force of arms. In spite of this, the tithings of Entremont, Martigny, St. Maurice and Monthey, in 1833, after the fall of the Sarnenbund, renewed their just demands in a petition breathing noble sentiments. The state-council again contemptuously rejected it. The same thing took place on the following year. But when the tithings of Sierre and Sion joined the western districts, a majority of the council granted that which could no longer be refused. A constituent-council framed a new constitution, which was accepted by a majority of the people on 17th February, 1839. But Upper Valais, which had voted against it, obstinately persisted in her opposition. The old government, unwilling to surrender their power, retired to Sierre; that chosen under the new constitution fixed its seat at Sion. A civil war was on the point of breaking out between them. To prevent this, the vorort Zurich sent mediators; and, when these could accomplish nothing with the embittered parties, the Diet decided that the work on the constitution should again be taken in hand. Lower Valais, though in the right, submitted to this decision, and sent deputies to the newly assembled constituent-council. But Upper Valais inexorably refused to do this also. The discussions began, nevertheless, and on the 3d of August, another constitution was completed, from which, to satisfy the opponents, the article on the freedom of the press was stricken out. The people accepted this also by an overwhelming majority, and even many of the communes of Upper Valais voted for it. The Confederate deputies declared that the legal approval had been given, that the object of their mission was accomplished, and returned home. But the state-council of Sierre, in conjunction with the bishop of Sion, resisted strenuously, and, in a circular letter to the cantons, demanded a separation of the upper district from the western tithings.

Thus stood matters in Valais when, in 1839, the vorort Zurich herself became the theatre of a bloody revolution, and reaction raised its head everywhere more boldly. The first consequence of this was that the Diet refused to the new constitution that guaranty which had been promised by the deputies of the Confederacy. The liberal Valaisian representatives were sent back, and a fresh mediation ordered. Now, the Lower Valaisians, indignant at this breach of faith, refused assent. "We prefer separation," said they, "rather than subjection to our old bondage." The state-council of Sierre, however, deemed themselves strong enough to enforce submission to their wishes. When a dispute respecting the trade in salt occurred between citizens of the commune of Evolenaz, which had voted for the constitution of 3d August, they hastily ordered out troops and occupied that village (March, 1840). Then the alarm-drum beat through all Lower Valais; the young men seized their arms with determination and hurried towards Sion. Their opponents, after a short fight, gave way before their furious onset. Now, the leaders of Lower Valais, Maurice Barmann and Joris, pressed irresistibly forward with their adherents. Sierre was taken; the old state-council fled; shouting treachery, the dispersed troops, in blind rage at their defeat, murdered grey-haired Peter of Curten, brother of the president of the council. All Upper Valais submitted to the government of Sion, which accomplished the work of victory by a noble moderation.

But, although the peace-giving promise of forgiveness for all past offences was made, no real peace was restored to the banks of the Rhone. The members of the old state-council, on their return home, cherished inveterate enmity in their hearts and awaited the moment for revenge. To them secretly adhered the numerous priesthood, whose power, worthy of the middle ages, had hitherto flourished here more than almost anywhere else. In the new rights of the people they saw danger to their own old supremacy. When, soon after, encouragement came from reactionary Lucerne, their opposition to the liberal government was more and more openly declared. This was especially the case in 1843, when propositions were made for two laws, one of which tended to the improvement of public education, and the other provided that, in case of military taxation, the clergy should also contribute. The Jesuit missions opposed both projects violently. The provost of St. Bernard, in his Whitsuntide sermon, expatiated on the injury done to the people by the public schools. The taxing of ecclesiastical property was openly declared to be contrary to catholic doctrine, and the government denounced as haters of religion. The consequence was that the frightened people at once rejected both propositions. This victory encouraged the clerical leaders to further steps. The society of "Young Switzerland" was especially a thorn in their sides, because the changes of 1839 were due to its activity and it now gave important support to the government. Against it the principal attack was directed. Its members were debarred from all the privileges of the church, from the confessional, from partaking of the sacrament, from acting as godfathers in baptism. The bishop even ordered that the reading of the "Echo of the Alps," published by that society, should be forbidden from all pulpits. In consequence of all this, bitter hatred again burned between the parties. It reached an unequalled height, when, towards the end of 1843, a new choice of legislators was to take place. It was known that the rich convent of St. Bernard, by distributing money, the abbey of St. Maurice, by means of emissaries, influenced the electors. No effort was left untried to spur the people to a raging fanaticism. Some liberals were even assassinated. Neither did the "Young Swiss" remain within the bounds of moderation. A band of these tumultuously destroyed the printing-office of the "Simplon Zeitung," an engine of the clergy, at the very moment when the people were on their way to the polls. Nothing, however, could now prevent the long-prepared revolution. The votes were given in great majorities for the friends of priestly supremacy, and the magistrates were almost passive tools in the hands of the obscurantist party, whose most influential leader at that time was the prebendary of Rivaz. Now the country was again rent by a fearful, inextinguishable hatred. The "Young Swiss" established a directing committee at Martigny. On both sides, citizens armed for another conflict with citizens. The outbreak followed, when, in Berrossaz, a murderous attack upon an unarmed old man was avenged by gun-shots from the opponents (1st May, 1844). Now, the state-council called forth troops, and, at the same time, requested Confederate interference. The vorort Lucerne sent her reactionary state-secretary, Bernard Meyer, with a double mission: ostensibly a mediator, he was to advise the adoption of bloody measures to subdue the liberals. From this moment the state-council pursued their arbitrary course without regard to law or constitution. The opposition-members were excluded from the sittings of the council; but almost unlimited power was conferred on William of Kalbermatten, the partisan leader of Upper Valais. At his command, masses of the landsturm and militia from Upper Valais rushed into Sion (18th May). Liberals from the western tithings, hastily assembled by the committee at Martigny, had come from the other side to the gates of the city, but could not maintain their ground against the overpowering force of their adversaries. Discouraged, they turned on their homeward march. But, on the dividing line between St. Maurice and Martigny, where the torrent of the Trient, rushing from the rugged mountain-valley, cuts through the highway to precipitate itself into the Rhone, a last fearful blow already awaited them. For here, a strong force had been placed in ambush under command of Major Jost. With shouts, these so styled "Old Swiss" attacked the unprepared and straggling band of those who were returning to their homes. From the covered bridge, from behind rocks and bushes, flashed their death-bearing shots. Soon man grappled with man. They killed with the rage of tigers. Thirty bodies of the "Young Swiss" bled upon the ground; the rest saved themselves over the swampy plain, or by swimming across the Rhone. But the conquerors followed them for some distance, and shockingly mutilated the already dead bodies. This was the fratricide on the Trient (20th May). It confirmed the victory to the old-party. The leaders of Lower Valais were outlawed and compelled to flee. Their work, the constitution of 1839, was annulled, and another established in its stead. By this, the former power of the priesthood was secured in exemption from all taxes and freedom from accountability to the civil tribunals. The task of instruction was confided to the Jesuits exclusively. The practice of private worship was no longer allowed to such Swiss citizens of the reformed faith as remained in the canton. Thus the assertion of the prebendary of Rivaz was made good: That Valais must first of all be catholic, then Swiss.

The peace of death thenceforward prevailed in the Rhone canton, which was now the seventh confederate of the Sonderbund.

CHAPTER LXXVIII.

THE JESUITS INVITED TO LUCERNE. FIRST FREE-CORPS EXPEDITION.

[A. D. 1844.]

As soon as the tidings of the butchery on the Trient spread through the Confederacy, thousands of voices were raised in denunciation of the followers of Loyola, as instigators of so horrid a crime. In the great-council of Aargau, Augustine Keller, who, full of noble daring, had first moved the suppression of the convents, now also stepped forward to propose the exclusion of that order from the Confederacy. In words of flame, he depicted their power and proceedings in the fatherland, and proved that their presence was incompatible with the public welfare. The great-council adopted his motion almost unanimously (29th May, 1844), and, in a circular letter, advised the other cantons of their proceeding. It found little favor, however, with the governments, but much more with the people of Switzerland. At the great shooting-festival at Bâle, where the four-hundredth anniversary of the hero-fight of St. Jacques was simultaneously celebrated, that proposition was the exciting watchword of the day.

Ever nearer approached the danger which threatened the Confederacy. Not only were Valais and Freiburg and Schwyz, where the Jesuits had long since secured a foothold, almost slavishly subjected to their influence, but even the vorort Lucerne now showed herself inclined to take to her bosom those bold champions of the papal see.

A large portion of her citizens had, indeed, long been struggling against such a design. In January, 1842, when it was proposed in the great-council to entrust to the

Jesuits the direction of the higher academies, that assembly had decided in the negative. It was convincingly demonstrated by enlightened men that several provisions of the constitution would thereby be violated. But Leu and Siegwart, the principal favorers of the Ultramontanes, did not allow themselves to be deterred by this. In order to persuade the people to support their plans, missions were commanded, and clever preachers of the order traversed the canton from place to place. Their eloquence, full of seductive images and fanatical hatred against those of a different persuasion, soon won over the ignorant masses. The followers of Loyola were regarded as the saviors and angels of the persecuted catholic faith.

Many publications, however, zealously and loudly exposed their deceptive fallacies. Then the political leaders tried to muzzle the press by multiplied legal proceedings. When it would not be silenced, force was employed, and, by a law, the masterpiece of complete tyranny over opinion, every free expression by word or pen was prohibited (8th March, 1843). In vain did many noble men, for the last time, raise their warning voices against the destruction of this, to a republic, most precious jewel; the submissive people permitted every thing. And now, in the territory of Lucerne, every opinion, except that of the rulers, was silenced. Even the newspapers of other cantons were forbidden to enter: the borders were to be enclosed as by a brazen wall. Step by step the leaders advanced towards their object. Liberal young men were sought out and deprived of employment; even the intercourse of trade with other districts was trammelled. Notwithstanding all this, however, when a second attempt was made, in November, 1843, to introduce the order of Jesus, the government still again refused, though but by the casting vote of the president. The bishop of Bâle also declared himself satisfied with the previous management of the higher academies, and most of the clergy of the canton voted with him. Only by the triumph of the "old Swiss" in Valais and the strengthening of the Sonderbund in consequence of the irresolution of their opponents, was the fulfilment of the designs of the church-party secured.

At the Diet of 1844, the old differences among the libe rals again manifested themselves. The deputy of the Valaisian government which originated in blood-stained injustice, was not forbidden to take his seat in the assembly. Bernard Meyer, who, as deputy of the Vorort, had advised that deed of violence, vindicated his ignominious conduct from the president's chair, without meeting with much opposition. When the proposition of Aargau respecting the Jesuits came under discussion, Bâle-country, only, voted with that canton. This disposal of the pending question of the day emboldened the Lucerners to proceed in their long-prepared work. Regardless of the lamentations of the fatherland, and in spite of the warnings and prayers of the best among their own party, the great-council, by seventy votes against twenty-four, decreed the invitation of the Jesuits (24th Oct.). Seven teachers of this society were to direct the youth in the study of the sciences. They were to be allowed to live and labor according to the rules of their order. For this purpose, considerable property and privileges were granted to them. Thus Lucerne sank entirely into a willing tool of the Roman court. The constitution was violated, and the old rights of the citizens seemed forever annihilated. A portion of the people still struggled courageously for the exercise of the veto. But in vain. The majority of the citizens, influenced by church-fanaticism, rose tumultuously in favor of the council's decree, and others, urged by threats, assented to what was inevitable. The whole country was rent by a deep schism; brothers were inflamed against brothers, sons against fathers; distrust of each other and fear for the future took possession of all minds.

Under the influence of this division in their own canton and of the fearfully increasing excitement among the neighboring Confederates, some bold men determined to compel a reversal of the decree respecting the Jesuits by force of arms. A committee of liberals, formed two years before at the baths of Knutwyl, again bestirred themselves. Near and distant alliances were made; and soon some opposed the government openly. But the latter held heedful watch upon the movements among the people, and, towards the end of November, introduced troops into the city for their protection. To prevent a surprise, they thought it advisable to remove into safer keeping the heavy artillery which, for years, had been confided to certain places in the country. In the night of 5th December their emissaries entered the little city of Willisau, to take possession of the cannon in the castle. But the citizens, awakened by the noise and seizing their arms, courageously drove them away. This occurrence precipitated the execution of the plans of the Knutwyl-union: all further delay now seemed dangerous. In the extremity of the occasion, on the 7th of December, they decided that an attack should take place the next day. The rising was to commence in the city and be supported by simultaneous advances from the country. Messengers hastened in every direction. Even the allies, in Aargau, Bâle-country and Solothurn, were notified to assist.

Notwithstanding the insufficient notice, bands of warlike men assembled in most places at the first call, and directed their march towards the city during the night. Long before the morning of Sunday, 8th December, dawned, the men from Rothenburg had occupied the Emmen-bridge before the city. The united bands from Hitzkirch and Hochdorf joined them. They awaited a signal to enter the city. There, an inn in the neighborhood of the arsenal had been taken possession of by the insurgents during the night. Towards morning, a large number of them also assembled on the Muhlenplatz. Some patrols of the government troops were dispersed by musket-shots. But when a superior force of the military appeared under command of lieutenant Jenni of Musswangen, the insurgents could no longer maintain their ground. In vain did a reinforcement come from the suburbs. They were compelled to flee; many were taken prisoners.

At news of this, the little band on the Emme bridge also fell back to Rothenburg. But when the forces from Munster and Neudorf appeared, and, shortly afterwards, information was received of the advance of fresh bands from Wiggerthal and even of stout men from Aargau under lead of government-councillor Waller, new courage was infused into all. The conspirators, now seven hundred in number, advanced a second time as far as the Emme. It was about 10 o'clock in the forenoon. Before taking a decisive step, they here halted, awaiting the men from Suhrenthal. Then the drums beat: major Schmidt of Hitzkirch, with the hastily-raised government troops, came from the valley of Emme towards the bridge, intending to cross it by a hurried march. After a vain attempt at negotiation, a short fight took place. Schmidt and his troops were compelled to flee; the blood of many fallen reddened the ground. Directly afterwards, the expected reinforcement from Suhrenthal appeared. But now, irresolution took possession of the leaders. The boldest, indeed, urged advance: the passage of the Reuss, the entrance to the city, lay open before them, and therein, notwithstanding the victory gained with so little exertion in the morning, helpless confusion prevailed. "Fortune favors the brave," said they. But others, frightened by the numerous fugitives from the city, and in apprehension of the landwehr (organized militia) which had been called out and was approaching under Leu, advised a retreat to Sursee. These carried the day. A large portion of the people at once turned on their backward march. And when the liberals from Aargau saw themselves almost entirely deserted, they hastened home over Munster. Their example was followed by the Solothurners and Olteners, who had come as far as Buron with two field-pieces. A band from Bâle-country also, which, in consequence of the distance, only entered the Lucerne territory on the following night, immediately left it again when they found their expectations disappointed. Thus did this desperate undertaking fail, more from the want of resolution in its leaders, than from the power of its adversaries.

But the more frightened the government of Lucerne had been, the more intoxicated were they now by victory. They determined to take a fearful revenge on the insurgents. The communes from which the insurrection proceeded were overwhelmed by armed forces. State-secretary Meyer and government-councillor Wendelin Kost made a hunt after the liberals. Innocent and guilty were imprisoned in great numbers; among them Dr. Robert Steiger, who was considered the principal promoter of what had taken place. Much real and personal property was confiscated. Great distress spread over the land. Many hundreds fled from their homes into the neighboring cantons. All entreaties from the other governments, in favor of clemency, were in vain; they were coldly rejected.

CHAPTER LXXIX.

REVOLUTION IN VAUD. SECOND FREE-CORPS EXPEDITION.

[A. D. 1845.]

THE unsisterly feelings of Lucerne towards the Confederates, and her heartlessness to her own citizens, excited great indignation. An indescribable bitterness of heart, such as had never before been known, prevailed, from the Rhine to lake Leman. In Berne, Aargau, Bâle-country, even in Zurich, meetings, attended by many thousands, were held in the open fields during the winter. At these appeared fugitives from Lucerne, beseeching assistance; and the sight of these men, driven from their homes and families, inflamed still more the indignation against their persecutors. Unions against the Jesuits were formed everywhere. Petitions, covered with numberless names, demanded of the great-councils the instant expulsion of the followers of Loyola. In case this was not decreed, it was to be feared that the people would rise a second time and try to effect it by violence. In this emergency, a new Diet was immediately summoned. In the mean while, Zurich, now the Vorort, endeavored to avert the imminent storm by mediation. But the words of her messengers of peace were not listened to by the rulers of Lucerne.

As the great-councils were now discussing the instructions to be given to their several deputies, the state-council of Vaud wished once more to attempt the path of conciliation. Already thirty-two thousand electors of the canton had voted for the entire expulsion of the order of Jesus from Switzerland; but, regardless of this, a majority of the council agreed with Zurich in proposing to address a friendly confederate request to Lucerne: any more decided action appearing to them an encroachment on the sovereign rights of that canton as guaranteed by the Confederacy. The great-council accepted the proposition (13th Feb). But half-measures are always ruinous in times of great emergency. The people said: "He who is not with us is against us;" and on the same evening the clash of arms resounded in the streets of Lausanne; alarm-fires blazed from height to height along the lake; a serious outbreak was prepared. The state-council, divided in itself, called for troops. They appeared; but with them long trains of people, with whom they fully fraternized. The council, terrified, abdicated; and, in their stead, the people held a session in arms, under the lime-trees of Montbenon. A new government was installed, under the lead of Henry Druey, who had drawn up the report of the minority in the state-council; and the decree for the expulsion of the Jesuits was announced amid immense rejoicings (15th Feb). Then the crowd returned peaceably to their homes.

Notwithstanding this triumph of the popular will in Vaud, the tidings of which were welcomed by the greater part of the nation, no majority in favor of the removal of the Jesuits could yet be united in the Diet at Zurich. To Aargau and Bâle-country, which had stood alone in the previous year, nine other cantons and one-half were now added. Even a request to Lucerne for milder treatment of her prisoners could not be agreed upon. The deputies of the Confederacy appeared helpless and undecided in this moment of most pressing danger to the fatherland. Only the notes received at this time from foreign powers, especially from the French minister Guizot, which, in the tone of a master to subject-vassals, forbade further free-corps expeditions, could rouse the national feelings of most of the deputies. Their reply, full of noble sentiments worthy of their ancestors, shone as a clear light through those days of darkest gloom. However, as public right required, the raising of free-corps was prohibited by thirteen votes. The deputies of the Sonderbund-cantons, who had earnestly urged this, rejoiced; the others returned home with anxious hearts.

A bloody encounter of the embittered parties had become unavoidable. Lucerne armed openly. General Sonnenberg was recalled from the service of the king of Naples; the defensive troops in service were daily exercised; the landwehr were freshly organized and trained; armed assistance from the Urcantons and Zug was secured for the hour of need. And all this was done in the name of endangered religion. The church-zeal of the people was inflamed to indescribable rage by the priests and their assistants. Whoever would not act with them was imprisoned or compelled to flee. The again menaced citizens, in bands, sought refuge in the neighboring cantons.

But here, the excitement of men's minds had reached its highest pitch. Since the deputies of the Confederacy had separated, unable to loose the tangled knot, a determination had been formed to cut it with the edge of the sword. In spite of the prohibition, new free-corps were zealously raised. By day and night, during the month of March, messengers hurried in every direction, strengthening the bonds between the unions. Leagues were made, weapons prepared, accomplices armed. Thousands were seized with an inexpressible enthusiasm to free the fatherland from her enemies and to restore the fugitives to their homes. This dazzling object, which they expected to accomplish almost without a contest, blinded their understandings to the injustice of their violent proceedings, so fraught with destruction to the Confederacy. Even the governments of Berne, Aargau and Bâle-country, where the expedition was prepared, carried away by the popular feeling, no longer attempted to oppose the current. Thus it happened that, when the cannon were taken away from the arsenal at Liestal, from the fortress at Aarburg and from the tower at Nidau, every remonstrance on the part of the government-commissioners proved of no avail. The leagues hurried in great numbers towards Zofingen, where the principal rendezvous was appointed. The Bernese partisans assembled at Huttwyl, on the western border of

Lucerne. The chief-command of these was given to Ulrich Ochsenbein of Nidau, who had, on a former occasion, led the way into the territory of Lucerne.

Before daybreak of 30th March, the imposing train, in military array, with banners flying, left the gates of Zofingen. On the evening before, the vanguard had advanced as far as the villages of Dagmersellen and Altishofen, and distributed printed addresses to the people of Lucerne. The plan was: to turn the government-forces posted on the lake of Sempach and the Reuss, to divide them, and to reach the city, the principal object, as quickly as possible. This was done. The free-corps advanced by a day-march, through ways which the enemy had not guarded. At Ettiswyl, the Bernese troop joined them from Huttwyl. Some bands of the landwehr were seen in the distance; but the invaders first came to a fight near Hellbuhl, with a body of troops which retreated at the first volley. It was a bad omen, however, that the citizens of the canton nowhere joined the expedition, as had been expected. When they reached the Emme, the force divided. The smaller portion hurried to the bank of the stream, swollen by the spring-rains, to make a sham attack upon the baths at Rothen on the other side. Here they were unexpectedly assailed from a masked battery. Thrown into confusion and without a position which they could maintain against the superior force, they retreated in the afternoon to Hellbuhl, vainly expecting further orders. The larger body, in the mean while, in spite of heavy discharges from field-pieces on the other side, had stormed the half-covered bridge near Thorenberg, and now advanced across the steep ridge against the churchyard of Littau. General Sonnenberg had, in great haste, called in a portion of his scattered forces to defend the capital-city, and had also received auxiliaries from the forest-cantons. He had stationed some companies of Lucerners and Unterwaldeners on the mountain-plain of Littau to resist the invaders. But the latter, outflanking them, at once forced them to a hurried flight. Now the free-corps advanced without further opposition. By nightfall, they occupied the Gutsch, a spur of the mountain over the city, and the clump of houses at Ladeli in the valley of the Reuss, close to the city-gate. At this moment, the fate of Lucerne and of the Confederacy wavered in the balance of Providence. Confusion and terror prevailed within the city; the government prepared for flight. A few cannon-shots from the Gutsch would probably have occasioned a surrender. But in the councils of God it was otherwise determined. A dangerous indecision took possession of the hitherto victorious invaders. Tired by their long day's-march, hungry, without military union as a whole, they lost order and presence of mind. Those on the Gutsch remained faithful at their posts, while most of the others, fearful of being surrounded by the enemy, retreated in the night to Littau. Their pusillanimity increased; orders were no longer obeyed; all discipline was at an end. The storm-bells sounded from all the church-towers; the alarm-signals of the landsturm blazed on all the mountain-tops. Those who had been waiting since evening at Hellbuhl, as they received no tidings whatever from the force that had advanced, had already commenced their backward march, and, though attacked on the way by the enemy's troops whom they bravely repulsed, regained Zofingen in good order on the following day. Even the leaders of the body on the heights of Littau gradually dispersed during the darkness. Their cause was hopelessly lost by reason of the increasing disorder. Finally, the whole force, conquered by destiny, not by the enemy, sought safety in flight. At midnight, the mob of fugitives, with field-pieces, came to Malters. Here they received a murderous fire from the windows and the rear of the houses. In spite of their despairing resistance, death so thinned their ranks that, panic-struck, they were obliged to disperse. Bloody bodies of men and horses covered the highways. Those who escaped death, fell into the hands of the armed peasants. The same result attended separate conflicts. When the morning of the 1st of April dawned, Sonnenburg also recovered courage, and, from the city, attacked the advanced posts which had remained on the Gutsch and at Ladeli. Their spirited defence was useless. A small body of them did indeed cut their way through and after many perils, wearied almost to death, succeeded in reaching the Bernese frontier, at Melchnau; but the rest were overpowered. Thousands of fugitives now wandered about in the woods and mountains, unacquainted with the country, without food, having thrown away their arms, and sought for safety. After them rushed the hordes of the fanatical landsturm, baiting and hunting them like wild beasts. Shocking cruelties were practised on some of the prisoners. Others, bound in gangs with ropes, were driven in savage triumphal procession to Lucerne. Here, no prison was large enough to contain them all. They were shut up in the Franciscan and Jesuit churches; the leaders imprisoned in the city-tower. Nearly four thousand had marched on the preceding day, confident of victory; hardly more than the half returned. Over two hundred had met their death from the balls of the enemy's cannon, or the fatal clubs of the landsturm, or in the waters of the Emme; eighteen hundred and thirty-six prisoners, badly fed, lay on straw in the jails of Lucerne. A higher power had condemned their rash undertaking.

As soon as the news of the defeat of the free-corps was received, the Vorort ordered out a large armed force to secure peace in the fearfully excited fatherland. The canton of Lucerne was surrounded by them in deep lines. The Diet, summoned by expresses, met immediately (5 April). The sorrowing nation turned their eyes towards them, as saviors in this unexampled misfortune. But in vain: more contemptuously than ever did the deputies of the victorious canton reject all entreaties for reconciliation and mercy. The victory, now in their hands, was to be used as a sword of destruction to annihilate their opponents. A few weeks afterwards, however, when the government of Lucerne required money and the maintenance of so many prisoners became too expensive, they began to treat about the ransom. This amounted to 350,000 Swiss francs,* of which Solothurn contributed 20,000, Bâle-country 35,000, Berne 70,000, Aargau 200,000, and other cantons 25,000. In addition to this the Confederacy had to pay 150,000 francs, war-expenses. In the last days of April, the released free-companions finally returned to their weeping families.

* The Swiss franc was equal to about 28 of our cents.

CHAPTER LXXX.

PAINFUL CONSEQUENCES.

[A. D. 1845 and 1846.]

THE tidings of the destruction of the free-corps had shaken all liberal Switzerland like a thunderbolt. The fruit of all the labors of long years seemed lost in a moment. And woe to the conquered! Everywhere their opponents rose exultingly and overwhelmed them with scoffs and curses. Here and there preparations were even made for a counter-revolution. The ferment of a second insurrection was already at work in the free-bailiwicks of Aargau, but when the troops of Zurich, suddenly ordered out by the Diet, unexpectedly crossed the Reuss from Ottenbach, and the roll of their drums was heard near Muri, the reäwakened desires were at once extinguished. Still more was this the case, when the government of Aargau was protected by the bayonets of her neighbors, and when, with noble candor respecting past errors, it paid the ransom for the prisoners out of the state-treasury, and at the same time forgave all offences committed in consequence of the former convent-troubles.

Not so quickly was the storm of popular commotion dispelled in Berne. Here, those who returned from Lucerne met with a chilling reception from the leaders of the people. Avoyer Neuhaus especially, who, by his previous inactivity, had rather favored than impeded the free-corps expedition, now gave utterance to extreme disapproval of it. He went still further. Officials who had taken part in the expedition were removed, foreign leaders of the popular unions expelled from the canton, and some journals, which were active in their opposition to the government, persecuted with endlessly accumulating law-suits. Such proceedings occasioned great bitterness of feeling. This statesman, shortly before loved and admired by all, sank rapidly in popular estimation. His friends angrily turned their backs upon him; his former enemies flocked closely around him. And as, at the same time, many instances of mal-administration came to light, the cry for a new and popular constitution increased. Those who had been defeated on the Jesuit-question, hoped to recover their influence by means of this. Long and bitter was the struggle of the parties, in the public prints as well as in the council-chamber and in the meetings of the unions. When Neuhaus saw that the revision of the constitution would inevitably take place, he insisted that it must be accomplished by the great-council, as the only competent authority. His opponents, on the other hand, demanded a constituent-council. The people voted decidedly in favor of the latter (1 Feb., 1846). This occasioned great irritation among those who had before possessed the power. They declared that this decision of the people was an outrageous violation of the existing constitution, and many of them abdicated their offices. Threats, even, were employed. But the choice of the constituent-council proceeded without disturbance, and their deliberations began. The once honored name of Neuhaus faded away, and to his former elevation was raised Ochsenbein, whose statesmanly work soon obscured the remembrance of the military misfortunes suffered in the free-corps expedition. The new constitution was elaborated by him and his friends. When it was accepted by the majority of the people (13 July), bonfires, from the Stockhorn to the slopes of the Jura, proclaimed this first victory in the cause which had been considered lost the year before.

In Vaud, also, a grudge remained on account of the mine which had been sprung in the contest about the Jesuits. After the decision of February, 1845, the work on the constitution did indeed proceed peacefully, till the news of the defeat on the Emme awakened fresh hopes in the discontented. The disaffection of many of the clergy towards the government, which showed itself no less unfavorably disposed towards them, occasioned a dangerous schism in the canton. When the state-council issued an official proclamation respecting the business of the constitution, and sent it to the clergy with directions to read it from the pulpits, many of them refused beforehand to do so. They said: "Not only is it at variance with existing laws, but the dignity of God's worship would be diminished thereby." In vain did the government attempt to enlighten and to pacify them; on the appointed Sunday (3d August), forty clergymen omitted the reading. Such contumacy could not be passed over unnoticed. The matter was referred to the clerical Classes for investigation, and at the same with this, numerous complaints respecting the private religious exercises termed oratorios, which were held by several clergymen and had quite often given rise to scandalous scenes. But when the Classes almost unanimously justified their brethren in office and the excitement in the country increased, the government decreed the temporary suspension of the recusants from their functions. Now the gauntlet was openly thrown down between the ministers of the state and those of the church. The clergy of the canton met in the city-hall of Lausanne for a solemn conference (11th and 12th November). It was opened with singing and prayer. Numerous speakers, among them Monnard, before honorably known as a deputy to the Swiss Diets, depicted in burning words the injustice which church-freedom had long suffered, and complained of the arbitrary encroachments of the civil power. At this moment of great excitement, 153 clergymen signed a pledge to surrender their benefices at once. Many may have been urged by their consciences to this step; others, probably, by the secret hope that the people would turn in their favor. In this difficult emergency, Druey, the president of the state-council, asked the representatives for extraordinary powers. They were granted. Once more an attempt was made at reconciliation, and when this failed, an immediate rigorous removal from office of all the signers of the pledge took place. The oratorios were closed at the same time. There was great excitement among the people at this. Many blamed, more applauded the decree of the state-council. Rough outbreaks of the people's anger against the deposed clergymen and their adherents often occurred. The irritation of men's minds lasted a long while. This matter made a great noise throughout Switzerland and through all Europe. The clergymen received approving and encouraging addresses from clergy and laity of many foreign lands, and even from king Frederic William of Prussia. The interest taken in the church-dispute of Vaud was only lost, by degrees, in the overpowering impression caused by after events.

But the painful consequences of the free-corps expedition were felt most keenly by Lucerne herself. Here, since that event, terror, under the name of holy religion, ruled more severely than before. After the prisoners from the other cantons had been released, still harsher measures were employed towards those of her own territory. Examining-judge Ammann from Thurgau was charged with the prosecution of the endless suits against them. The curse of many unhappy families still hangs about his name: for bare suspicion was enough to bring confiscation and fines, imprisonment and severe suffering upon the heads of disliked opponents. No page in the history of Switzerland is stained with blacker sins in the administration of public justice. And amid the lamentations of the whole nation, the fathers of the society of Jesus made their entrance into this canton whelmed in blood and tears (29th June, 1845). But shortly after this took place came the news: "Robert Steiger is free!" He had been again taken prisoner in the second free-corps expedition. Against him, as the principal leader, the anger of his adversaries was most fierce. The court condemned him to be shot. But when the most touching entreaties in his behalf were received from individuals and from governments, from the Vorort, from the bishops of Solothurn and Freiburg, even from foreign embassadors, the government of Lucerne decided not to execute the sentence of death but to render this dangerous man forever innocuous. He was to expiate his offence by confinement for life in a Sardinian fortress. But three land-yagers, devoted to him, rescued him by night through the walls of the Kesseltower (19th June), and brought him in safety to Zurich. A loud cry of joy greeted the success of this enterprise from all countries, even from the United States of America. But the tidings of another occurrence excited abhorrence in even a greater degree. The man of the people, Joseph Leu of Ebersoll, the most influential favorer of the Jesuits, was found dead in his bed, shot through the heart (night of 19th July). The consequence of this crime was almost as horrible as the crime itself. For the rulers of Lucerne laid to the charge of the whole party of their opponents the unrighteous deed which a single individual had perpetrated. A fresh course of prosecutions and imprisonments ensued, which was continued for years. Examining-judge Ammann had plenty of work. But Leu's name, thenceforth, shone among the popular saints; incessant pilgrimages to his grave were made by the pious. Thus his death did more to strengthen his work than he could have done if living.

CHAPTER LXXXI.

THE CRISIS APPROACHES.

[A. D. 1846 to 1847.]

In the mean while the Sonderbund of the seven cantons was knit more and more closely. But the world had as yet only conjectures, rather than certainty, about their designs. The leaders were seen to meet frequently, but no information respecting their deliberations transpired. Men knew of the missions of the Jesuit-preachers, of the numerous assemblages for devotion, the pilgrimages and other priestly machinery to excite popular fanaticism; they saw the continuous military preparations; but the object of all this remained in doubt. Then the veil of the secrecy suddenly fell, and the transactions of the conference at the baths of Rothen were unexpectedly revealed. The great-council of Freiburg at last discussed in open session the matter of their connection with the Sonderbund. The existence of a vast conspiracy against the unity and safety of the Confederacy was now apparent. The vorort Zurich immediately questioned Lucerne respecting the nature of this dangerous compact; and, when the answer removed all doubt, required the cantons to give instructions on this point to the next Diet. But, at the regular yearly session of the latter, no twelve votes could be united for any decision. They could not agree: either upon an edict to expel the Jesuits, or to remodel the confederate compact according to the spirit of the times, or to dissolve the Sonderbund. Zurich, Berne, Glarus, Schaffhausen, Grisons, Aargau, Thurgau, Ticino, Vaud, with Bâle-country and Outer-Appenzell, did indeed come forward with determination to assert the rights and honor of the fatherland. Against them stood the catholic seven in immovable obstinacy. The rest were rendered powerless by division. The deputy of Geneva, a docile scholar of the French minister Guizot, openly testified his inclination towards the party of the Sonderbund. He even urged the plan to appoint a committee of representatives from the cantons as supervisors to the future vorort Berne, from whose boldness some decisive action was feared.

Thereat a wild storm burst forth at Geneva. The union of the Third of March was still strong. The members now roused themselves to fresh activity. When the council of representatives issued new instructions in accordance with the sentiments of their deputy, the minority protested, left the council-hall and called upon the people to decide (3d October). The citizens hastily assembled on the square of the Temple, in spite of a stormy rain. Here, the champion of liberty, James Fazy, stood forth, and, with triumphant eloquence, exposed the treachery intended against the Confederacy. Amid loud shouts of the crowd, the decision of the council was declared null, and a committee of the people charged to draw up a new constitution (5th October). Then the government hurriedly prepared to quell the outbreak. But the liberals betook themselves to St. Gervais, the little city on the other side of the Rhone, and there threw up barricades during the night. A requirement from the state-council to demolish these and to surrender their leaders, was decisively rejected. When the time allowed (till three o'clock in the afternoon of 7th October) had elapsed, the government-troops brought their field-pieces to the bank of the river

2H

and directed a heavy connonade against St. Gervais. It was answered by rifle-shots from the windows and roofs of the opposite houses. An attempt of the troops to storm the bridge was repelled by the bravery of their opponents Finally, after a bloody fight of three hours the troops re turned sullenly to their barracks. The excitement still increased. On the next day, the burghers of the larger city also deserted the government; then the latter abdicated. The victors of St. Gervais joyfully crossed the half-burned bridge to unite with their fellow-citizens. A great assembly on the place-Molard installed a provisional government under the lead of Fazy. The accession of Geneva to the liberal cantons in the Jesuit and Sonderbund question was at the same time unanimously decided upon by the people.

On the other hand, however, a movement in the canton of Freiburg, occurring almost immediately after, did not produce a similar result. Here, the citizens of the reformed district of Morat had already, in June, addressed to the Diet fruitless complaints respecting the decision of the great-council in favor of Lucerne. Now, encouraged by the tidings of success at Geneva, they presented fresh petitions urging withdrawal from the Sonderbund. The patriots of the French districts of Estavayer, Surpierre and Dompierre also joined those of Morat. In the popular assemblies, the inimical feeling of a large portion of their inhabitants against the Jesuits was manifested more openly than before. When some of the principal speakers in those assemblies were arrested on that account by the police, they were rescued by a tumultuous mob, singing liberty-songs. But the government, assured of the fidelity of the catholic, German, portion of the country, assembled troops. The insurrection now burst forth, but it wanted order and union in itself. A body of insurgents marched from Morat against the capital-city; another from Estavayer (7th Jan., 1847); but they soon dispersed, all chance of success being destroyed by their own imbecility and want of prudence. The troops of the government immediately occupied the seditious districts. Here, also, prosecutions and imprisonments took place. The Sonderbund enjoyed a new triumph.

Even in recently-quieted Berne, the discontented sought, about this time, to open the way for a counter-revolution. The opportunity seemed favorable, when the government appointed the free-thinking minister, Dr. Zeller of Tubingen, as professor in the university. Immediately, in opposition to him, as in the time of Strauss at Zurich, a loud cry of danger to religion rose from ecclesiastical and laical opponents over city and country. But it was soon seen that the attempt was powerless against the steady persistency of the Bernese people. The great-council passed over the motion presented to them to the order of the day (24th March), and the opposed professor entered upon his office without further disturbance.

St. Gallen, also, had her day of trial. Her great-council had for many years been without influence, almost null, in Confederate matters: for parties were always so equally divided, almost to a man, that a valid decision could seldom be obtained. Now, a new choice of members, according to the constitution, drew near. There was a hot election-contest in all the communes, as to whether the cause of the common fatherland or of the Sonderbund should prevail. The priest-party made great efforts to secure a preponderance of votes. The eyes of all in the Confederacy were turned towards this canton, upon whose cast the result again depended, as in the time of the convent-question. It was in favor of the honor and rights of the fatherland. The catholic district of Gaster turned the scale by the votes of her liberal citizens (2d May). Thereat loud rejoicing was heard throughout Switzerland, for now brightened the hope of a union of the majority of the cantons in coming eventful days.

CHAPTER LXXXII.

THE SONDERBUND-WAR.

[A. D. 1847.]

CALAMITY after calamity afflicted the fatherland. Two winters of severe scarcity had turned the cares of government and people almost exclusively to the relief of the necessitous. But a more imperious anxiety soon overpowered all others. In the summer of 1847, Lucerne, with her co-leaguers, prepared for war more openly than ever. A committee of war from the seven cantons was now actually established; stores of arms and munitions were collected in great quantities; the work on the fortifications at the frontiers of the Sonderbund-cantons and at some points within their territories was pressed by day and night; their active defensive force incessantly exercised in arms; the landsturm disciplined; and Ulrich of Salis-Soglio invited from Grisons to take the chief command of their formidable army. If any one asked the object of such unusual preparations, the answer was: "To repel a new free-corps attack." And yet everybody knew that such a thing could not again occur, for the bloody lesson on the Emme had been more effectual than all the prohibitions of the governments. The real intentions of the Sonderbunders were no longer a secret, however. Their scornful defiance betrayed them: they prepared for open rebellion against the Confederacy. The rule of the liberal governments was to be put an end to by force of arms, and the recent constitutions abolished. Into their schemes, as afterwards discovered, also entered a plan for the partition of the territories of Aargau, Berne, Zurich and other cantons. Jesuitism, everywhere predominant, was to give laws to all Switzerland for the future. The conspirators hardly entertained a doubt of the success of their designs. They reckoned upon division and consequent impotency among the other cantons, while they confidently relied on the invincibility of their own people, united by identical fanaticism. They even counted, treasonably, on foreign assistance. The courts of Vienna and Paris, favoring their plans, had already forwarded the accomplishment by supplies of arms. The embassador of France, Bois le Comte, to sound men's minds and to advance the undertaking, busily travelled through the cantons. But the soul of the whole was avoyer Constantine Siegwart of Lucerne. He, by birth a foreigner, for his own ambitious purposes staked the happiness of his new country, to which he felt no attachment, upon the perilous hazards of a game of chance.

The Diet assembled at Berne early in July. Never had their proceedings been expected with so much anxiety and never did they fulfil their duties with more manly decision. A series of important decrees proclaimed to the nation the intention of the liberal cantons, twelve and two halves, to meet the danger with bold determination. And the tutelar genius of the fatherland stretched over them his strength-giving arms. At the very first sitting, the matter of the catholic Sonderbund was discussed. Noble Confederates, especially Furrer of Zurich, Kern of Thurgau and Naff of St. Gallen, demonstrated unanswerably the illegality of its existence, as well as the danger to the fatherland with which it was fraught. In vain did the seven strive against them; in vain did Bâle-city, Neuchâtel and Inner-Appenzell attempt to mediate; it was solemnly decreed: "The Sonderbund is dissolved." (20th July.) When, shortly after, the news came that a quantity of arms sent by Austria for the Urcantons had been seized in Ticino, not only was this approved of, but the seizure of all future consignments of a similar character ordered throughout the whole circumference of the Confederacy. At the same time, orders were sent to the Sonderbund-cantons to desist from their warlike preparations, lest the peace of the country should be thereby endangered (11th Aug.). Then Geneva proposed: that the names of all Confederate staff-officers who remained in the service of the Sonderbund, should be erased from the army-list. This also was decreed. Finally, the Jesuit-cantons were requested to dismiss the order, and its further admittance (into other cantons) was prohibited (3d Sept.). After accomplishing this work, the deputies adjourned for six weeks, to await the fulfilment of their decrees and to take the sense of the nation.

The gloomy stillness which precedes the bursting of a storm lowered over Helvetia. The people and councils of the cantons met, to lay their last word, for or against, in the balance. In Uri, Schwyz and Unterwalden, the leaders announced to the general assemblies that freedom and religion would be alike destroyed, if the Confederates were not withstood, as Austria had formerly been at Morgarten. A furious shout on all sides approved their course. It was almost unanimously decided to hold fast by the Sonderbund; those who opposed were threatened with punishment in life or property. The same was the case in Valais and Freiburg. Zug alone, divided in herself, began to waver. In the great-council of Lucerne, only seven worthy men dared to advise loyalty to the Confederacy. With open contempt of the Diet, the government here continued its military preparations; the frontiers were, by degrees, entirely closed against those without. Many, favorable to the Confederacy, again fled from their homes before the renewed prosecutions. The friends of the Sonderbund began to stir in the other cantons also. But all their endeavors to provoke confusion and disunion were vain. After the great-council of Zurich first declared their decision to insist on the fulfilment of the Diet's decrees by force of arms if need should be, one canton after another of the majority of the Confederacy courageously followed the example. St. Gallen was the last. Here the priest-party hoped, even at the last moment, to give a turn to affairs by a rising of the catholic population. But disjointed attempts at so unrighteous an enterprise were speedily put down. Then, after four days of a protracted, excited and memorable session, in which the parties measured their greatest strength against each other, it was decided here also: that the way of conciliation should first be tried; but, if this proved impracticable, that the recusants should be brought back to their duty by force of arms. Thus the required number of twelve cantonal votes was again complete; respecting which many had hitherto doubted. But the nation which surrenders in the hour of danger no longer deserves to exist.

Now, the Diet met again (18 Oct.). They were still disposed to conciliation. They sent some of their own members as messengers of peace to all the seven refractory cantons to move the hearts of the rulers. They solemnly assured the people in a proclamation: "The rights and freedoms inherited from your fathers shall remain unaltered, your faith untouched. The Diet desire no oppression of their Confederate brothers, no nullifying of cantonal sovereignty, no forced change in the present Confederate compact. But the existence of a separate league, endangering the welfare of the whole, can never be allowed. Dissolve it, while there is yet time!" (20 Oct.) Vain efforts! As the deputies of the seven cantons had foretold: the messengers were rejected with scorn; even the circulation of the proclamation was strictly forbidden. Zug alone listened to milder counsels. Her deputy to the Diet at Berne endeavored to restore union. So, finally, did Bâle-city. But every endeavor failed before the obstinacy of the Sonderbunders. Now that all attempts at reconciliation had proved fruitless, the assembly of the Confederacy proceeded to serious measures. They issued an order for troops, to the number of 50,000 only at first, to secure the peace of the country against the continued military preparations of the Sonderbunders. William Henry Dufour of Geneva was chosen by them as commander-in-chief, Frederic Frey-Herose of Aargau as chief of the staff. All this was violently opposed by the deputies of the seven, who insisted that it was a commencement of hostilities. But the Diet remained firm in their decision. Then rose Bernard Meyer of Lucerne in behalf of the Sonderbund-deputies, and said: "The moment has come for us to depart from the Diet." Invoking God's name, he cast upon their opponents all present and future responsibility for coming events. Then the seven deputies left the hall of session and the city of the Confederacy (29 Oct.). The bond of century-old fidelity seemed forever broken. But, strong in their good right, the other deputies continued their deliberations.

On the fourth of November it was solemnly decreed: to dissolve the Sonderbund by force of arms. A proclamation announced this to the people and to the army. Now, the statesmen had done their part; the drawn sword must give the fatal blow.

In the mean while, grey-haired Dufour had already begun to assemble his force. The people, with ready and earnest minds, left their firesides to range themselves under his banner. Bitter though the task might be to march against their brothers of the same country, each, nevertheless, answered the call of duty with determination. Only in the bailiwicks of Aargau, and more violently in some catholic districts of St. Gallen, were attempts again made to resist. But the insurrection was quickly repressed. Even Bâle-city, though delaying, now sent a battery to the Confederate army. Inner-Appenzell, on the other hand, and Neuchâtel, refused all participation, and declared themselves neutral. Yet the government of Neuchâtel secretly granted passage through her territory to a quantity of arms sent by France and intended for Freiburg. They were, however, discovered by the patriotic mountaineers, carried over into the territory of Vaud and there retained. Some bold Vaudois then seized the steamboat, in order to cruise upon the waters of the lake of Neuchâtel and prevent any more such smuggling. In spite of the refusal of these cantons, the force of the Confederates quickly swelled to more than ninety thousand men, who were formed into six divisions, under the lead of officers of proved experience. Two hundred and sixty pieces of heavy artillery were at their command. The speedy preparations, the host of able officers, the spirit of discipline which prevailed in so great an army, astonished foreigners doubtful of the result.

The Sonderbunders had called out their forces even earlier. Volunteers and deserters from the other cantons, foreign officers also, among them even the Austrian prince Schwarzenberg, had joined them. The greater part of their troops were filled with raging enthusiasm. The bloodthirstiness evinced so long beforehand by the self-styled avenging corps of examining-judge Ammann, was horrible. All means were employed to excite fanaticism. The papal nuncio himself blessed the banners of those going to the frontiers, as formerly, before the fratricidal war of Villmergen. Jesuits were appointed field-chaplains. Blessed amulets were distributed to the hordes of the landsturm, to protect them from shot and sword, and preachers from the pulpits assured all the people of the assistance of the Virgin Mary to preserve them from death and make their victory sure.

Even before the Confederate army was fully arrayed, blood already flowed. On the same day that the proclamation for the armed execution of the Diet's decree was published at Berne, the outposts of the Sonderbunders penetrated over the heights of the St. Gotthard into the territory of Ticino. Two of their leaders paid for their temerity with their lives.

Dufour delayed the onset for a long while. Disposed to carry on the war with extreme forbearance, he said to his soldiers in an order of the day: "I place under your protection, children, women, old men, and the ministers of the church. You must come from this conflict victoriously, but without stain." Then he surrounded the territories of the Sonderbund with an immense chain of troops, closing every exit. The recusants were to be brought back to their duty more by the determination displayed in the overpowering force than by bloody violence. The soldiers shared the humane disposition of their general. The advanced posts handed their drinking-flasks to each other over the boundary-lines.

While the principal force of the Confederates marched first to subdue Freiburg, the Sonderbunders began the assault from Lucerne upon comparatively unprotected Aargau. The village of Kleindietwyl, the outer post in the free-bailiwicks, was unexpectedly surprised by them, and the advanced guard there, forty in number, taken prisoners and carried in triumphal procession to Lucerne (10th Nov.). This success encouraged them to bolder attempts. A portion of the people of the free-bailiwicks seemed only to await a favorable moment in order to declare openly for the cause of the Sonderbund. Salis-Soglio therefore made incursions into this territory at two separate points simultaneously, on the morning of 12th Nov. One body of troops, commanded by himself, advanced by a forced march, over Sins and Merenschwanden, towards Lunnern, where the Confederates had thrown a bridge of boats across the Reuss. But the small troop of Zurichers stationed there maintained their post with old Swiss valor. They destroyed the bridge under a storm of balls and compelled the enemy, three times their number, to retreat. No better success attended the other expedition under colonel Elgger. He ascended the Lindenberg, and surprised two Aargau companies at dinner in Geltwyl. But these also, quickly falling into ranks repelled the attack after a hard fight; so that the Lucerners fled back to Hitzkircherthal, in great disorder. On the same day, a third attack was made from Beromunster upon Menzikon and Reinach. But the Aargau-landwehr opposed the invaders with such courage and vigor that the latter retreated at once. Thus the bloody ventures of that day failed everywhere.

In the mean while, Dufour had directed his principal force upon Freiburg. This canton, the district of the capital-city especially, is strongly fortified by nature and art, and the latter was secured against any desperate assault on the part of the people. The Confederates, therefore, were the more astonished at being allowed to enter unopposed by Staffis and Chatel St. Dennis (10 Nov.). Three days afterwards, the city was closely beleaguered. Then the Confederates demanded its surrender (13 Nov.). The Freiburg state-council, disappointed in their expectations of aid from Valais or Lucerne, requested a suspension of arms. It was granted till the morning of the next day. But colonel Rilliet, who knew nothing of this agreement, began to storm two redoubts with a body of fiery Vaudois. His loss in killed and wounded was great; but the result was not decisive. The rest of the army passed the night quietly at their watch-fires; then, when morning broke, prepared to storm the city. They were only waiting for the command to advance, when negotiators appeared on the part of the government, humbly announcing their wish to capitulate. The convention was executed in the head-quarters at Belfaur (14 Nov.): Freiburg withdrew from the Sonderbund, and the city-gates were opened to the Confederates. When this was made known, the Freiburg troops shouted treason, and dispersed in disorder. The landsturm rushed raging through the streets. The Jesuit-fathers, however, protected by the forethought of the French envoy, were happily enabled to escape, though much wanton injury was done to their deserted palace. But tears of joy flowed, when the prison-doors were opened for those confined on account of the January-insurrection. Soon, while the city was occupied by the Confederates, a provisional government was formed, all the old magistrates having fled together. Composed of liberal men, it proclaimed the rule of moderation and justice, and banished the Jesuits, as causers of all this trouble, forever from the canton.

As soon as Freiburg had fallen, the main army of the Confederates directed its march upon Lucerne and the Forest-cantons. Here the governing party were intoxicated by a triumph which the men of Uri and Valais had just then (18 Nov.) obtained at the St. Gotthard pass. Favored by the mist, they penetrated as far as Airolo, and, surprising the Ticinese under Luvini, put them to flight. The latter first made a stand on the Moesa, entrenched themselves and called on the Grisons for assistance. But the conquerors, abstaining from further pursuit, were satisfied to occupy the mountain-passes of St. Gotthard and Furka. Notwithstanding this favorable news, great dissension prevailed among the people of Lucerne. Many citizens who were mistrusted, were disarmed, and all assemblages in the streets dispersed. Many of the necessaries of life were already wanting. All desired a speedy deliverance from their intolerable condition.

The columns of the Confederate army began to enter the territories of the Sonderbund on several sides: through the March into Schwyz, through the bailiwick of Knonau into Zug, and by three roads into the canton of Lucerne. When Zug saw herself seriously threatened, she hastily sent messengers to Dufour at his head-quarters in Aarau, in order to capitulate and declare her withdrawal from the Sonderbund (21st Nov.). The Confederates, who now advanced peacefully into her territory, were received with joy. But Abyberg, with the Schwyzers, as soon as he saw the pass by Arth and Goldau thus left open, hastily returned to the defence of his own country and remained an inactive spectator of the combats which followed.

The 23d of November, the great decisive day, dawned. Dufour directed his chief attack against the Rothenberg and the fortifications near Gislikon, the key of Lucerne. Here the principal force of the Sonderbunders was arrayed. The Confederate brigadiers, Isler and Ritter, were ordered to turn the Rothenberg from the side of the lake of Zug. In the vicinity of Meyerskappel, they encountered the troops of the Urcantons, advantageously posted on the sheltered rising ground. At sight of the advancing Confederates, the mountaineers knelt and told their beads, then rushed with war-cries to the fight. The Confederates answered with hearty shouts. Both sides fought valiantly, and the combat was a hot one. But the Confederates succeeded in breaking the ranks of the men of the Urcantons. The latter retreated, fighting, behind Udligenschwyl to the Kiemenberg, where they formed again in order of battle. Their resistance was overcome here also, and, before nightfall, the victors took possession of the heights.

Ziegler's division had advanced at the same time from the free-bailiwicks, passing the Reuss over a hastily-constructed bridge of boats, on the road by Honau, up the north side of the Rothenberg. Here and on the hill-sides, a warm fight immediately took place. The Sonderbunders retreated, step by step, to Gislikon, where strong fortifications with heavy artillery commanded the banks of the Reuss. In the trenches which traversed the rising ground, the riflemen of Unterwalden were posted, and the ridges of the hill were covered with masses of the landsturm. The advancing battalions of the Confederates, under Egloff, Hausler, Einsberg, Benziger and Morf, were now received with a terrible fire from large and small arms. Some portions soon wavered, and the Solothurn-artillery, which had pushed too far ahead, was compelled to give ground. At this decisive moment, the Bernese howitzer-battery sprang forward and cast death and destruction into the enemy's ranks. Colonel Ziegler ordered a bayonet charge; with him, his adjutant, landammann Siegfried of Aargau, dismounted and encouraged the troops by word and example. Like lions they advanced. Then Salis-Soglio, vanquished—it was nearly half-past four in the afternoon—abandoned the fortifications of Gislikon. The Confederates rushed, storming, into them. There was fighting on the hill, however, until nightfall. Near a chapel dedicated to St. Michael, the Unterwaldeners fought with praiseworthy courage, until they also yielded to the fate of the day.

Now confusion prevailed, and a general fight towards Lucerne took place. When the defeated troops, covered with dust and blood, reached the city, and wagons full of wounded and dead increased the terror, Siegwart hastily entered an already prepared steamboat, and fled during the night over the lake of the four cantons to Uri. With him were the other members of the Sonderbund council of war, the government, the Jesuits, and even the nuns of Eschenbach and Mariahilf. They carried with them the treasure and seals of the state, and stores of grain. Twenty land-yagers served as a guard to the fugitives. Salis-Soglio, wounded, also escaped, and the auxiliaries from the Urcantons, with depressed spirits, returned home that same night. But the city-council of Lucerne, to avert serious injury from the city, sent negotiators to Dufour. The grey-haired general demanded an unconditional surrender, and that which was unavoidable was assented to.

On the next morning, the almost endless train of victors entered the city amid thousand-voiced acclamations of the people. All the buildings were decorated with Confederate flags. With those Confederates who had fought on the Rothenberg were already united that portion of the army which had passed unopposed through the valley of Hitzkirch, and the reserve division of Bernese under Ochsenbein. The latter had entered the canton through Upper Entlibuch, fighting their way step by step. They had encountered a slight resistance at the very frontiers, near Escholzmatt (22d Nov.); one still more serious on the day after, at Schupfheim. But they overcame their opponents everywhere with great valor, and were thus enabled to reach the common object, the city, at the same time with the other troops.

Now, only the Urcantons and Valais remained to be subdued. Unterwalden, however, capitulated in the night of 25th Nov. Schwyz, where Keller's brigade had victoriously entered the March, on the 26th; and Uri, also, on the same day. From here, the leaders of the Sonderbund had issued fresh calls for steadfast perseverance; but when they saw that all fell away from them, they fled over the Furka into Valais, and thence into Piedmont. Then Valais, also, had neither strength nor courage to hold out. Rilliet-Constant was already on the point of opening hostilities from Vaud, when petitions for an agreement were presented (29th Nov.). As at Freiburg and Lucerne, the government fled hence also. But the Confederate troops were received with joy.

Thus in the course of surprisingly few days, the Sonderbund suddenly came to an end. That which had been proclaimed before Europe as the rock of religion and of true freedom, collapsed at the first dash of the waves, like a house built upon the sand. Too late did the French envoy, from Neuchâtel, whither he had retired with the other diplomatists at the beginning of the war, proffer foreign assistance. Too late, also, did the same envoy finally propose to mediate between the Diet and the council of war of the seven cantons. Siegwart had already fled over the frontier with his colleagues, when the French messenger went to seek him. But the Swiss people, full of joyful courage as never before, recognized in all these events the intervention of a higher hand for the salvation of their fatherland.

CHAPTER LXXXIII.

THE NEW SWISS CONFEDERATE-BOND.

[A. D. 1848.]

GREAT reforms now took place in all the cantons of the former Sonderbund. The feelings of the people were suddenly changed. As had been the case at Freiburg, so also in Lucerne, a provisional government was formed of a committee of worthy citizens. Here, as there, the constitution of 1830 was restored to its former validity. A similar revolution was effected in Valais. Zug, also, and the Ur cantons immediately went to work to improve the order of their states. Even in Uri, where, since Tell's time, no written constitution had ever existed, one was now drawn up and accepted by the communes. Men favorable to the Confederacy took the helm. The Jesuits had everywhere fled on the entrance of the Confederates; now they were forever banished from Swiss soil. Men tried to efface, as far as possible, by means of improved arrangements, the marks of the recent doings of the order and its adherents. But this was a tedious task and did not proceed without encountering much opposition. The prosperity of many of those cantons was long impeded. Now the bad management of the former governments first came to light. The public treasuries stood empty; charges, before unknown, oppressed the land. These were, moreover, greatly increased, when the Confederacy demanded from the Sonderbund-districts repayment of the war-expenses, amounting to five millions (of Swiss francs). Until the receipt of the first instalment and of security for the others,* the armed occupation was to continue. All this caused great embarrassment to the new governments. Lucerne instituted judicial suits against the members of her former council, for embezzlement of the public money, and confiscated the estates of those who provoked the war. Shortly

* The last instalments were remitted by the Federal government in 1852.

afterwards she sought a doubtful remedy by suppressing the convents, that she might be indemnified by their property (13th April, 1848); and the people, before whose veto the decree was laid, did not refuse their consent. Still greater were the necessities of Freiburg, and with them increased the indignation against those members of the council who had voted for the Sonderbund. They were brought to a most severe account in discharging the war-expenses. Many of the discontented among their adherents opposed this violently, and disturbances even took place, which had to be settled by Confederate interference. Valais, also, laid almost all her share of the expenses upon those who had voted for, advised and preached the war. The convents of St. Bernard and St. Maurice were especially hard pressed, and the monks of the former removed their property to Sardinian soil. The demands of the Diet were with difficulty fulfilled. Before the coming of spring, however, the last of the army of occupation were enabled to return to their homes. Neuchâtel and Inner-Appenzell, which had refused to perform their duty as Confederates during the war, were only freed from similar occupation by the payment of a heavy fine into the treasury of the Confederacy.

While past offences against the fatherland bore such bitter fruits, loyalty to the fatherland, on the contrary, reaped great glory. The returning warriors were welcomed by their compatriots as men who had saved the country from a great danger, and the names of the fallen were perpetuated on marble monuments. A feeling of pride in her strength inspirited the nation. The report of the fall of the Sonderbund stirred all Europe also. The people rejoiced. From Germany, France and Italy, even from more distant lands, congratulations poured in, and large sums for the support of the wounded. The victory of general Dufour and his army was the signal for a reäwakening of the spirit of liberty throughout the whole continent. But the opponents, also, were not silent. Full of vexation that the interference of foreign powers had been prevented, they did not, on this account, give up their already lost cause. Austria readily opened an asylum for the fugitive

Jesuits and Sonderbunders. Pope Pius IX., in whose hands the power for a peaceful settlement had shortly before lain, overwhelmed the victors with complaints and reproaches. But the doings of Switzerland were most severely handled in the French chambers, whence the count of Montalembert, with the rage of a defeated partisan, fulminated the thunders of his eloquence against the conquerors. They found many echoes in the gazettes of the courts and clergy. It soon became evident that a violent storm against the rejuvenating Confederacy was brewing on all sides. This was especially seen to be the case when the long-entertained desire of all Swiss patriots drew nearer to fulfilment: the desire to establish, after such long conflicts, a new and internally stronger bond in the place of that recently sundered. The cabinets of the princes combined to prevent this, and in notes of very threatening tone presented their protest against it. "As," they insisted, "we have guaranteed the covenant of 1815, therefore, without our consent and the united votes of all the twenty-two cantons, no alteration shall be made therein."

When the Diet received these messages, conscious of strength and moved by a noble sense of dignity, they answered: "We are the vassals of no foreign power; a free people must frame their own laws." Then, undisturbed by the threatenings from without, they formed a commission from the deputies of all the cantons to draw up the new bond of confederation, and these immediately began their work (16th February).

The monarchs would, most probably, have given effect to their threats, had not world-stirring events of greater importance intervened. Paris and France cast off their fetters in wild insurrection. King Louis Philippe was driven into exile, and the republic again took the place of the shattered throne (24th February). The news of this sped like lightning through the other monarchies, crashing and kindling as it went. The day of universal destruction seemed to have dawned, to light the way for incoming popular freedom. Every mail brought astonishing accounts of bloody street-fights in the capital cities, of the trembling of kings and their concessions to their subjects, of war and cries of war in all places in Germany and Italy. The year 1848 is marked with brazen pen upon history's tablet of memorabilia. But while the world-storm thus raged, Switzerland stood like an island of peace amid the roaring waves. She did not, however, remain entirely unmoved by their mighty influences. Neuchâtel, especially, felt them.

Here, the valiant mountaineers had long unwillingly endured their condition: having the distant king of Prussia for their prince, and not being independent, like the rest of the Swiss. Especially were they indignant that, in the time of the Sonderbund-war, the high-council of the state, yielding to the wishes of the king, had renounced their duty to the Confederacy. Therefore, when the call to freedom sounded from France, they felt that the right moment had come for them also to shake off the hated yoke. The insurrection began at La Chaux-de-fonds, by the rescue of some men of Swiss sentiments, who had been imprisoned by the police (27th February). Encouraged by this success, crowds of people, on the next day, summoned the unpopular communal council to abdicate. When the latter refused, the people called to arms; the council-hall was stormed: now the Swiss-cross banner floated high, where before the Prussian eagle had his stand. Simultaneously, the citizens of Locle rose, and the valley-districts of Travers and Les Brenets joined them. A committee of enterprising men was at the head of all. The valley of La Sagne, favorable to the kingly rule, was entered, and the inhabitants disarmed. All this terrified the state-council of Neuchâtel, and they sent the lord-chamberlain with proposals for accommodation. But in vain. The government, in haste, called upon the citizen-troops of the capital to defend the castle and council-hall. But the men of the Jura were already advancing in three bodies from different sides. Then, reduced to extremity, and without hope of protection, as the troops manifested little zeal in their cause, the government abdicated their offices, but with reservation of the royal rights. On the evening of the same day (1st March), the republicans, eighteen hundred strong, without stroke of sword, entered the city. Here, a provisional government was instituted, and, by this, the discontinuance of the princely rule solemnly proclaimed. Soon, deputies came from almost all the communes with assurances of joyful acquiescence. The vorort Berne, also, which had sent commissioners on the outbreak of the insurrection, recognized the new order of things, and replied to the Prussian envoy, von Sydow, when he presented a protest in the name of his master: "Switzerland acknowledges no covenant with any prince of Neuchâtel. That canton entered the Confederacy equal in rights with all the others, and we cannot oppose her when she changes her government to suit herself." Thus matters remained. A republican constitution was now drawn up and accepted by the people (30th April). But many of those who had hitherto basked in the sunshine of royal favor, still bore ill-will to the new Swiss rule, and did not lose their hopes of returning once more under the sceptre of the prince, in more favorable times.

With firmness equal to that displayed in their answer to Prussia, did the Diet reject a request shortly afterwards made to them by Sardinia. The king of this country, Charles Albert, had declared for the Lombard party which stood in open insurrection against the supremacy of Austria, and wished to strengthen his power by an offensive and defensive alliance with the Confederates. There were many among the latter, especially in those districts where French and Italian are spoken, who, enthusiastic for popular liberty, shouted approval of such a proposition. But far more said: "Why should we mix in foreign disputes and bind the fortunes of our fatherland to those of other states? Switzerland has always fared badly when she served others. The highest duty of every people is invariably towards their own welfare and independence." And the Diet, without delay, declared: "That Switzerland would favor no one and injure no one, but remain strictly impartial in the disturbances of Europe." (18th April.) There were some, nevertheless, who, desirous of combat, hastened across the Alps, on their own responsibility, to the Lombard battle-fields; the greater portion, however, disappointed in their expectations, returned home at once.

The name of the Confederates was far otherwise notorious in the Italian combats of those days. This was especially the case when the Swiss hirelings, in the service of Ferdinand, king of Naples, contended in terrible street-fights with the insurgent populace of his capital-city (15th April). Their death-despising valor did indeed win the victory; but it was a victory for royal power against the rights of the people. Therefore a cry of imprecation against these degenerate sons of Helvetia rose throughout the whole peninsula, and, in their own fatherland, the popular voice loudly demanded the abrogation of the ancient unworthy capitulation. More honor, on the other hand, fell to the lot of those Swiss troops who, in the pay of the papal government, fought against Austria at Vicenza (10th June). The valor of these heroes, who bore unwavering the storm of balls from a force four times their superior, recalled the deathless deeds of their ancestors. When, in spite of their efforts, the papal general Durando surrendered the city, the enemies themselves praised the courage of the Swiss lions and carefully nursed their wounds.

Soon afterwards, the fortune of war changed entirely in upper Italy, and Austria's field-marshal, grey-haired Radetzky, returned to Milan as conqueror. The resistance of individual adventurers was prolonged as far as the borders of Grisons and Ticino. At the same time, a great host of Lombard fugitives swarmed into those cantons. The Diet immediately ordered out troops to protect the soil of the fatherland. The same thing had already taken place on the Rhine, when an insurrection of republicans occurred in the highlands of Baden, under Hecker (last of April). There also the unsupported rising failed, and many of the fugitives sought refuge in the northern cantons. Their incessant endeavors to rekindle the war from their post of safety at last involved the Swiss magistrates in a long interchange of notes with the German governments. In this case, also, the dignity of the Confederacy was firmly and boldly maintained.

Thus, in spite of all attacks, internal peace remained undisturbed during all the bloody commotions of the nations, and the commission of the Diet quietly elaborated the new bond of confederation. When they had completed their work, the great councils of the cantons met to deliberate upon it. Much was said for and against it everywhere, but over this difference of opinion prevailed the unanimous desire to establish a foundation on which internal welfare and external independence might rest forever secure. After the cantons had uttered their opinions, the Diet again met to give the finishing hand to the great work (15th May to 17th June). Thus was produced the new national constitution, the first which had been formed by the Swiss alone and without foreign intervention since the destruction of the old Confederacy in 1798, and which united the twenty-two free commonwealths into a nation of brothers. Concluded in the name of Almighty God, it was then laid before the people for their acceptance or rejection. In the days of August, the citizens, assembled in their primary communal meetings in the cantons of Geneva, Berne, Zurich, Solothurn, Bâle, Glarus, Lucerne, Aargau, St. Gallen, Schaffhausen, Thurgau, Grisons, Outer-Appenzell, Vaud and Neuchâtel, at once, with overwhelming majorities and joyous approval, declared their acceptance. The great council of Freiburg did the same in the name of her people. Only in a part of the former Sonderbund-cantons: in Zug, Uri, Schywz, Unterwalden and Valais, as well as in Inner-Appenzell, did the councils and communes vote for rejection. Here the shortly-before dispirited party had again, since Austria's victory over Sardinia, raised their heads boldly, and hoped for a change in their own fatherland. Zealous priests had again attempted to foment disturbance by awakening anxiety for religion. Ticino wished to make some stipulations respecting the pecuniary loss she feared from the surrender of her tolls, and therefore voted to reject; but at the same time declared her willingness to accept the decision of the majority, for the welfare of the common fatherland. As a majority of fifteen cantons and one half, with a population of 1,897,887 souls, had voted to accept, and a minority of only six cantons and one half, with a population of 292,371 souls, had voted to reject, the Diet, in solemn session (12th September), declared the new Swiss constitution to be in force. The tidings were immediately promulgated by messengers and telegraphs, and, on that very evening, innumerable bonfires blazed on the mountain-tops from the Doie to the Santis, while the rejoicings of all the people resounded from the valleys. Never had Switzerland seen a day of more beautiful fraternization since the commencement of her history.

Thus have the feeling of common citizenship and love for the fatherland refortified the liberty which our fathers won with their hearts' blood at Sempach and Grandson. Helvetia stands again, more nobly than ever, the rock of freedom among the nations. But the happiness of no people can continue steadfast on the earth, if trust in God and brotherly love be not its guardian angels. The enemy of Swiss independence still prowls about like a roaring lion, and awaits the moment when he can destroy it. Be watchful therefore, O Confederates; hold unchangeably true to each other, and forget not God; so will He not forget you in the hour of conflict.

THE END

INDEX.

Aargau, subject to Habsburg—Austria, 26. 45. 76; conquered by the Confederates, 77; a canton, 272; a Confederate. 280; arms for independence, 286; liberal constitution, 296; religious difficulties, convents suppressed, 338-341; votes the expulsion of the Jesuits, 357; national constitution, 393.
Abacker, Anthony, 138.
Abandonment of principle, 78.
Abyberg, Theodore, of Schwyz, 328–384.
Ackermann of Unterwalden, 202.
Act of Mediation, Napoleon's, 279; annulled, 285.
Adam the Camogaster, 84.
Adolf of Nassau, 36.
Agnes of Hungary, 43.
Albert of Austria, emperor, 36; assassination, 43.
Allemanni The, subdue Helvetia, 14; vanquished by the Franks, 16.
Allemannia, Dukes of, 17.
Allied cantons and cities, 126.
Allobroges, The, 7.
Alps, The, 1.
Am Buel, Matthias, 64.
Ammann, Examining judge, 371, 372–380.
Am Stalden, Peter, 116.
Amstein, John, 57.
Anabaptists, The, 135.
Ancient noble families, 27.
Ancient traditions, 5.
Appenzell, foundation of, 32; heroic deeds, independence and league with Confederates, 67–73; a Confederate, 125; religious division, 135; separation into Inner and Outer-rhodes, 155, 156, 244; canton of Santis, 272; national constitution, 393.
Armagnacs, The, 96.
Arnold of Cervola, 56.
Augusta Rauracorum, 11.
Augustus the emperor, 9, 10.
Aulus Cecina, 11.
Austria, Dukes of; counts of Habsburg, great possessions, 26; designs upon the Confederates, 37; defeated at Morgarten, 44–54; Sempach, 61; by Appenzell, 71, 72; peace, 73; lose Aargau, 76–78, 91–98; Thurgau also, 104; Treaty, 113; war with Grisons and Confederates, 122–125, 167–175; threaten, 295; protest, 341.
Aventicum, 11; destroyed, 14.
Aymar, French general, 330.

Baden, 11, 77, 201.
——— Canton of, 272, 280.
——— Capuchins at, 339.
——— conference, 320–325.
Bailiwicks, see Common and Italian.
Baldiron, Austrian general, 165–168.
Bâle, 23–28; independence, 29, 97; a Confederate, 125; protestant, 134; reforms, 193; civil war, division into Bâle-city and Bâle-country, 297–300.
Bâle, Bishopric of, 252; annexed to Berne, 288.
——— Bishops of, 158, 176, 210, 252, 252, 253.
Bâle-city, 300; Sarnen-league, 302, 305, 306; national constitution, 393.
Bâle-country, 300, 305, 316, 317, 336; national constitution, 393.
Balthazar, Felix, of Lucerne, 243.
——— Urs, ——— 237.
Bannerets of Berne, 225.
Barmann, Maurice, of Valais, 354.
Baselga, Caspar, 161.
Battle of Airolo, 383; Arbedo, 82; Arth, 273; Bibracte, 8; Bicocca, 130; Boetzberg, 12; Brolla-bridge, 346; Bruderholz, 125; Buttisholz, 56; Donnerbuhl, 37; Dornach, 125; Emme, 361, 365; Ezel, 91; Frastenz, 124; Fraubrunnen, 57; Gelterkinden, 299; Geltwyl, 382; Giornico, 115; Gislikon, 385; Grandson, 109; Grauholz, 271; Gubel, mount, 142;

Hauptlisberge, 71; Herzogenbuchsee, 187; Hessingen, 100; Hutten, 202; Ins, 37; Kappel, 141; Kussnacht, 52; Lake Leman, 4; Laupen, 48; Liestal, 298, 299; Lunnern, 382; Luziensteig, 123; Malserhaide, 124; Malters, 366; Marignano, 130; Morat, 111; Morgarten, 44; Nafels, 64; Nancy, 112; Neuenegg, 271; Novara, 130; Oehrli, 305; Pavia, 130; Prattelen, 96; Ragatz, 98; Raschnals, 168; Rothenberg, 384; St. Gervais, 374; St. Jacques, 97; St. James, 93; St. John's, 123; Schindellegi, 273; Schwaderlochs, 123; Sempach, 61; Sins, 202; the Stoss, 71; Tatwyl, 52; Tenero, 346; Tirano, 165; Treisen, 123; Ulrichen, 81; Vicenza, 392; Villmergen, 191, 208; Voglinseck, 69; Weidikon, 94; Wolfshalde, 72; Wollrau, 273.
Battles in the Grison bailiwicks, 172.
——— Lombardy, 129, 130, 391.
——— Nidwalden, 276.
——— of the French and Austrians, 277.
Battle-fields, Foreign, 151, 154.
Baumgartner of St. Gallen, 342.
Beccaria, 149.
Beda, the wise abbot of St. Gallen, 263.
Beeli, George, 160, 161.
Belet, Vicar, 325.
Bellinzona, 81; canton of, 272; canton of Ticino, 280.
Berne, 23; defeats the nobles, 37, 48; a Confederate, 54; increase of territory, 55; reforms, 58, 59; ambition, 75; conquests in Aargau, 76; quarrel between nobles and commons, 106; protestant, 134; conquests in Vaud, 147; revolt of subjects, 179, 181–189; defeated by the catholic cantons, 191; superiority in arms, 197–204; Henzi's conspiracy, 225–229; dispute with Vaud, 254; taken by the French, 271; loses Aargau and Vaud, 272; bishopric of Bâle annexed, 288; liberal constitution, 294–296; quarrel with Germany, 314, 315; religious disturbances, 324; false step, 325; commotion and new constitution, 368, 369; national constitution, 393.
Bero, Count, 20.
Beroldingen, Hector of, 159.
——— John Conrad, 166.
Berthelier, of Geneva, 145–147.
Bienne, 158, 159, 288.
Bishoprics, Ancient, 18.
Black Death, The, 159.
Blanschli, councillor of Zurich, 350.
Blasius, John, 134.
Bleuler-Zeller, of Zurich, 332.
Blood-thirsty justice, 118.
Bodmer of Zurich, 198.
——— treasurer of Stafa, 267, 271
Bois le Comte, 377.
Bombelles, Count, Austrian envoy, 315.
Bonnivard, prior of St. Victor, the prisoner of Chillon, 146.
Booty, Immense, at Grandson, 110.
Borelli, Count, 114.
Bormio, Grison bailiwick, 129, 162; Cisalpine republic, 269; annexed to Austria, 288.
Borromean League, 153.
Borromeo, Cardinal Charles, his virtues and influence, 151–153.
Bossi, bishop of Coire, 326.
Brandenburg, The elector of, 54.
Brandis, Louis of, 123.
Brantschen, Thomas, the lion of Vaud, 81.
Breitenlandenberg, Hans of, the Savage, 94.
Brettigauers, The, 163, 168, 169.
Brommer, Secretary, 188.
Bruchenburen, The, 5, 30.
Brugg, destroyed by the nobles, 95.
Brun, Rudolf, of Zurich, 49, 50.
Brune, French general, 270.
Bubenberg, John of, 47, 48.
——— Henry, 98.
——— Adrian, 110.
Bugle-call, 307.
Bullinger, Pastor Henry, 138.
Burgisser, Leodegar, abbot of St. Gallen, 196–203.
Burgler, Henry, of Obwalden, 116.
Burgundians, The, subject Vaud and Valais, 14; lose their power, 16.
Burgundy, Dukes of, 22.
——— Little, 17.
——— Upper, 112.

Caddean league of Rhetia, 86.
Calendar, Dispute about the, 153.
Calvin, John, 147, 149.
Camogast, Adam of, 84.
Campobasso, Count Cola, 112.
Cantonalism, 90.
Capitulations with foreign princes, 102, 129, 150; abrogation demanded, 392.
Caraccioli, papal nuncio, 204.
Castelberg, Sebastian of, abbot of Discutis, 166.
Castellaz of Greyerz, 248, 249.
Catholic cantons, 135, 138, 191; 197–204.
——— unions, 321.

Celestin, abbot of Einsiedeln, 321.
Celier, burgomaster of Neustadt, 212.
Censorship of the press, 235.
Chaldar John, 85.
Charlemagne and his successors, 21, 22.
Charles the Bold, duke of Burgundy, 107–112.
Charles X. of France, 293.
Charles Albert of Sardinia, 391.
Chateauneuf, French envoy, 260.
Chenaur, Peter Nicholas, of Freiburg, 248; his death, 249.
Chiavenna, Grison bailiwick, 129, 162, 165; Cisalpine republic, 269; annexed to Austria, 288.
Christianity, its introduction and beneficial effects, 18–21.
Church-dispute in Vaud, 369–371.
Church-question, 133, *passim.*
Cilano, Destruction of, 163.
Cisalpine republic, 269.
Cities are walled and organized, 24; increase in franchises and power, 29; league with each other, 30.
Clergy, Fanaticism of the, 161.
Coeuvres, Count of, 170.
Coire, Bishops of, 33, 83, 85, 168.
——— City of, 33, 83.
Columban, 19.
Comander, John, 134.
Committee of faith in Zurich, 332 to 335.
————— in Lucerne, 344.
——— The Bunzner, of Aargau, 338, 339.
Common bailiwicks, Aargau, 76; Thurgau, 103; Rheinthal, 121; partly protestant, 135; form cantons, 272.
Commotion of the nations, 390.
Communes on the lake of Zurich, revolt and are subdued, 265–267.
Compact, nature of the, 126; of 1815, 288, 289, 292; new, rejected, 304; of the liberal cantons, 301.
Confederates, The original, expel the Austrian bailiff, 42; defeat Austria at Morgarten, 44; assist Berne, 47; occupy Glarus, 52, and Zug, 53; Confederacy of eight cantons, 54; strength, increase of territory, justice, 55–56; victorious at Sempach, 61; in numerous battles, 65; peace and its fruits, 66; conquer Aargau and establish common bailiwicks, abandon principle, 73 to 78; invade Valais, 80; become proud, 89; war against Zurich, barbarity, 92 to 95; heroes' death at St. Jacques, 97; first treaties with France and Milan, 102; conquer Thurgau, 103; war with Burgundy, 108 to 112; treaty with Austria, 113; military pride, arrogance, 114; petty wars, 118; bad blood, 121; refuse to become a circle of the German empire, 122; defeat the Austrians and Suabians, 123-124; Confederacy of thirteen cantons, 125; serfdom of the people, 126; demoralized, debased by love of money, 128; mercenary wars, 129; Italian bailiwicks, 130; disputes, wars, and consequent alienation between protestants and catholics, 134, *passim;* subserviency to foreign envoys, 178; independence recognized, 180; arbitrary rule, 181; insurrection of the subjects, 186–188; religious civil wars, 190-192, 197–204; reciprocal distrust, 205; general corruption, 233–236; weakened by division, 254; universal confusion, 270; conquered by the French, and all Swiss made equal in the Helvetian republic, 271–274; Confederacy of nineteen cantons, 280; intrigues of the nobles, restoration of servitude, quarrels and conflicts, Confederacy of twenty-two cantons, 285–288; cantonalism, familism and favoritism, 292; peaceful revolutions, commotions, 293–300; energetic measures, firmness and moderation, 305, 306; threats from abroad, 313; education and skill in arms encouraged, 316; blockade, 319; martial enthusiasm, 330; quarrels and disputes, question apparently religious, but really political, 336-350; the Sonderbund, 351; civil war, 376–386; dignity preserved, 392; national constitution, 393; universal rejoicing, 394.
Congress of Vienna, 287.
Conseil, Case of, 318, 319.
Conspiracy of the nobles of Lucerne, 45.
Constance purchases peace, 102.
Conto, Slide of mount, 163.
Convention of Sempach, 65.
————— Waldmann, 120.
Convents suppressed in Aargau, 340, 341.
—————— in Lucerne, 388.
Council of Constance, 74.
Covenant of Stanz, 117.
Crivelli of Uri, 201.
Crusades, The, 28.
Curten, Peter of, 354.

Cuttat, priest of Pruntrut, 325.
Cymbri, The, overrun Gaul, are joined by Helvetians, defeated by the Romans, find refuge in Helvetia, 4, 5.

Dagobert, 16.
Demoralization of the Swiss, 127.
Diesbach, Nicholas of, 170.
Diplomatic notes, 313.
Disregard of the Bond, 236.
Divikon, leader of the Tigurins, 4–7.
Dolder, landammann of Switzerland, 273.
Dominicans, The, 132.
Dorrenberg, Peter of, 57.
Druey, Henry, of Vaud, 363, 370.
Ducrest, Michael, 227, 257.
Dufour, William Henry, of Geneva, Confederate-general, 379–386.
Durando, papal-general, 392.
Du Terreil, 159.

Early Christian teachers, 19.
Einsiedeln, Convent of, 20, 31, 176, 290, 327.
Emanuel Philibert, duke of Savoy, 151.
Enderli, Thuring, 168.
Enemy of Switzerland, The real, 308.
Engadine, 122, 161, 163, 169, 174.
Engelberg, Convent of, 3.
———— Abbot, 137.
English envoy assassinated, 207.
Enlistment for foreign service, 101, 113, 118, 127–130, 154, 290.
Entlibuchers, The, 56.
Erlach, Ulrich of, 37.
———, Rudolf of, 47, 48.
———, Sigismund of, 186–188.
Escher, stadtholder of Zurich, 223.
Escalade of Geneva, 157.
Evangelical preachers, 134.
Evangelicals expelled from Arth, 190.
Execution on the wheel, 43.
Extinction of patriotism, 235.

Falkenstein, Thomas of, 95.
————, John of, 98.
Familism and favoritism, 292.
Farel, Nicholas, 134.
——, William, 147.
Fatherland, The, 309.
Fatio, John, of Bâle, 193, 194.
Fazy, James, of Geneva, 373, 374.
Federal constitution, 393.
Felber, Major, 199; death, 200.
Ferdinand of Austria, emperor, 315.
——— ——— Naples, 392.
Feria, Duke of, 167.
Feudal organization, 17.

Finningers, The, of Muhlhausen, 154.
First settlers, 2.
Fischingen, The abbot of, 176.
Florin, Colonel, 172.
Flugi, John, bishop of Coire, 162.
Fontana, Benedict, 124.
Francis I. of France, 130.
Franks, The, vanquish the Allemanni, Burgundians, and Goths, and organize the country feudally, 16, 17.
Fratricide on the Trient, 356.
Frederick of Austria, 74.
Frederick the Great, 238–240.
Frederick William of Prussia, 297, 371.
Free-corps expeditions against Lucerne, first fails from irresolution, 360, 361; second organized in other cantons, totally defeated, prisoners ransomed by their governments, 364–367.
Freedom's New Year, 42.
Freiburg, 23; falls into the power of Savoy, 101; independnet, 114; a Confederate, 117; divided in religion, 135; increase of territory, 147, 148; disturbances and insurrections, 247–251; taken by the French, 271; admits the Jesuits, 291; new constitution, 296; the Sonderbund, 351; revolt subdued, 374; war, 380; surrenders to the Confederates, 383; results of the war, 387, 388; national constitution, 393.
French, The, help the Grisons, 170–172; occupy the bishopric of Bâle, 253; intervene at Geneva, 259; conquer and plunder the country, fight with the Austrians, 271–277; finally withdraw, 280; blockade Switzerland, 319.
French revolution of 1790, 251.
——————— of 1830, 293.
——————— of 1848, 389.
Frey-Herose of Aargau, 340, 379.
Froideville of Berne, 249.
Fuchs, Aloys, 322.
——— Christopher, 344.
Fuentes, governor of Milan, 160.
Fueter, Emanuel, of Berne, 228.
Furno of Leventina, 231, 233.
Furst, Walter, 39, 40.
Furstenberg, Henry of, 125.
Fussli, Henry, of Zurich, 264.
——— Archdeacon, 332.

Galba, the Roman emperor, 11.
Gallus, 19.
Gardovall, Castle of, 84.
Gaudot, Prussian chargé, 239.

Gauls, The, drive the Rhetians from Italy, are plundered by the Cymbri, 3, 4.
Geiger, John Jacob, 243, 244.
Geisberger, Francis, abbot of St. Gallen, 139.
Geneva, 7, 14, 17; compact with Berne and Freiburg, assaulted by Savoy, protestant, independent, 144–147; compact with Zurich, 151; escalade, 157; constant quarrels, interference of French and Confederates, rising of the people, revolutionary misrule, order restored, 256–262; incorporated with France, 272; a Confederate, 287; disturbances, new constitution, 347, 348; bloody revolution, 373, 374; national constitution, 393.
Geneva, Bishops and counts of, 144.
German envoys leave Berne, 314.
Gersau, Commune of, 55.
Gessler, Hermann, of Brunegg, 37, 38, 40; death, 41.
Giornico, Incredible feat at, 115.
Girard, Ignatius, of Freiburg, 250, 251.
Glarus, 26; a Confederate, 52; despair, valour and victory, 63, 64; purchases her independence, 67; divided in religion, 135; subjects revolt, 213–216; constitutional quarrel, 326, 327; national constitution, 393.
God's-house league of Rhetia, 86.
Goldau destroyed, 282.
Goths, The, subjugate Rhetia, and make the people serfs, 15; vanquished by the Franks, 16.
Grafenried, Colonel, of Berne, 271.
Grandson, capture, massacre, and battle of, 108–110.
Gregory XVI., pope, 323.
Greifensee, Massacre at, 94.
Grey league of Rhetia, 87.
Grindelwald, 137.
Grisons, Confederacy of the three leagues, 88; democratic republic, 105; defeat Austria, 124; establish bailiwicks, 129; partly protestant, 143; violent disputes, 152; civil war, interference of Spain, war with Austria, woe to the conquered, Hungarian plague, great misery, the emperor's sword gives the law, freedom recovered by help from France, and the old leagues renewed, 160–175; party quarrels, 255, 256; invited to join the Helvetian republic, 272; compelled to, 277; a Confederate, 280; unjustly treated, 288; national constitution, 393.
Grossi, Judge of Geneva, 145.
Growth of liberty, 30.
Grunenberg, William of, 99.
Gruyero, Counts of, 148.
Guglers, The, 57.
Guisolan of Freiburg, 250, 251.
Guizot, French minister, 363.
Guler, John, 165, 175.
———, Peter, 168, 172.
Gustavus Adolphus of Sweden, 171.

Habsburg, Counts of, large domains, 26; dukes of Austria, 36.
Haller, Berchtold, 134, 139.
Hallwyl, Thuring of, 92, 98, 100.
———, John of, 109–111.
Harten, The, of Zug, 218.
————, of Appenzell, 222.
Hartmann, bishop of Coire, 85.
Hartsch, Jacob, 69.
Hasenburg, Hans of, 60.
Hatred against Austria, 62.
Hecker in the grand duchy of Baden, 392.
Hegetschwyler, Councillor, of Zurich, 335.
Heimathlosen, The, 179, 290.
Helvetia, Ancient, 1; a prey to foreign nations, 13.
Helvetians, The, first exploits, 3; emigrate into Gaul, defeated and sent back by Julius Cesar, 7, 8; civilization and effeminacy, 12; slain or made slaves, 14.
Helvetian republic, The, 272; impotence of the government, 275; repeated changes, 278; comes to an end, 279.
Helvetian Society, The, 237.
Henry the Fowler, 22.
——— II., of France, 150.
——— IV., of France, 157.
Henzi, Samuel, of Berne, his conspiracy and death, 226–229.
Hertenstein, Caspar of, 111.
Herzog, Marianus, 278.
Hess, burgomaster of Zurich, 334, 335.
Hirzel, of Zurich, 237.
———, Bernard, pastor of Pfeffikon, 334, 335.
Holy alliance, The, 289, 293.
Holzach, of Menzingen, 94.
Holzhalb, John Henry, 169.
Horn, The Swedish general, 177.
Horners of Schwyz, The, 328.
Hortense, Queen, 329.
Hug, John, 142.
Huguenots, The, of Geneva, 146.
———— of France, 153, 154.

Hungarians, The, 22.
Huns, The, sweep over the country, 14.
Hurliman, Landis, 332.
Huss, John, 74.

Ida of Toggenburg, 27.
Imgrund, Henry, 116.
Imperial domains, 31.
——— tribute, 29.
Imposing spectacle, 232.
Increase of franchises, 35.
Independence of Switzerland acknowleged, 180.
Ingelram of Coucy, 56, 57.
Inner-rhodes of Appenzell, 155; party-disputes, 243–246; neutral in Sonderbund-war, 380; fined by the Diet, 388.
Interference, Foreign, 202, 306,313,386.
Interlaken, Convent of, 136.
Iselin of Bâle, 237.
Italian bailiwicks, 130; protestants banished, 150; canton of Ticino, 280.

Jenatsch, George, 161, 166, 170, 172, 174.
Jenni, of Musswangen, 360.
Jesuits, The, in Freiburg and Valais, 291, 321; in Schwyz, 325, 327, 328; in Valais, 354–356; in Lucerne, 357–359; banished from Switzerland, 387.
Jobst of Rudenz, 48.
Joris of Valais, 354
Jost, Major, of Valais, 356.
Journeymen's banquet, 314.
Joyous band, The, 113.
Julia Alpinula, 12.
Julius Cesar defeats the Helvetians and occupies their country, 7–9.

Kaiser, pastor of Uznach, burnt at the stake, 138.
Kalbermatten, William of, 356.
Keller of Lucerne, 243.
———, avoyer, 291.
——— of Zurich, 319.
———, Augustine of Aargau, 340, 357.
Kistler, Peter, of Berne, 106.
Klauens, The, of Schwyz, 328.
Knutwyl-union, 359, 360.
Kolin, Peter, 82.
Kost, Wendelin, of Lucerne, 361.
Kruss, Casimir, 243.
Kuno, abbot of St. Gallen, 67–73.
Kunzli, John, 263.
Kyburg, Counts of, 26, 57, 58.

La Barde, French envoy, 184.
La Basside, 159.
Landenberg, Beringer of, 37; his expulsion, 42.
Landsturm, 64; cruelty, 199, 367.
Landwehr, 361.
Lanier, French envoy, 173.
Lausanne, 14, 23, 36; protestant, 144; retains her franchises under Berne, 148; commotions, 254.
———, bishop of, 26, 148.
Lavater, John Caspar, of Zurich, 264.
League of Wollhausen, 182.
——— of the subjects, 185.
——— of Sarnen, 302–305; dissolved by the Diet, 306.
Lecques, French marshal, 174.
Lenzburg, Counts of, 31, 32.
Leo X, pope, 132.
Leopold of Austria, at Sempach,60, 61.
Leu, Joseph, of Ebersoll, 343; his assassination, 372.
Leuenberger, Nicholas, chief of the people's league, 185, 186; executed, 188.
Leventina, Italian bailiwick, 66, 81, 91; revolts and loses her franchises, 230–232; canton of Ticino, 280.
Linth canal, 282.
Little Burgundy, Dukes of, 17.
Louis of Bavaria, emperor, 44, 46.
——— the Dauphin, 97.
——— XI. of France, 107; perfidy, 108.
——— XVI. ——— 253, 254.
——— XVIII. ——— 285.
——— Philippe, 313, 317, 330, 389.
——— Napoleon, 329, 330.
Love of money, 128.
Lowenbrugger, Nicholas, von der Flue, 116.
Lowerz destroyed, 282.
Lucerne, 20, 23; a Confederate, 45; saved by a boy, 46; increase of territory, 55; conquests from Austria, 76; holds fast to the catholic faith, 135; subjects revolt, 182–189; party-quarrels, 241–243; liberal constitution, 296; reaction and revolution, 343, 344; Sonderbund, 351; admits the Jesuits, prohibits free expression, defeats the free-corps and prosecutes the liberals, 357–362; arms, 364; defeats the second free-corps, 365–367; fresh prosecutions, 372; war, 380; surrenders to the Confederates, 385; results of the war, 387, 388; national constitution, 393.
Lugano, Italian bailiwick, 130; canton of Ticino, 280.
Lugnetzers, The, 163.
Lupulus, 134.

Luther, Martin, 133; writings burned, 135.
Luvini, Colonel, of Ticino, 345, 346, 383.

Maggia-thal (Val maggia), Italian bailiwick, 130; canton of Ticino, 280.
Maillardon, Emanuel of, 251.
Mamelukes, The, of Geneva, 146.
Mangold, 19.
Manesse, Rudiger, 49–52.
Manuel, Nicholas, 134.
Maple tree of Truns, 87.
March-union of Geneva, 347, 373.
Mariastein, abbey of, 337.
Massacre at Reichensee, 60.
——— Grandson, 109, 110.
——— Greifensee, 94.
——— Tirano, 164.
——— in Nidwalden, 276.
Massena, French general, 277.
Massner, Thomas, 206, 208.
Maximilian I. of Austria, emperor, 122.
Mazza, The, of Valais, 79.
Meggelin, landammann of Appenzell, 155.
Meinrad, 19
Meier of Coire, 173.
Melchthal, Arnold, of Anderhalden, 38–40.
Mercenary wars of the Swiss, 129, 290.
Merveilleux, French chargé, 206.
Meyer, Bernard, of Lucerne, 344, 355, 356, 359, 379.
——— Leodegar, 241.
——— Valentine, 242, 243.
Milan, the Schwyzer's grave, 129, 130.
——— Dukes of, 81, 91, 115.
Military school at Thun, 290.
Mob-law, 335.
Monier, Colonel, of Berne, 202.
Monnard of Lausanne, 319, 370.
Montalembert, Count, 389.
Montebello, Duke of, French envoy, 318, 319.
Morat, 107, 110.
Muhlhausen, 103; ally of the Confederates, 126, 154, 155, 177; incorporated with France, 272.
Mullinen, Nicholas of, 165.
Muralte, The, 160.
Muri, Abbey of, 27, 324, 341.

Nabholz of Zurich, 197–200.
Napoleon Bonaparte annexes the Grison bailiwicks to the Cisalpine republic, 269; gives to the Swiss an act of mediation, 279.
Narrow policy of the artisans of Zurich, 50.

National constitution, 393.
Negative party of Geneva, 257, 258.
Nessi, Joseph, of Ticino, 346.
Neuchâtel, 26; subject to Austria, 45; falls to Prussia, franchises increased, 238–240; a Confederate, 287; insurrection, 297; Sarnen league, 302; neutral in Sonderbund war, 380; fined, 388; a republic, 390, 391; national constitution, 393.
Neuchâtel, Counts of, 26.
Neuhaus, Carl, avoyer of Berne, 342, 368, 369.
Neutrality of the Swiss, 177, 284; guaranteed by the Congress of Vienna, 288; in 1848, 391.
Nicholas von der Flue, 116, 117.
Nidau, Count Rudolf of, 47, 48.
Nidwalden, 31; valour and massacre, 276.
Nobles and signiors revolt against their feudal lords, and make themselves independent, 22; jealous of the cities, 24; ruined by the crusades, 28; all-powerful in Rhetia, 33; war against Berne, 37; Lucerne, 45; Berne, 46–48; Zurich, 51, 54; Solothurn and Berne, 58; the Confederates, 59; Glarus, 63; impoverished, sell their estates to the Confederates, 66; or ask for the rights of citizenship, 78.
Nullification, 302.
Nuncio, The papal, 149–152, 204, 322, 325, 327; at Lucerne, 350.
Nuremberg, Diet of, 133.

Oath, The, 39, 40.
Oberhasli, 137.
Oberland, Canton of, 272.
Obwalden, 31.
Ochsenbein, Ulrich of Nidau, 365; avoyer of Berne, 369, 385.
Oecolampadius, 134.
Orelli, The, 150.
Orgetorix, projects and suicide, 6.
Ospenthal, Henry of, 44.
Ossola, Valley of, 78, 79, 81.
Ossuary at Morat, 112.
Osterwald, banneret of Neuchâtel, 240.
Outer-rhodes of Appenzell, 155; quarrel between Harten and Linden, 221–225.

Pancratius, abbot of St. Gallen, 277, 286–288.
Paritat of Aargau, 338.
Peace and its fruits, 66, 67.
Pecolat of Geneva, 145.

People's fortresses, 23.
——— league, 186–188.
Perpetual Bond of the three primitive cantons, Uri, Schwyz, and Unterwalden, 36; with Lucerne, 45; Zurich, 51; Glarus, 52; Zug, 53; Berne, 54; Solothurn and Freiburg, 117; Bâle, Schaffhausen, and Appenzell, 125; dissolved by the French invasion, 273.
Peter of Pultinga, abbot of Disentis, 86.
Petty wars, 118.
Pfyffer of Lucerne, 191, 242.
Pius IX., pope, 389.
Planta, John, of Rhezuns, 152.
——— Pompey, 162, 164, 166.
——— Rudolf, 160, 164, 167, 174.
——— party in Grisons, 255, 256.
Plappart-war, 102.
Plater, Thomas, 143.
Plurs, Terrible destruction of, 163.
Poles, The, in Switzerland, 303, 311, 313, 317, 318.
Popes, The, hire Swiss life-guards, 128.
Priesthood, The Catholic, 132, 291, 321–326.
Primitive cantons, The, settled by the Cymbri, 5; originally one community, 30; form a Confederacy, 36; resist the French, 273.
Propaganda, The Roman, 321.
Protestant cantons, 134, 138, 189–191, 197–194.
Pruntrut, 212.

Raccaud, John Peter of Freiburg, 248, 249.
Radetzky, Austrian field-marshal, 392.
Rahn-Escher of Zurich, 332.
Rapperswyl, 51, 103.
——— Counts of, 27.
Raron, Wichard of, 79.
Rauracia, The short-lived republic of, incorporated with France, 253.
Rechberg, John of, 95, 98, 99.
Reding of Biberegg, 44.
——— Itel, 89, 93, 94.
——— Rudolf, 128.
——— Aloys, 273, 278.
——— Nazar, 328.
Reduction of the currency, 181, 182.
Refugees, 179, 303, 311, 313, 317, 318, 392.
Reinach, John Conrad of, 211.
——— Jacob Sigismund, 212.
——— bishops of Bâle.
Religious schism, 133, *passim*.
Réné, duke of Lorraine, 107, 112.
Rengger, Von, councillor, 252, 253.
Representative party of Geneva, 257, 258.
Revolt of vassal-nobles and bishops against their feudal lords, 22.
Revolt of the subjects of Berne, 181.
——— ——— of Zurich, 264-267.
Rey of Freiburg, 250, 251.
Rheinfelden, 45, 98, 99.
Rhetians, The, 3; subjugated by the Romans, 8; by the Goths and Franks, 15, 16; generally serfs, 33; sufferings, individual resistance, early alliances, the three leagues, are called Grisons, 83–88.
Rilliet, Colonel, of Vaud, 382, 386.
Rivaz, The prebendary of, 355, 356.
Robustelli, Jacob, 164, 165.
Roggenbach, Joseph of, bishop of Bâle, 252, 253.
Rohan, Duke Henry of, 172–177.
Romain idiom and districts, 15, 17.
Romans defeated by the Tigurins, 4; subdue Helvetia, Valais, and Rhetia, dominion, overpowered by the Allemanni, 8–14.
Roman court, plans and action, 320, 348.
Romantsch idiom, 33.
Romarino, General, 312.
Rossberg, capture of the castle, 42.
——— slide of the mountain, 282.
Rossier, Henry, 249.
Rott, John, 57.
Rousseau, Jean Jacques, 257.
Rudolf of Habsburg, the good emperor, 34–36.
Rusca, Nicholas, 162.
Rutli, The meadow of, 39.
Rysig, Petermann, of Schwyz, 82.

Safety-unions of Berne, 319, 320.
St. Bernard, Convent of, 354, 355, 388.
St. Gallen, Abbey and Abbots of, 19, 21, 32, 67, 73, 121, 139, 143, 176, 195, 204, 263, 287.
St. Gallen, City and district, 23; league with Appenzell, 68; dispute with the abbey, 121; partly protestant, 134; canton of Santis, 272; canton of St. Gallen, a Confederate, 280; anarchy, 287; new constitution, 296; casting vote in favour of liberal measures, 351, 375, 378; national constitution, 393.
St. Jacques, Heroes' death at, 97.
St. Maurice, Abbey of, 355, 388.
Sale of indulgences, 132.

Salis, Hercules of, 160.
——, Ulysses of, 165.
——, Rudolf of, 168, 170.
——, Lords of, 255, 256.
Salis-Soglio, Ulrich of, general of the Sonderbund, 376, 381, 382, 385.
Samson, Bernardin, 132.
Santis-alp, 244.
Santis, Canton of, 272.
Sarasin of Geneva, 205.
Sarnen, Capture of the castle of, 42.
———, League of, 302–305.
Sartori of Leventina, 231, 233.
Saunier, Anthony, 147.
Savage manners of the Swiss, 127.
Savoy, Counts of, 26, 34, 144; dukes, 145–147, 157.
———, Invasion of, 311.
Schaffhausen, 23; independent, 29; subject to Austria, 45; fights against the Confederates at Sempach, 61; freed by the emperor, 75; a Confederate, 125; protestant, 134; reforms and disturbances, 209; liberal constitution, 296; national constitution, 393.
Scharnachtal, Nicholas of, 109.
Schauenberg, French general, 270, 276.
Schauenstein, Thomas of, 164.
Scherr, Thomas, of Zurich, 331, 332.
Schik, Arnold, of Schwyz, 97.
Schiker, Josias, of Zug, 218.
Schinner, Cardinal, 129.
Schmidt, Major, of Hitzkirch, 361.
Schmied, Colonel Caspar, 170, 173.
Schmucker, Thomas and Lienhard, 135.
Schon, Rudolf, 65.
Schumacher, Anthony, Ammann of Zug, 217–220.
——————, Placidus, 241, 242.
Schwyz, 5, 30–32; perpetual bond, 36; renowned for valour, and gives name to the Confederacy, 44; takes the March and Uznach, 89; holds fast to the catholic faith, 135; canton of Waldstatten, 272; disturbances and temporary division, 296; Sarnen-league, 302; breaks the peace and is occupied by Confederate troops, 306; admits the Jesuits, 325; The Horner and Klauen quarrel, 327, 328; Sonderbund, 351; war, 380; capitulates, 386; results of the war, 387, 388; national constitution, 393.
Schybi, 186, 188.
Seckingen, Abbey of, 26.
Seldenburen, Konrad of, 31.
Serfs, lamentable condition, 17; dues to their signiors, 25; benefited by the crusades, 28; majority of the country-people, 126.
Sforza, Maximilian, duke of Milan, 130.
Siegfried, landammann of Aargau, 385.
Siegwart, Constantine, of Lucerne, 344; chief of the Sonderbund, 377, 386.
Sigibert, 19.
Sigismund, emperor, 74.
Signioral rights, 25.
Sion, Bishop of, 34.
Socinius, Lelius and Faustus, 149.
Solothurn, 23; independent, 28; assists Berne, 47; saved by John Rott, 57; a Confederate, 117; partly protestant, 135; catholic worship reëstablished, 143; taken by the French, 271; liberal constitution, 296; disturbances, new constitution, 337; national constitution, 393.
Sonderbund: separate league of Uri, Schwyz, Unterwalden, Lucerne, Zug and Freiburg, 351; secret plans, 352; Valais joins, 357; conspiracy against the Confederacy, 372; schemes and preparation for war, 376; arms from Austria, dissolution decreed by the Diet, 377; representatives quit the Diet, 379; arms from France, 380; early successes, 381; subsequent reverses and surrender of Freiburg to the Confederate army, 382; withdrawal of Zug, 383; defeat at Gislikon, 384; surrender and capitulation of the other cantons, and end of the league, 386.
Sonnenberg, general of Lucerne, 364. 366.
Sources of the glory and subsequent debasement of the Swiss, 194.
Spaniards in Grisons, 160–170.
Sprecher, Fluri, 165.
Spreiter, Henry, 134.
Stafa, Revolt and subjection of, 265. 267.
Stanz, Covenant of, 117.
Staub, John Peter, 219.
Stauffacher, Werner, 38, 42.
Steiger, Dr. Robert, 362, 371.
Steiner, Jacob, 165.
Steinholzlein, Banquet at, 314.
Strassburg, Count Otto of, 44.
——————, Festival at, 102.
Strauss, David Frederick, 331–333.
Strebel, Berthold, 43.
Street-fights in Naples, 392.
Strength of Confederates, 55.
Stussi, Rudolf, 89, 93; death, 94.
Suabia, Dukes of, 17, 22.

Suabia, John of, 42.
Suabians, The, attack Appenzell, 69; Switzerland, 122; assist the abbot of St. Gallen, 199.
Subserviency to foreigners, 178.
Sumptuary-law of Berne, 106.
Suter, Joseph Anthony, landammann of Appenzell, 243–246.
Suwarrow, Russian general, 277.
Swedish family names, 5.
Swiss life-guards, 254.
Switzerland, boundaries of, 2; in great danger, 123; independence acknowledged, 180; limits contracted, 269.

Tanner, landammann of Appenzell, 156.
Tell, William, the archer of Burgen, 40, 41.
Ten-jurisdictions, League of the, in Grisons, 88; rights of Toggenburg bought by Austria, 122; subjugated by Austria, 169; purchase of freedom, 174.
The Three men of Rutli, 39.
Theilig, Frischhans, 115, 119.
Thirty years' religious war of Germany, 176.
Thorberg, Peter of, 59.
Threats from abroad, 318, 389.
Thun, Military school at, 290.
Thurgau, a bailiwick of the Confederates, 103; great mortality, 159; a canton, 272; a Confederate, 281; liberal constitution, 296; national constitution, 393.
Ticino, Canton of, a Confederate, 280; civil war prevented, 287; liberal constitution, 296; bloody change of government, 345–347; national constitution, 393.
Tigurins, The, 3; join the Cymbri and defeat a Roman army, 4.
Todfalls, 25.
Toggenburg, Counts of; great possessions in Rhetia, 27.
——— Frederick of, dies childless, 87; war for his estates, 88–91.
Toggenburgers, The, 138, 195–203.
Travers, Anthony, 161.
——— Augustin, 161, 162.
Treasures carried away by the French, 272.
Treaty of Aarau, 203; Amiens, 279; of Bâle, 125; Cherasco, 171; Feldkirch, 174; Lausanne, 151; Monzona, 170; Rorschach, 222; St. Julian, 146; Teynikon, 142; Westphalia, 180.
Tribunals of the Grisons, 152, 160, 161, 164.
Trient, Fratricide on the, 356.
Trumpi, Caspar of Glarus, 213, 214.
Tscharner of Berne, president of the Confederacy, 318.
Tschudi, priest of Glarus, 326.
Tyrolese, The, 72, 122.

Uechtland, 23.
Ulli Galli, 186, 188.
Unequal rights, 126.
Unterwalden, 30; divides, 31; perpetual bond, 36; holds to the Catholic faith, 135; canton of Waldstatten, 272; Sarnen league, 302; Sonderbund, 351; war, 380; capitulates, 386; results of the war, 387, 388; national constitution, 393.
Uri, 30; perpetual bond, 36; scrupulous justice, 77; holds to the Catholic faith, 135; deprives Leventina of her franchises, 232; canton of Waldstatten, 272; Sarnen league, 302; Sonderbund, 351; war, 380; capitulates, 386; results of the war, 387, 388; national constitution, 393.
Urs of Leventina, 231, 233.
Utiger, Beat Caspar, 218.

Valais, subdued by the Romans, 9; signiors, 26; upper Valais free, 34; invaded by Confederates, 80; aids them against Savoy, 108; partly protestant, 143; extends her boundaries, 147; protestants expelled, 158; a canton, 272; a prey to the French, 278; a Confederate, 287; admits the Jesuits, 291; Sarnen-league, 302; civil war, fratricide, Sonderbund, 352–357; war, 380; capitulates, 386; results of the war, 387, 388; national constitution, 393.
Valtelina, Grison bailiwick, 129; commotions and massacre, 160–167; Cisalpine republic, 269; annexed to Austria, 288.
Vaud, 26; protestant, 144; subdued by Berne, 147; calls in the French, and declares herself independent, 270; a canton, 272; a Confederate, 280; arms for independence, 286; liberal constitution, 296; change of government, 363; church dispute, 369–371; national constitution, 393.
Vendome, Duke of, 207.
Venice and Grisons, 160.
Vergennes, French envoy, 258.
Vindonissa, 11, 14.

Vitellius, 11.

Wahl, Brothers, 317.
Wala, John, of Glarus, 124.
Waldmann, John, burgomaster of Zurich, 111, 112; arrogance, 119; execution, 120.
Waldmann, Convention of, 120.
Waldstatten, Canton of, 272.
Waller, of Aargau, 339, 360.
Walsors, The, 33.
War not the greatest of evils, 208.
Wart, Rudolf of, 43
Wasser, John Henry, of Zurich, 175.
Weimar, Duke Bernard of, 178.
Wendell, Clara, 291.
Wengi, avoyer of Solothurn, 143.
Werdenberg, Counts of, 27, 86.
———— Rudolf of, 70–72.
Werdenbergers, Revolt of the, 213–216.
Werli, avoyer of Unterwalden, executed by the protestants, 138.
Wernier, Samuel, of Berne, 228.
Wertmuller of Zurich, 186–188, 201–202.
Wesen, 62; treachery, 63.
Wetters, The, of Appenzell, 221–223.
Wettingen, Abbey of, 138, 340.
Wettstein, John Rudolf, 180.
Wieland, Dr., of Aargau, 341.
Wigoldingen, Fray at, 192.
Wilchingen, Revolt in, 210.
Willi, John Jacob, 281.
Willisau, Attack on, 360.
Winkelried, Arnold Struthahn of, 61.
Wisard, banneret of Munsterthal, 231.
Wolleb, Henry, 124.
Wyler, John, 109.
Wyttenbach, Thomas, 134.

Zahringen, Dukes of, 23, 26.
Zambra, (John Baptist Prevost), 162.
Zeller, Dr., of Tubingen, 375.
Zellwegers, The, of Appenzell, 221–223, 237.
Ziegler, Colonel, 384.
Zoppo, Lord, 82.
Zug, a Confederate, 53; holds to the catholic faith, 140; party-rage and disturbances, 216–220; canton of Waldstatten, 272; Sonderbund, 351; wavers, 378, withdraws, 383; national constitution, 393.
Zurich, 23, 26, 28; change of government, 49, 50; plot of the nobles defeated by an apprentice, 51; a Confederate, Vorort, 52; besieged by Austria, 54; increase of territory, 55; conquests in Aargau, 77; Toggenburger-quarrel, 88; takes the oath to Austria, and breaks the bond, 92; defeated by the Confederates, 93; besieged, 95; peace, 98; revolt of subjects, 119, 120; protestant, 134; defeated by the catholic cantons, 141; revolt of subjects, 179; with Berne defeats the catholics, 197–204; reforms, 209; revolt of subjects, 264–267; liberal constitution, 296; reaction and revolution, 331–336; repentance, 349; national constitution, 393.
Zurlauben, Fidelis, 217, 218.
Zwier of Evenbach, 186, 192.
Zwingli, Ulrich, 132; death, 141.

THE END.

JOSEPHUS' WORKS.

JOSEPHUS.—A New and Elegant Library Edition. Explanatory Notes, Observations, and complete Index. On tinted paper. 4 vols., crown 8vo, cloth . . 9 00

——— Library sheep, ... 10 00

——— Half calf, gilt, or antique, . . 16 00

JOSEPHUS.—A Popular Edition. 2 vols., crown 8vo, cloth, . 4 50

——— Library sheep, ... 5 00

———Half calf, gilt, or antique, . . 8 00

ANNUAL OF SCIENTIFIC DISCOVERY.

A Year-Book of Facts in Science and Art, exhibiting the most important Discoveries and Improvements in Mechanics, Useful Arts, Natural Philosophy, Chemistry, Astronomy, Meteorology, Zoology, Botany, Mineralogy, Geology, Geography, Antiquities, etc., together with a List of Recent Scientific Publications. Edited by David A. Wells, late U. S. Commissioner, and Samuel Kneeland, M.D. 21 vols. Price, in cloth, $2.00 per vol. Sold either in sets or by single volume.

We shall issue early in the spring of 1875 a new volume, which will contain all the Discoveries and Improvements in the various branches of Science, from the year 1871 to 1874 inclusive, and will be edited by a well-known author and leading professor in Science.

WORKS OF LORD MACAULAY.

Critical, Historical and Miscellaneous Essays. By Lord Macaulay. With a Memoir and Index, and a Portrait of Macaulay. Riverside Edition. In 6 vols., crown 8vo, extra cloth . . 12 00

Half calf, gilt, or antique 24 00

History of England. Riverside Edition. In 8 vols., crown 8vo, with a new Portrait of Macaulay. Extra cloth, . . 16 00

Half calf, gilt, or antique, ... 32 00

The Complete Works of Lord Macaulay. Containing the History of England, Essays, Poems and Speeches. Riverside Edition. In 16 vols., crown 8vo, extra cloth, . . . 32 00

Half calf, gilt, or antique, ... 64 00

The Complete Works of Lord Macaulay. Students' Edition. In 8 vols., extra cloth, ... 16 00

Half calf, gilt, or antique, ... 32 00

SCOTT'S POEMS.

SCOTT'S Poems. Library edition, 2 vols., 16mo, in black and gilt. New style. Illustrated, . . . $4 00
" " In half calf. . 7 50
" Lay of the Last Minstrel. 1 vol., 16mo, in black and gilt. New style 1 25
" Marmion. 1 vol., 16mo, in black and gilt. New style. 1 25
" Lady of the Lake. 1 vol., 16mo, in black and gilt. New style, . . . 1 25
" Rokeby. 1 vol., 16mo, in black and gilt. New style, . 1 25
" Lord of the Isles. 1 vol., 16mo, in black and gilt. New style, ... 1 25
" Poems. 5 vols. Holiday edition, bound in cloth, full gilt sides and edges, in box, . . . 8 75
" The same, in half calf, ... 12 50

MOORE'S POEMS.

MOORE'S Lalla Rookh. 1 vol., 16mo, in black and gilt. New style . . 1 25
" Irish Melodies. 1 vol., 16mo, in black and gilt. New style . . . 1 25
Holiday edition of the above two volumes, bound in cloth, full gilt sides and edges, . . 3 50

MACDUFF'S WORKS.

THE WORDS AND MIND OF JESUS AND FAITHFUL PROMISER. 1 vol., 18mo, red edges, 75
The same. 1 vol., 32mo, red edges, . . . 50

ASTRONOMIES.

MITCHEL'S Planetary and Stellar Worlds. 1 vol., 12mo, . 1 75
" Popular Astronomy. 1 vol., 12mo, illustrated . 1 75
" Astronomy of the Bible. 1 vol., 12mo, . . 1 75
The above 3 vols., in half calf, per set . . . 10 50
By O. M. Mitchel, formerly Director of the Cincinnati and Dudley Observatories, late Major-General U. S. Volunteers.

NATURAL HISTORY.

MARTIN'S Natural History. Containing 262 Beautiful Colored Illustrations. 1 vol., crown 8vo, ... 3 50

FRENCH.

All the French Verbs at a Glance. By Lambert and Sardou. 1 vol., 12mo, ... $50

Idiomatic Key to the French Language. By Lambert and Sardou. 1 vol., 12mo, ... 1 50

Keetels' Analytical and Practical French Grammar. 1 vol., 12mo, ... 2 00

Key to the English Exercises contained in above, . . 75

Keetels' Elementary French Grammar. 1 vol., 12mo, . 1 25

MISCELLANEOUS BOOKS.

STEARNS. THE CONSTITUTION OF THE UNITED STATES, with a CONCORDANCE and Classified Index, and Questions for Educational Purposes. 1 vol., 8vo, library edition, 1 50

" The same. One vol., 12mo, college edition, . 1 00

PIERSON'S System of Questions in Geography, Adapted to Any Modern Atlas. 1 vol., 12mo, . . . 75

MASON. The Story of a Workingman's Life. 1 vol., 12mo, 490 pp., ... 2 00

TROWBRIDGE. The Excelsior Cook-Book and Housekeeper's Aid. 1 vol., 12mo, 288 pp., ... 1 25

WILKINSON. The Dance of Modern Society. 16mo, paper, . 25

" The same. 16mo, cloth, ... 50

NEWHOUSE. The Trapper's Guide. 1 vol., 8vo, 216 pp. With 34 full-page illustrations, ... 1 5(

WIDOW BEDOTT PAPERS. With 8 spirited illustrations. 12mo, cloth, gilt back 1 75

TAYLOR'S January and June. 1 vol., 12mo, 280 pp., . . 1 50

COOPER'S Naval History. 1 vol., 8vo, sheep. A new edition, continued to 1860, ... 3 75

KINGLAKE. Eothen; or, Traces of Travel brought home from the East. By Alexander Wm. Kinglake, 12mo, . 1 25

SAINTINE. Picciola, the Prisoner of Fenestrella; or, Captivity Captive. By X. B. Saintine. A new edition, with illustrations, 12mo, muslin, ... 1 00

TRUE STORIES OF THE DAYS OF WASHINGTON. 1 vol., 16mo, 1 50

BOB AND WALTER. With a Story of Breakneck Ledge. A beautifully illustrated Juvenile for Little Folks, 85

WEE-WEE SONGS FOR OUR LITTLE PETS. By Leila Lee. Beautifully illustrated. Bound in fancy muslin, with gilt back, . . . 75

FARRAR.	Julian Home. 1 vol., 12mo.	$1 7[illegible]
"	St. Winifreds, " "	1 75
"	Eric; or Little by Little. 1 vol., 12mo,	1 75
FRANKLIN.	Life of Benjamin Franklin, 1 vol., 16mo,	1
ALLEN.	Life of Ethan Allen, " "	1 50
WASHINGTON.	Lives of Mary and Martha, " " . .	1 50
WEBSTER.	Daniel Webster and his Contemporaries. 1 vol., 16mo, . .	1 50
DE STAËL, MADAME.	Corinne, or Italy, translated by Isabel Hill One volume, 12mo, cloth, . .	1 75

THE COLLEGE LIBRARY.

COMPRISING

JULIAN HOME,

ERIC,

ST. WINIFREDS,

Put up in neat boxes, Price per set, - - 5 25

THE CONTINENTAL LIBRARY.

COMPRISING

[T]RUE STORIES OF THE DAYS OF WASHINGTON,

LIVES OF MARY AND MARTHA WASHINGTON,

LIFE OF BENJAMIN FRANKLIN,

LIFE OF ETHAN ALLEN,

Put up in neat boxes. Price per set 6 00

THE DANCE

OF

MODERN SOCIETY.

BY W. C. WILKINSON.

One Volume, 16mo, paper, 25 cents.
One Volume, 16mo, cloth, 50 cents.

OPINIONS OF THE PRESS.

"We do not know who Mr. W. C. WILKINSON is, but we do not hesitate to say that this little essay entitles him to a front rank among American essayists. He is quite as sparkling and more sententious than Parton. He is immeasurably stronger and more vigorous than Timothy Titcomb. His earnestness is not surpassed by that of Mrs. Stowe. We know no writer who equals him in the courage with which he handles the most delicate and difficult of subjects. If his essay is not exceptional—if it be not the burst of a manly indignation that can no longer withhold its protest against a wrong on which it has long looked with accumulating hate—if the author is able to throw himself with any analogous power into the discussion of other topics—there is no reason why he should not become an acknowledged leader in a kind of writing which the public increasingly demand. Macaulay's *critique* on the Puritans has never been more happily responded to than it is incidentally in a single paragraph of this essay. A keener and more caustic exposure of the current plans for the conversion of the drama, the dance, and the billiard-room we have never read, than in his flashing and trenchant pages."—*Independent.*

"Mr. WILKINSON handles his subject boldly, without coarseness; wittily, without flippancy; piously, without cant. * * * Whether his readers agree with him or not, they will admire the evident sincerity and vigor of his ideas, and the terse, trenchant style in which he sets them forth."—*N. Y. Daily Times.*

OPINIONS OF THE PRESS.

"Merely a headlong hammer-and-tongs schedule of abuse. Leaves one with the impression that the author failed in his attempt at a waltz, or polka, or galop."—*Cleveland Leader.*

"One of the most forcible appeals against dancing we have ever read. * * * Those who deprecate dancing, and yet hardly know how to frame arguments against it, will here find a whole magazine full, ready to their hands. It can hardly have been written by a novice in the Terpsichorean art, and the author must even have had some practice in 'round dances.'"—*Lowell Courier.*

"'THE DANCE OF MODERN SOCIETY,' by W. C. WILKINSON, New York (Albert Mason, pp. 77), is the best tractate we have seen against this iniquity, which, more than any popular amusement, sets on fire the course of nature, and is set on fire of hell. How Christians and Methodists even can indulge in this devil's sport, is only to be solved after Wesley's 'Sin in Believers.' The modern dance is the most complete and successful form of diabolical seduction in vogue in respectable places. With the social glass, its steps take hold on hell Rare, most rare is it, that they that go in thereat, at either of these gates, return again. This work is admirably written, with great cogency and elegance. We give an extract elsewhere. Read it, and circulate it. Let every father and mother beset by this popular sin buy it, and give it to their tempted child. It costs but a trifle, and will be found of great price."—*Zion's Herald.*

"Clever and sensible."—*Press* (*Philadelphia*).

"The writer has great command of forcible and terse English. * * * He leaves little to be said from his stand-point, and he who would overthrow him must be equally devoted to principle and science, and a most cogent and candid reasoner."—*Albany Evening Journal.*

"It is only within the past week that one of our most experienced and sagacious physicians uttered, in our hearing, sentiments precisely in accordance with those here affirmed."—*Christian Secretary* (*Hartford*).

"Whoever begins this book will be likely to read it through. It is the very reverse of mealy-mouthed."—*Free Press* (*Burlington*).

"Pastors, parents! here is a magazine of argument for you. Get this book."—*Methodist Home Journal.*

OPINIONS OF THE PRESS.

"The views of the author are extreme, but they are worthy of serious consideration."—*Chicago Daily Republican.*

"If there is in our language any better discussion of the subject, we would be glad to have it pointed out."—*Baptist Quarterly.*

"The bray and the ass are inseparable. We leave our readers to discover what connection all this has with 'THE DANCE OF MODERN SOCIETY.'"—*Liberal Christian.*

Rev. Dr. Cuyler, in *The Evangelist:* "That most pungent and powerful little book, 'THE DANCE OF MODERN SOCIETY.' * * * Those who wish to see the 'Dance' well dissected, should read Mr. WILKINSON'S little work."

"Although embraced within brief compass, the discussion is thorough, and well nigh exhaustive. * * * We wish that this essay might be read in every Christian household, and we would commend it also to those who are just entering upon the Christian ministry, as well as to religious teachers of all kinds."—*National Baptist.*

"Deserving of extensive circulation and perusal."—*Standard* (*Chicago*).

"Written with unusual vigor of speech and thought."—*Congregationalist* (*Boston*).

"If any one wishes to see how modern fashionable dancing appears from a Christian point of view, they need only to peruse this little volume, earnestly and forcibly written."—*Evangelist* (*New York*).

"Mr. WILKINSON writes with vivacity."—*Commonwealth* (*Boston*).

"'THE DANCE OF MODERN SOCIETY,' when it first appeared, attracted a good deal of attention by the thoroughness, the vigor, the combination of effective satire and solemn earnestness with which the author assailed a popular amusement. * * * * The additions strengthen the argument at its strongest point."—*Examiner and Chronicle.*

"Certainly worthy of a careful reading."—*Pittsburg Gazette.*

"It is the best arraignment of the dance that we have ever seen." —*Utica Observer.*

"He writes earnestly but temperately, without any show of fanaticism, and in a fair and candid spirit."—*Salem Register.*

"Well worth reading."—*Patriot* (*Harrisburg*).

OPINIONS OF THE PRESS.

"His views are strongly expressed, and carry much weight with them."—*Transcript* (*Portland*).

"Members of any church who send their children to dancing-schools, would do well to read it; to ponder its startling facts; to heed its solemn warnings."—*Christian Advocate* (*Pittsburg*).

"Argues the case with irresistible logic."—*Christian World* (*Cincinnati*).

"We like his style. He strikes to hit. He 'goes for' his opponent."—*Troy Press.*

"Hard to answer."—*Central Baptist* (*Chicago*).

"Hard to escape the points of his logic. * * * Full of ideas. * * * Will do good and not harm."—*Republican* (*Binghamton*).

"Can be read at a sitting. Those who read it will find material for profitable meditation."—*Spy* (*Worcester*).

"Much superior in style as well as argument, to the bulk of the attacks on popular amusement. * * * Makes out a stronger case than most readers will anticipate."—*Newark Daily Journal.*

"Asks one pertinent question which is the key to his entire book: 'Why do dancers take no pleasure in dancing, unless when dancing with others of the opposite sex?' "—*N. Y. World.*

"A philippic."—*N. Y. Tribune.*

"The philippic is well written."—*North Am. and U. S. Gazette* (*Phila.*).

"A noted and powerful article."—*Boston Traveler.*

"Everywhere acknowledged to be able and incisive."—*Advance.*

"The most pungent attack on the modern dance we have ever read. We have looked with some interest, but in vain, for a defence of the accused against this most eloquent indictment."—*Harper's Magazine.*

The Dance of Modern Society is for sale by Booksellers generally, or will be sent by mail, prepaid, on receipt of price.

Address, ALBERT MASON, Publisher,
129 Grand Street, New York

www.ingramcontent.com/pod-product-compliance
Lightning Source LLC
LaVergne TN
LVHW021149110826
845150LV00005B/1170

* 9 7 8 1 4 2 5 5 4 7 0 6 6 *